Snow Drop

Volume Four
by Choi Kyung-ah

English Adaptation
by Sarah Dyer

TOKYOPOP®

Los Angeles • Tokyo • London • Hamburg

ALSO AVAILABLE FROM  TOKYOPOP®

MANGA

.HACK//LEGEND OF THE TWILIGHT
@LARGE
ABENOBASHI: MAGICAL SHOPPING ARCADE
A.I. LOVE YOU
AI YORI AOSHI
ANGELIC LAYER
ARM OF KANNON
BABY BIRTH
BATTLE ROYALE
BATTLE VIXENS
BRAIN POWERED
BRIGADOON
B'TX
CANDIDATE FOR GODDESS, THE
CARDCAPTOR SAKURA
CARDCAPTOR SAKURA - MASTER OF THE CLOW
CHOBITS
CHRONICLES OF THE CURSED SWORD
CLAMP SCHOOL DETECTIVES
CLOVER
COMIC PARTY
CONFIDENTIAL CONFESSIONS
CORRECTOR YUI
COWBOY BEBOP
COWBOY BEBOP: SHOOTING STAR
CRAZY LOVE STORY
CRESCENT MOON
CROSS
CULDCEPT
CYBORG 009
D•N•ANGEL
DEMON DIARY
DEMON ORORON, THE
DEUS VITAE
DIABOLO
DIGIMON
DIGIMON TAMERS
DIGIMON ZERO TWO
DOLL
DRAGON HUNTER
DRAGON KNIGHTS
DRAGON VOICE
DREAM SAGA
DUKLYON: CLAMP SCHOOL DEFENDERS
EERIE QUEERIE!
ERICA SAKURAZAWA: COLLECTED WORKS
ET CETERA
ETERNITY
EVIL'S RETURN
FAERIES' LANDING
FAKE
FLCL
FLOWER OF THE DEEP SLEEP
FORBIDDEN DANCE
FRUITS BASKET
G GUNDAM

GATEKEEPERS
GETBACKERS
GIRL GOT GAME
GIRLS' EDUCATIONAL CHARTER
GRAVITATION
GTO
GUNDAM BLUE DESTINY
GUNDAM SEED ASTRAY
GUNDAM WING
GUNDAM WING: BATTLEFIELD OF PACIFISTS
GUNDAM WING: ENDLESS WALTZ
GUNDAM WING: THE LAST OUTPOST (G-UNIT)
GUYS' GUIDE TO GIRLS
HANDS OFF!
HAPPY MANIA
HARLEM BEAT
I.N.V.U.
IMMORTAL RAIN
INITIAL D
INSTANT TEEN: JUST ADD NUTS
ISLAND
JING: KING OF BANDITS
JING: KING OF BANDITS - TWILIGHT TALES
JULINE
KARE KANO
KILL ME, KISS ME
KINDAICHI CASE FILES, THE
KING OF HELL
KODOCHA: SANA'S STAGE
LAMENT OF THE LAMB
LEGAL DRUG
LEGEND OF CHUN HYANG, THE
LES BIJOUX
LOVE HINA
LUPIN III
LUPIN III: WORLD'S MOST WANTED
MAGIC KNIGHT RAYEARTH I
MAGIC KNIGHT RAYEARTH II
MAHOROMATIC: AUTOMATIC MAIDEN
MAN OF MANY FACES
MARMALADE BOY
MARS
MARS: HORSE WITH NO NAME
MINK
MIRACLE GIRLS
MIYUKI-CHAN IN WONDERLAND
MODEL
MY LOVE
NECK AND NECK
ONE
ONE I LOVE, THE
PARADISE KISS
PARASYTE
PASSION FRUIT
PEACH GIRL
PEACH GIRL: CHANGE OF HEART
PET SHOP OF HORRORS
PITA-TEN

04.23.04T

ALSO AVAILABLE FROM 🍥 TOKYOPOP®

PLANET LADDER
PLANETES
PRIEST
PRINCESS AI
PSYCHIC ACADEMY
QUEEN'S KNIGHT, THE
RAGNAROK
RAVE MASTER
REALITY CHECK
REBIRTH
REBOUND
REMOTE
RISING STARS OF MANGA
SABER MARIONETTE J
SAILOR MOON
SAINT TAIL
SAIYUKI
SAMURAI DEEPER KYO
SAMURAI GIRL REAL BOUT HIGH SCHOOL
SCRYED
SEIKAI TRILOGY, THE
SGT. FROG
SHAOLIN SISTERS
SHIRAHIME-SYO: SNOW GODDESS TALES
SHUTTERBOX
SKULL MAN, THE
SNOW DROP
SORCERER HUNTERS
STONE
SUIKODEN III
SUKI
THREADS OF TIME
TOKYO BABYLON
TOKYO MEW MEW
TOKYO TRIBES
TRAMPS LIKE US
UNDER THE GLASS MOON
VAMPIRE GAME
VISION OF ESCAFLOWNE, THE
WARRIORS OF TAO
WILD ACT
WISH
WORLD OF HARTZ
X-DAY
ZODIAC P.I.

NOVELS

CLAMP SCHOOL PARANORMAL INVESTIGATORS
KARMA CLUB
SAILOR MOON
SLAYERS

ART BOOKS

ART OF CARDCAPTOR SAKURA
ART OF MAGIC KNIGHT RAYEARTH, THE
PEACH: MIWA UEDA ILLUSTRATIONS

ANIME GUIDES

COWBOY BEBOP
GUNDAM TECHNICAL MANUALS
SAILOR MOON SCOUT GUIDES

TOKYOPOP KIDS

STRAY SHEEP

CINE-MANGA™

ALADDIN
CARDCAPTORS
DUEL MASTERS
FAIRLY ODDPARENTS, THE
FAMILY GUY
FINDING NEMO
G.I. JOE SPY TROOPS
GREATEST STARS OF THE NBA
JACKIE CHAN ADVENTURES
JIMMY NEUTRON: BOY GENIUS, THE ADVENTURES OF
KIM POSSIBLE
LILO & STITCH: THE SERIES
LIZZIE MCGUIRE
LIZZIE MCGUIRE MOVIE, THE
MALCOLM IN THE MIDDLE
POWER RANGERS: DINO THUNDER
POWER RANGERS: NINJA STORM
PRINCESS DIARIES 2
RAVE MASTER
SHREK 2
SIMPLE LIFE, THE
SPONGEBOB SQUAREPANTS
SPY KIDS 2
SPY KIDS 3-D: GAME OVER
THAT'S SO RAVEN
TOTALLY SPIES
TRANSFORMERS: ARMADA
TRANSFORMERS: ENERGON
VAN HELSING

**You want it? We got it!
A full range of TOKYOPOP
products are available now at:
www.TOKYOPOP.com/shop**

04.23.04T

Translator - Jennifer Hahm
English Adaptation - Sarah Dyer
Copy Editor - Suzanne Waldman
Retouch and Lettering - Riho Sakai
Cover Layout - Anna Kernbaum
Graphic Designer - James Dashiell

Editor - Julie Taylor
Digital Imaging Manager - Chris Buford
Production Coordinator - Antonio DePietro
Production Managers - Jennifer Miller and Mutsumi Miyazaki
Art Director - Matt Alford
Managing Editor - Jill Freshney
VP of Production - Ron Klamert
President & C.O.O. - John Parker
Publisher & C.E.O. - Stuart Levy

JAN 2 9 2016

Email: editor@TOKYOPOP.com
Come visit us online at www.TOKYOPOP.com

A  Manga

TOKYOPOP Inc.
5900 Wilshire Blvd. Suite 2000
Los Angeles, CA 90036

Snow Drop Vol. 4

ISBN: 1-59182-687-X

First TOKYOPOP printing: July 2004

10 9 8 7 6 5 4 3 2 1

Printed in the USA

Previously in

As Hae-Gi and So-Na's relationship continues to grow, Sun-Mi schemes to tear them apart! Meanwhile, So-Na feels strongly that there is a connection between Hae-Gi and the book, Snow Drop, and sets out to solve the mystery behind its missing pages. But after So-Na discovers a revealing secret about Hae-Gi, will the book of love have to be rewritten?

C·O·N·T·E·N·T·S

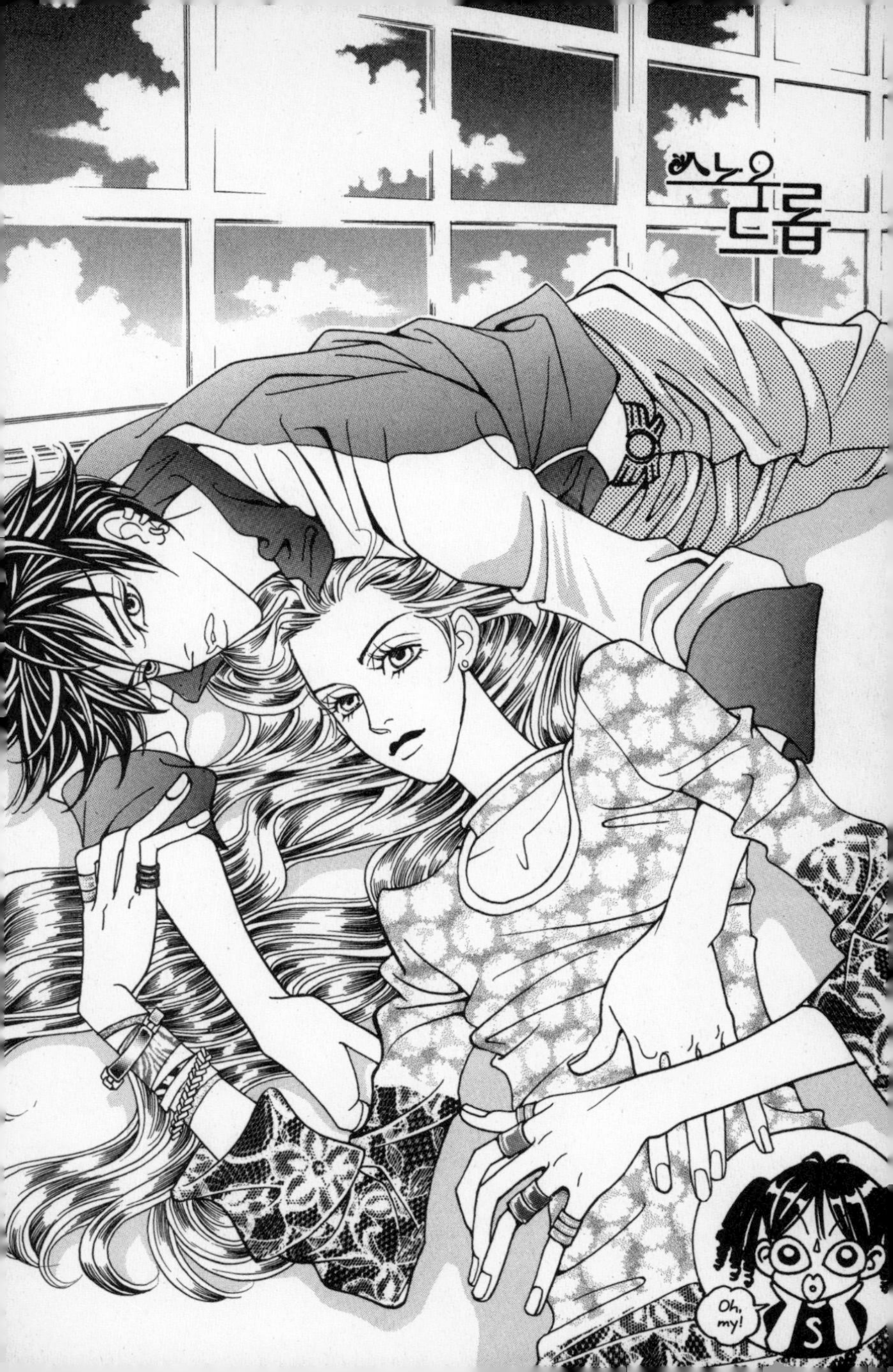
스노우 드롭
Oh, my!

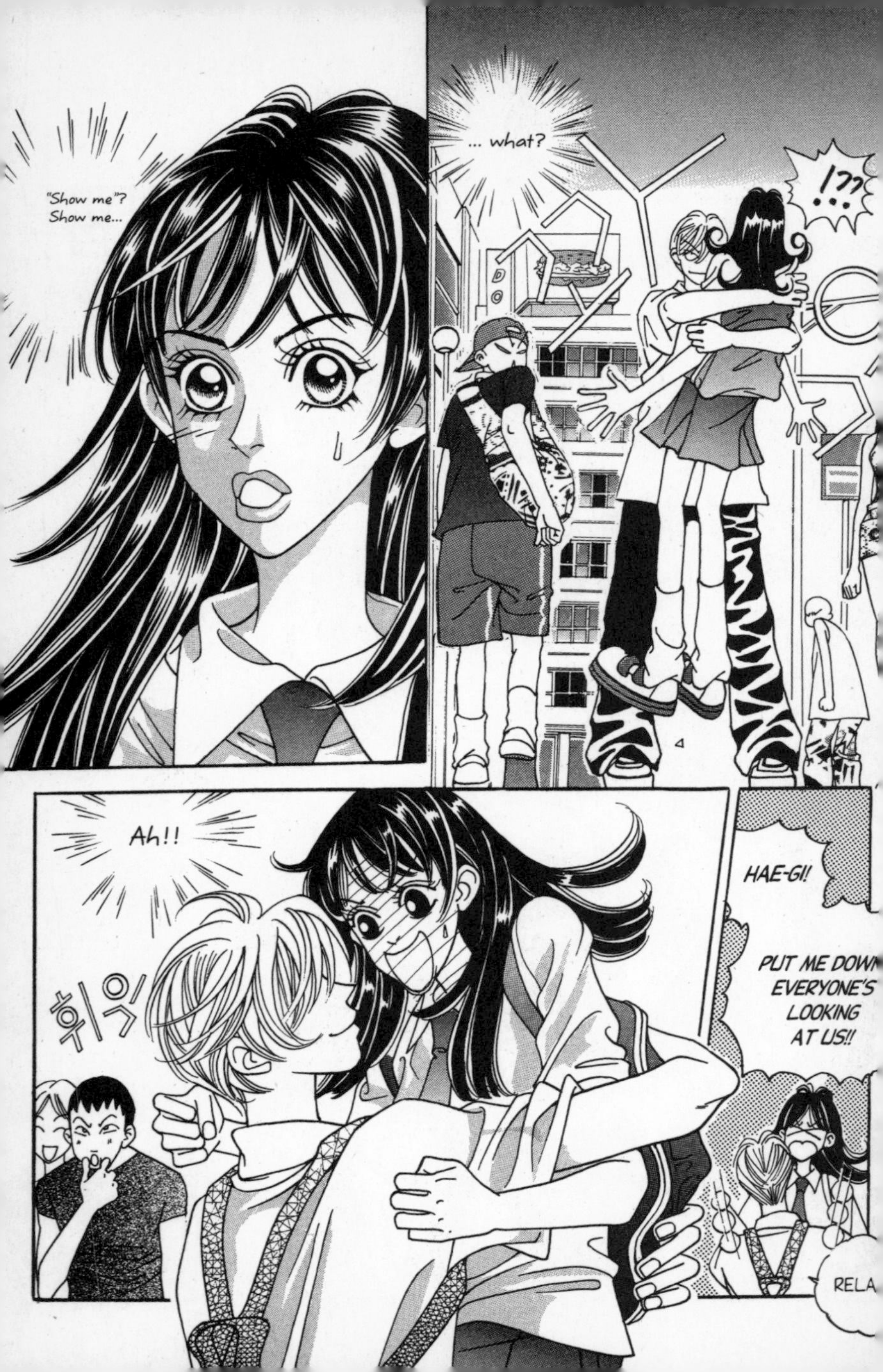
"Show me"? Show me...
... what?
!??...
Ah!!
휘잉
HAE-GI!
PUT ME DOW
EVERYONE'S LOOKING AT US!!
RELA

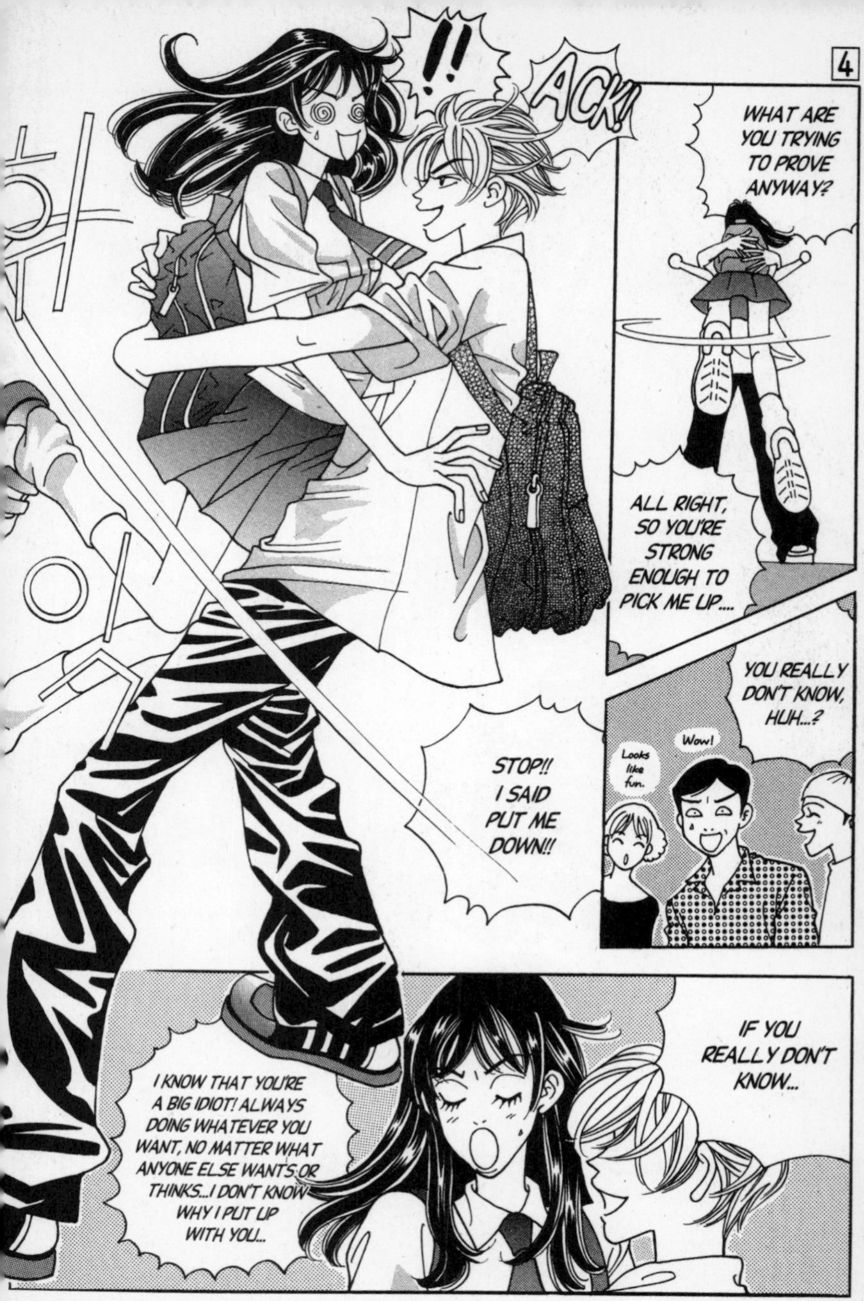

4
!!
ACK!
STOP!! I SAID PUT ME DOWN!!
WHAT ARE YOU TRYING TO PROVE ANYWAY?
ALL RIGHT, SO YOU'RE STRONG ENOUGH TO PICK ME UP....
YOU REALLY DON'T KNOW, HUH...?
Looks like fun.
Wow!
I KNOW THAT YOU'RE A BIG IDIOT! ALWAYS DOING WHATEVER YOU WANT, NO MATTER WHAT ANYONE ELSE WANTS OR THINKS...I DON'T KNOW WHY I PUT UP WITH YOU...
IF YOU REALLY DON'T KNOW...

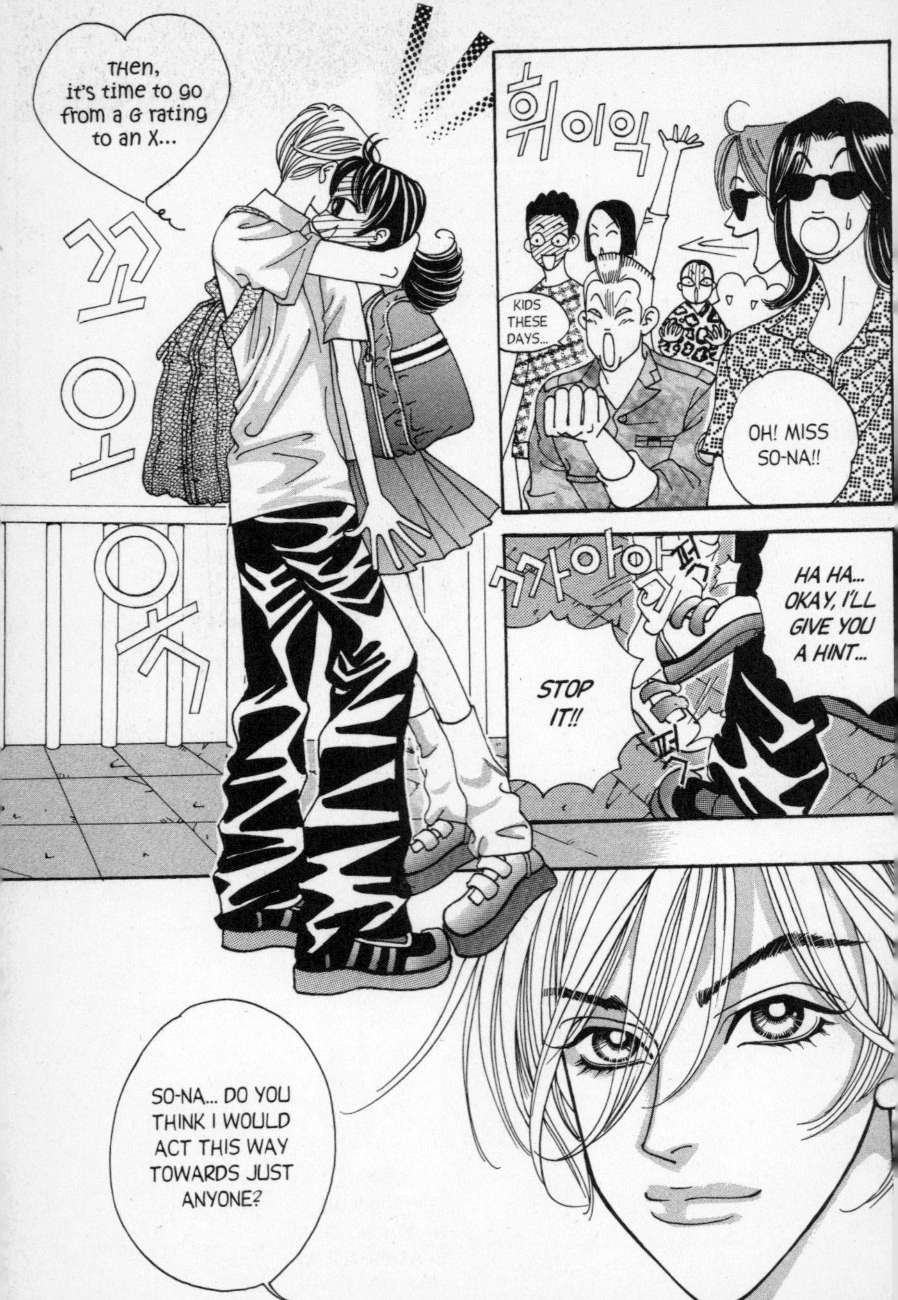
THEn, it's time to go from a G rating to an X...
꼬오옥
휘이익
KIDS THESE DAYS...
OH! MISS SO-NA!!
HA HA... OKAY, I'LL GIVE YOU A HINT...
STOP IT!!
퍽
퍽
SO-NA... DO YOU THINK I WOULD ACT THIS WAY TOWARDS JUST ANYONE?

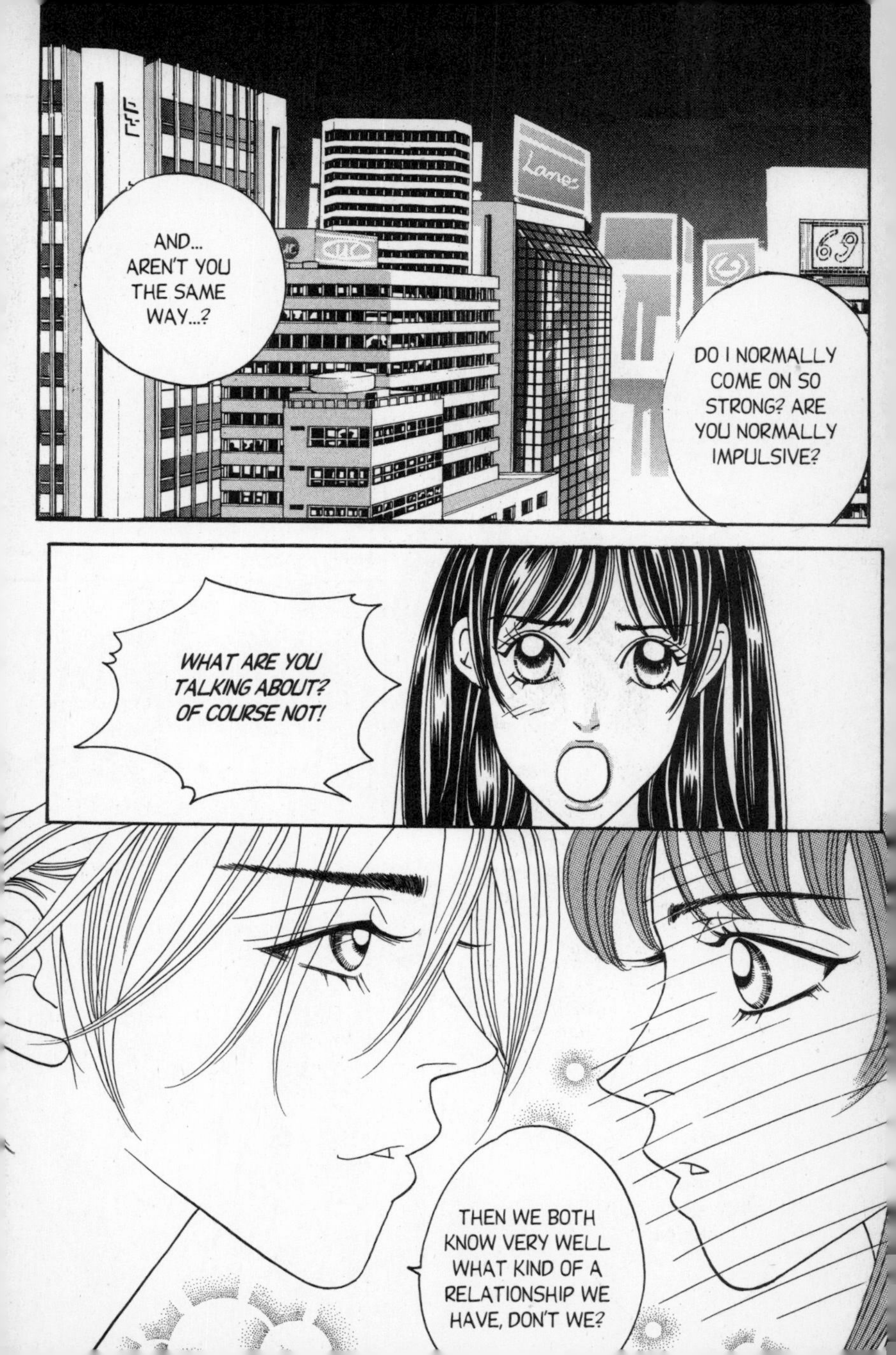
AND... AREN'T YOU THE SAME WAY...?
DO I NORMALLY COME ON SO STRONG? ARE YOU NORMALLY IMPULSIVE?
WHAT ARE YOU TALKING ABOUT? OF COURSE NOT!
THEN WE BOTH KNOW VERY WELL WHAT KIND OF A RELATIONSHIP WE HAVE, DON'T WE?

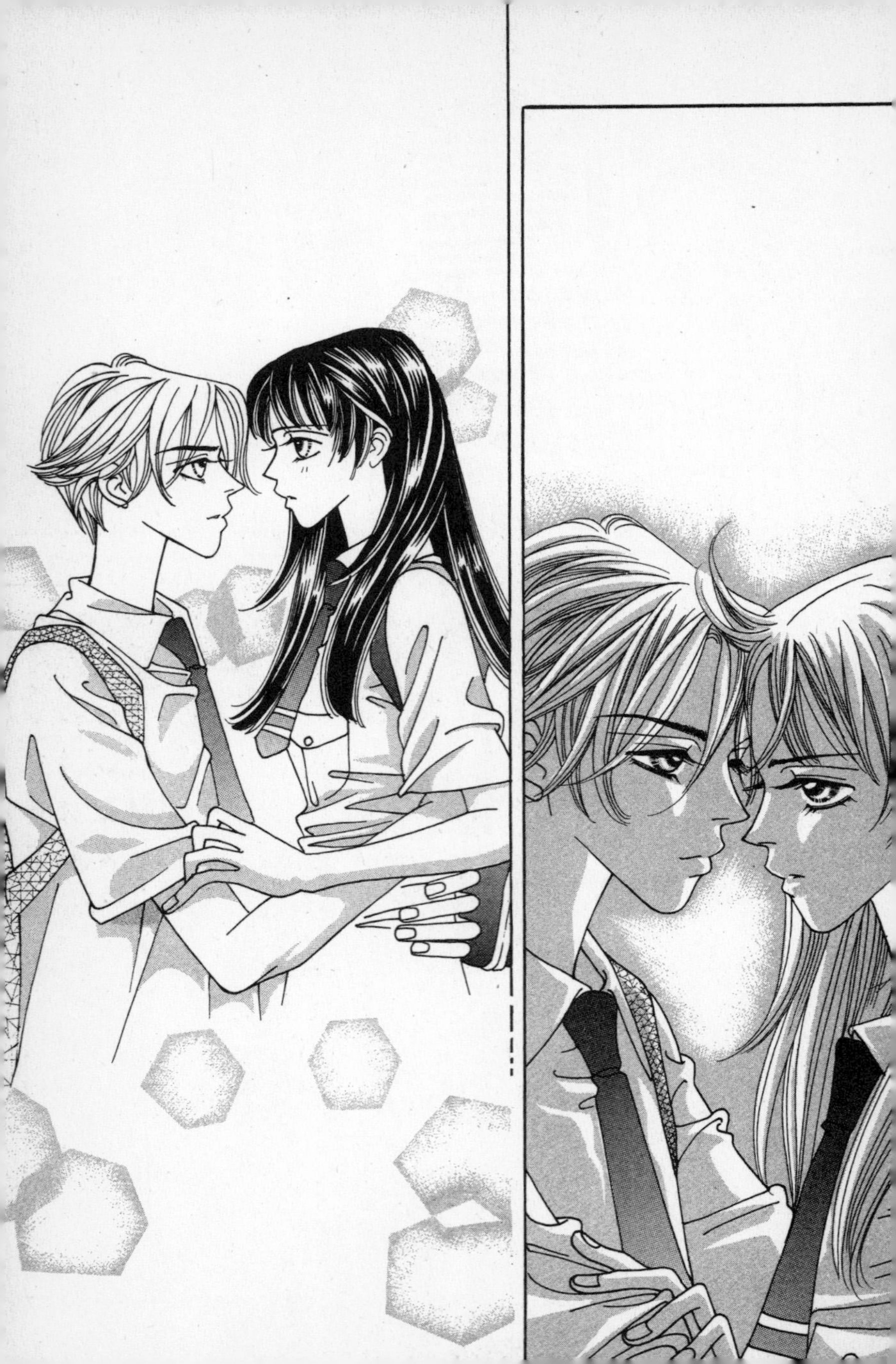

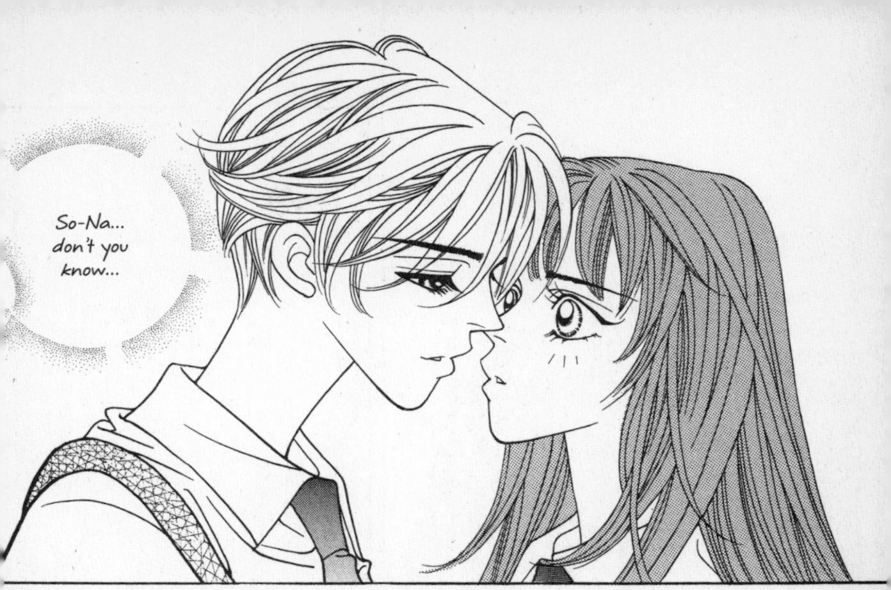
So-Na...
don't you
know...

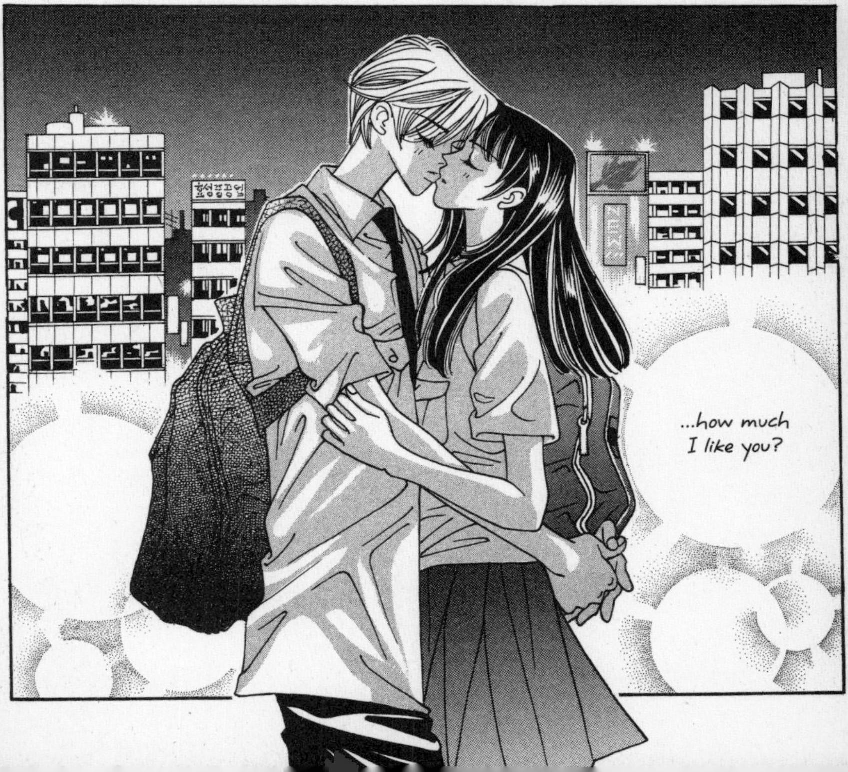
...how much
I like you?

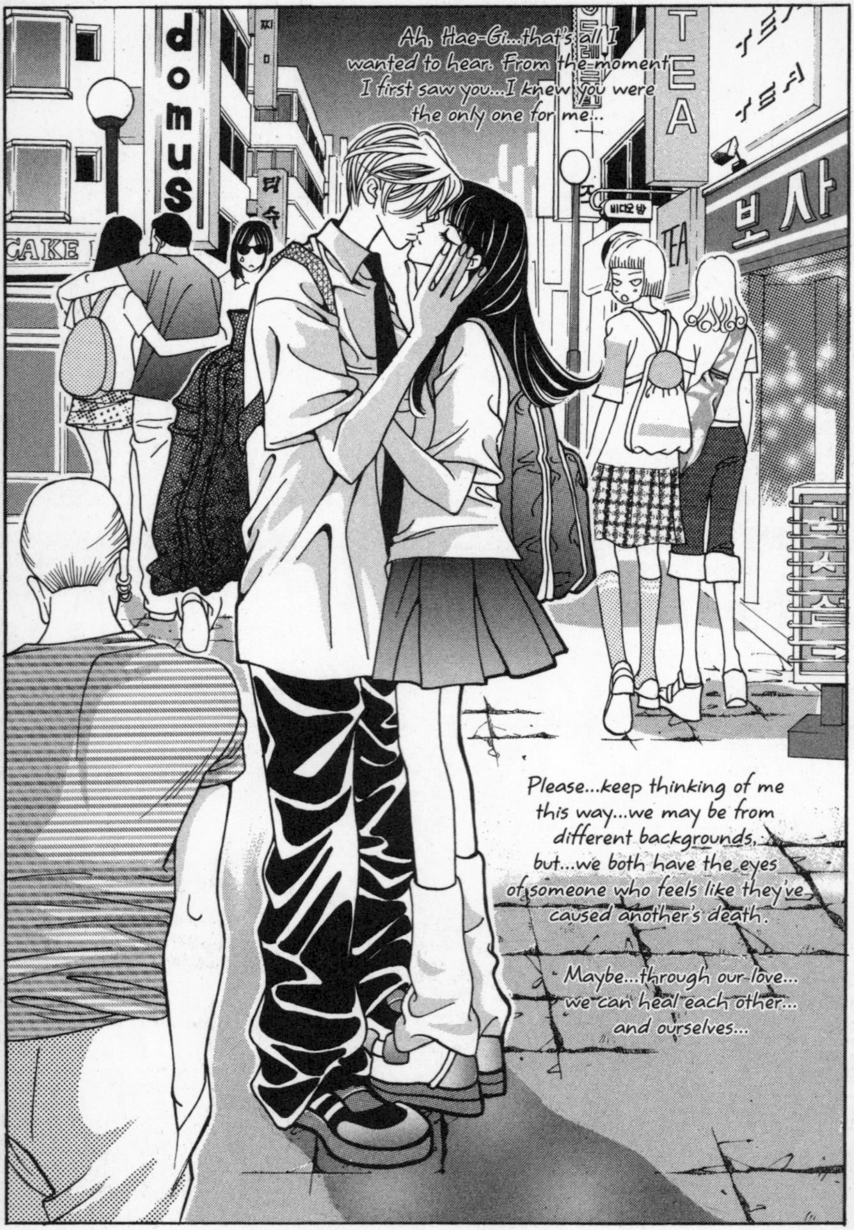
Ah, Hae-Gi...that's all I wanted to hear. From the moment I first saw you...I knew you were the only one for me...
domus
TEA
Please...keep thinking of me this way...we may be from different backgrounds, but...we both have the eyes of someone who feels like they've caused another's death.
Maybe...through our love... we can heal each other... and ourselves...

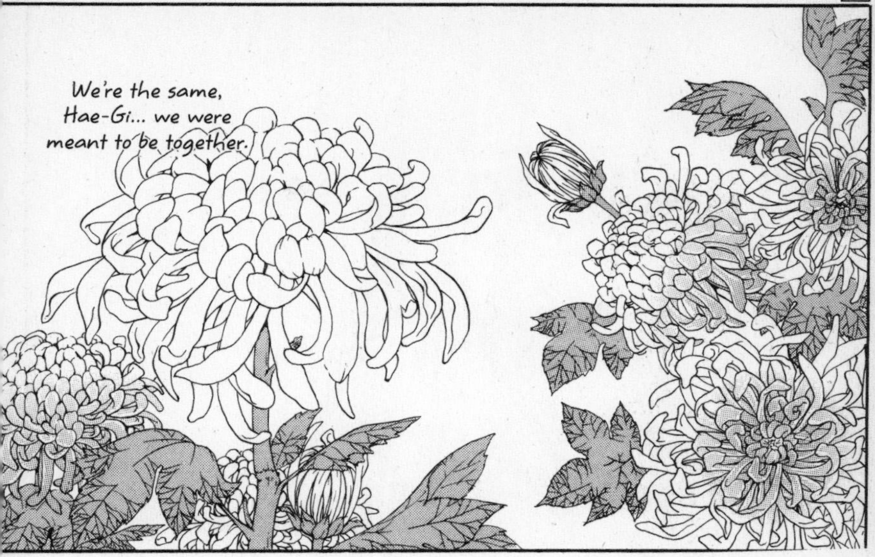
We're the same,
Hae-Gi... we were
meant to be together.

Part 14: **Sunflower**

You're So High-and-Mighty

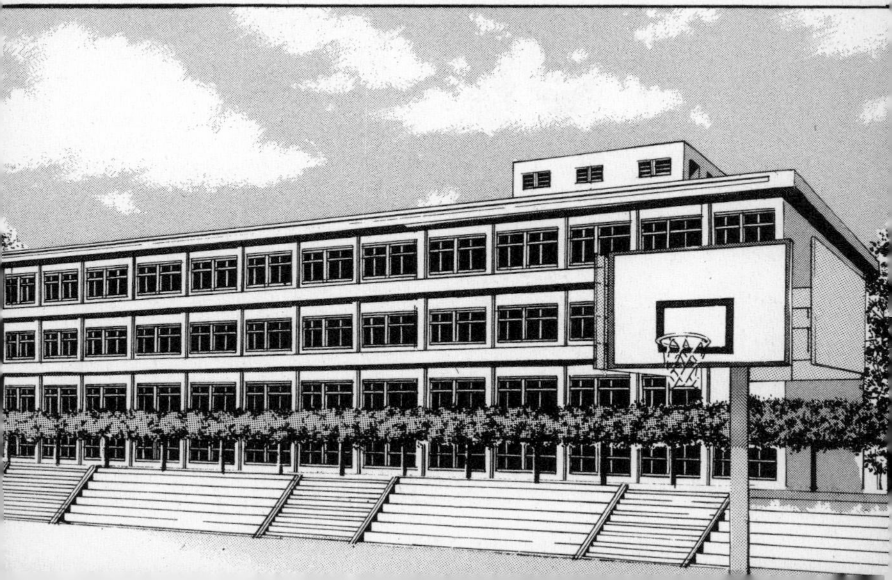

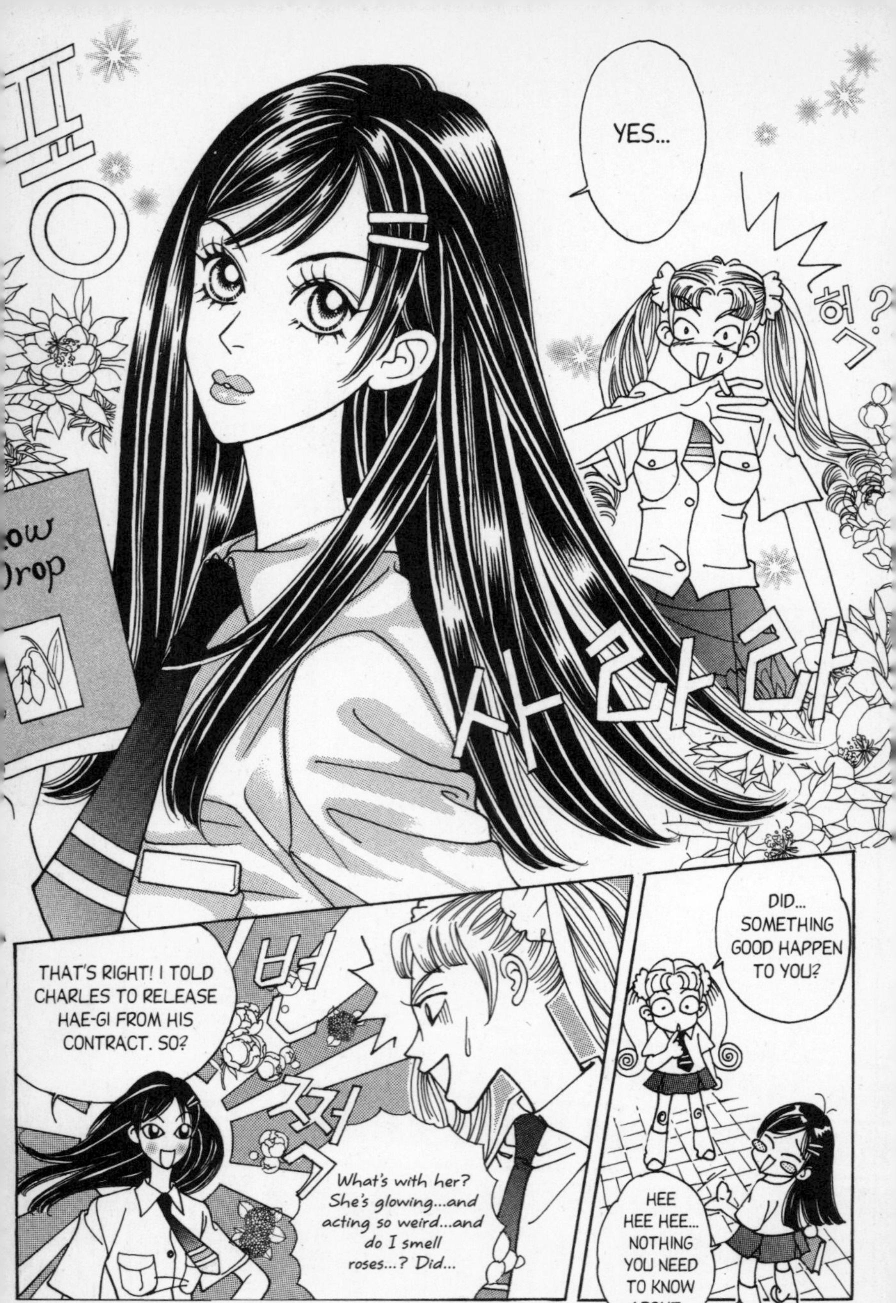
YES...
헉?
THAT'S RIGHT! I TOLD CHARLES TO RELEASE HAE-GI FROM HIS CONTRACT. SO?
What's with her? She's glowing...and acting so weird...and do I smell roses...? Did...
DID... SOMETHING GOOD HAPPEN TO YOU?
HEE HEE HEE... NOTHING YOU NEED TO KNOW ABOUT...

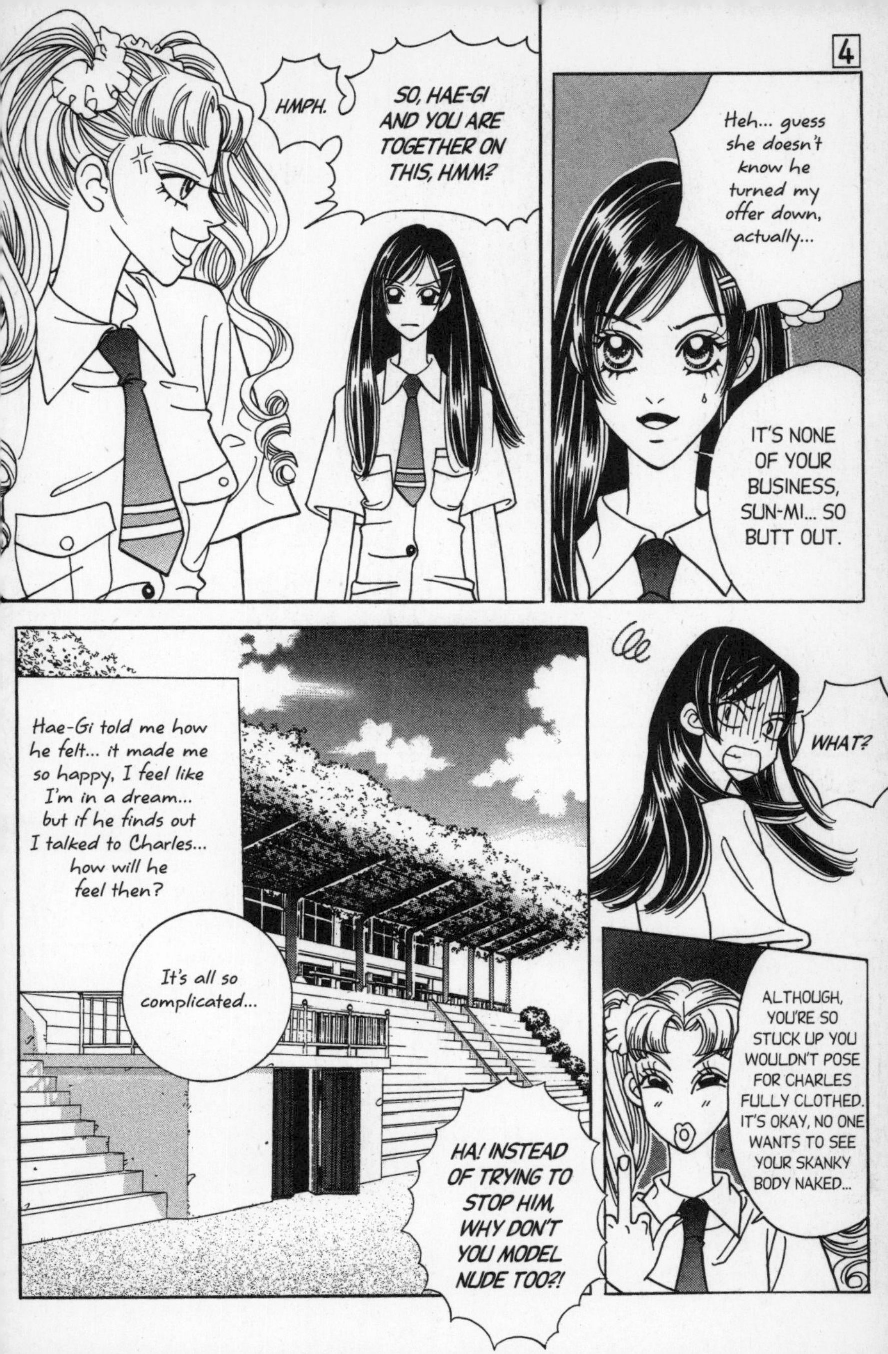
4
HMPH.
SO, HAE-GI AND YOU ARE TOGETHER ON THIS, HMM?
Heh... guess she doesn't know he turned my offer down, actually...
IT'S NONE OF YOUR BUSINESS, SUN-MI... SO BUTT OUT.
Hae-Gi told me how he felt... it made me so happy, I feel like I'm in a dream... but if he finds out I talked to Charles... how will he feel then?
It's all so complicated...
HA! INSTEAD OF TRYING TO STOP HIM, WHY DON'T YOU MODEL NUDE TOO?!
WHAT?
ALTHOUGH, YOU'RE SO STUCK UP YOU WOULDN'T POSE FOR CHARLES FULLY CLOTHED. IT'S OKAY, NO ONE WANTS TO SEE YOUR SKANKY BODY NAKED...

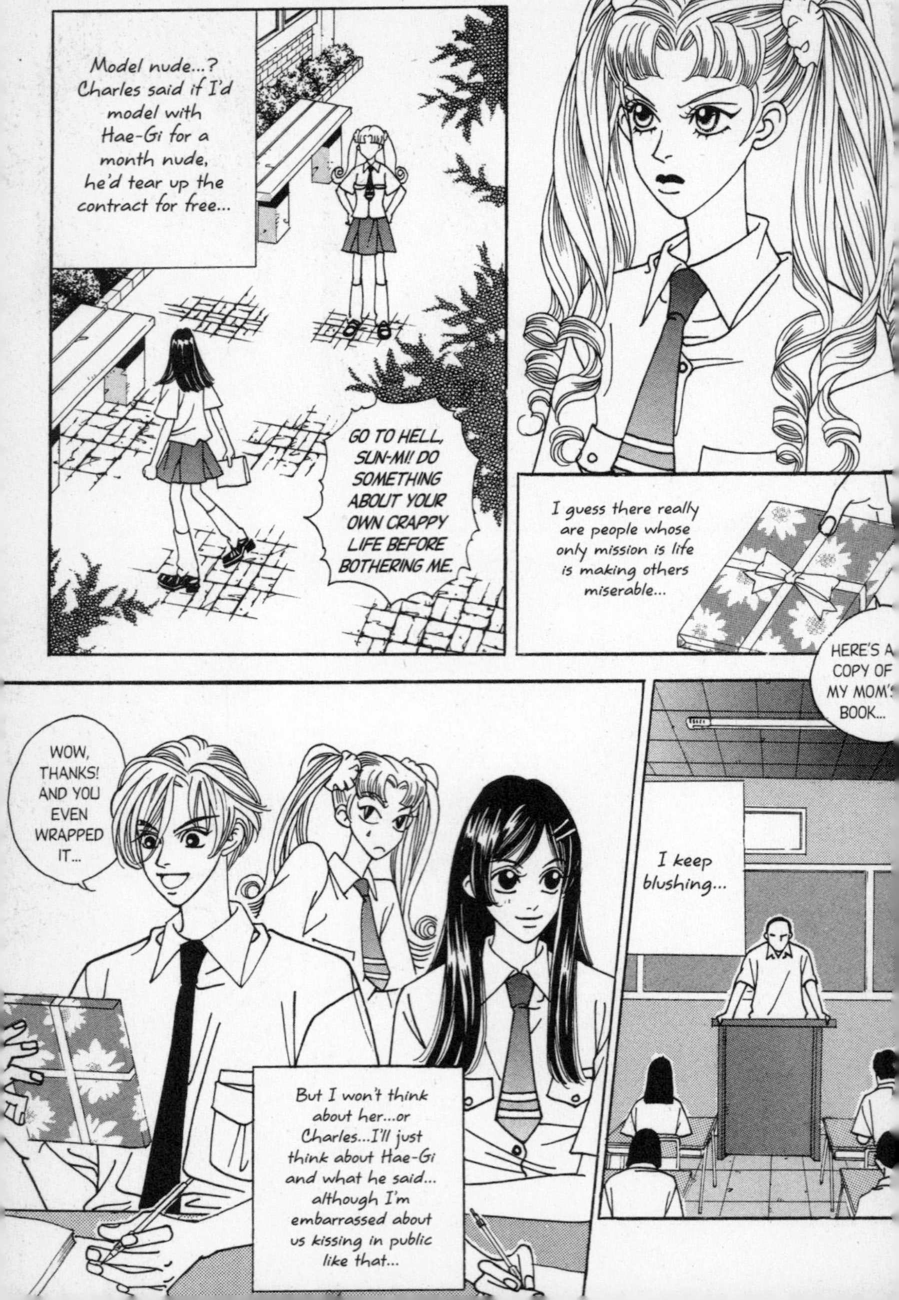
Model nude...? Charles said if I'd model with Hae-Gi for a month nude, he'd tear up the contract for free...
GO TO HELL, SUN-MI! DO SOMETHING ABOUT YOUR OWN CRAPPY LIFE BEFORE BOTHERING ME.
I guess there really are people whose only mission is life is making others miserable...
HERE'S A COPY OF MY MOM'S BOOK...
WOW, THANKS! AND YOU EVEN WRAPPED IT...
But I won't think about her...or Charles...I'll just think about Hae-Gi and what he said... although I'm embarrassed about us kissing in public like that...
I keep blushing...

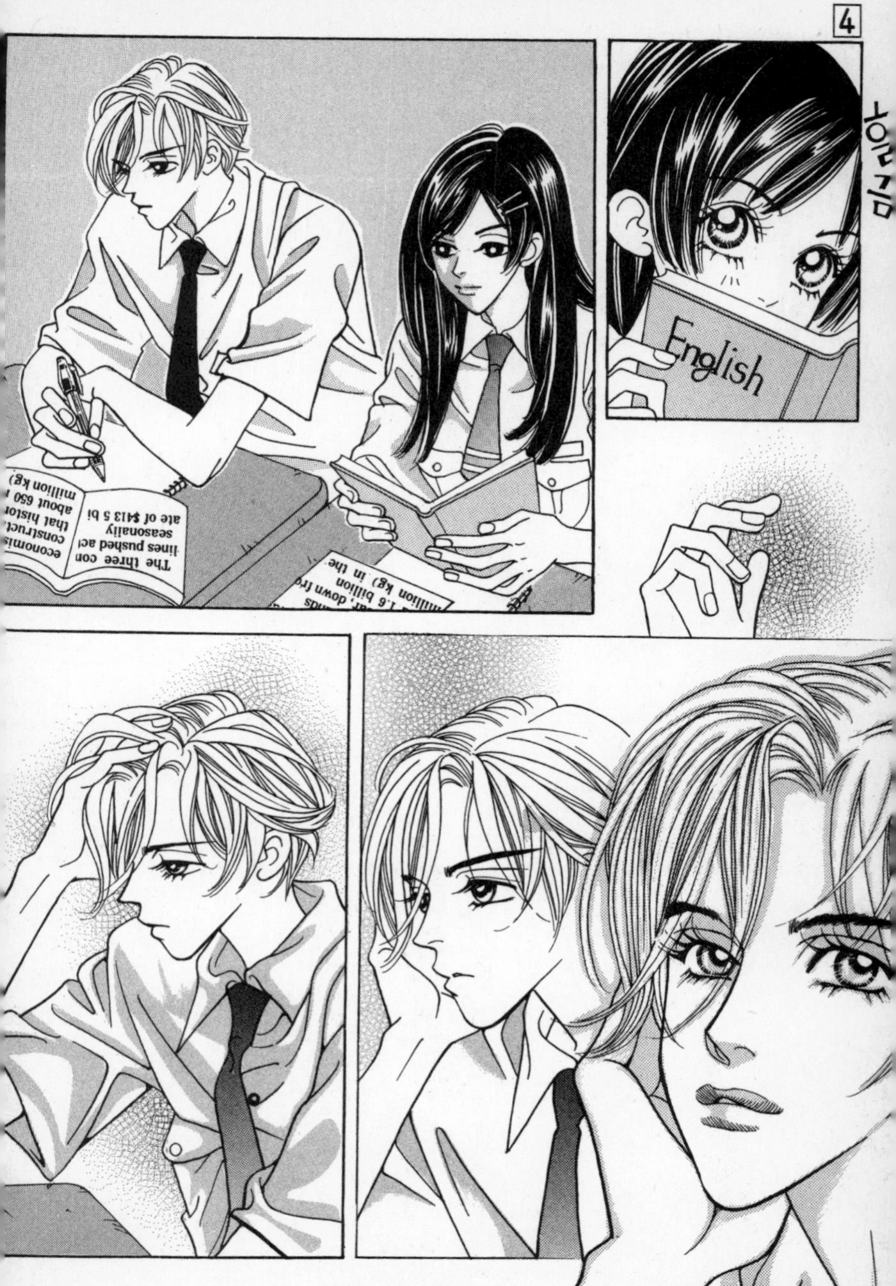
4
English

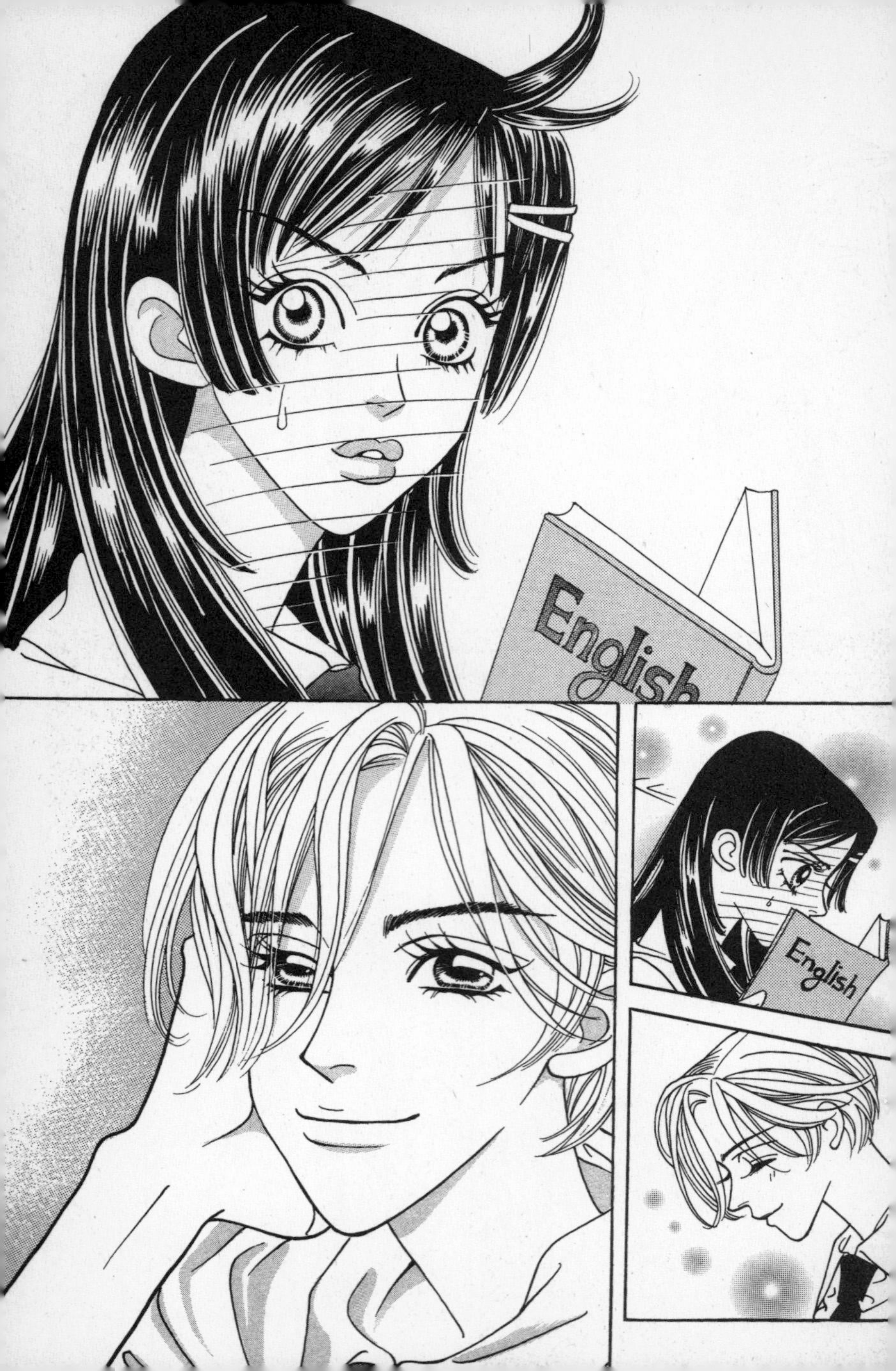
English
English

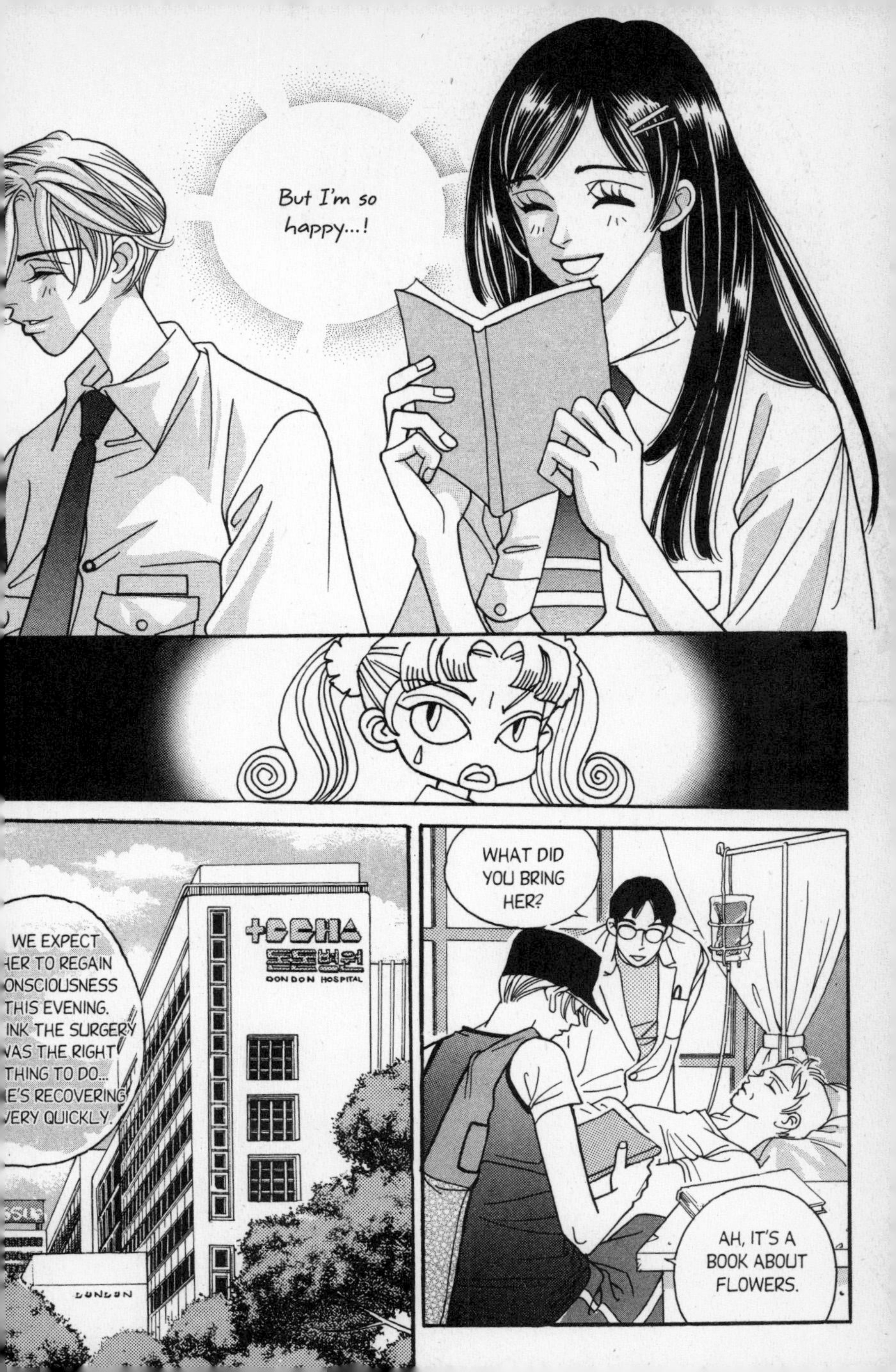
But I'm so happy...!
WE EXPECT HER TO REGAIN ONSCIOUSNESS THIS EVENING. INK THE SURGERY WAS THE RIGHT THING TO DO... E'S RECOVERING VERY QUICKLY.
DONDON HOSPITAL
DONDON
WHAT DID YOU BRING HER?
AH, IT'S A BOOK ABOUT FLOWERS.

FLOWERS?

IT WAS WRITTEN BY MY FRIEND'S MOTHER... MY MOM WAS A BIG FAN OF THE BOOK WHEN IT FIRST CAME OUT.

Snow Drop

BOY

I SEE... SO YOU BROUGHT HER SOMETHING SHE USED TO LIKE, THAT SHE'LL SEE WHEN SHE WAKES UP? THAT'S A GREAT IDEA.

JUST MAKE SURE IT CAN'T BRING BACK ANY BAD MEMORIES...

NO... IT'S JUST A BOOK ABOUT FLOWERS.

BOY

...

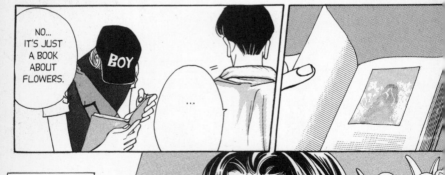

Ah... this is the page that was ripped out of my mom's copy... it's So-Na's mother...

I wonder wh this was take She looks l So-Na. A li nicer, mayb

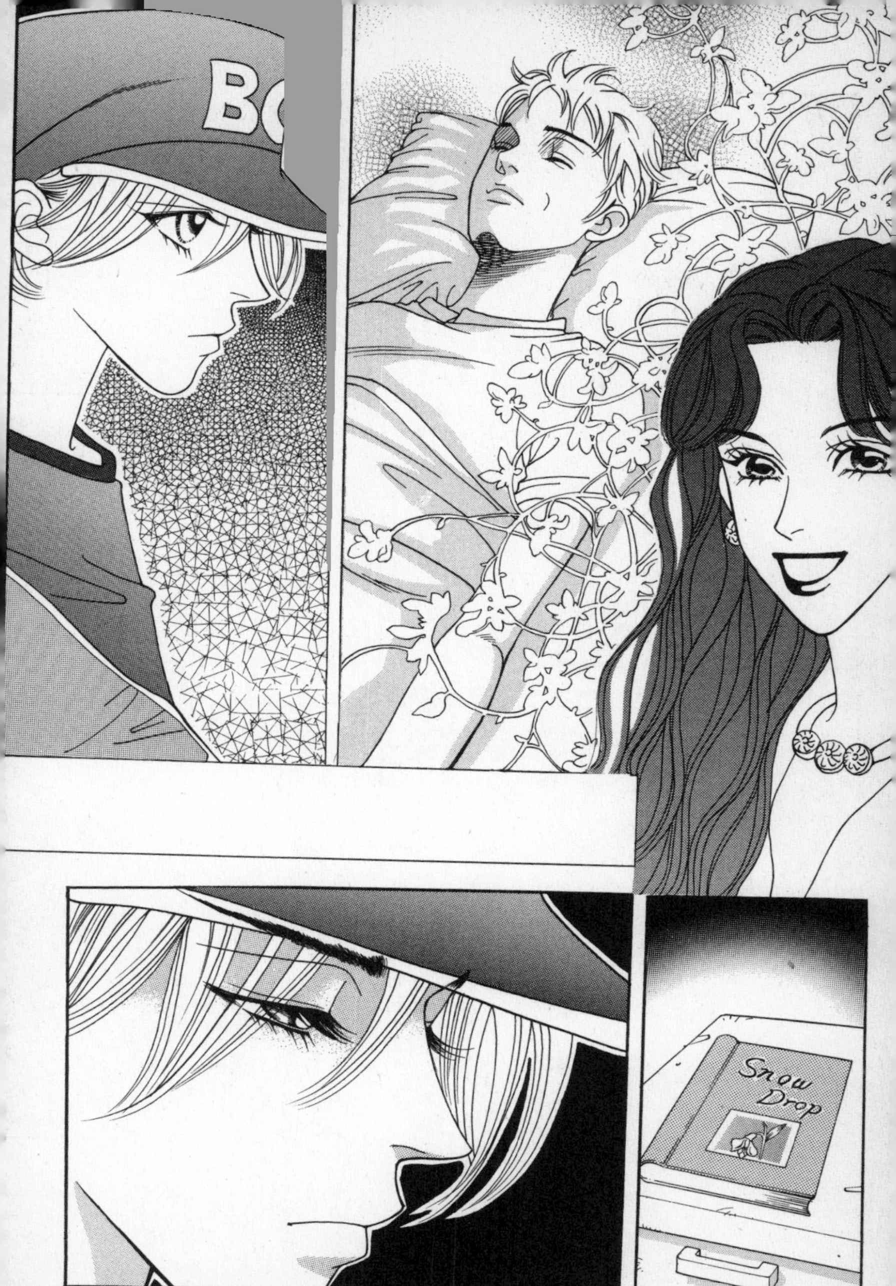
Snow Drop

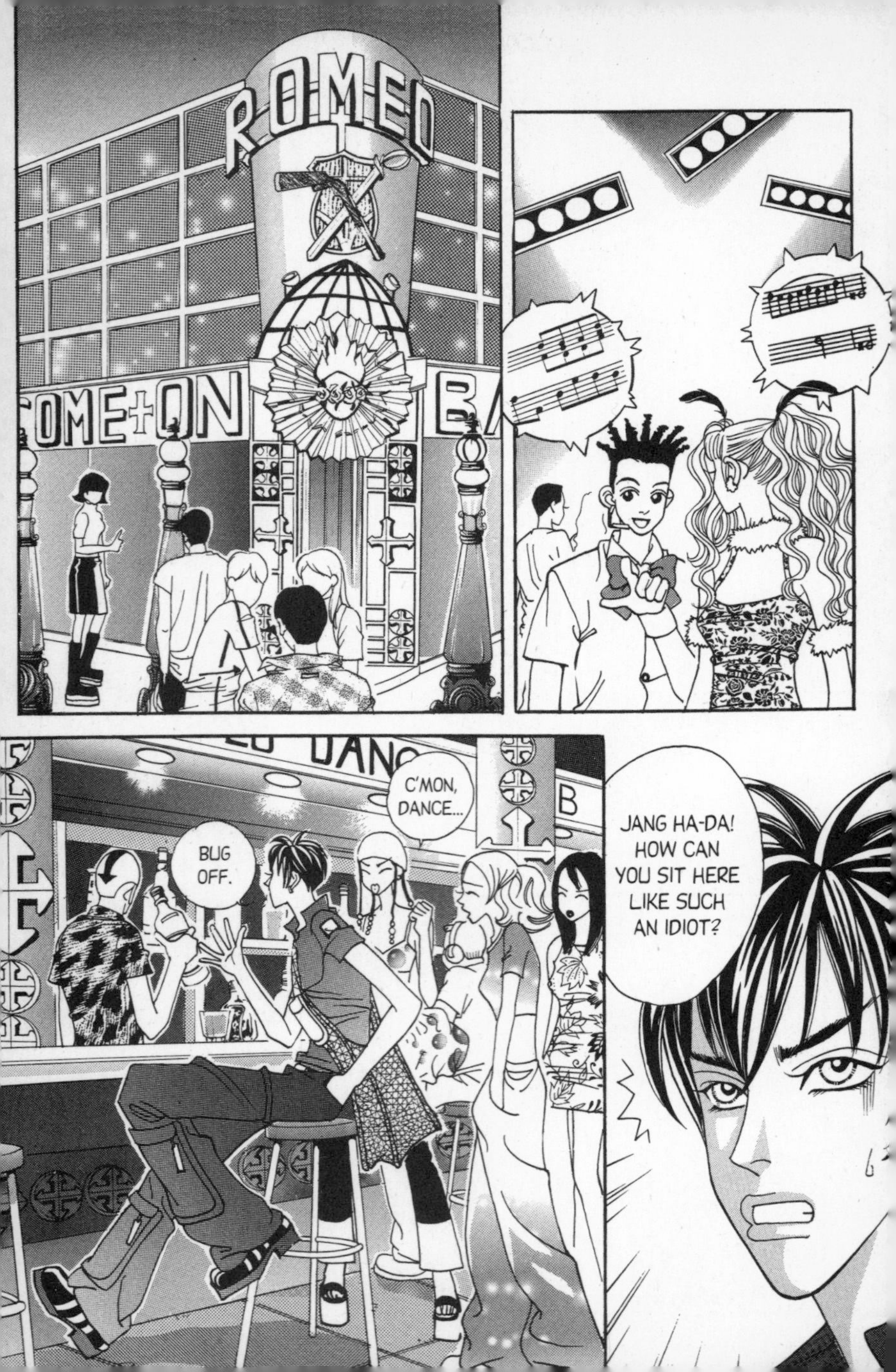
ROMEO
C'MON, DANCE...
BUG OFF.
JANG HA-DA! HOW CAN YOU SIT HERE LIKE SUCH AN IDIOT?

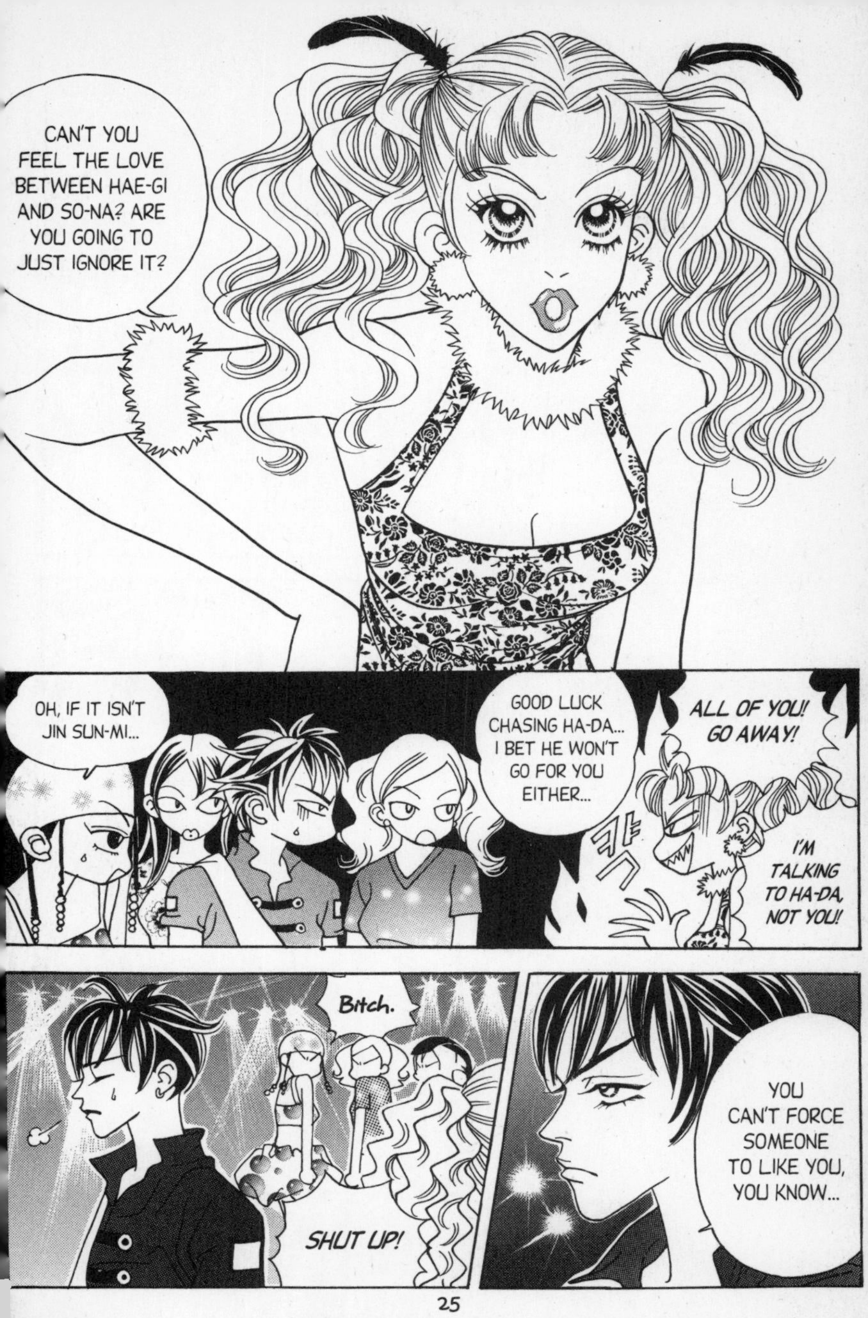
CAN'T YOU FEEL THE LOVE BETWEEN HAE-GI AND SO-NA? ARE YOU GOING TO JUST IGNORE IT?
OH, IF IT ISN'T JIN SUN-MI...
GOOD LUCK CHASING HA-DA... I BET HE WON'T GO FOR YOU EITHER...
ALL OF YOU! GO AWAY!
I'M TALKING TO HA-DA, NOT YOU!
Bitch.
SHUT UP!
YOU CAN'T FORCE SOMEONE TO LIKE YOU, YOU KNOW...

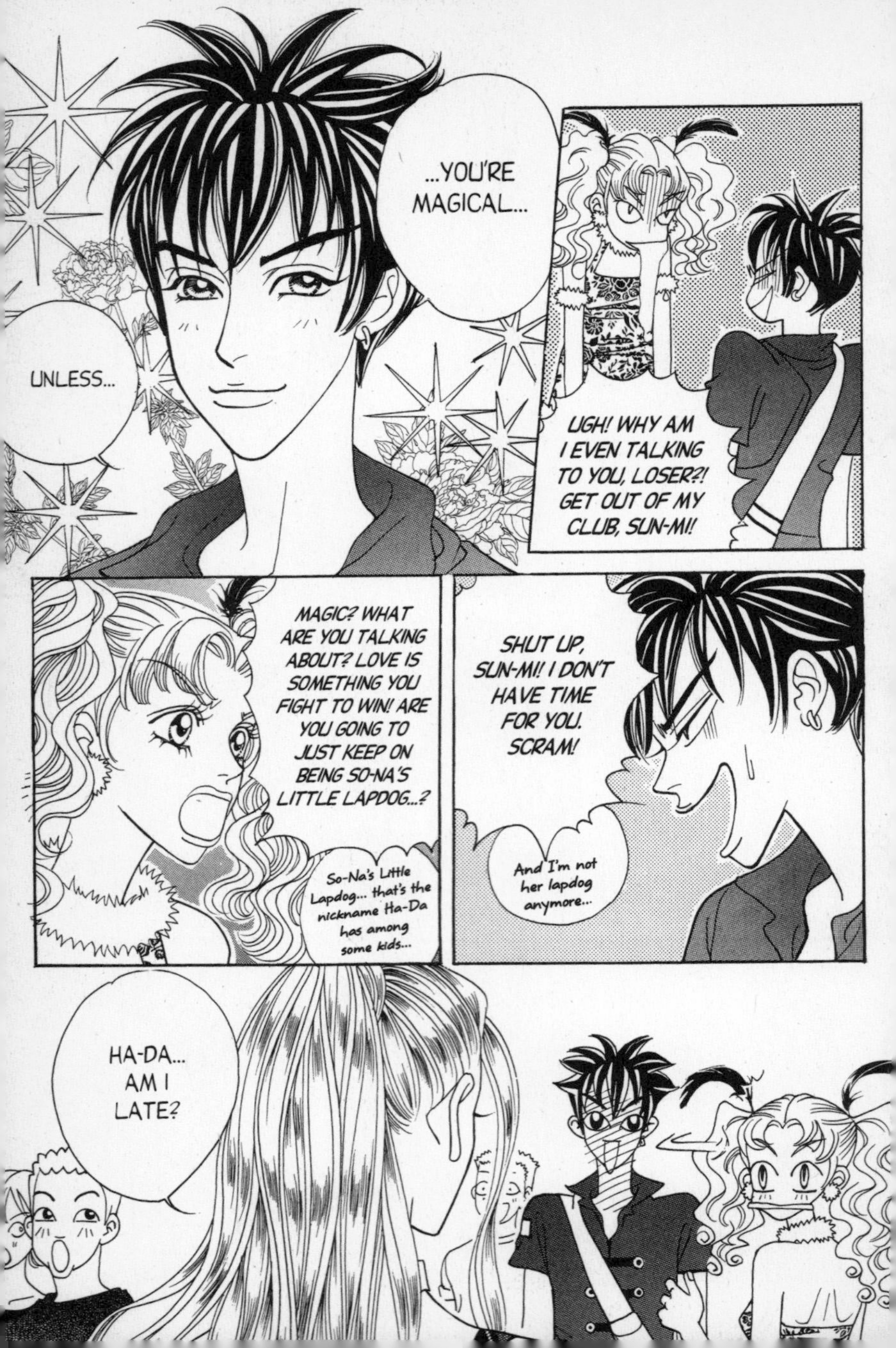

UNLESS...
...YOU'RE MAGICAL...
UGH! WHY AM I EVEN TALKING TO YOU, LOSER?! GET OUT OF MY CLUB, SUN-MI!
MAGIC? WHAT ARE YOU TALKING ABOUT? LOVE IS SOMETHING YOU FIGHT TO WIN! ARE YOU GOING TO JUST KEEP ON BEING SO-NA'S LITTLE LAPDOG...?
So-Na's Little Lapdog... that's the nickname Ha-Da has among some kids...
SHUT UP, SUN-MI! I DON'T HAVE TIME FOR YOU. SCRAM!
And I'm not her lapdog anymore...
HA-DA... AM I LATE?

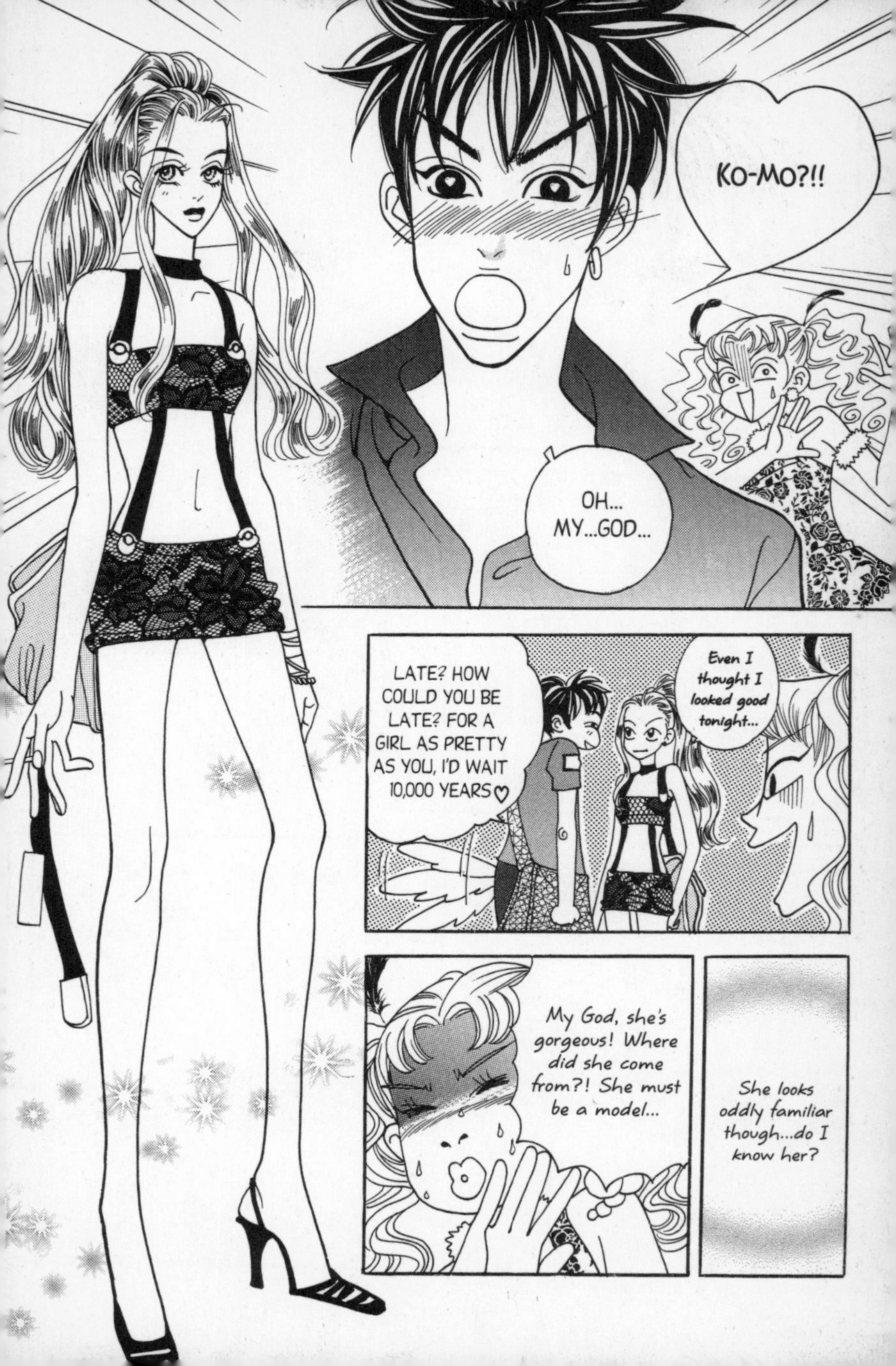
KO-MO?!!
OH... MY...GOD...
LATE? HOW COULD YOU BE LATE? FOR A GIRL AS PRETTY AS YOU, I'D WAIT 10,000 YEARS♡
Even I thought I looked good tonight...
My God, she's gorgeous! Where did she come from?! She must be a model...
She looks oddly familiar though...do I know her?

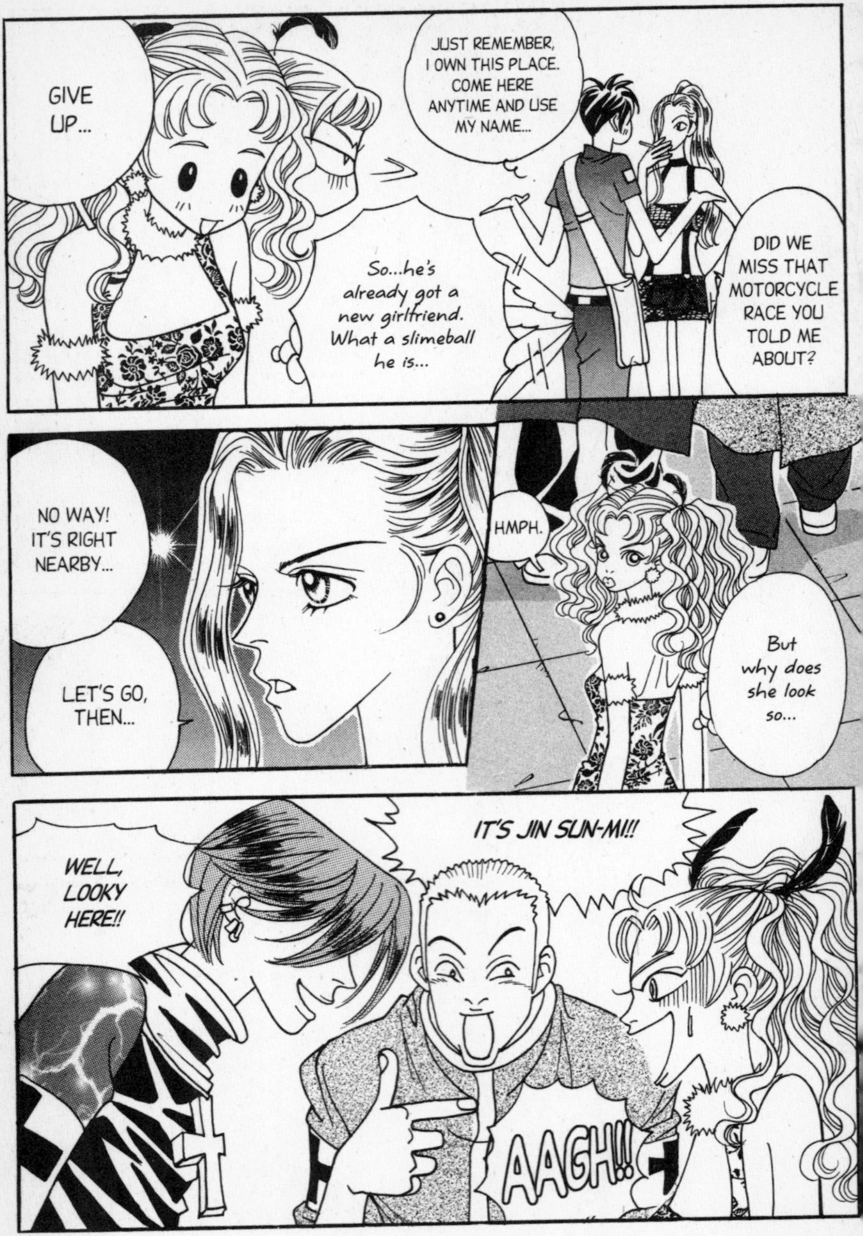
GIVE UP...
JUST REMEMBER, I OWN THIS PLACE. COME HERE ANYTIME AND USE MY NAME...
So...he's already got a new girlfriend. What a slimeball he is...
DID WE MISS THAT MOTORCYCLE RACE YOU TOLD ME ABOUT?
NO WAY! IT'S RIGHT NEARBY...
LET'S GO, THEN...
HMPH.
But why does she look so...
WELL, LOOKY HERE!!
IT'S JIN SUN-MI!!
AAGH!!

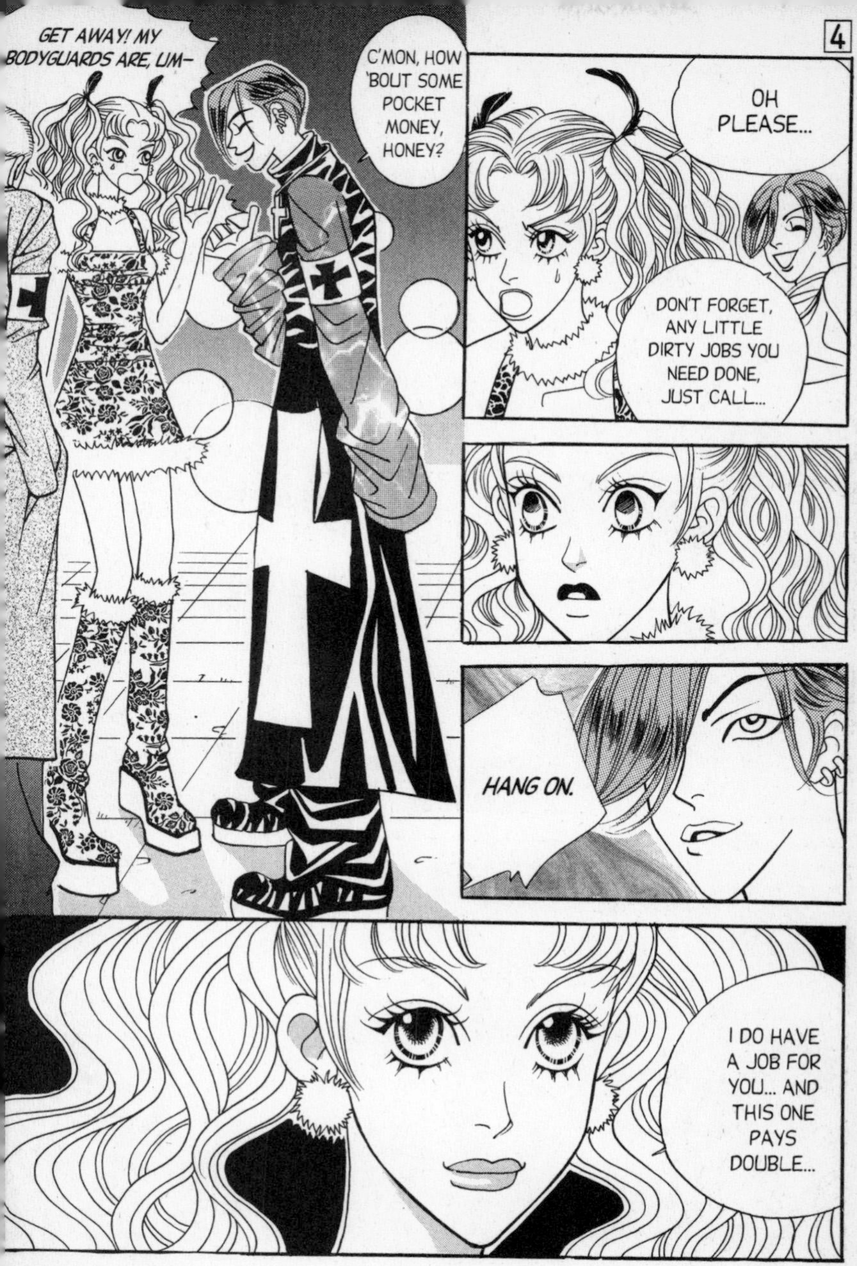
4
GET AWAY! MY BODYGUARDS ARE, UM-
C'MON, HOW 'BOUT SOME POCKET MONEY, HONEY?
OH PLEASE...
DON'T FORGET, ANY LITTLE DIRTY JOBS YOU NEED DONE, JUST CALL...
HANG ON.
I DO HAVE A JOB FOR YOU... AND THIS ONE PAYS DOUBLE...

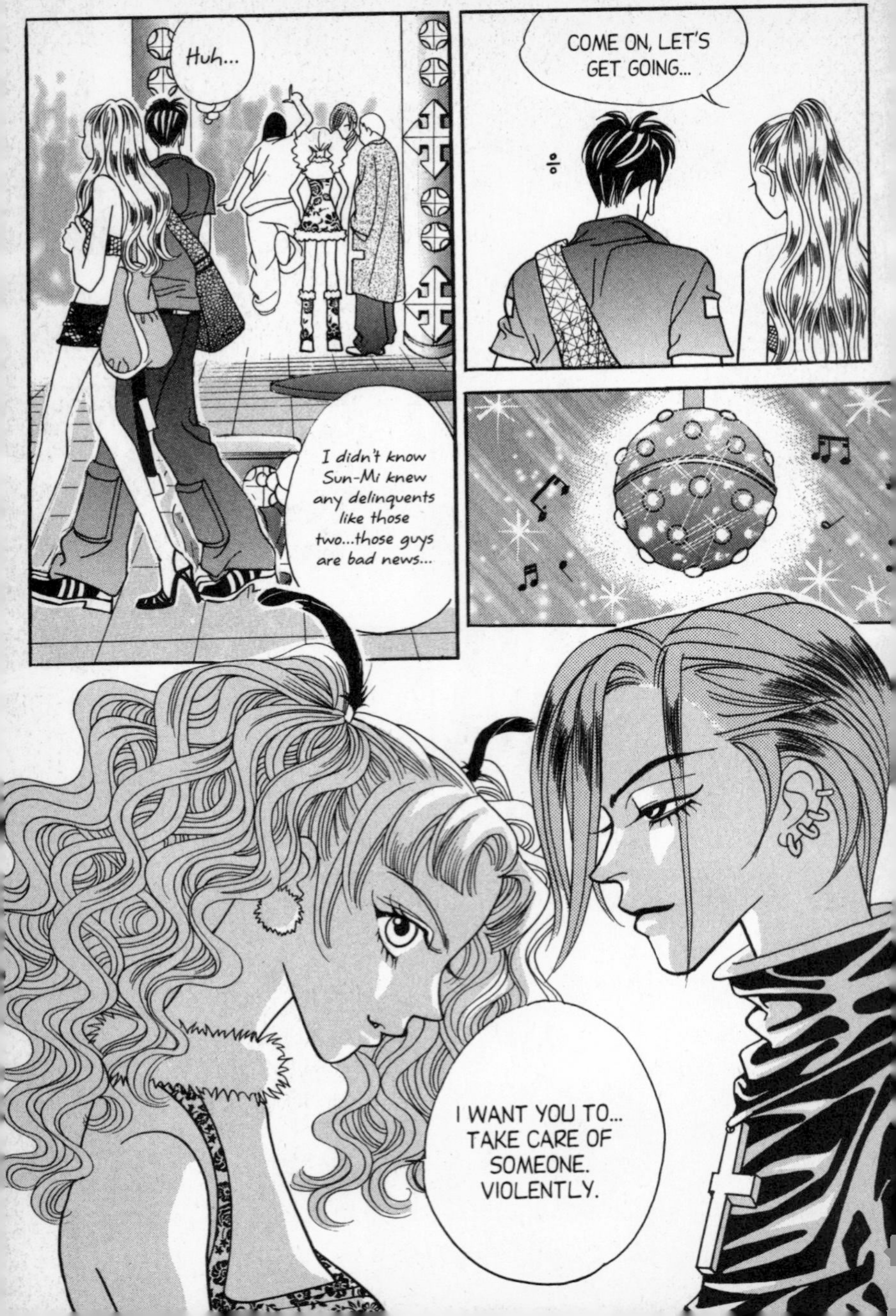

Huh...
I didn't know Sun-Mi knew any delinquents like those two...those guys are bad news...
COME ON, LET'S GET GOING...
I WANT YOU TO... TAKE CARE OF SOMEONE. VIOLENTLY.

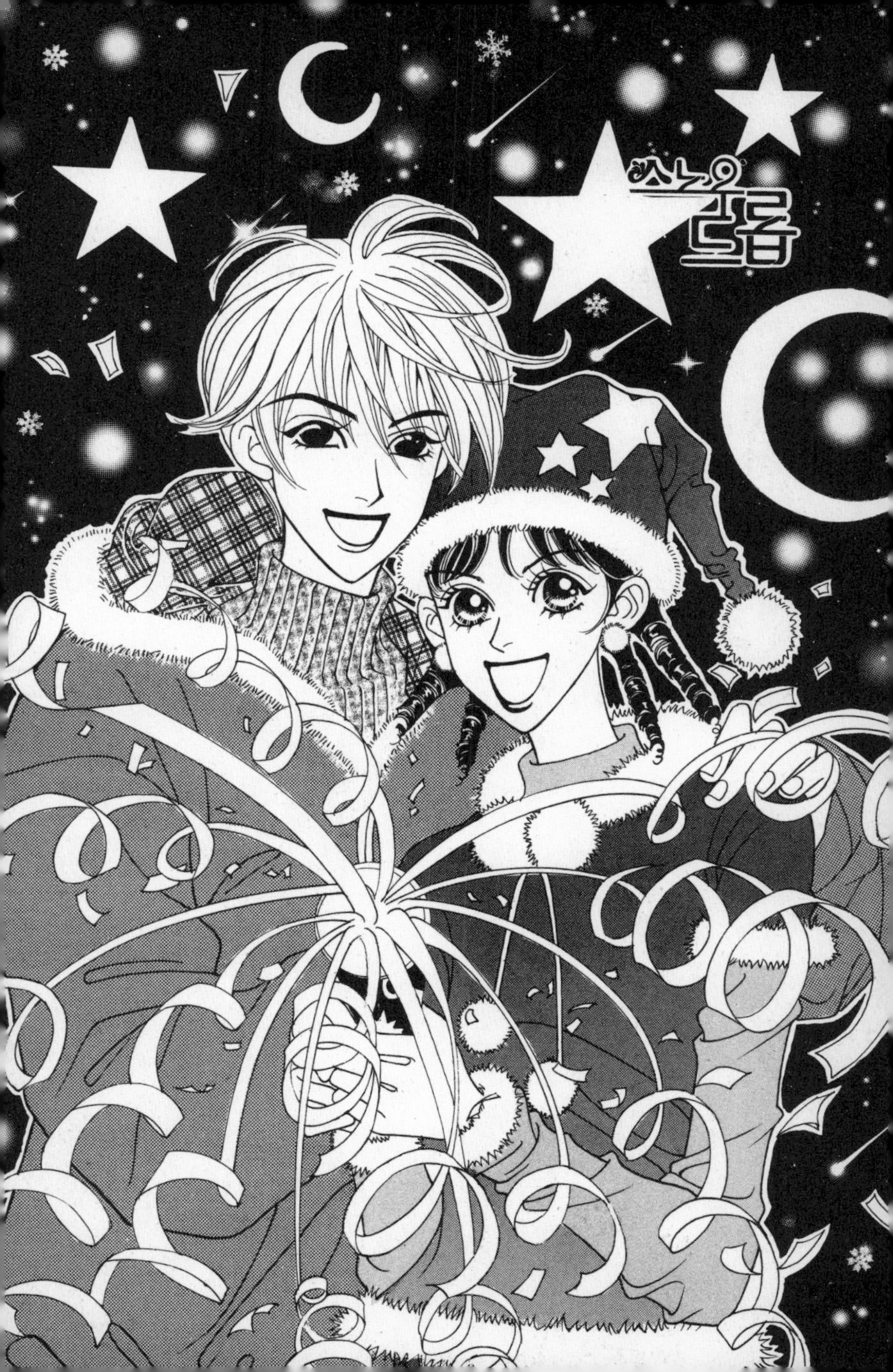
스노우 드롭

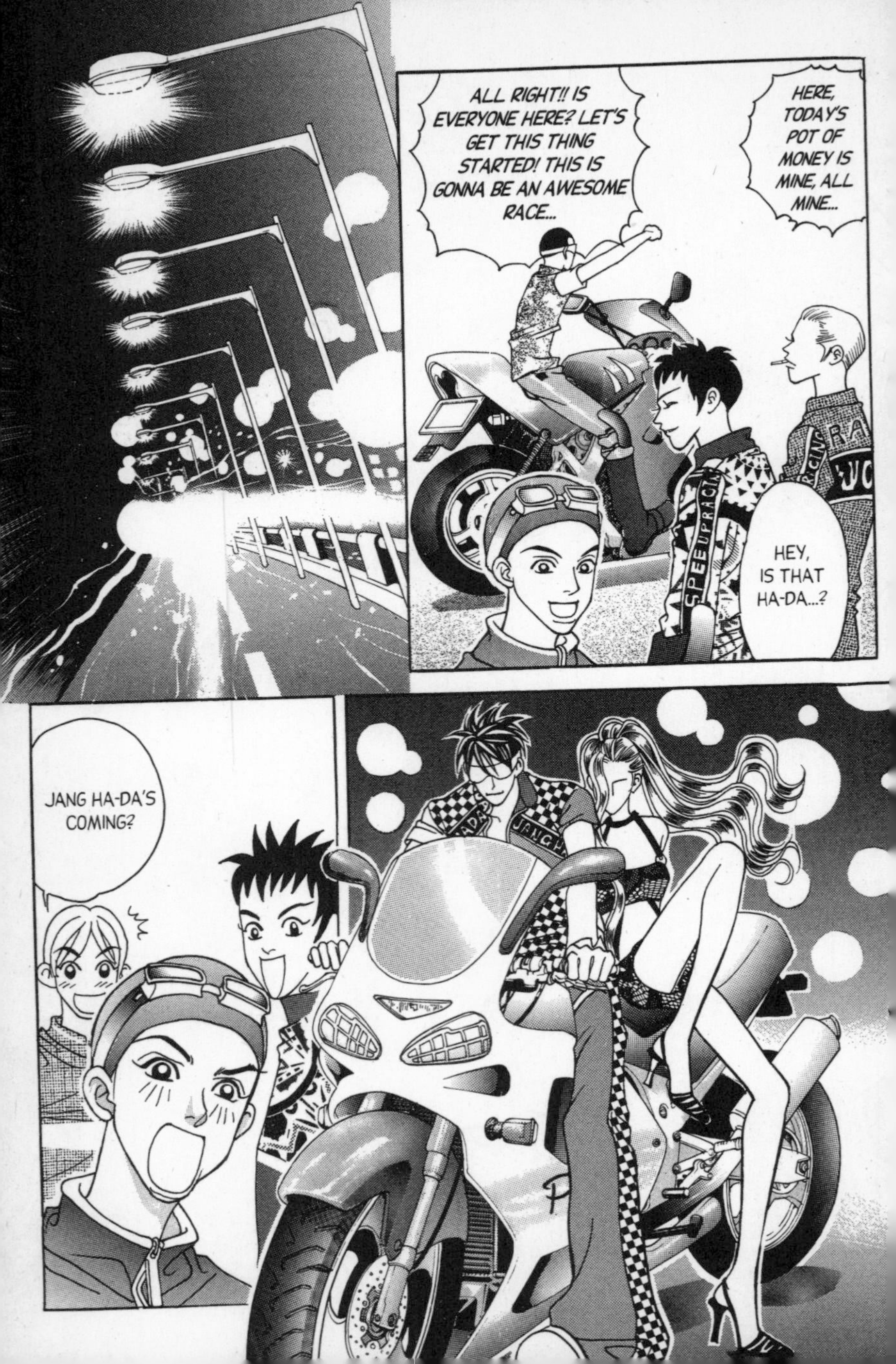
ALL RIGHT!! IS EVERYONE HERE? LET'S GET THIS THING STARTED! THIS IS GONNA BE AN AWESOME RACE...
HERE, TODAY'S POT OF MONEY IS MINE, ALL MINE...
HEY, IS THAT HA-DA...?
JANG HA-DA'S COMING?

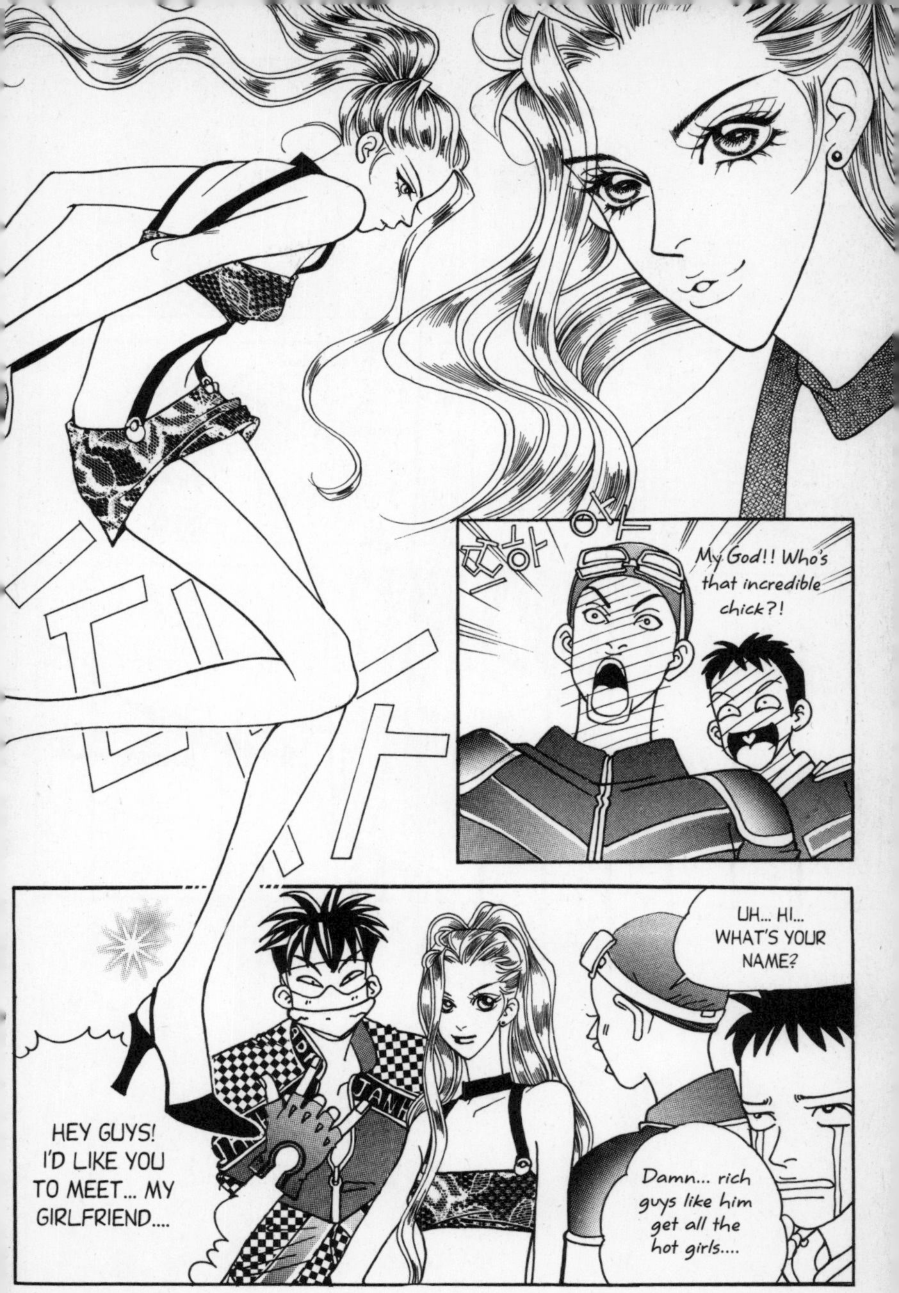
My God!! Who's that incredible chick?!
HEY GUYS! I'D LIKE YOU TO MEET... MY GIRLFRIEND....
UH... HI... WHAT'S YOUR NAME?
Damn... rich guys like him get all the hot girls....

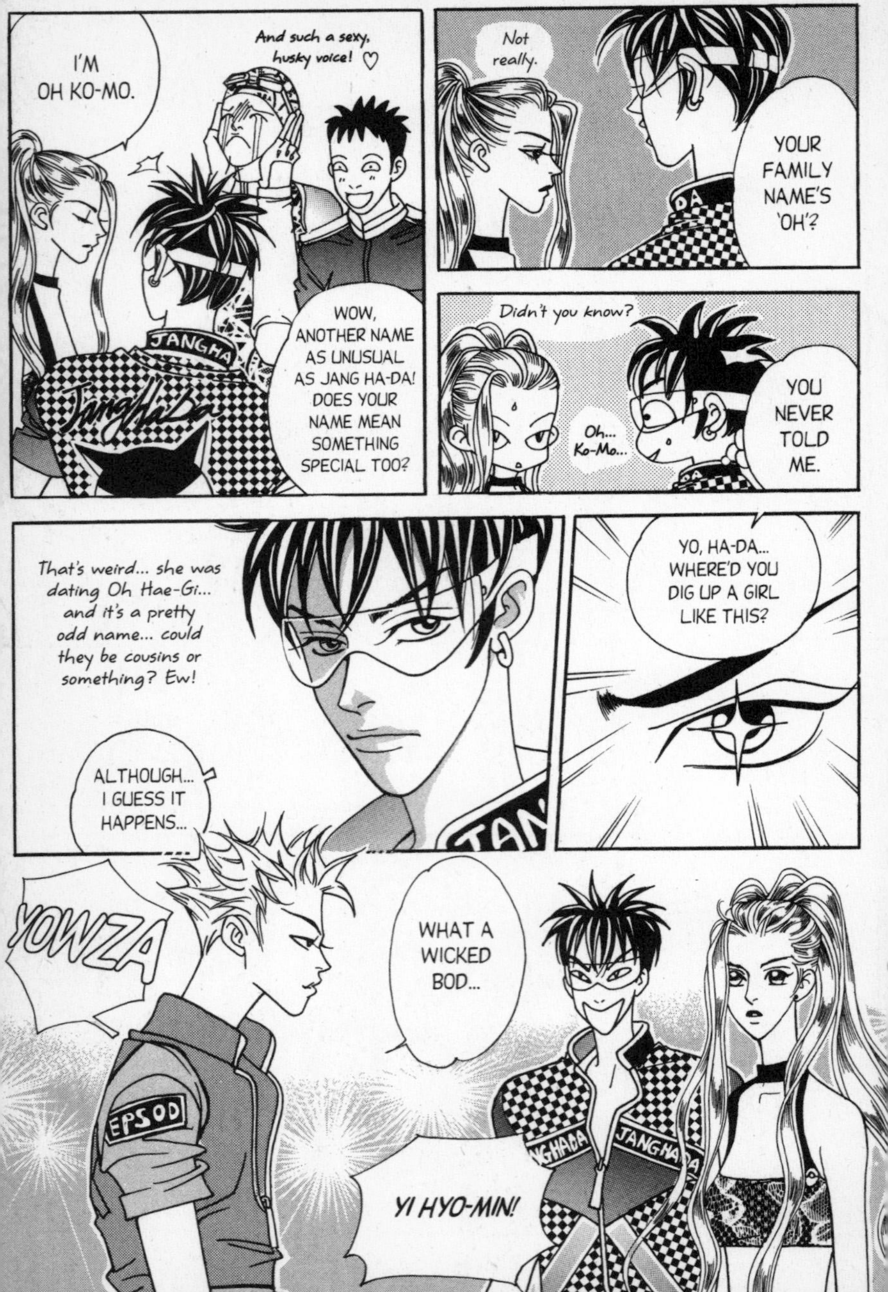
I'M OH KO-MO.
And such a sexy, husky voice! ♡
WOW, ANOTHER NAME AS UNUSUAL AS JANG HA-DA! DOES YOUR NAME MEAN SOMETHING SPECIAL TOO?
Not really.
YOUR FAMILY NAME'S 'OH'?
Didn't you know?
Oh... Ko-Mo...
YOU NEVER TOLD ME.
That's weird... she was dating Oh Hae-Gi... and it's a pretty odd name... could they be cousins or something? Ew!
ALTHOUGH... I GUESS IT HAPPENS...
YO, HA-DA... WHERE'D YOU DIG UP A GIRL LIKE THIS?
YOWZA
WHAT A WICKED BOD...
YI HYO-MIN!

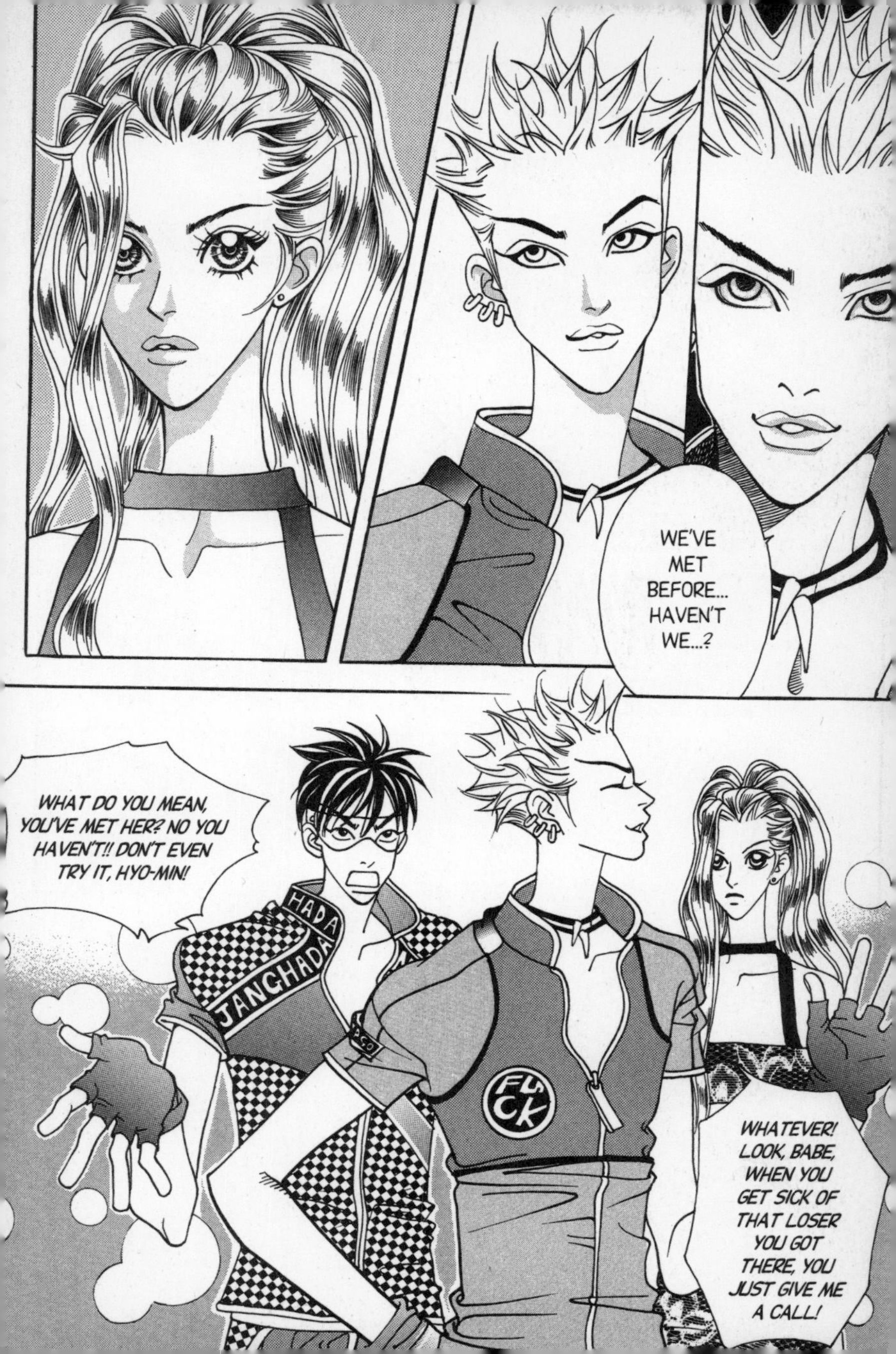
WE'VE MET BEFORE... HAVEN'T WE...?
WHAT DO YOU MEAN, YOU'VE MET HER? NO YOU HAVEN'T!! DON'T EVEN TRY IT, HYO-MIN!
HADA
JANGHADA
FUCK
WHATEVER! LOOK, BABE, WHEN YOU GET SICK OF THAT LOSER YOU GOT THERE, YOU JUST GIVE ME A CALL!

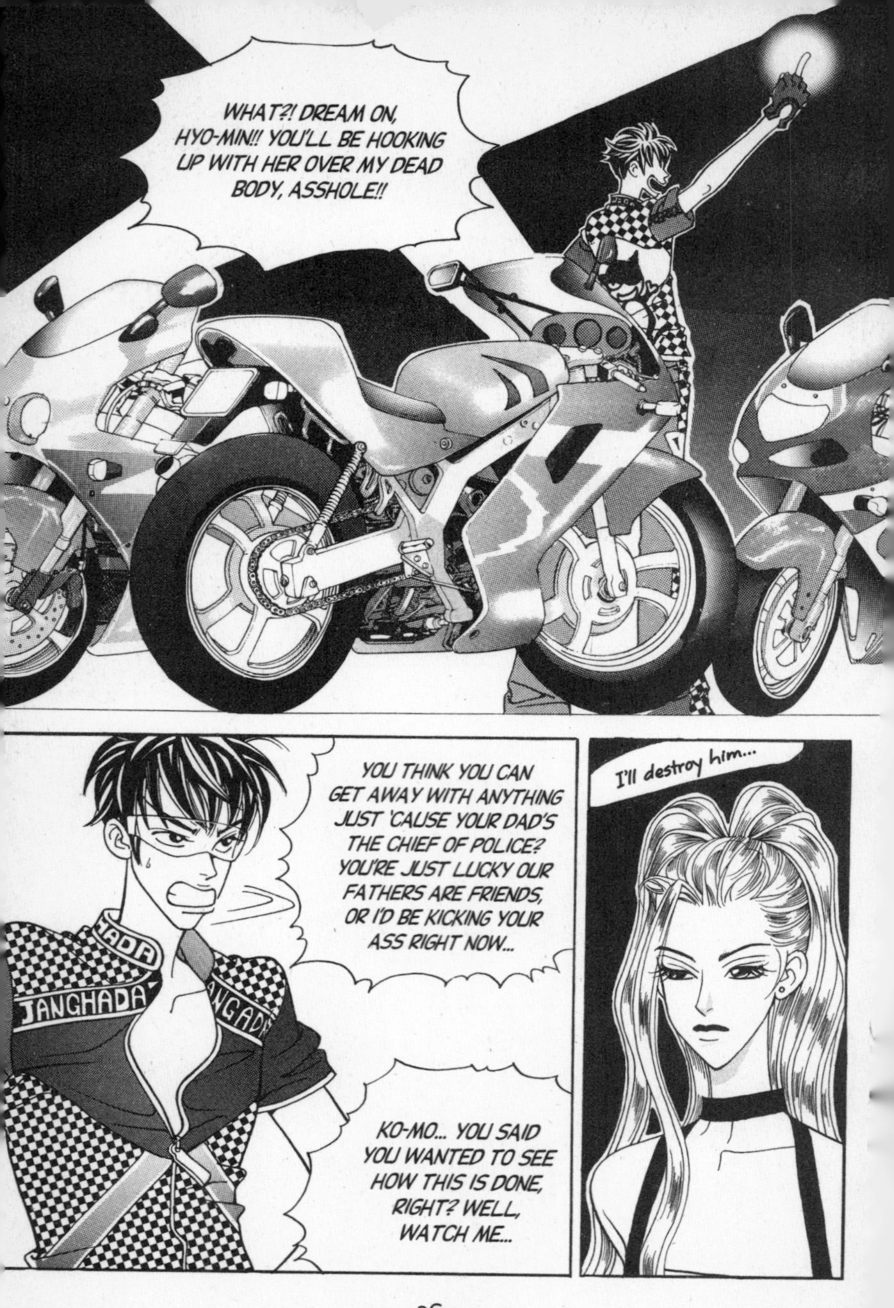
WHAT?! DREAM ON, HYO-MIN!! YOU'LL BE HOOKING UP WITH HER OVER MY DEAD BODY, ASSHOLE!!
YOU THINK YOU CAN GET AWAY WITH ANYTHING JUST 'CAUSE YOUR DAD'S THE CHIEF OF POLICE? YOU'RE JUST LUCKY OUR FATHERS ARE FRIENDS, OR I'D BE KICKING YOUR ASS RIGHT NOW...
KO-MO... YOU SAID YOU WANTED TO SEE HOW THIS IS DONE, RIGHT? WELL, WATCH ME...
JANGHADA
I'll destroy him...

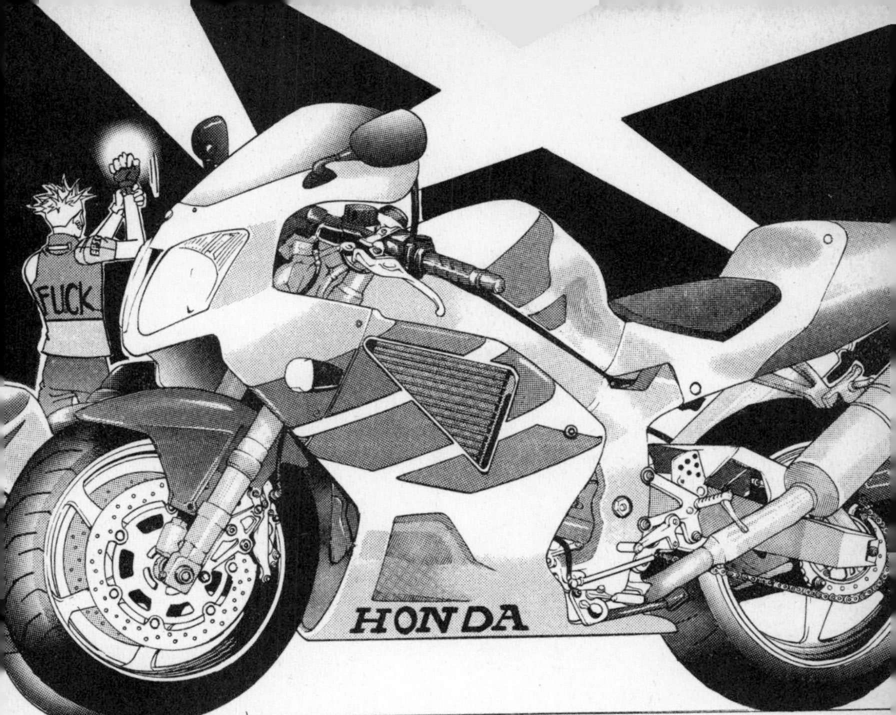
FUCK
HONDA

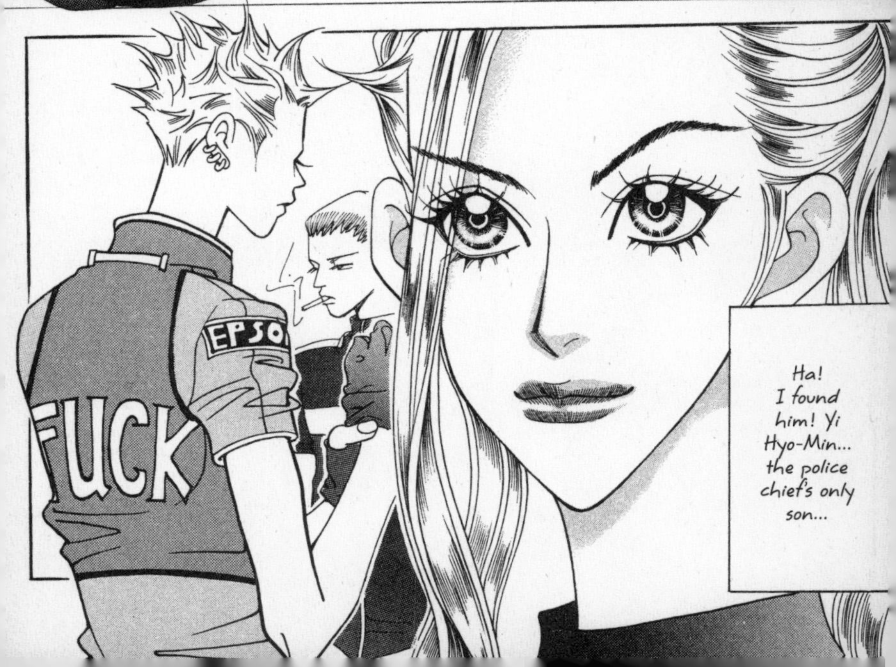
EPSO
FUCK
Ha! I found him! Yi Hyo-Min... the police chief's only son...

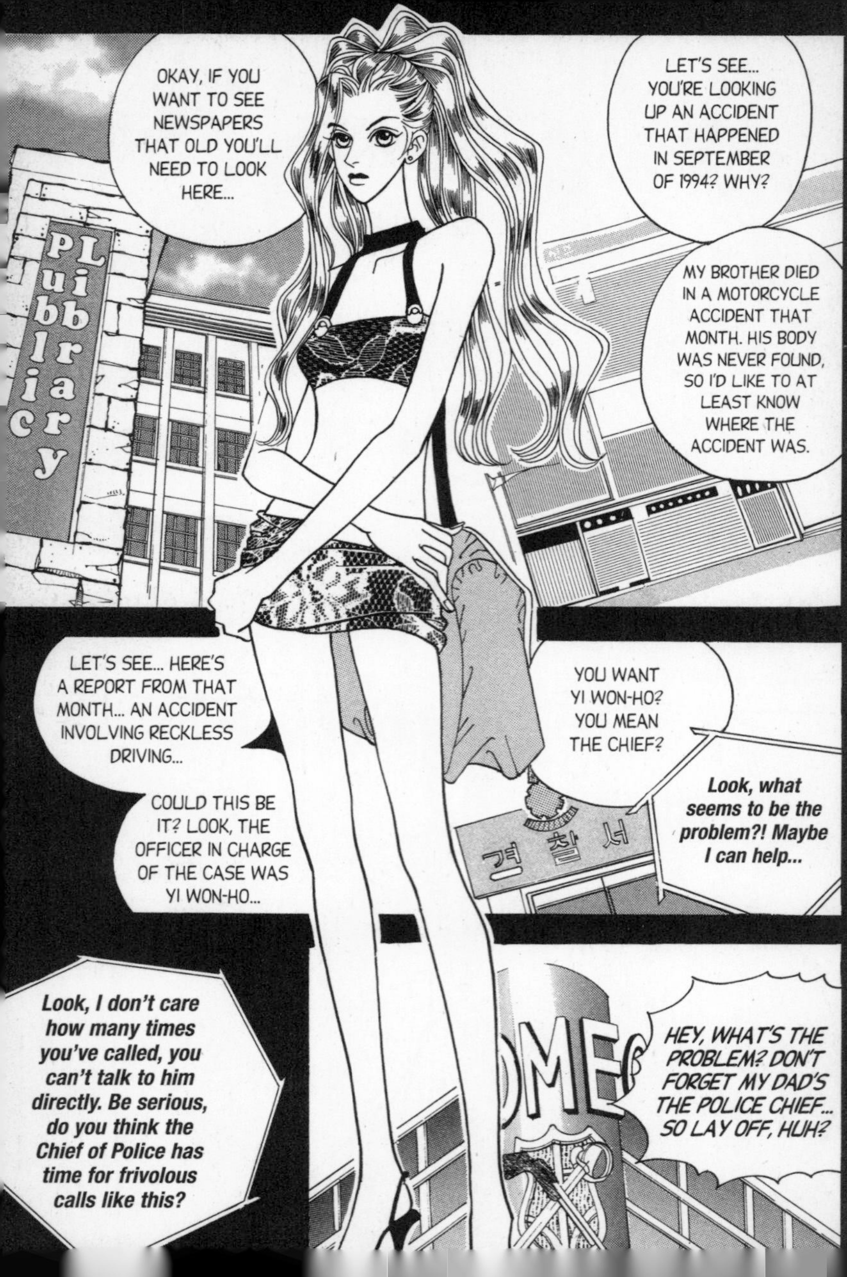
OKAY, IF YOU WANT TO SEE NEWSPAPERS THAT OLD YOU'LL NEED TO LOOK HERE...
Public Library
LET'S SEE... YOU'RE LOOKING UP AN ACCIDENT THAT HAPPENED IN SEPTEMBER OF 1994? WHY?
MY BROTHER DIED IN A MOTORCYCLE ACCIDENT THAT MONTH. HIS BODY WAS NEVER FOUND, SO I'D LIKE TO AT LEAST KNOW WHERE THE ACCIDENT WAS.
LET'S SEE... HERE'S A REPORT FROM THAT MONTH... AN ACCIDENT INVOLVING RECKLESS DRIVING...
COULD THIS BE IT? LOOK, THE OFFICER IN CHARGE OF THE CASE WAS YI WON-HO...
YOU WANT YI WON-HO? YOU MEAN THE CHIEF?
Look, what seems to be the problem?! Maybe I can help...
경찰서
Look, I don't care how many times you've called, you can't talk to him directly. Be serious, do you think the Chief of Police has time for frivolous calls like this?
HEY, WHAT'S THE PROBLEM? DON'T FORGET MY DAD'S THE POLICE CHIEF... SO LAY OFF, HUH?

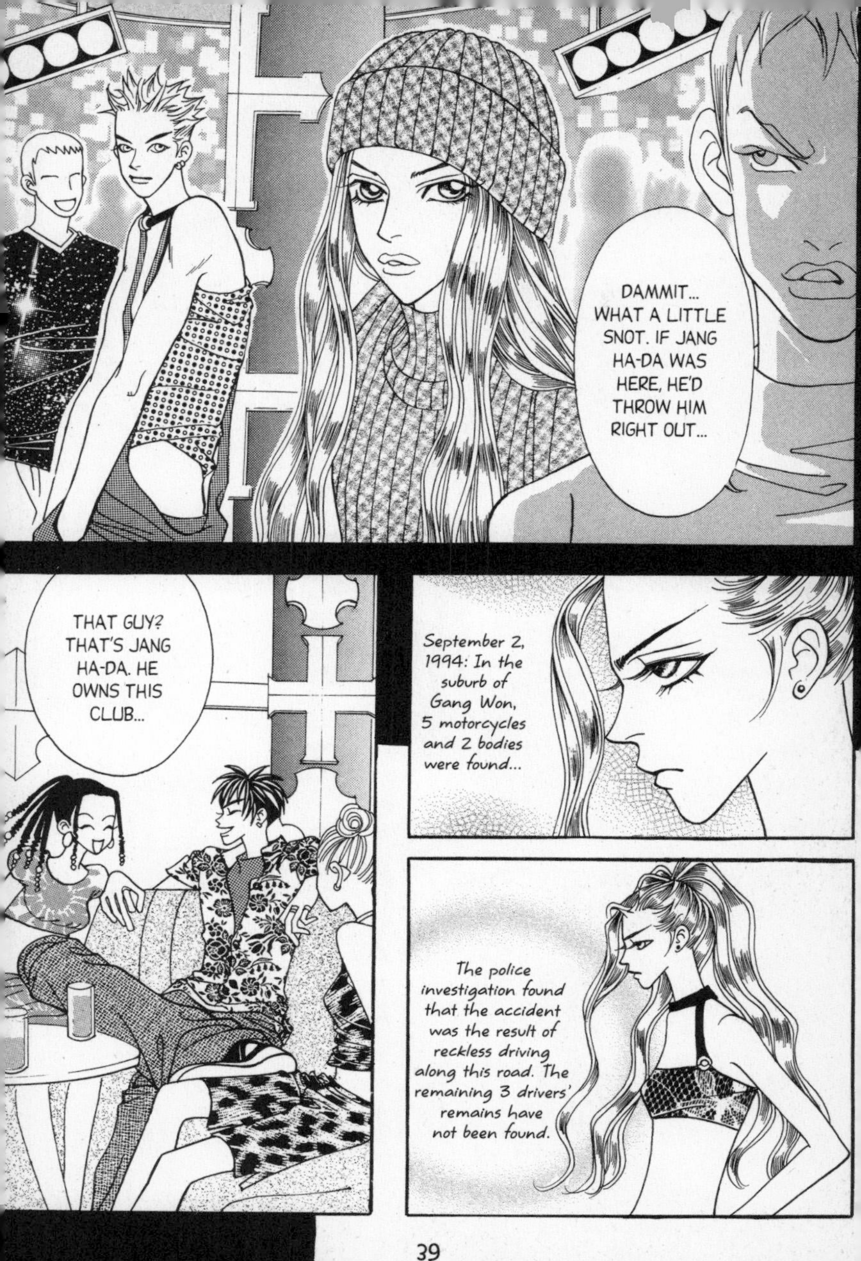
DAMMIT... WHAT A LITTLE SNOT. IF JANG HA-DA WAS HERE, HE'D THROW HIM RIGHT OUT...
THAT GUY? THAT'S JANG HA-DA. HE OWNS THIS CLUB...
September 2, 1994: In the suburb of Gang Won, 5 motorcycles and 2 bodies were found...
The police investigation found that the accident was the result of reckless driving along this road. The remaining 3 drivers' remains have not been found.

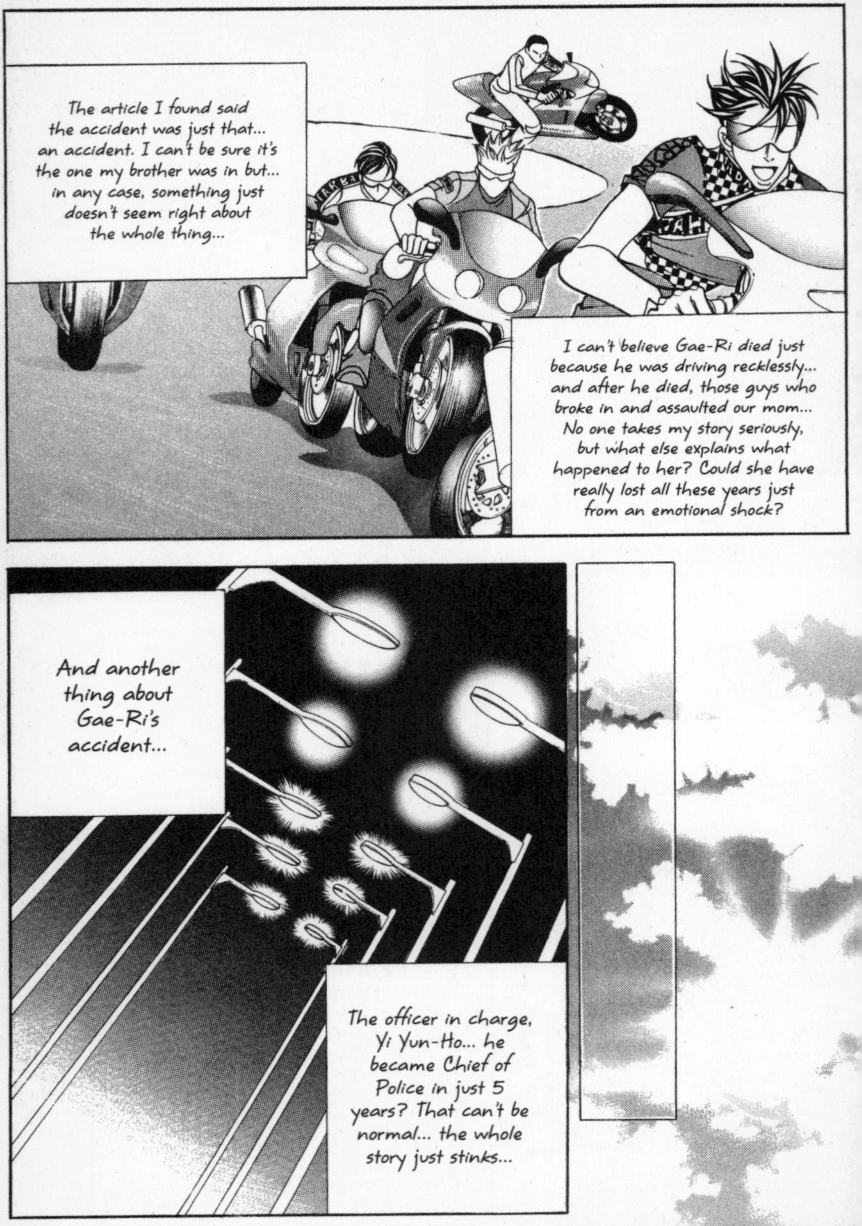
The article I found said the accident was just that... an accident. I can't be sure it's the one my brother was in but... in any case, something just doesn't seem right about the whole thing...
I can't believe Gae-Ri died just because he was driving recklessly... and after he died, those guys who broke in and assaulted our mom... No one takes my story seriously, but what else explains what happened to her? Could she have really lost all these years just from an emotional shock?
And another thing about Gae-Ri's accident...
The officer in charge, Yi Yun-Ho... he became Chief of Police in just 5 years? That can't be normal... the whole story just stinks...

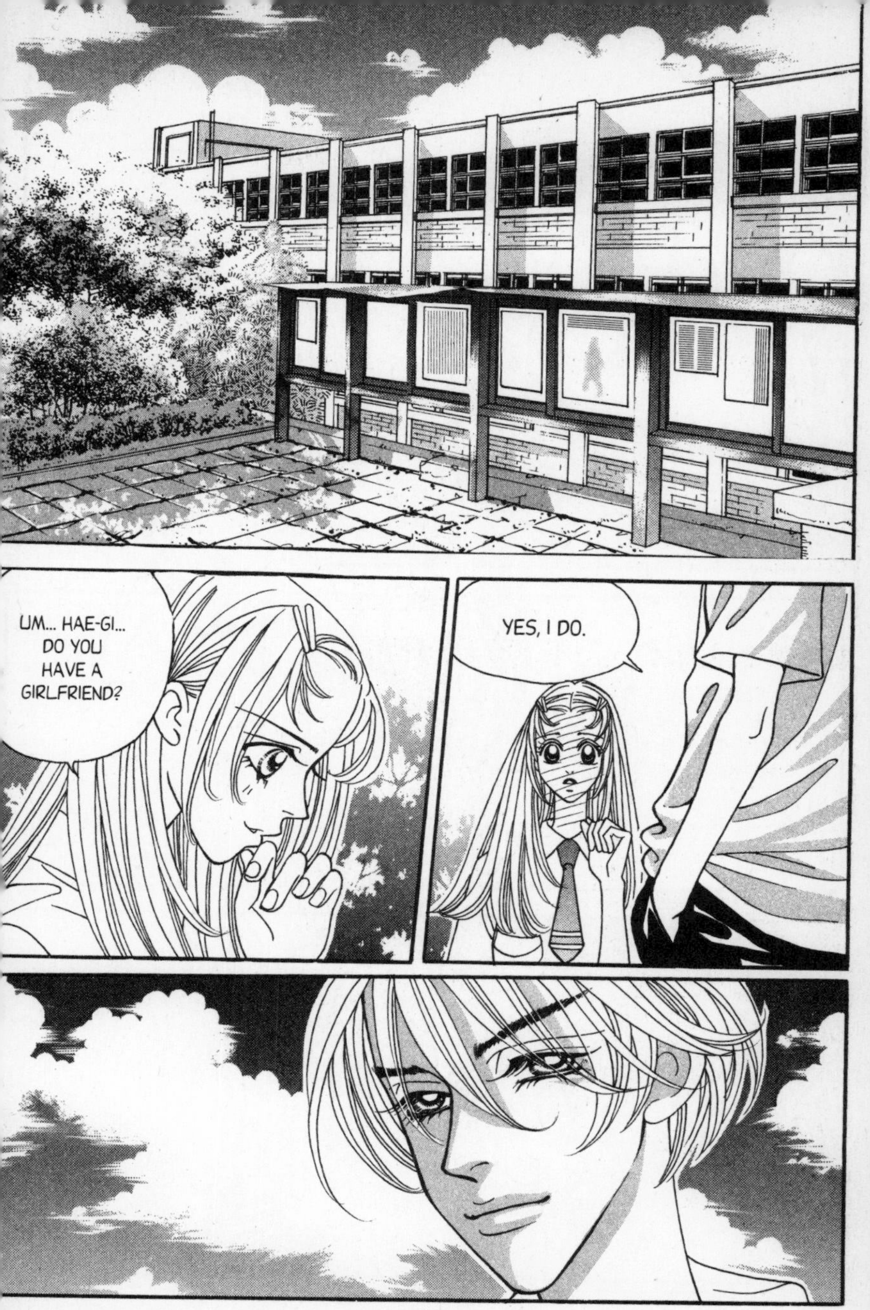
UM... HAE-GI... DO YOU HAVE A GIRLFRIEND?
YES, I DO.

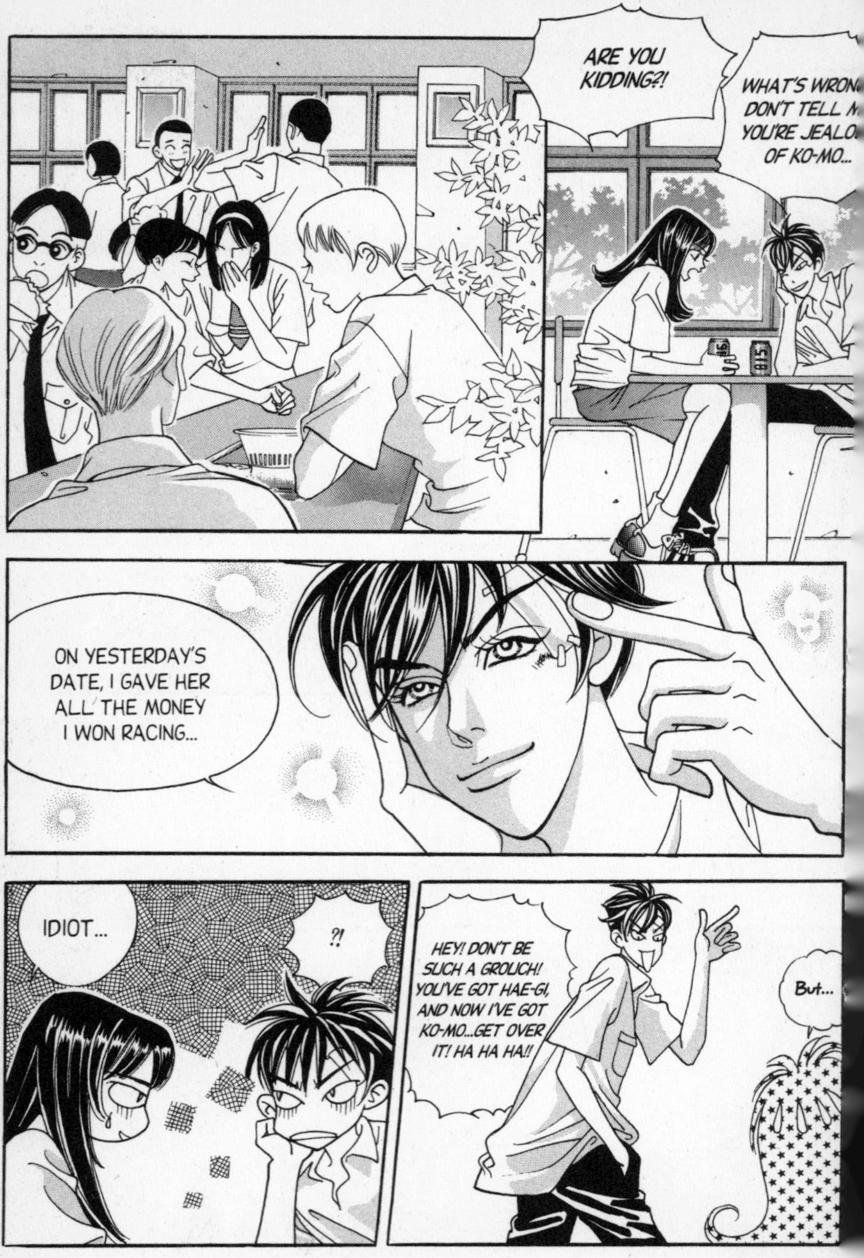
ARE YOU KIDDING?!
WHAT'S WRON DON'T TELL M YOU'RE JEALO OF KO-MO...
ON YESTERDAY'S DATE, I GAVE HER ALL THE MONEY I WON RACING...
IDIOT...
?!
HEY! DON'T BE SUCH A GROUCH! YOU'VE GOT HAE-GI, AND NOW I'VE GOT KO-MO...GET OVER IT! HA HA HA!!
But...

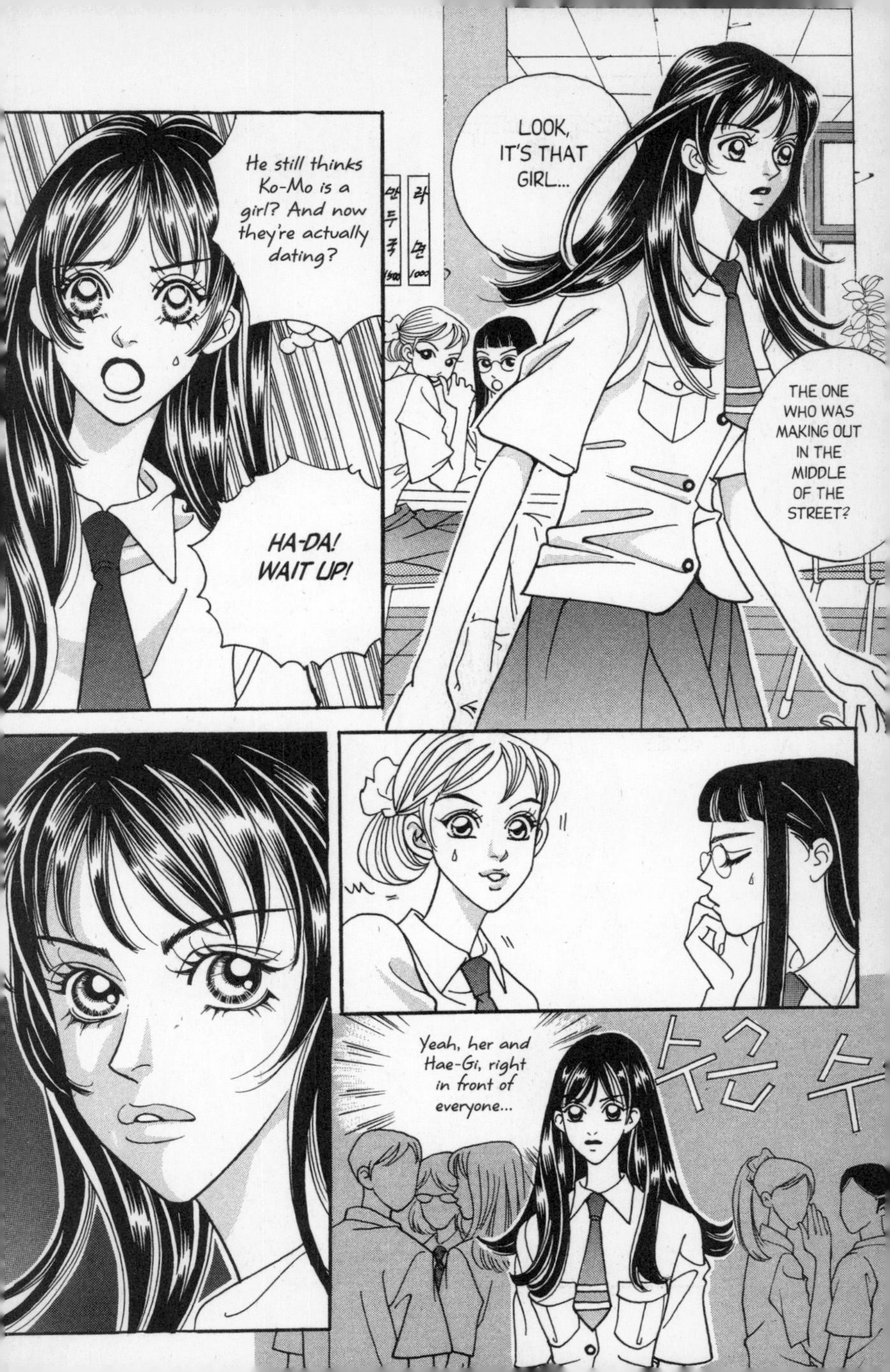
He still thinks Ko-Mo is a girl? And now they're actually dating?
HA-DA! WAIT UP!
LOOK, IT'S THAT GIRL...
THE ONE WHO WAS MAKING OUT IN THE MIDDLE OF THE STREET?
Yeah, her and Hae-Gi, right in front of everyone...

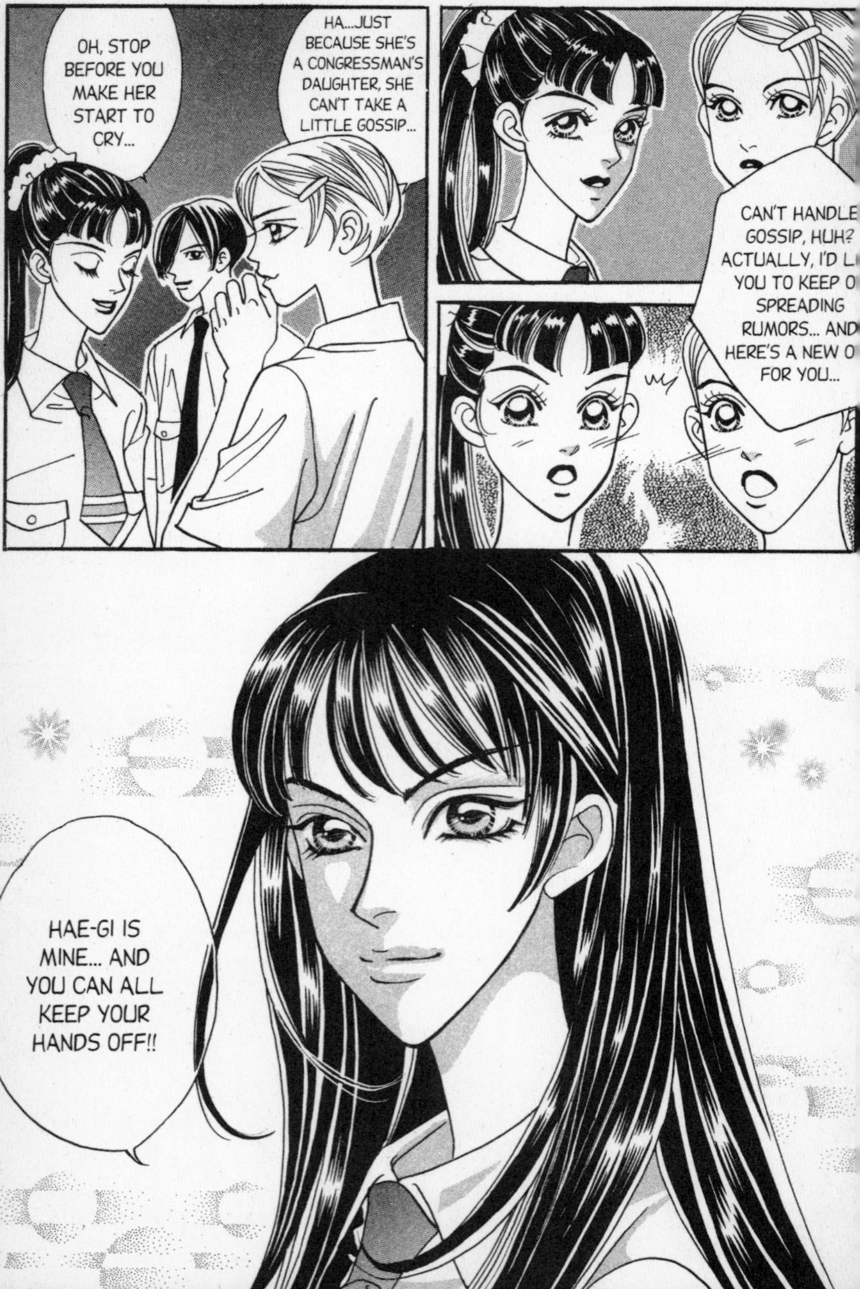
OH, STOP BEFORE YOU MAKE HER START TO CRY...
HA...JUST BECAUSE SHE'S A CONGRESSMAN'S DAUGHTER, SHE CAN'T TAKE A LITTLE GOSSIP...
CAN'T HANDLE GOSSIP, HUH? ACTUALLY, I'D L YOU TO KEEP O SPREADING RUMORS... AND HERE'S A NEW O FOR YOU...
HAE-GI IS MINE... AND YOU CAN ALL KEEP YOUR HANDS OFF!!

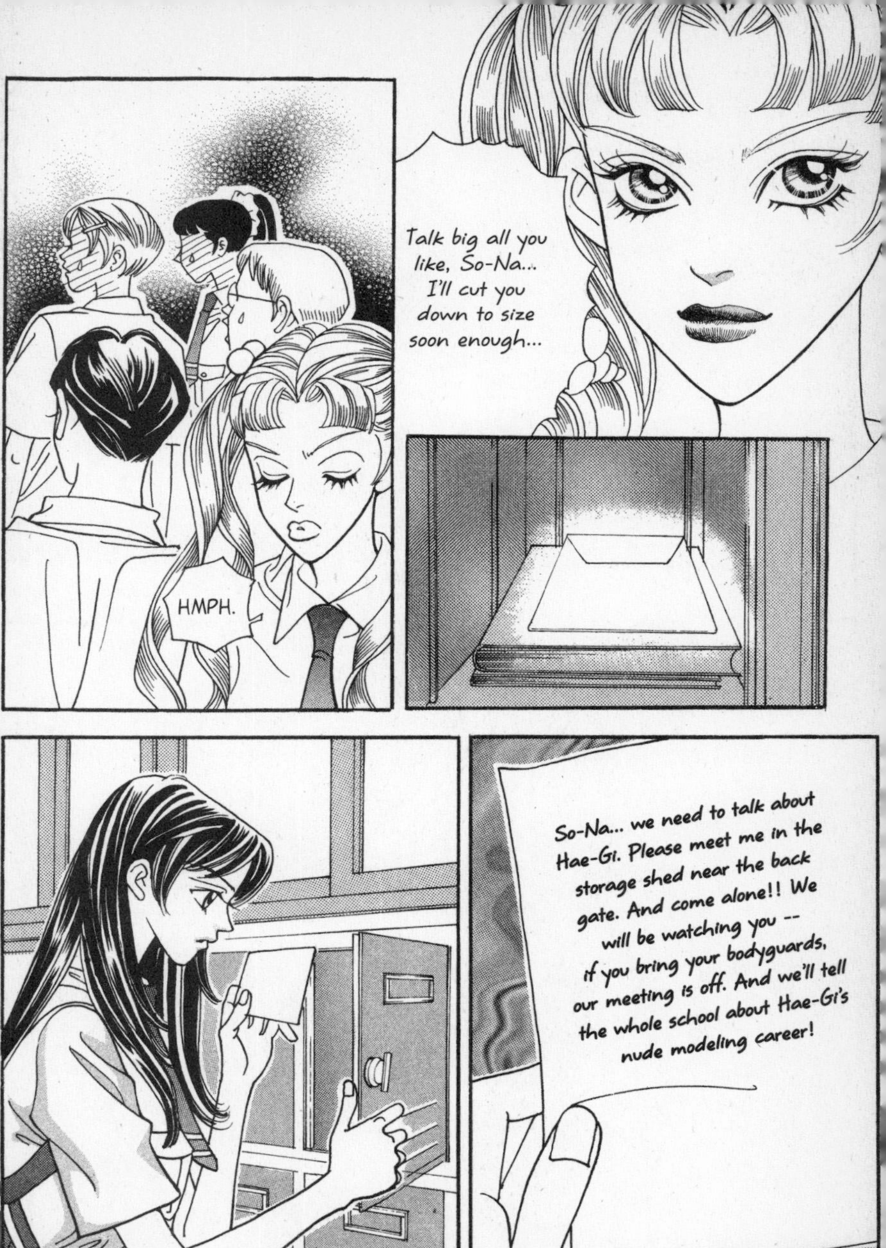
HMPH.
Talk big all you like, So-Na... I'll cut you down to size soon enough...
So-Na... we need to talk about Hae-Gi. Please meet me in the storage shed near the back gate. And come alone!! We will be watching you -- if you bring your bodyguards, our meeting is off. And we'll tell the whole school about Hae-Gi's nude modeling career!

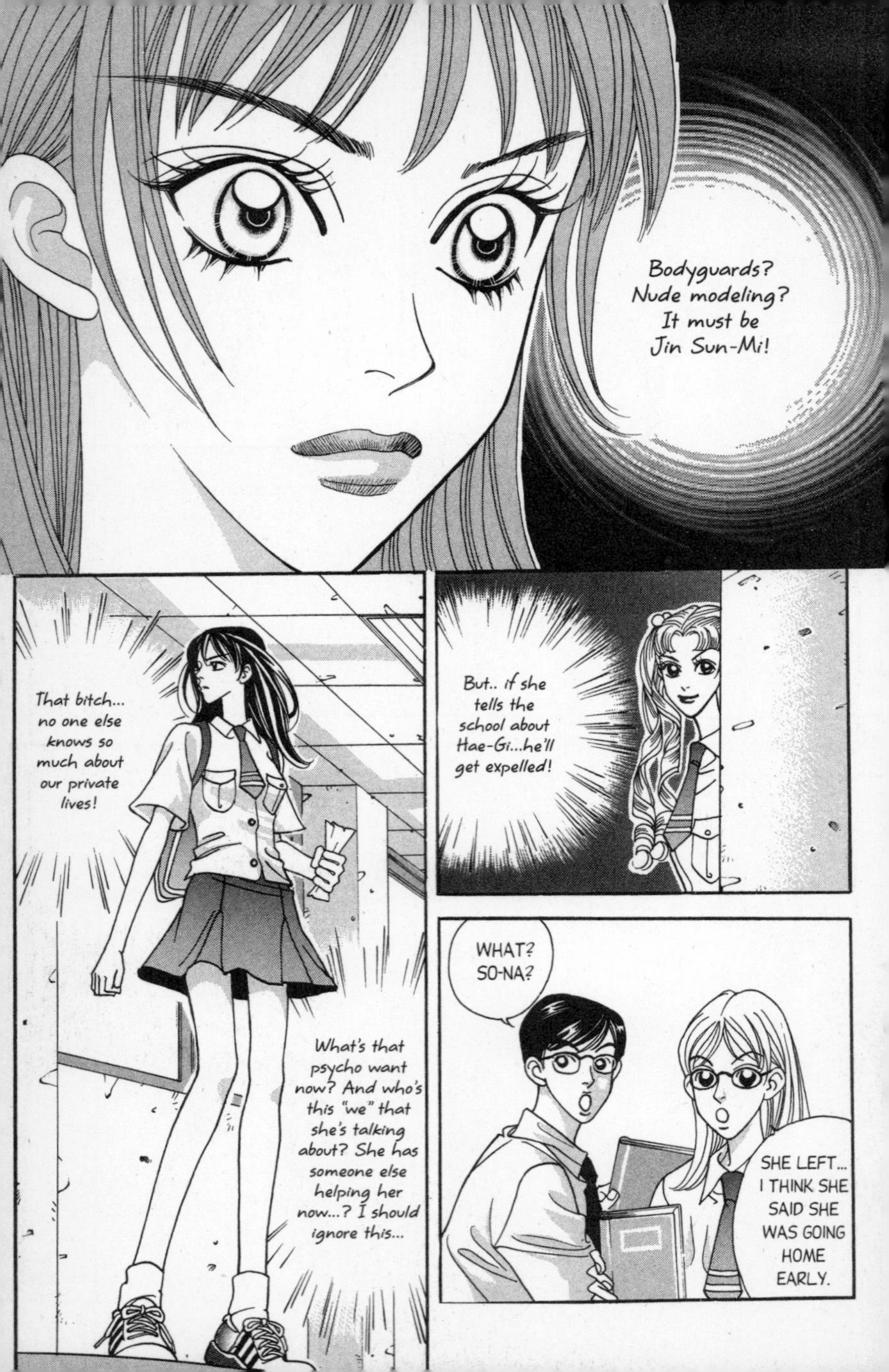
Bodyguards? Nude modeling? It must be Jin Sun-Mi!
That bitch... no one else knows so much about our private lives!
What's that psycho want now? And who's this "we" that she's talking about? She has someone else helping her now...? I should ignore this...
But.. if she tells the school about Hae-Gi...he'll get expelled!
WHAT? SO-NA?
SHE LEFT... I THINK SHE SAID SHE WAS GOING HOME EARLY.

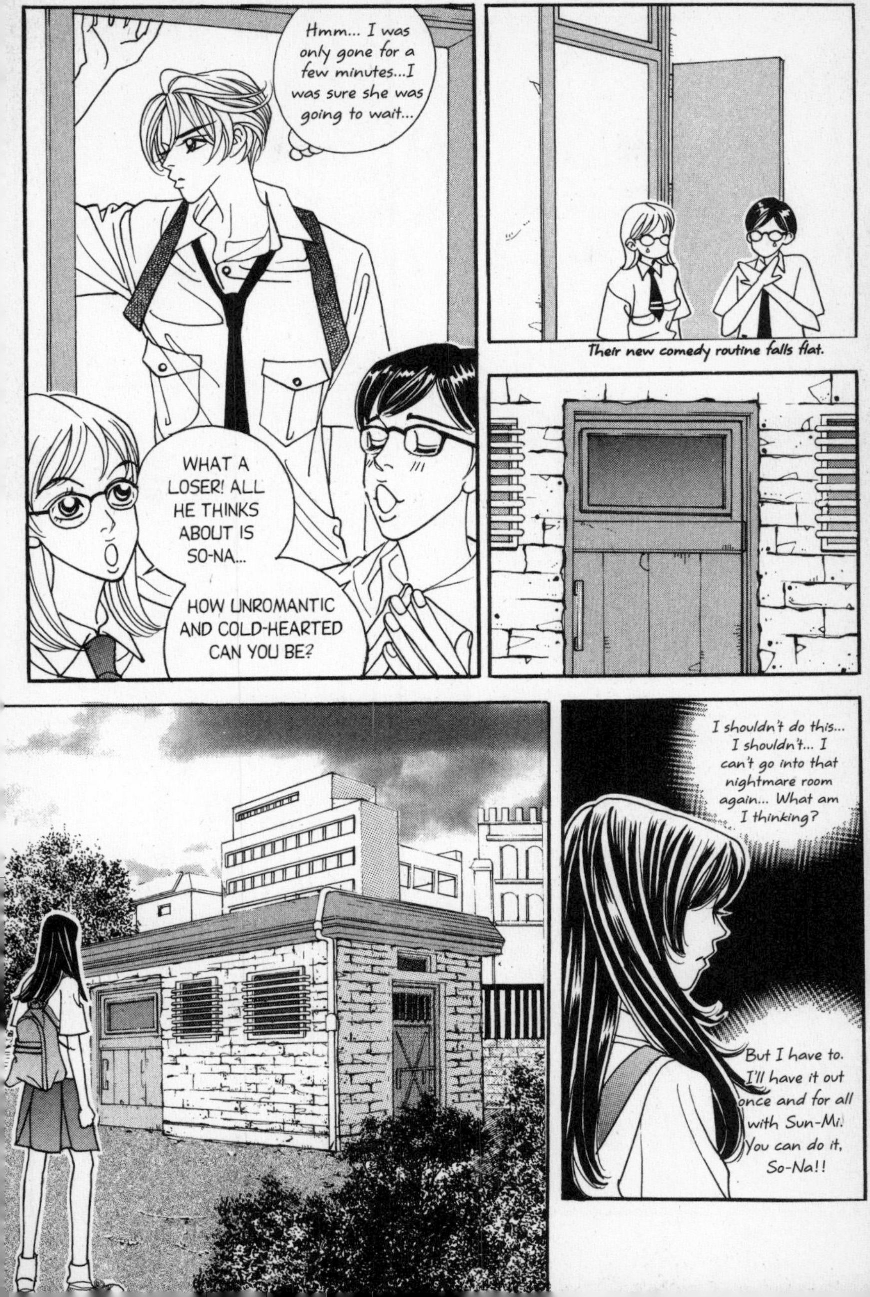
Hmm... I was only gone for a few minutes...I was sure she was going to wait...
WHAT A LOSER! ALL HE THINKS ABOUT IS SO-NA...
HOW UNROMANTIC AND COLD-HEARTED CAN YOU BE?
Their new comedy routine falls flat.
I shouldn't do this... I shouldn't... I can't go into that nightmare room again... What am I thinking?
But I have to. I'll have it out once and for all with Sun-Mi. You can do it, So-Na!!

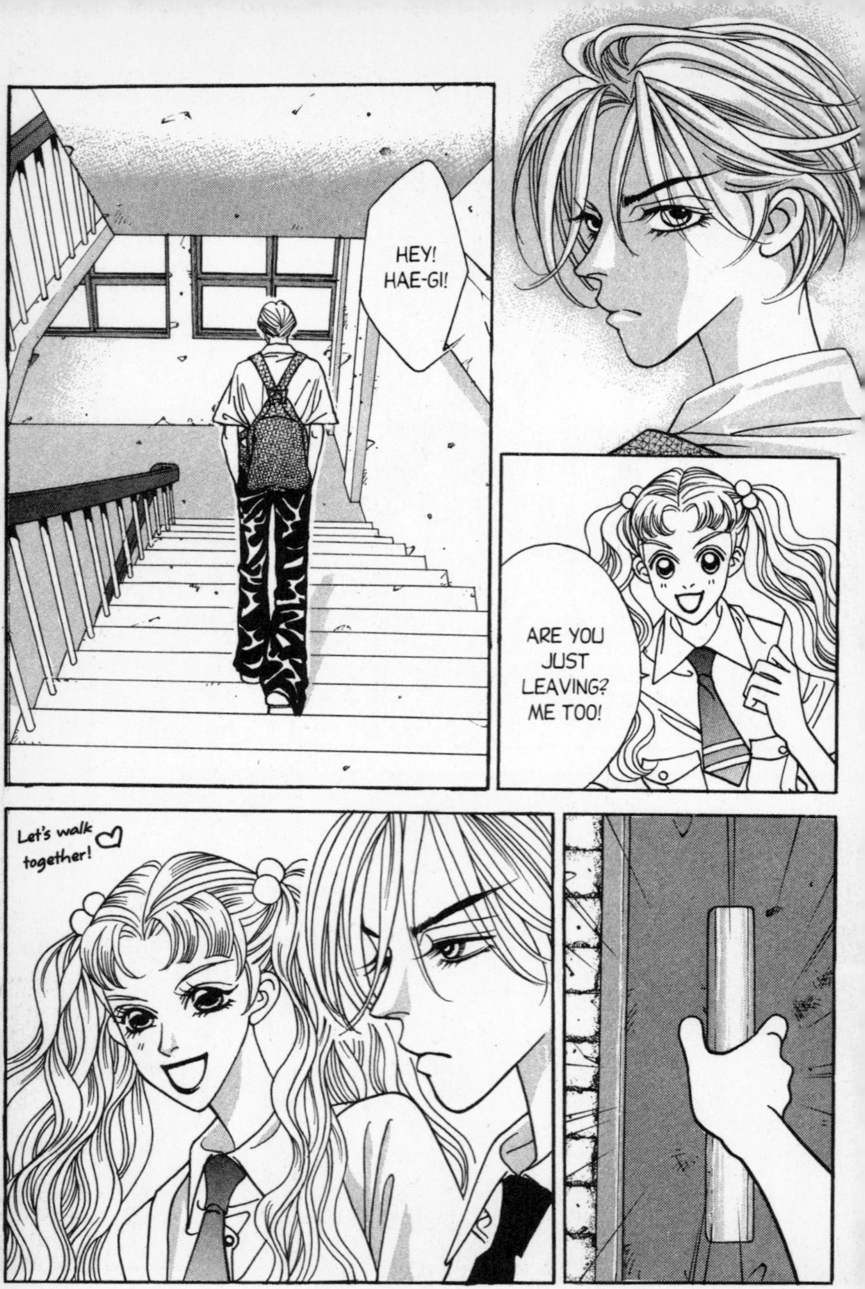
HEY! HAE-GI!
ARE YOU JUST LEAVING? ME TOO!
Let's walk together!

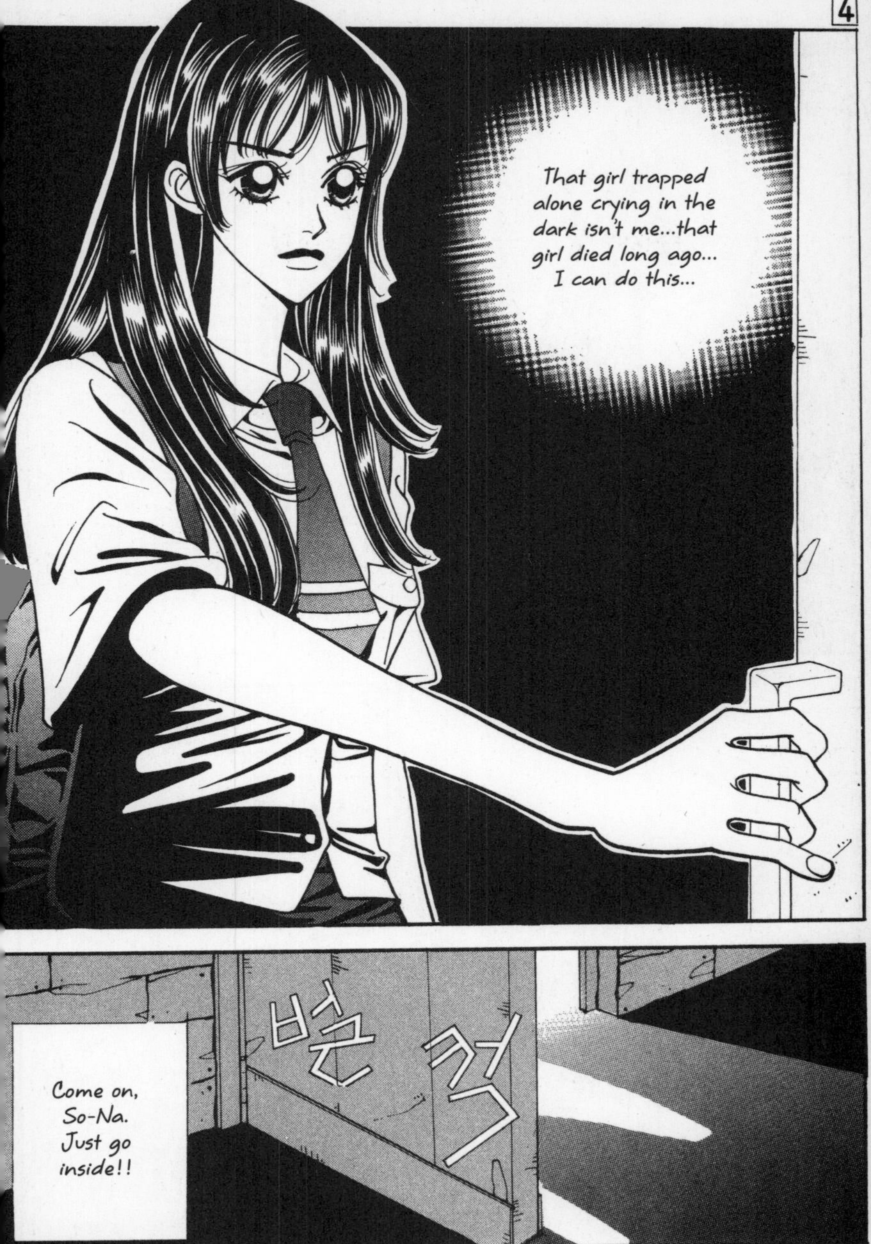
4
That girl trapped alone crying in the dark isn't me...that girl died long ago... I can do this...
Come on, So-Na. Just go inside!!

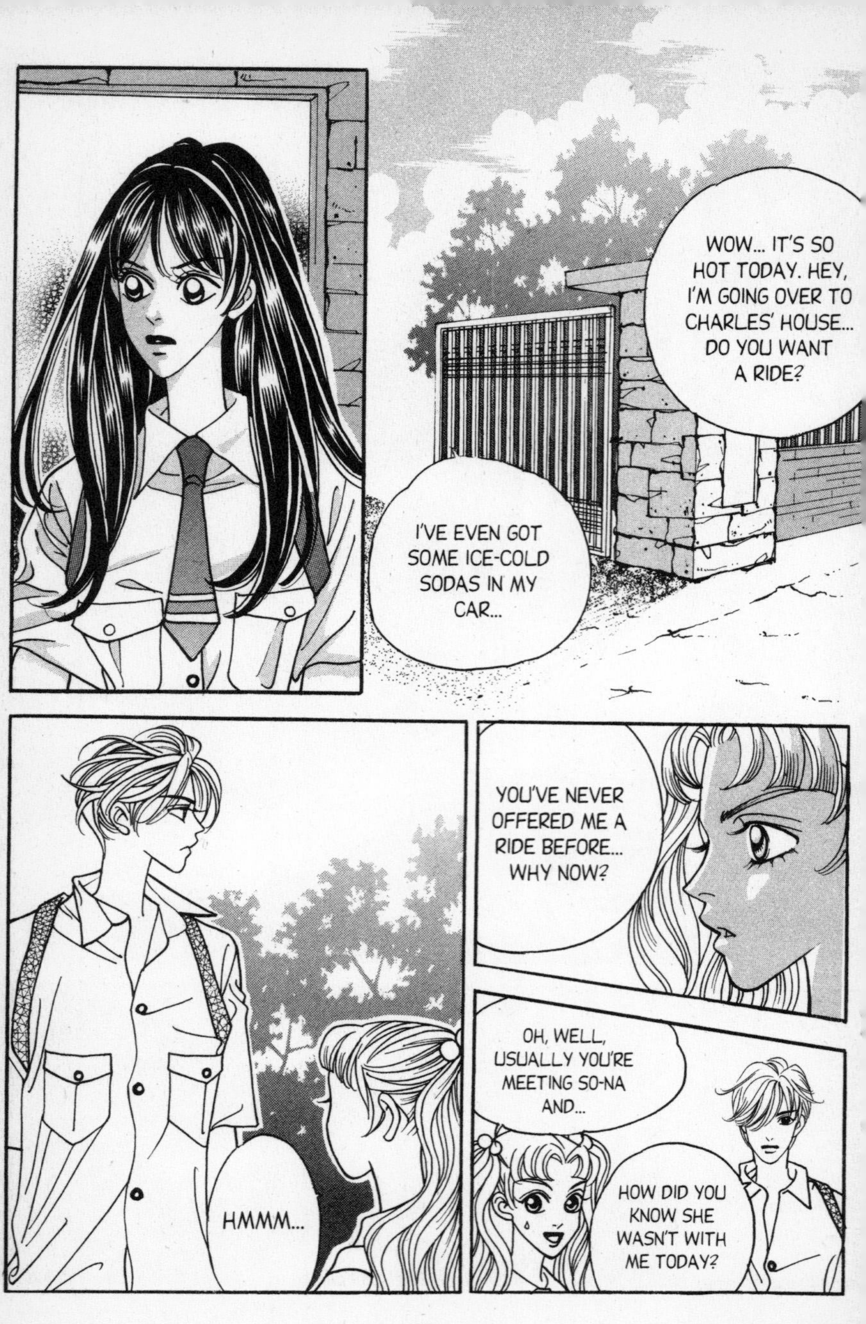
WOW... IT'S SO HOT TODAY. HEY, I'M GOING OVER TO CHARLES' HOUSE... DO YOU WANT A RIDE?
I'VE EVEN GOT SOME ICE-COLD SODAS IN MY CAR...
HMMM...
YOU'VE NEVER OFFERED ME A RIDE BEFORE... WHY NOW?
OH, WELL, USUALLY YOU'RE MEETING SO-NA AND...
HOW DID YOU KNOW SHE WASN'T WITH ME TODAY?

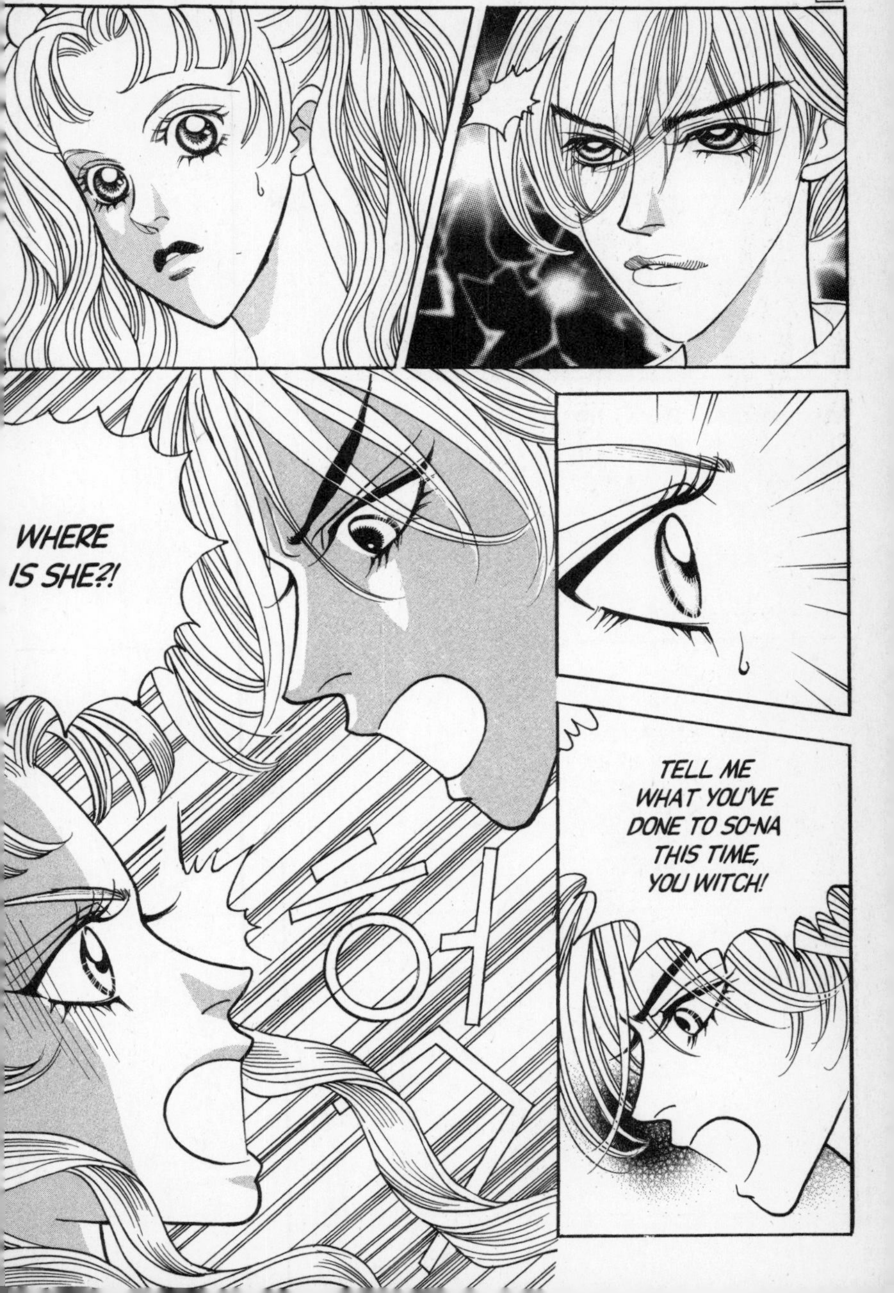
WHERE IS SHE?!
어
TELL ME WHAT YOU'VE DONE TO SO-NA THIS TIME, YOU WITCH!

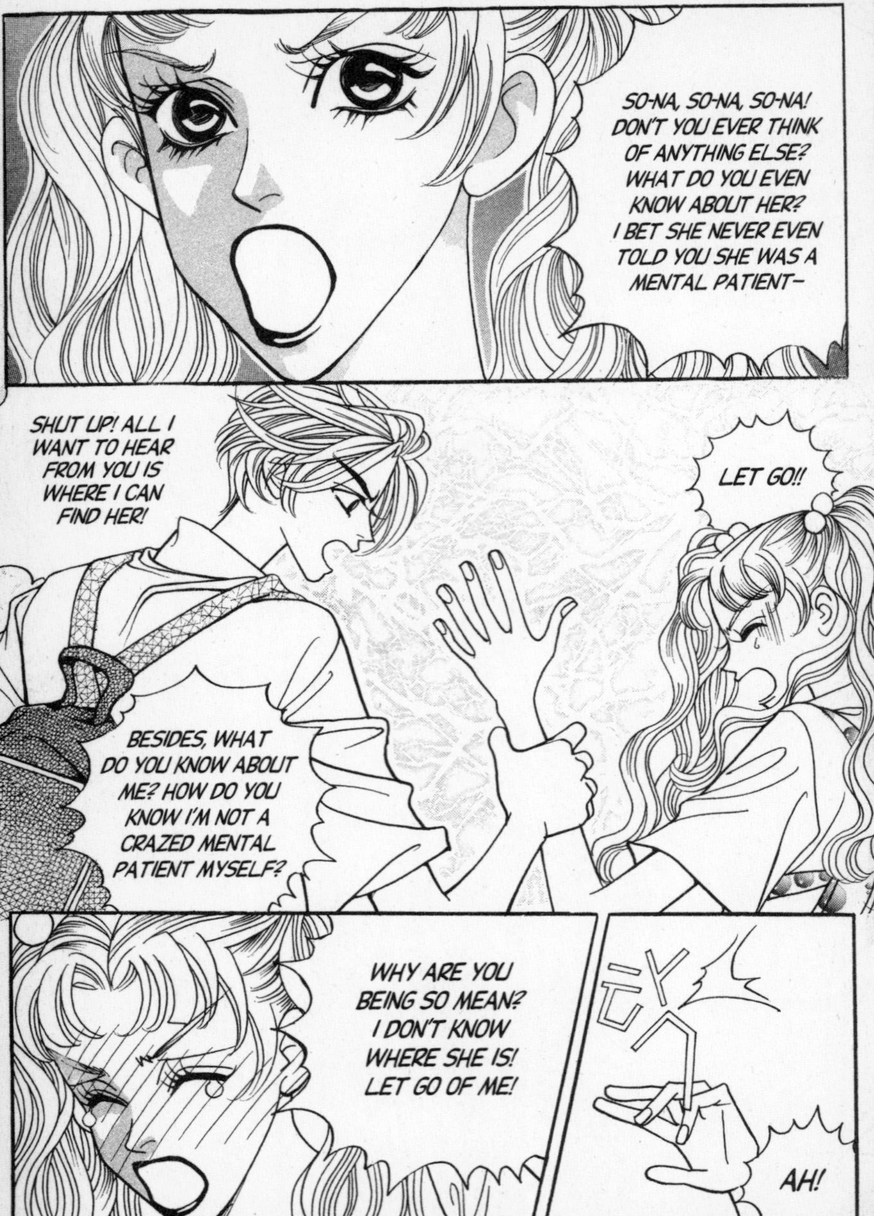
SO-NA, SO-NA, SO-NA! DON'T YOU EVER THINK OF ANYTHING ELSE? WHAT DO YOU EVEN KNOW ABOUT HER? I BET SHE NEVER EVEN TOLD YOU SHE WAS A MENTAL PATIENT–
SHUT UP! ALL I WANT TO HEAR FROM YOU IS WHERE I CAN FIND HER!
LET GO!!
BESIDES, WHAT DO YOU KNOW ABOUT ME? HOW DO YOU KNOW I'M NOT A CRAZED MENTAL PATIENT MYSELF?
WHY ARE YOU BEING SO MEAN? I DON'T KNOW WHERE SHE IS! LET GO OF ME!
AH!

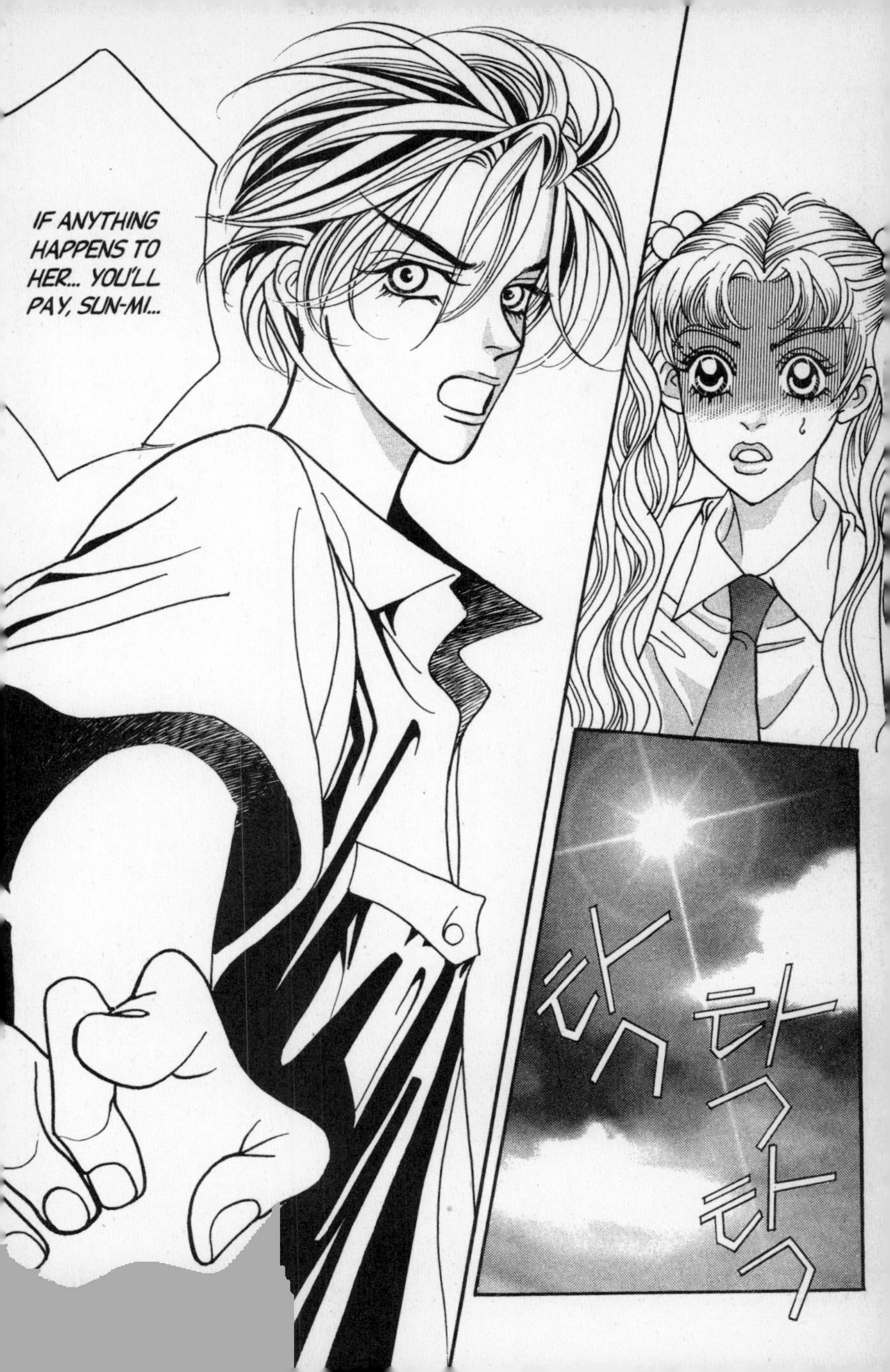
IF ANYTHING HAPPENS TO HER... YOU'LL PAY, SUN-MI...

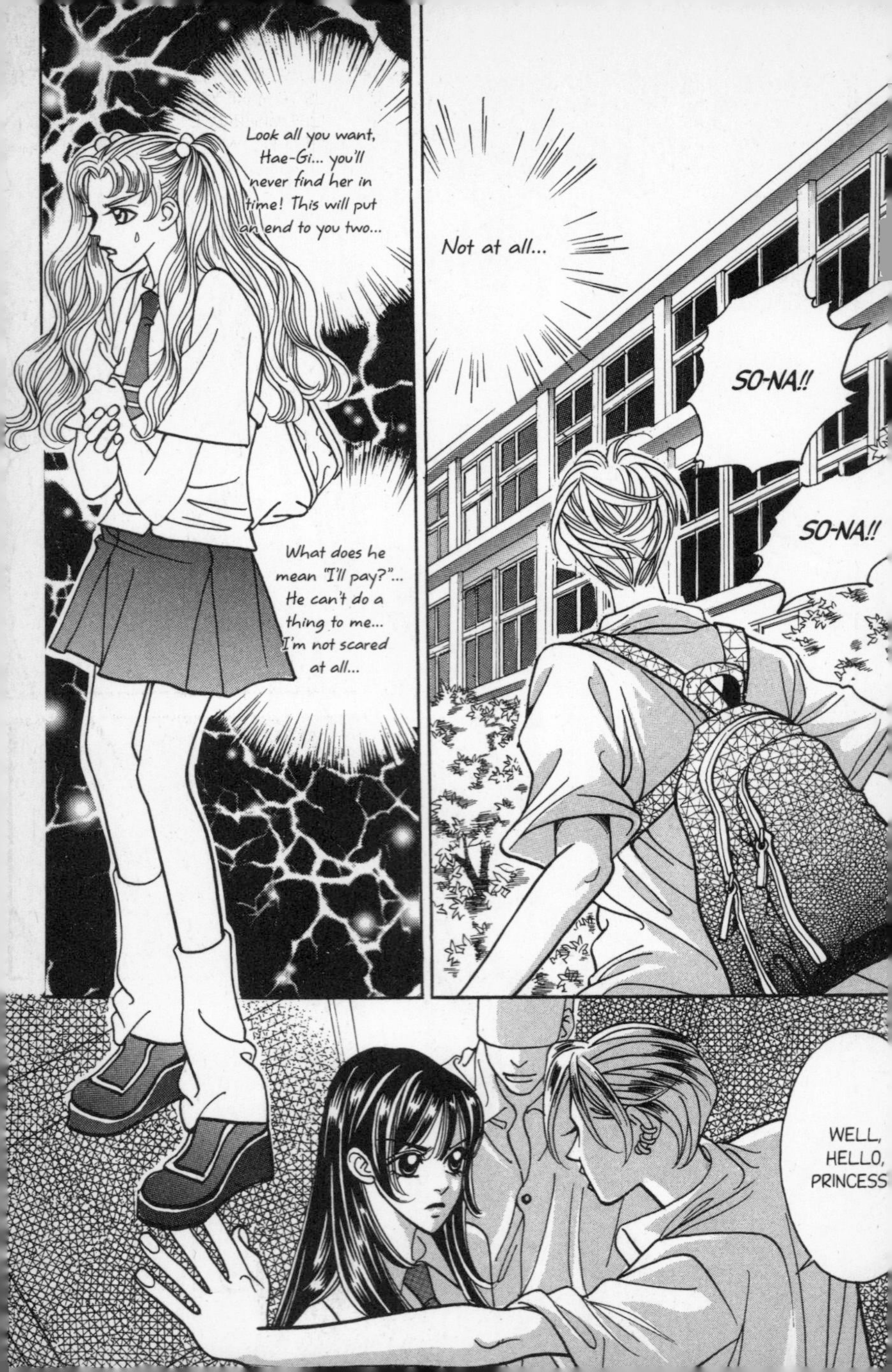

Look all you want, Hae-Gi... you'll never find her in time! This will put an end to you two...
What does he mean "I'll pay?"... He can't do a thing to me... I'm not scared at all...
Not at all...
SO-NA!!
SO-NA!!
WELL, HELLO, PRINCESS

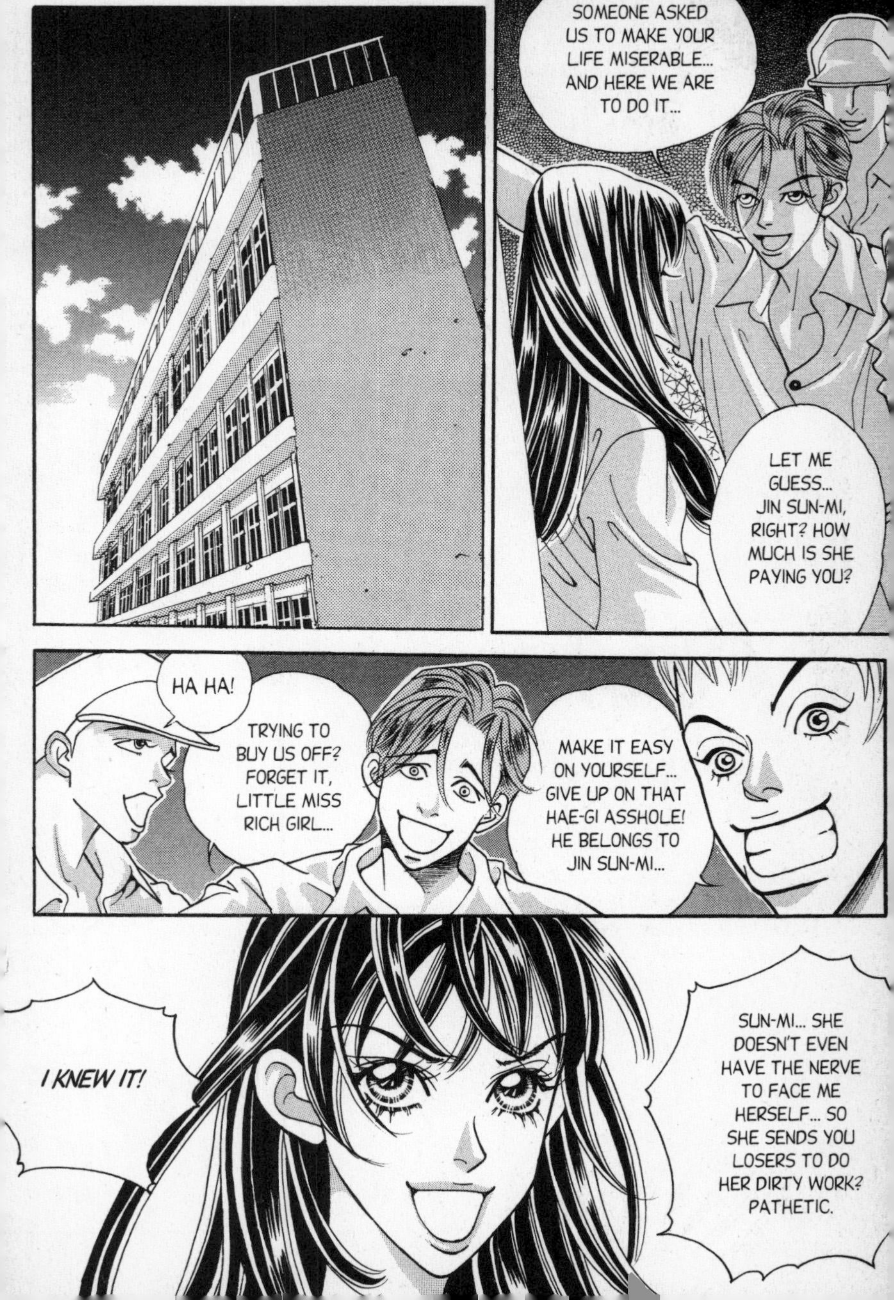
SOMEONE ASKED US TO MAKE YOUR LIFE MISERABLE... AND HERE WE ARE TO DO IT...
LET ME GUESS... JIN SUN-MI, RIGHT? HOW MUCH IS SHE PAYING YOU?
HA HA!
TRYING TO BUY US OFF? FORGET IT, LITTLE MISS RICH GIRL...
MAKE IT EASY ON YOURSELF... GIVE UP ON THAT HAE-GI ASSHOLE! HE BELONGS TO JIN SUN-MI...
I KNEW IT!
SUN-MI... SHE DOESN'T EVEN HAVE THE NERVE TO FACE ME HERSELF... SO SHE SENDS YOU LOSERS TO DO HER DIRTY WORK? PATHETIC.

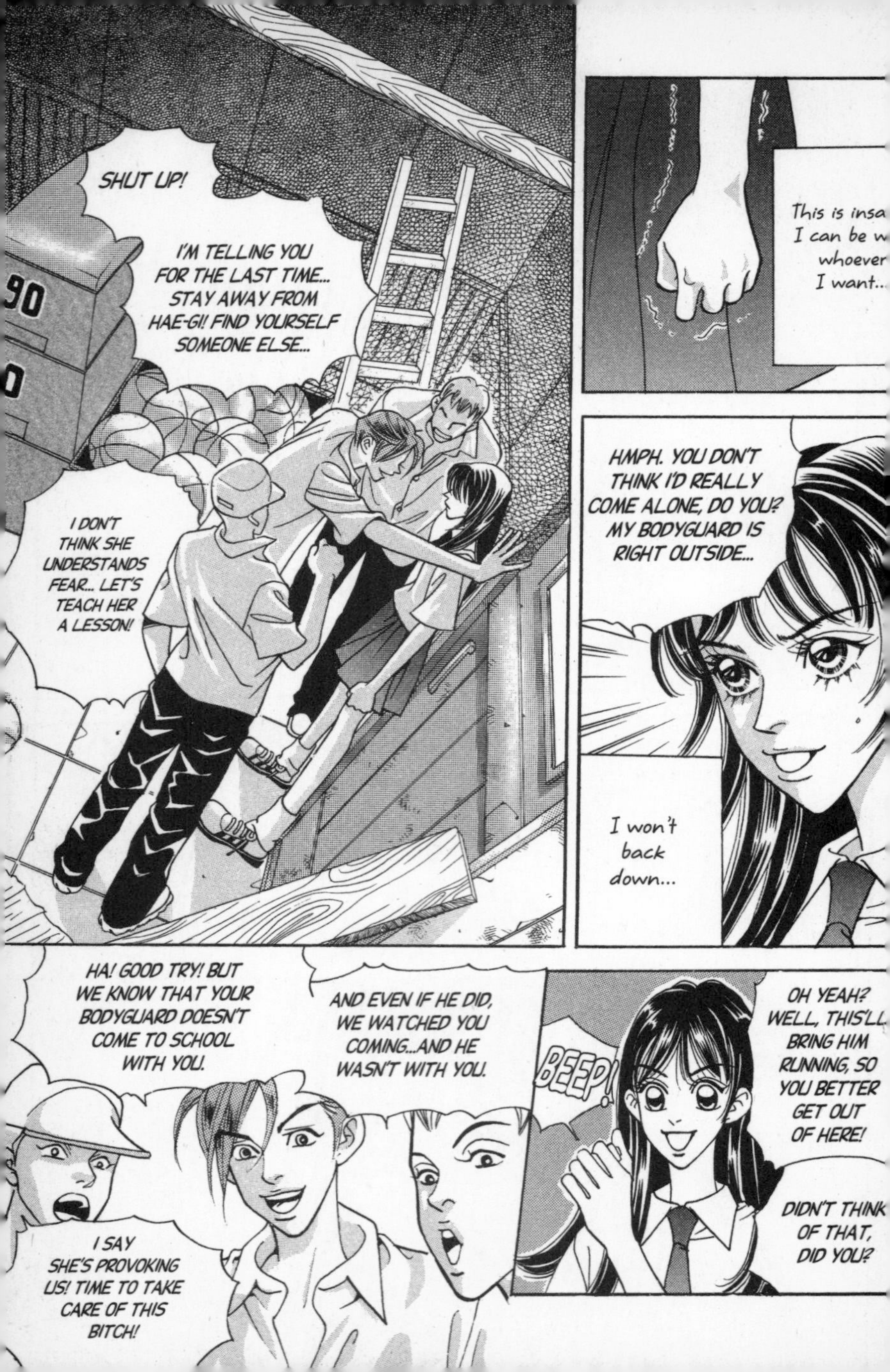
SHUT UP!
I'M TELLING YOU FOR THE LAST TIME... STAY AWAY FROM HAE-GI! FIND YOURSELF SOMEONE ELSE...
I DON'T THINK SHE UNDERSTANDS FEAR... LET'S TEACH HER A LESSON!
This is insa I can be w whoever I want...
HMPH. YOU DON'T THINK I'D REALLY COME ALONE, DO YOU? MY BODYGUARD IS RIGHT OUTSIDE...
I won't back down...
HA! GOOD TRY! BUT WE KNOW THAT YOUR BODYGUARD DOESN'T COME TO SCHOOL WITH YOU.
AND EVEN IF HE DID, WE WATCHED YOU COMING...AND HE WASN'T WITH YOU.
I SAY SHE'S PROVOKING US! TIME TO TAKE CARE OF THIS BITCH!
BEEP!
OH YEAH? WELL, THIS'LL BRING HIM RUNNING, SO YOU BETTER GET OUT OF HERE!
DIDN'T THINK OF THAT, DID YOU?

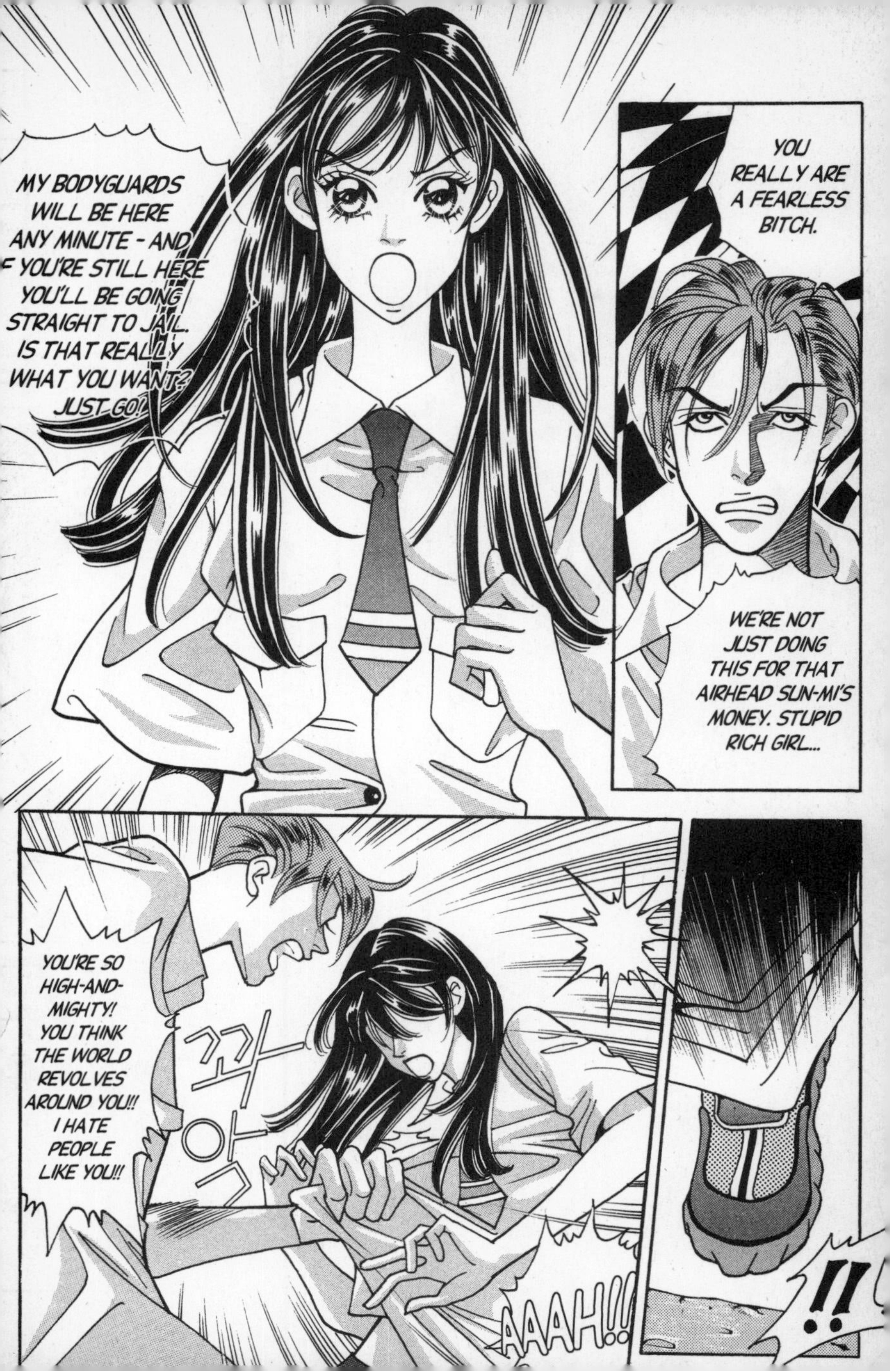
MY BODYGUARDS WILL BE HERE ANY MINUTE - AND IF YOU'RE STILL HERE YOU'LL BE GOING STRAIGHT TO JAIL. IS THAT REALLY WHAT YOU WANT? JUST GO!
YOU REALLY ARE A FEARLESS BITCH.
WE'RE NOT JUST DOING THIS FOR THAT AIRHEAD SUN-MI'S MONEY. STUPID RICH GIRL...
YOU'RE SO HIGH-AND-MIGHTY! YOU THINK THE WORLD REVOLVES AROUND YOU!! I HATE PEOPLE LIKE YOU!!
AAAH!!
!!

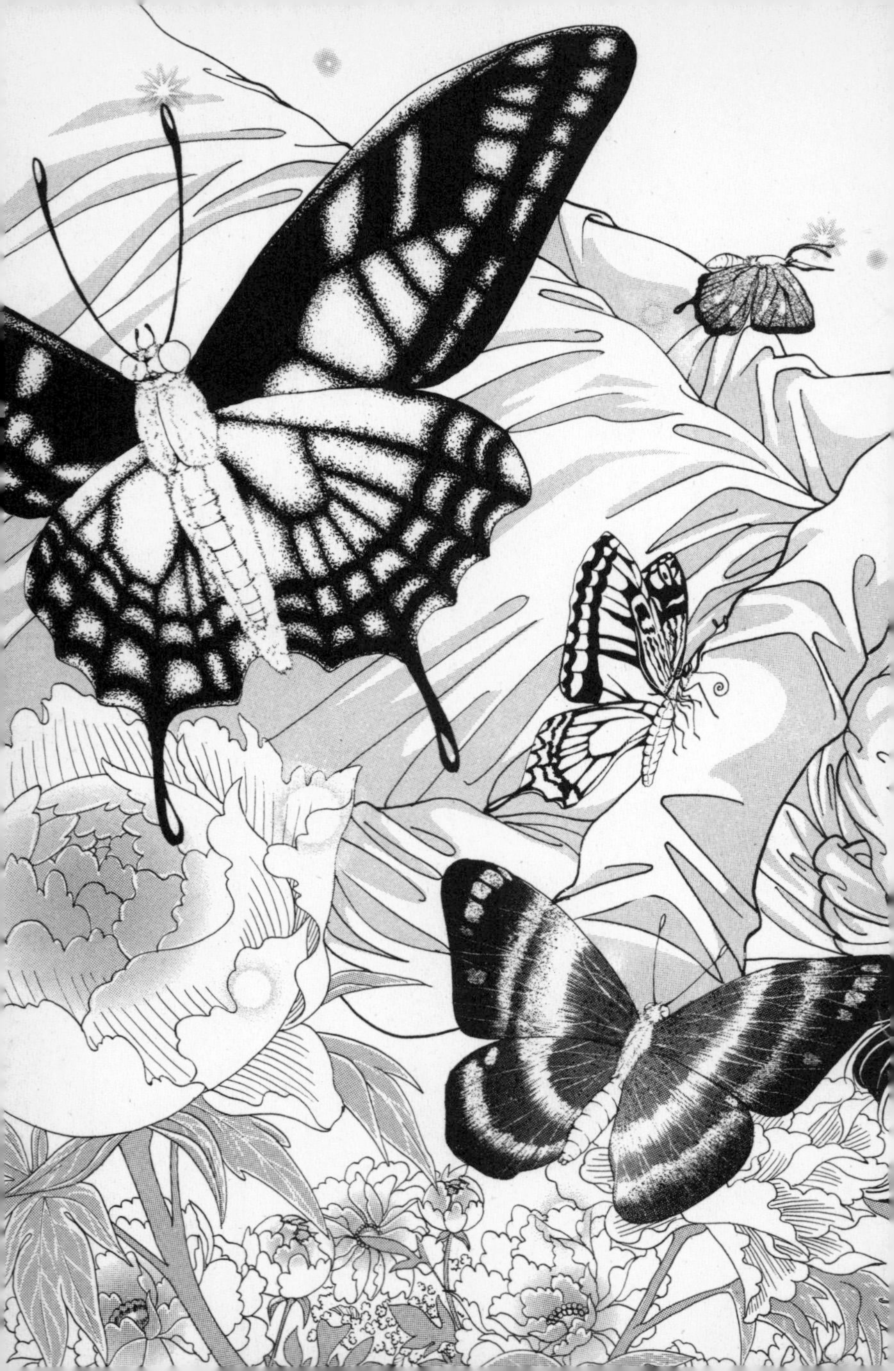

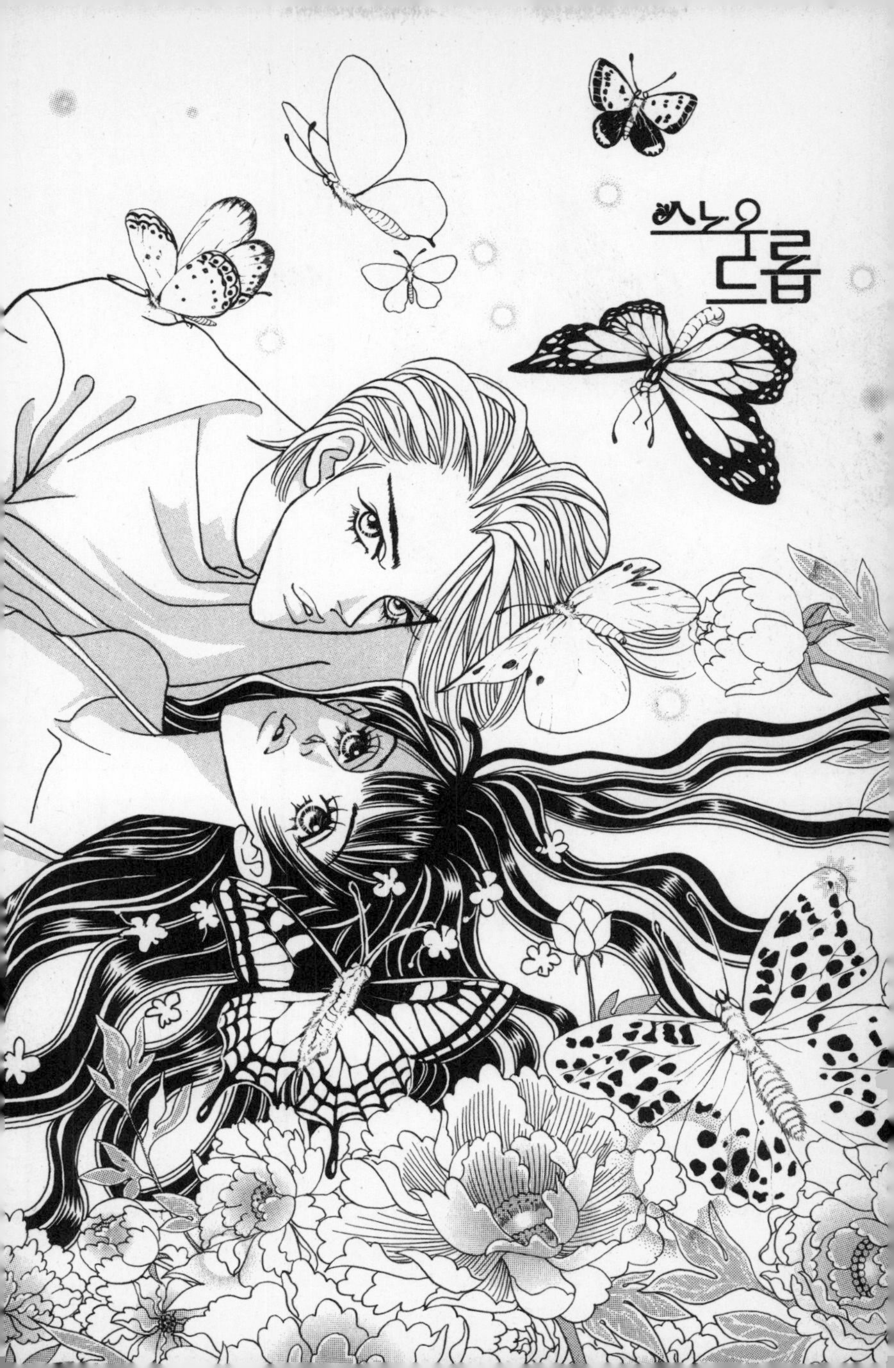
스노우 드롭

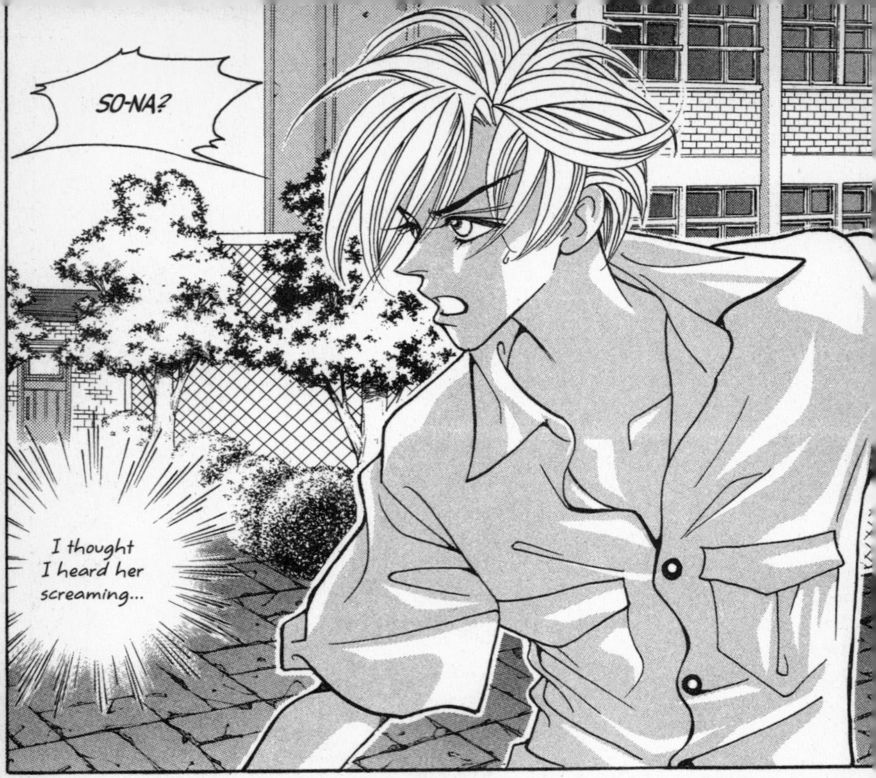
SO-NA?
I thought I heard her screaming...

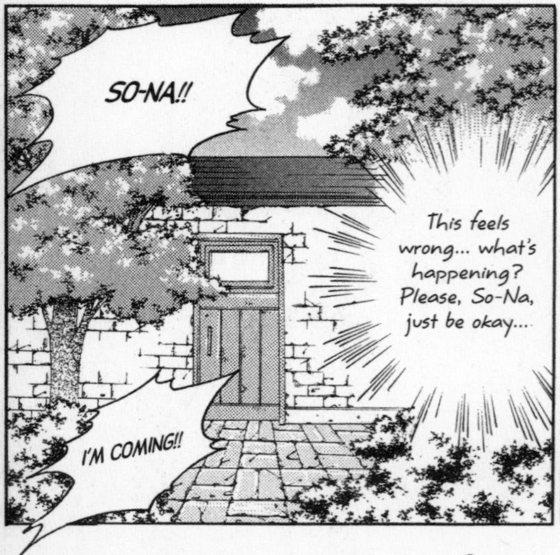
SO-NA!!
This feels wrong... what's happening? Please, So-Na, just be okay...
I'M COMING!!

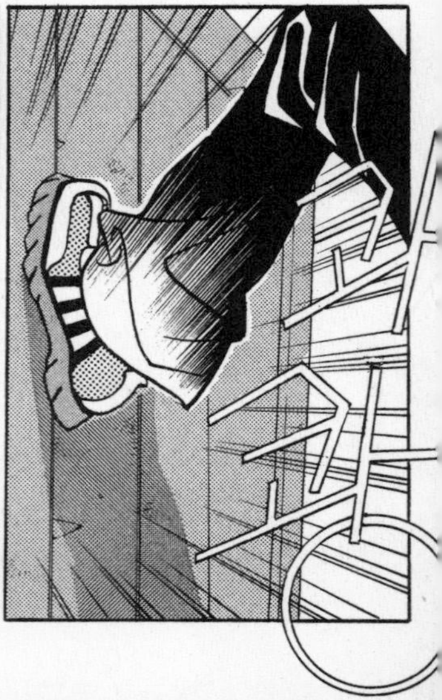

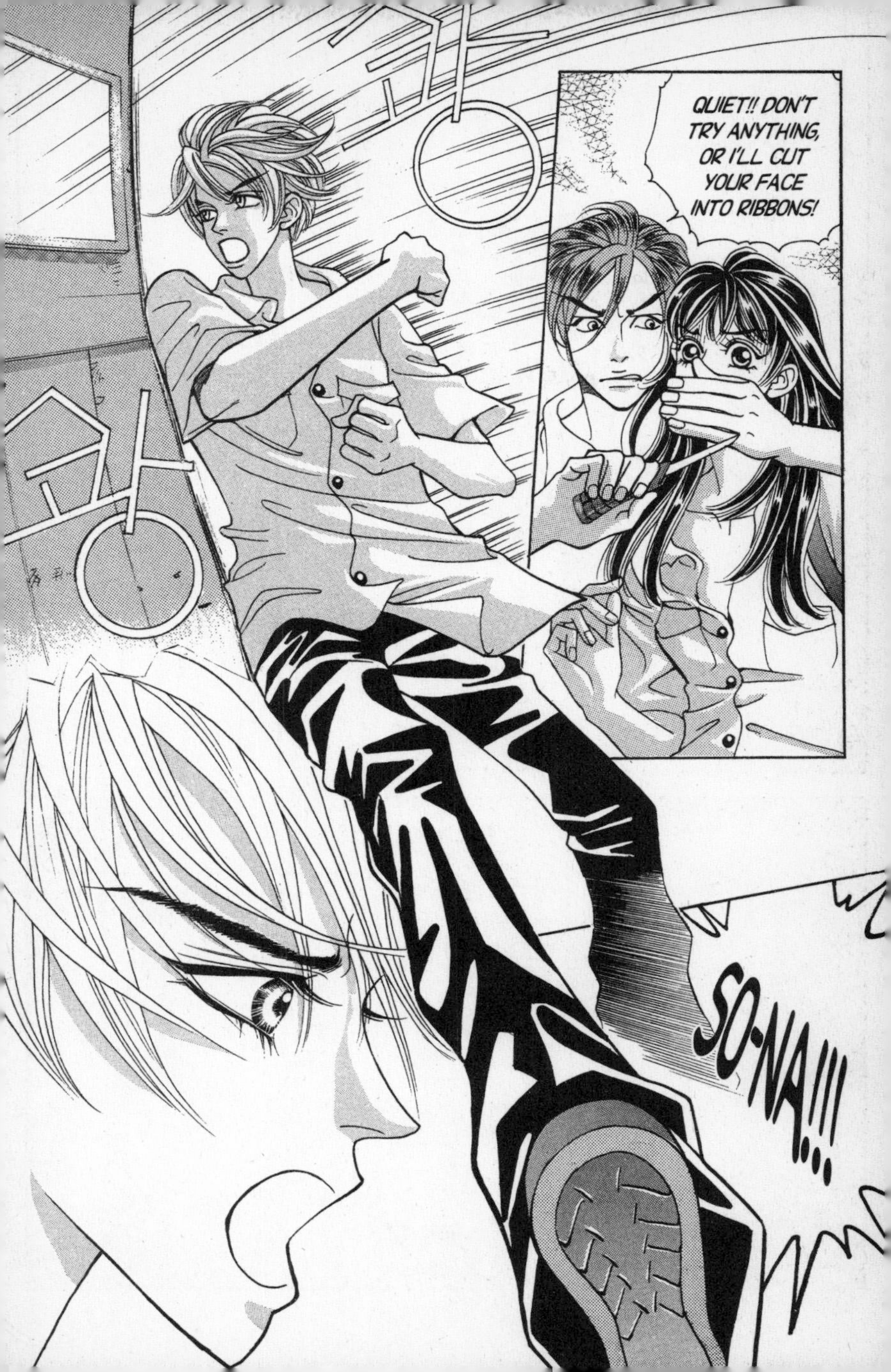
QUIET!! DON'T TRY ANYTHING, OR I'LL CUT YOUR FACE INTO RIBBONS!
SO-NA!!!...

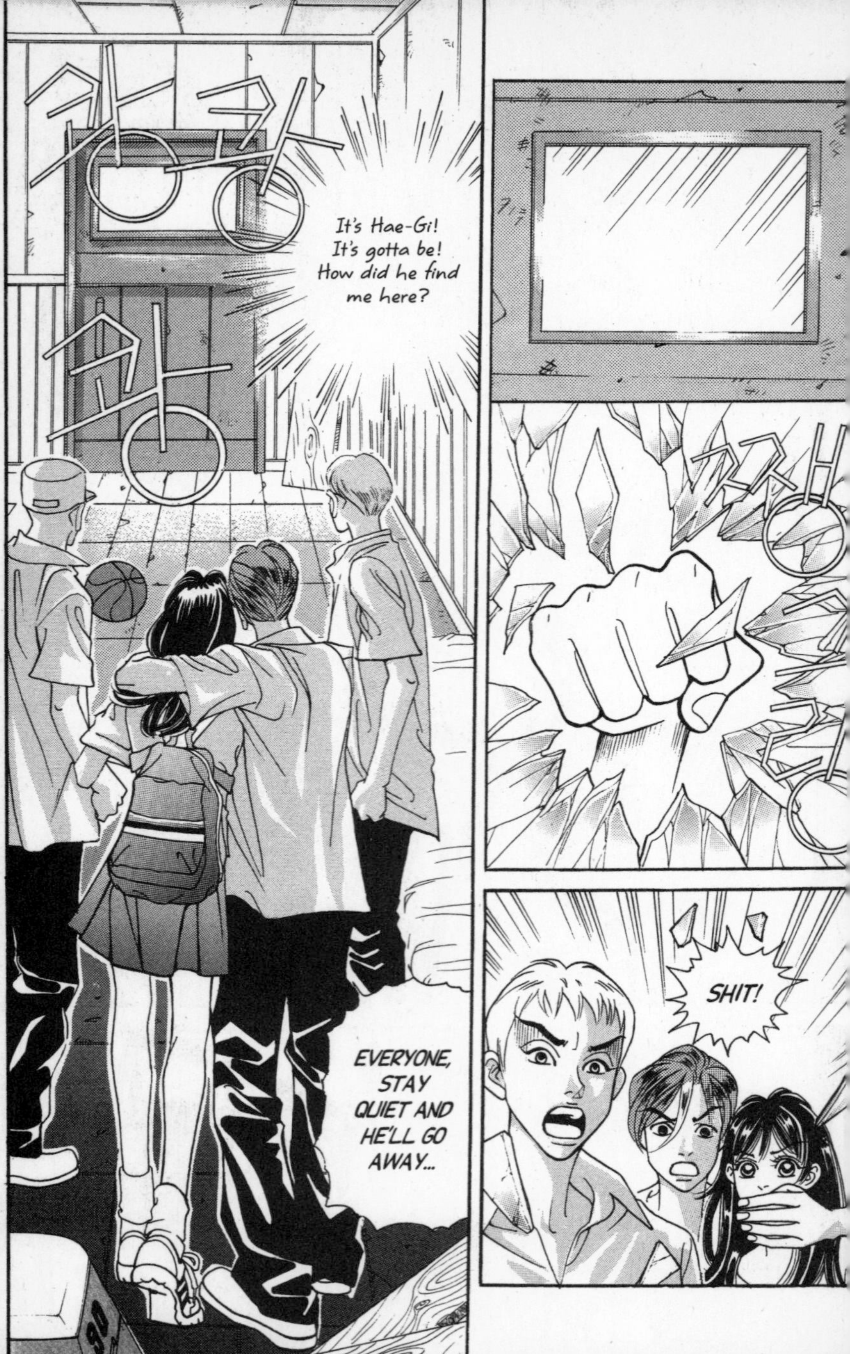
It's Hae-Gi! It's gotta be! How did he find me here?
EVERYONE, STAY QUIET AND HE'LL GO AWAY...
SHIT!

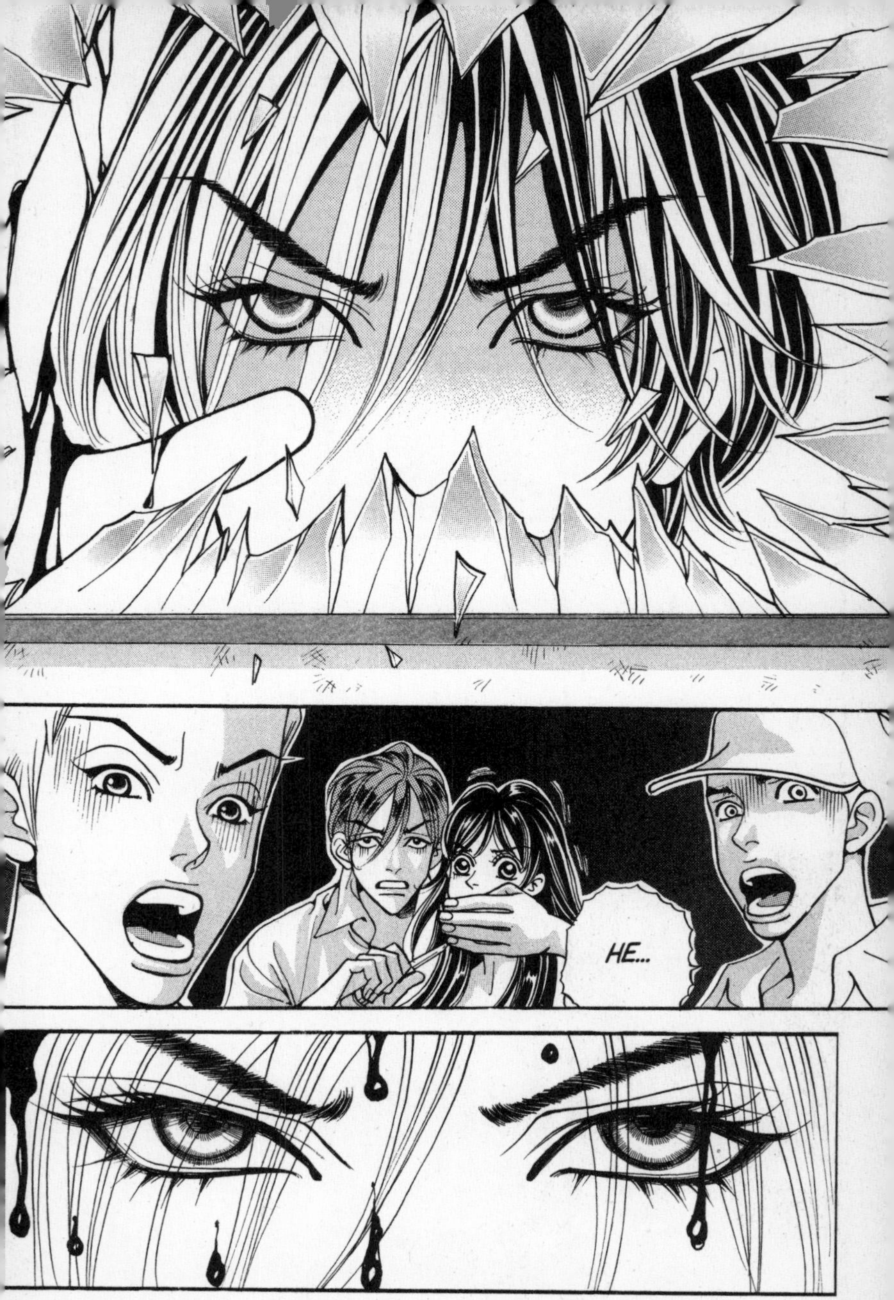
HE...

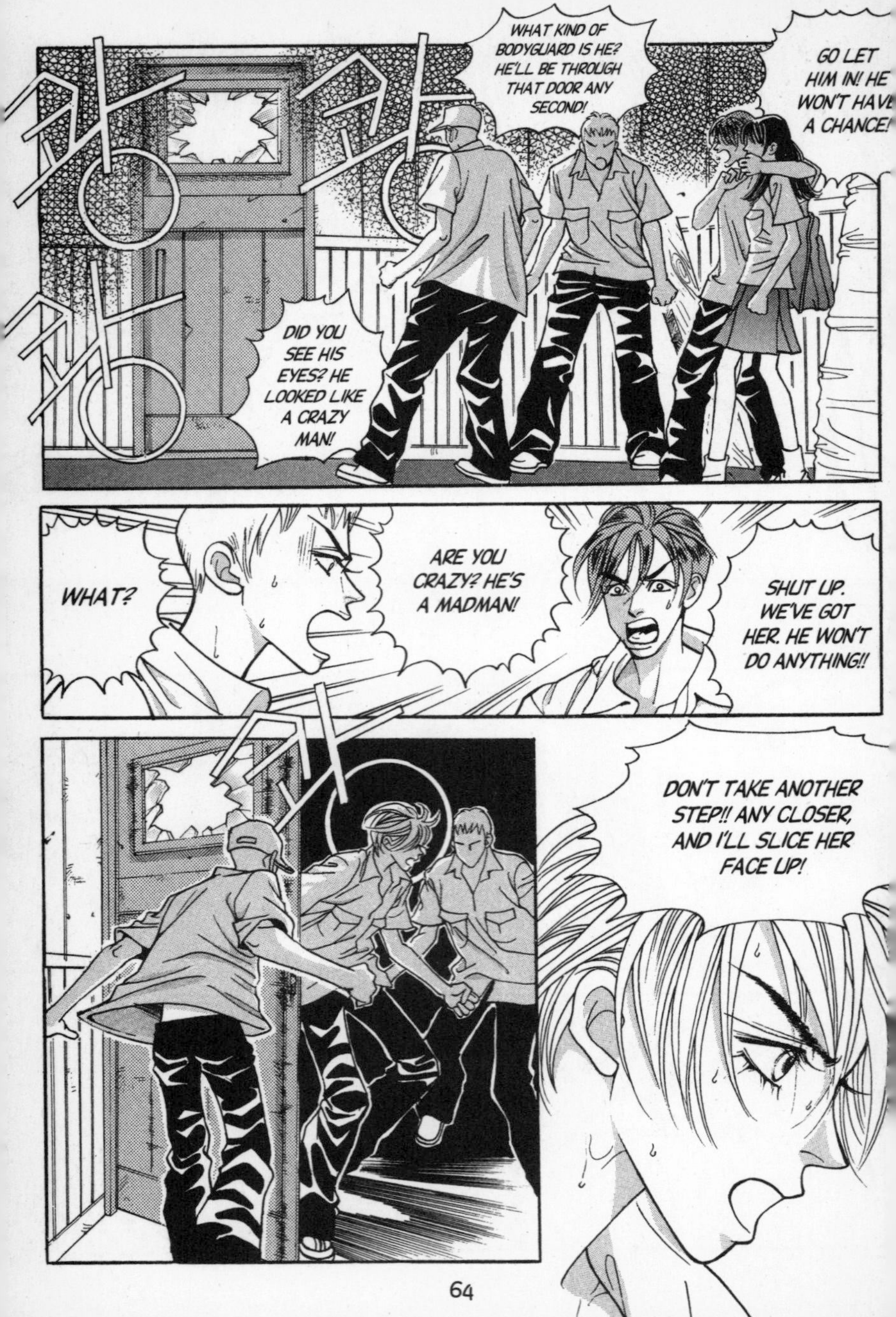
WHAT KIND OF BODYGUARD IS HE? HE'LL BE THROUGH THAT DOOR ANY SECOND!
GO LET HIM IN! HE WON'T HAVE A CHANCE!
DID YOU SEE HIS EYES? HE LOOKED LIKE A CRAZY MAN!
WHAT?
ARE YOU CRAZY? HE'S A MADMAN!
SHUT UP. WE'VE GOT HER. HE WON'T DO ANYTHING!!
DON'T TAKE ANOTHER STEP!! ANY CLOSER, AND I'LL SLICE HER FACE UP!

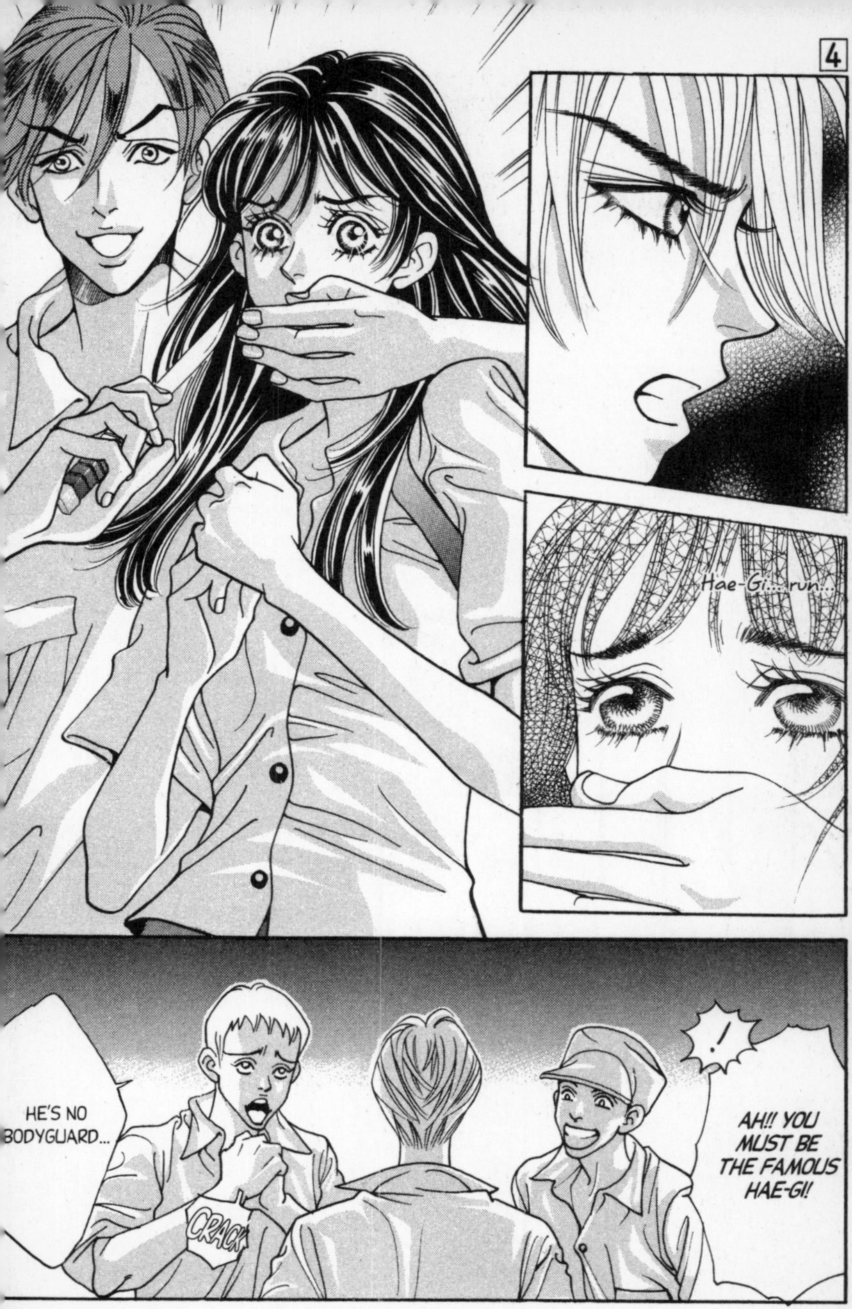
4
Hae-Gi... run...
HE'S NO BODYGUARD...
CRACK
!
AH!! YOU MUST BE THE FAMOUS HAE-GI!

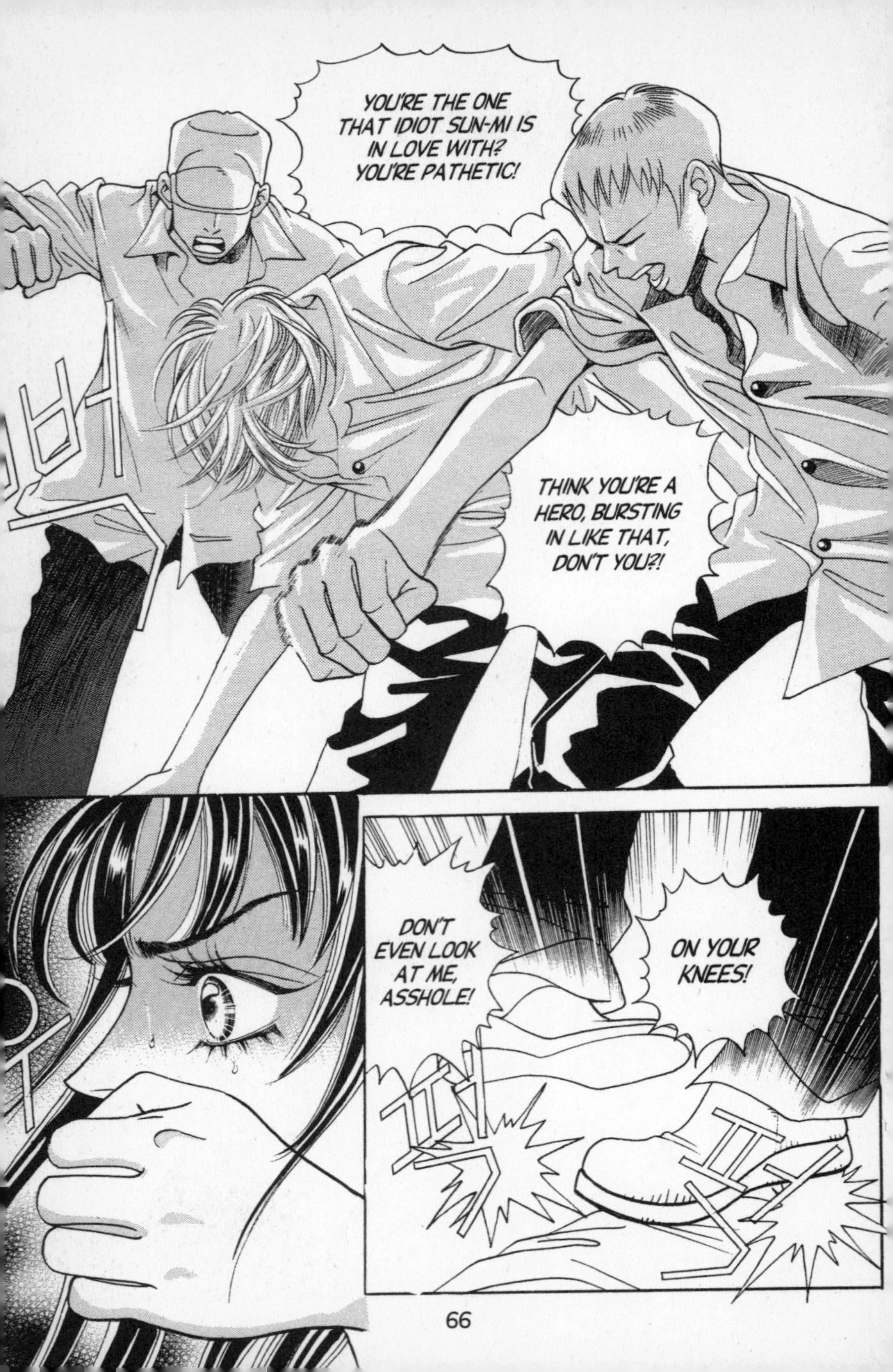
YOU'RE THE ONE THAT IDIOT SUN-MI IS IN LOVE WITH? YOU'RE PATHETIC!
THINK YOU'RE A HERO, BURSTING IN LIKE THAT, DON'T YOU?!
DON'T EVEN LOOK AT ME, ASSHOLE!
ON YOUR KNEES!

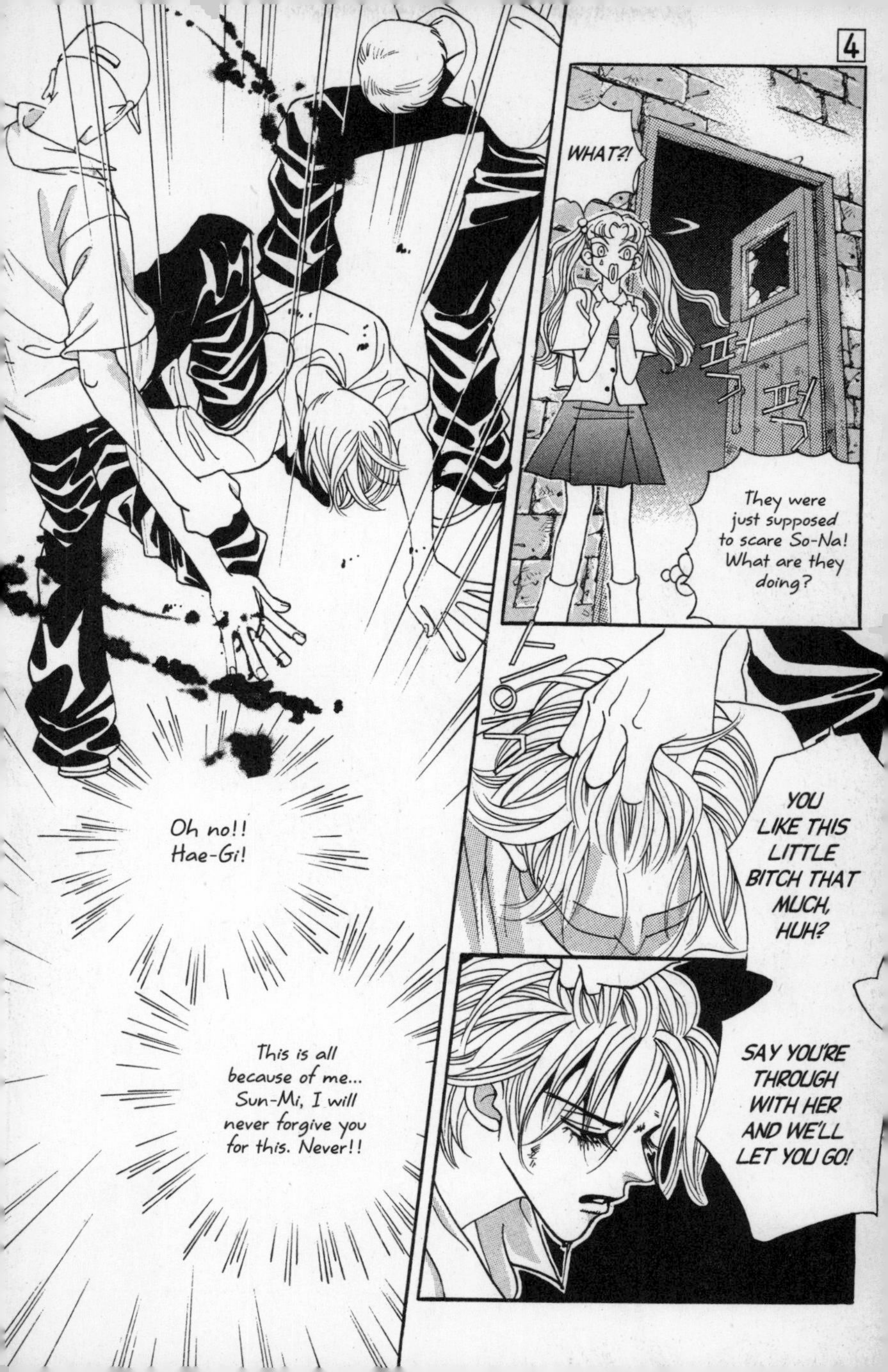
Oh no!! Hae-Gi!
This is all because of me... Sun-Mi, I will never forgive you for this. Never!!
WHAT?!
They were just supposed to scare So-Na! What are they doing?
YOU LIKE THIS LITTLE BITCH THAT MUCH, HUH?
SAY YOU'RE THROUGH WITH HER AND WE'LL LET YOU GO!

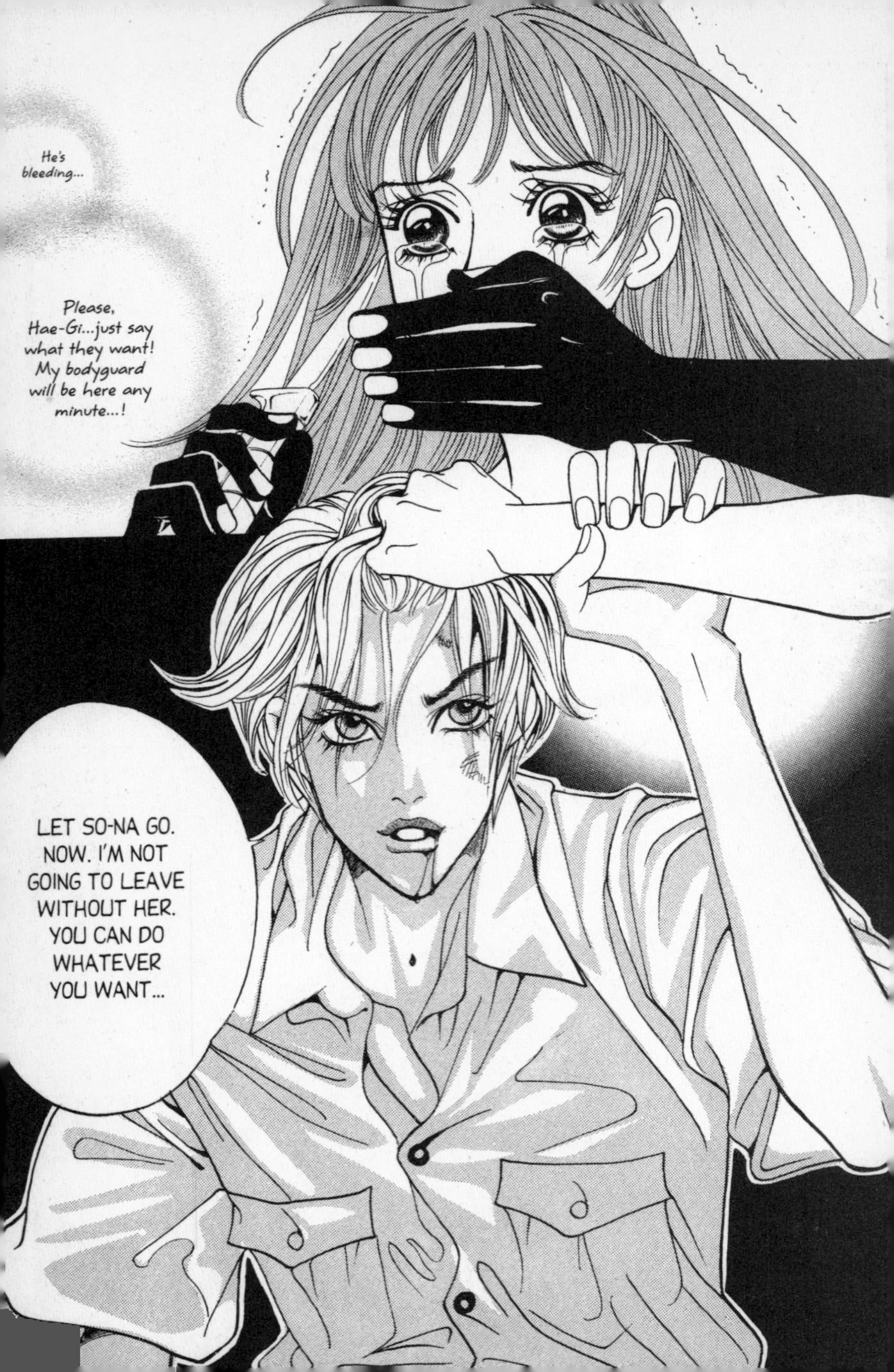
He's bleeding...
Please, Hae-Gi...just say what they want! My bodyguard will be here any minute...!
LET SO-NA GO. NOW. I'M NOT GOING TO LEAVE WITHOUT HER. YOU CAN DO WHATEVER YOU WANT...

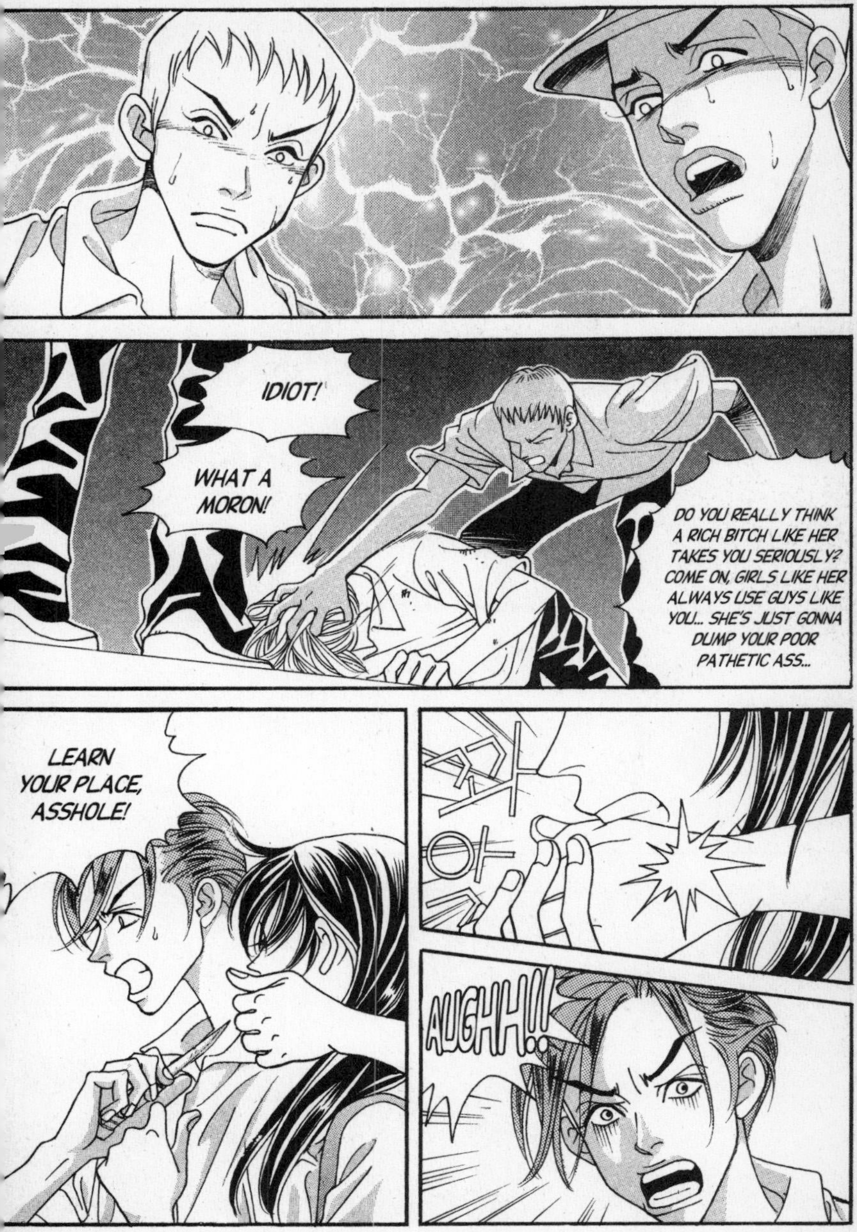
IDIOT!
WHAT A MORON!
DO YOU REALLY THINK A RICH BITCH LIKE HER TAKES YOU SERIOUSLY? COME ON, GIRLS LIKE HER ALWAYS USE GUYS LIKE YOU... SHE'S JUST GONNA DUMP YOUR POOR PATHETIC ASS...
LEARN YOUR PLACE, ASSHOLE!
AUGHH!!

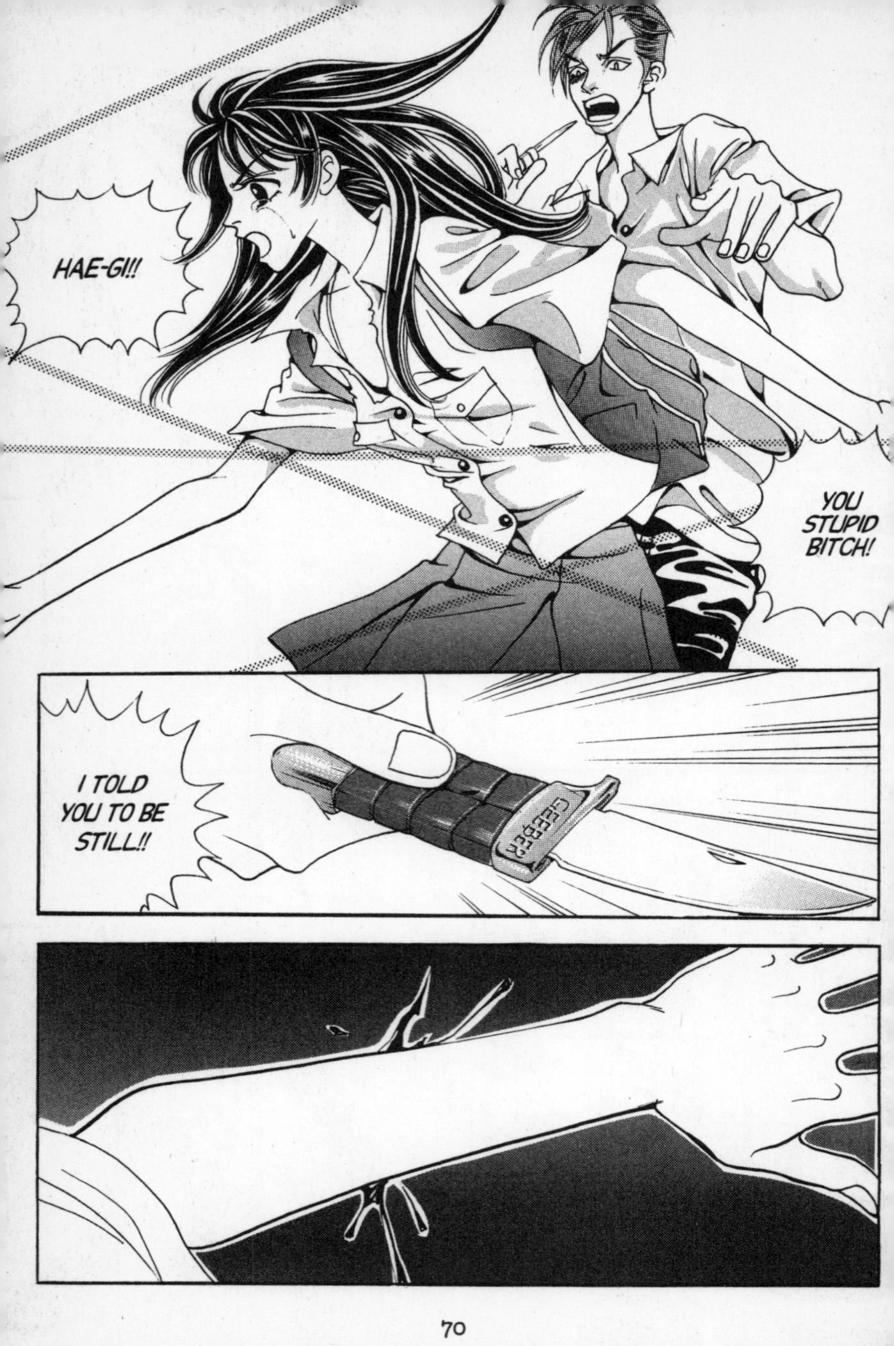
HAE-GI!!
YOU STUPID BITCH!
I TOLD YOU TO BE STILL!!

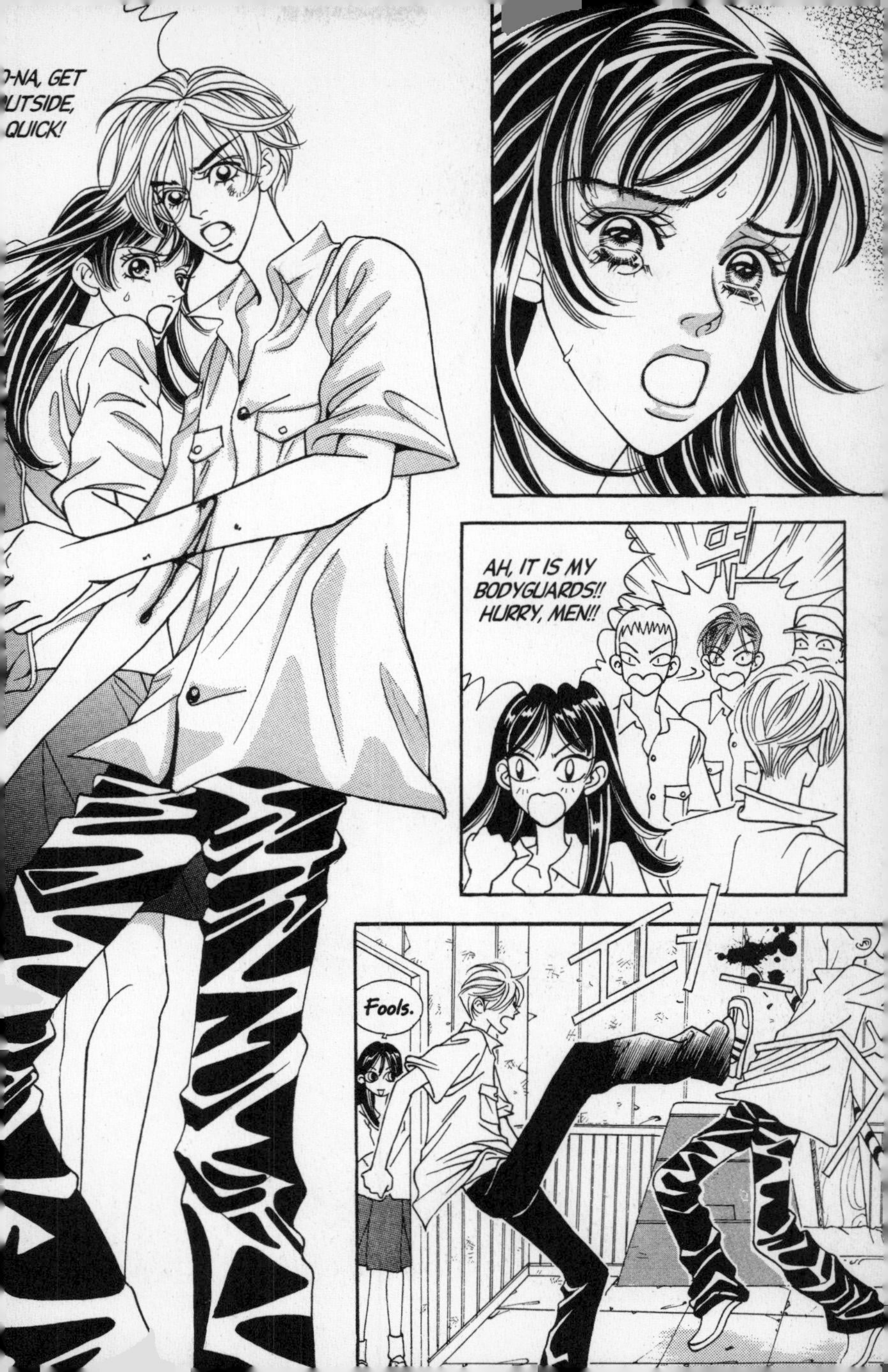
-NA, GET UTSIDE, QUICK!
AH, IT IS MY BODYGUARDS!! HURRY, MEN!!
Fools.

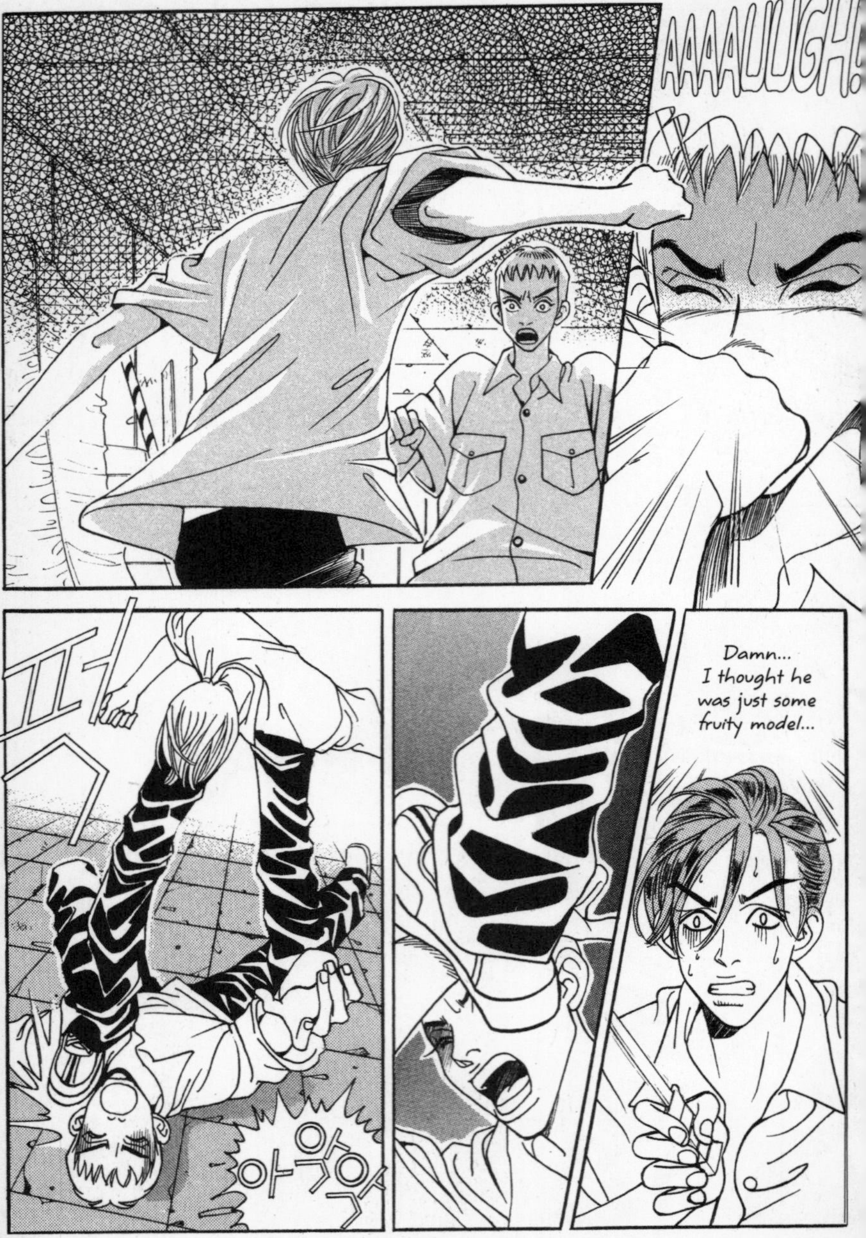
AAAAUUGH!
Damn... I thought he was just some fruity model...

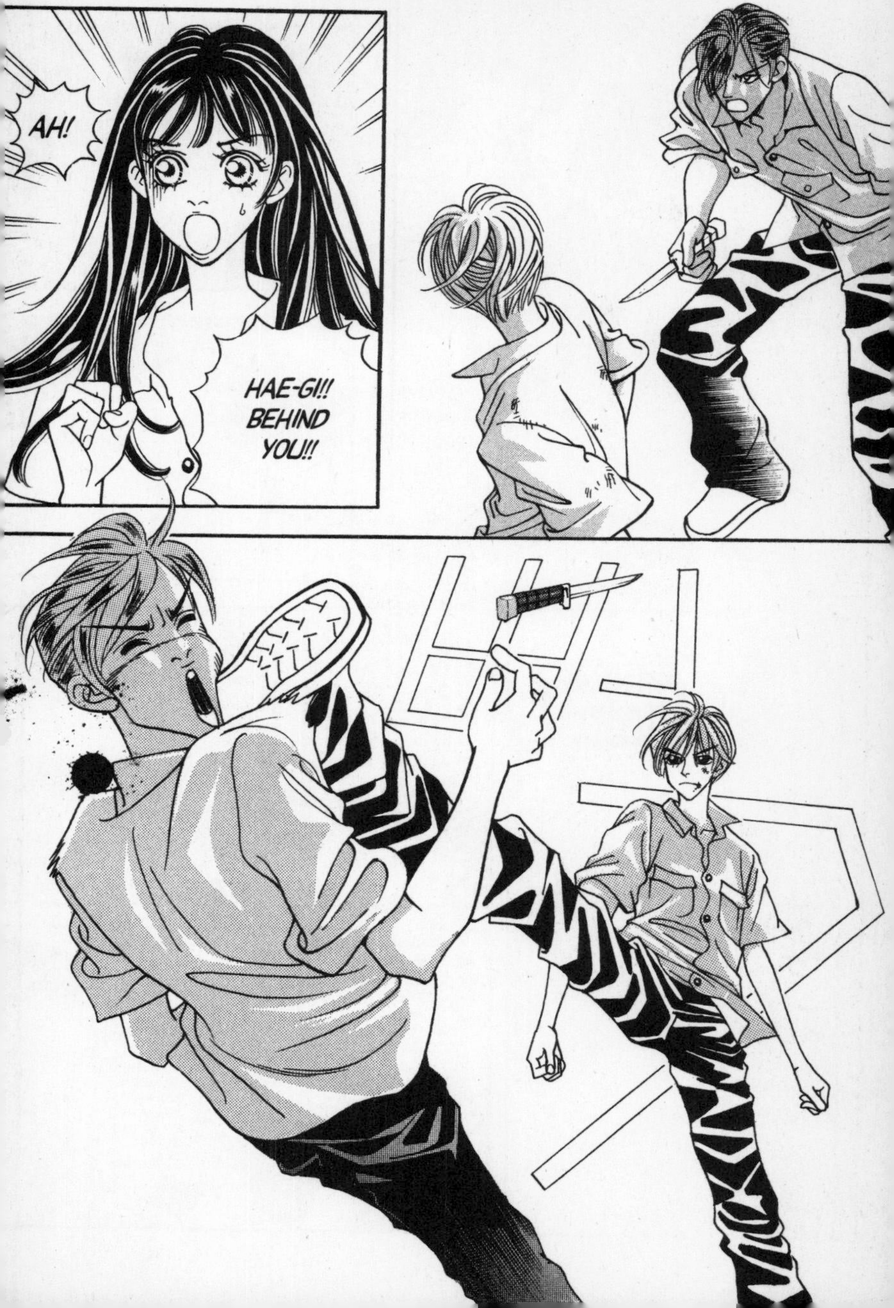
AH!
HAE-GI!! BEHIND YOU!!

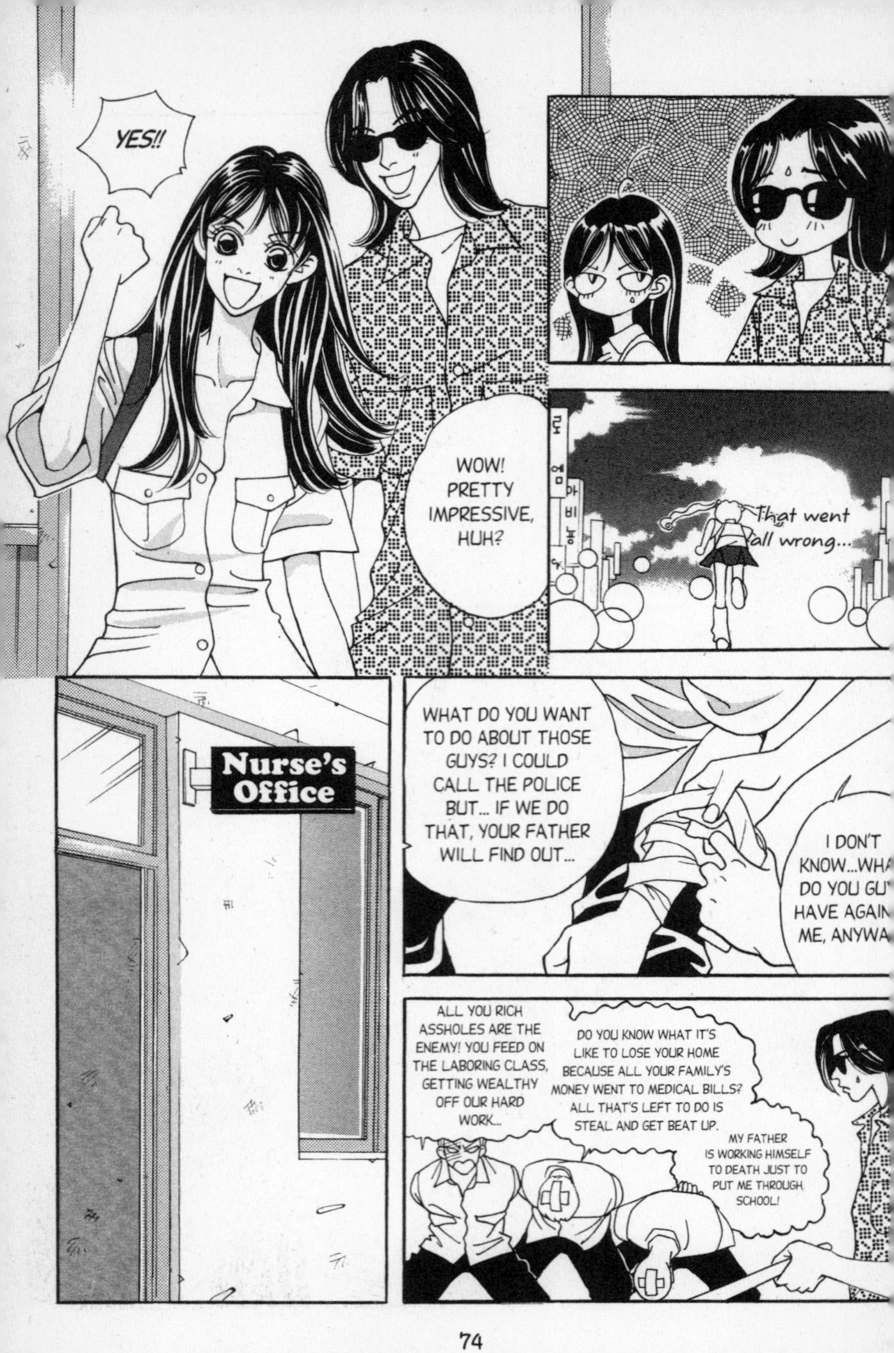

YES!!
WOW! PRETTY IMPRESSIVE, HUH?
That went all wrong...
Nurse's Office
WHAT DO YOU WANT TO DO ABOUT THOSE GUYS? I COULD CALL THE POLICE BUT... IF WE DO THAT, YOUR FATHER WILL FIND OUT...
I DON'T KNOW...WHA DO YOU GU HAVE AGAIN ME, ANYWA
ALL YOU RICH ASSHOLES ARE THE ENEMY! YOU FEED ON THE LABORING CLASS, GETTING WEALTHY OFF OUR HARD WORK...
DO YOU KNOW WHAT IT'S LIKE TO LOSE YOUR HOME BECAUSE ALL YOUR FAMILY'S MONEY WENT TO MEDICAL BILLS? ALL THAT'S LEFT TO DO IS STEAL AND GET BEAT UP.
MY FATHER IS WORKING HIMSELF TO DEATH JUST TO PUT ME THROUGH SCHOOL!

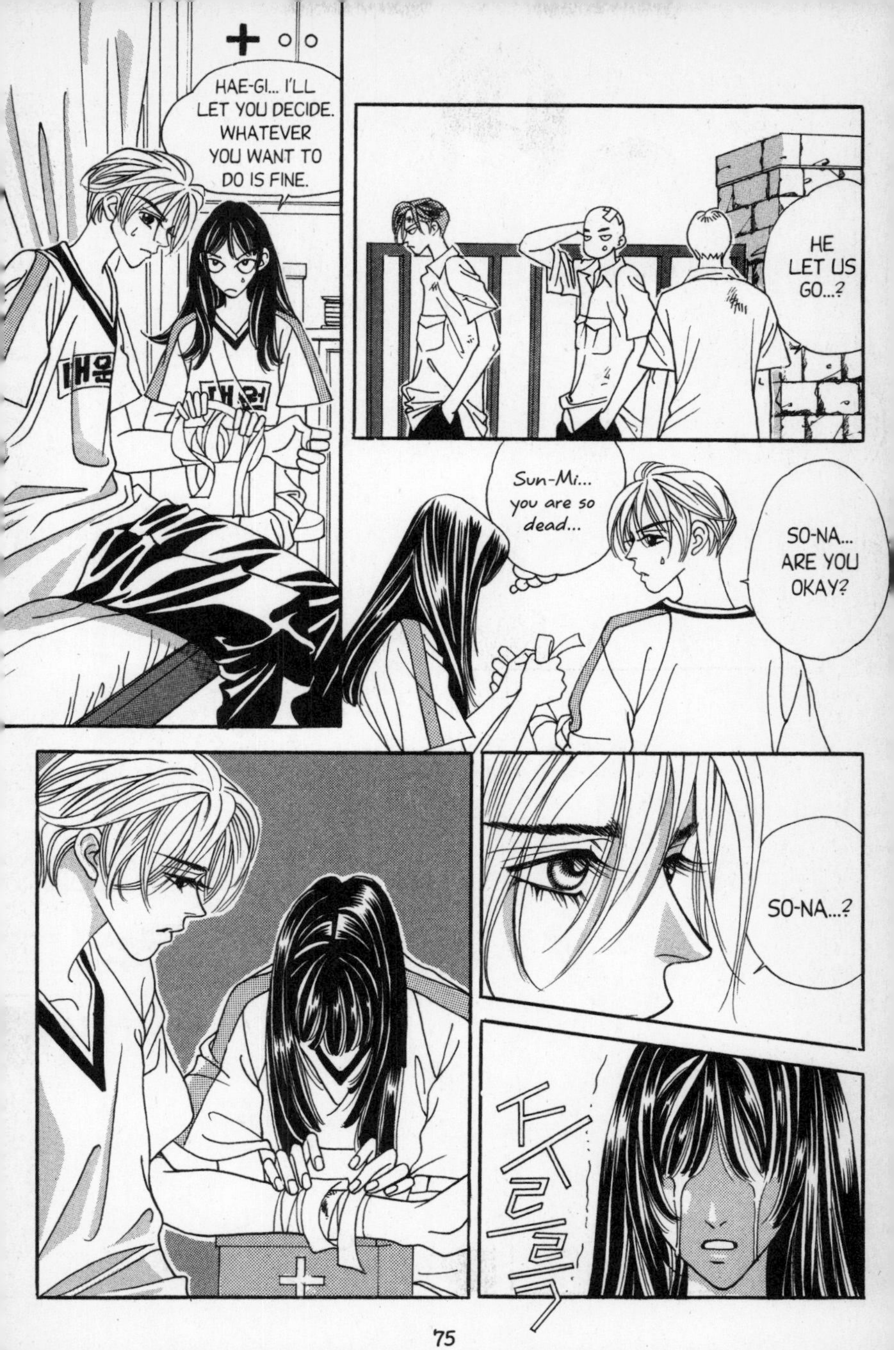
HAE-GI... I'LL LET YOU DECIDE. WHATEVER YOU WANT TO DO IS FINE.
HE LET US GO...?
Sun-Mi... you are so dead...
SO-NA... ARE YOU OKAY?
SO-NA...?

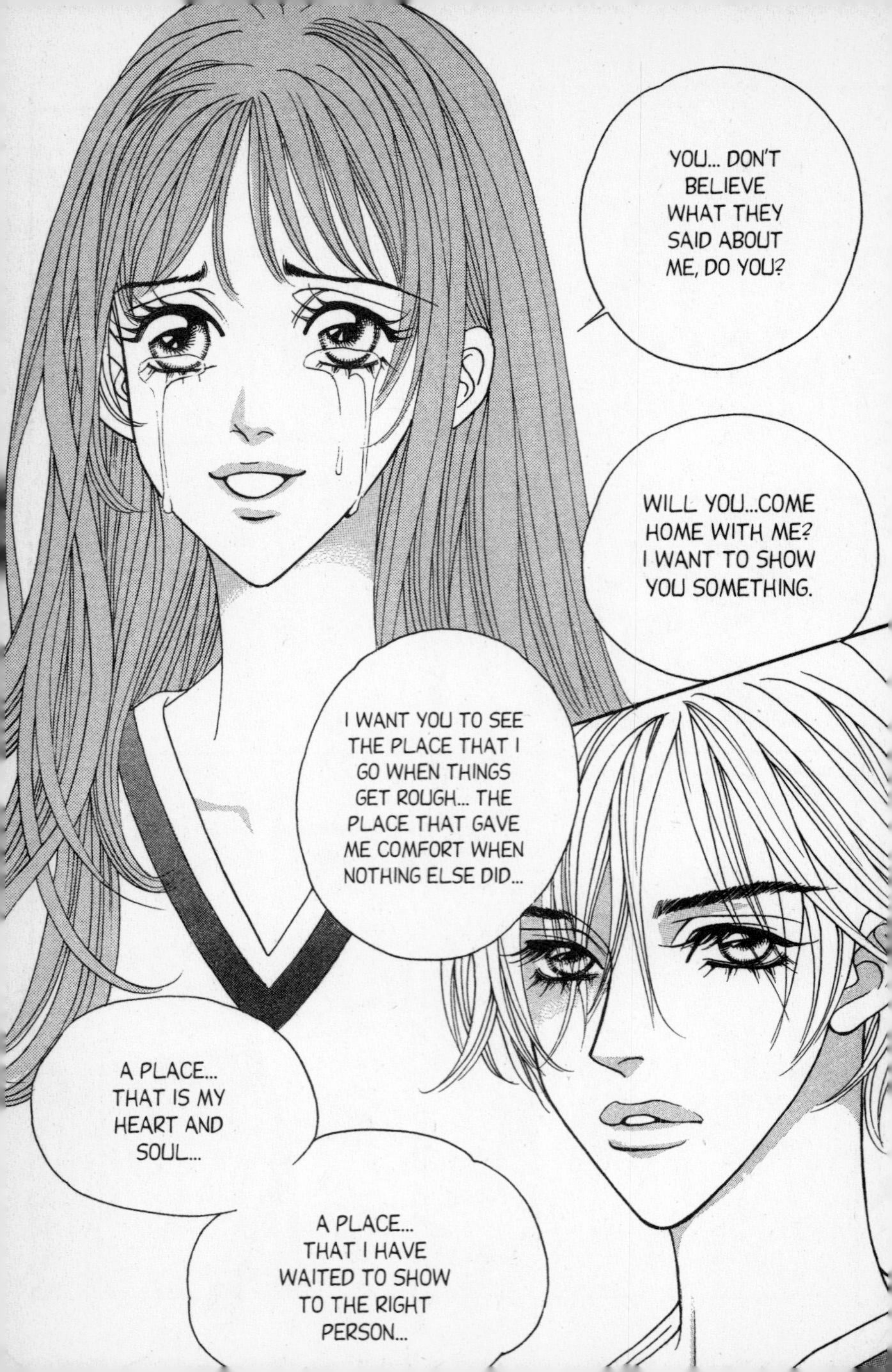
YOU... DON'T BELIEVE WHAT THEY SAID ABOUT ME, DO YOU?
WILL YOU...COME HOME WITH ME? I WANT TO SHOW YOU SOMETHING.
I WANT YOU TO SEE THE PLACE THAT I GO WHEN THINGS GET ROUGH... THE PLACE THAT GAVE ME COMFORT WHEN NOTHING ELSE DID...
A PLACE... THAT IS MY HEART AND SOUL...
A PLACE... THAT I HAVE WAITED TO SHOW TO THE RIGHT PERSON...

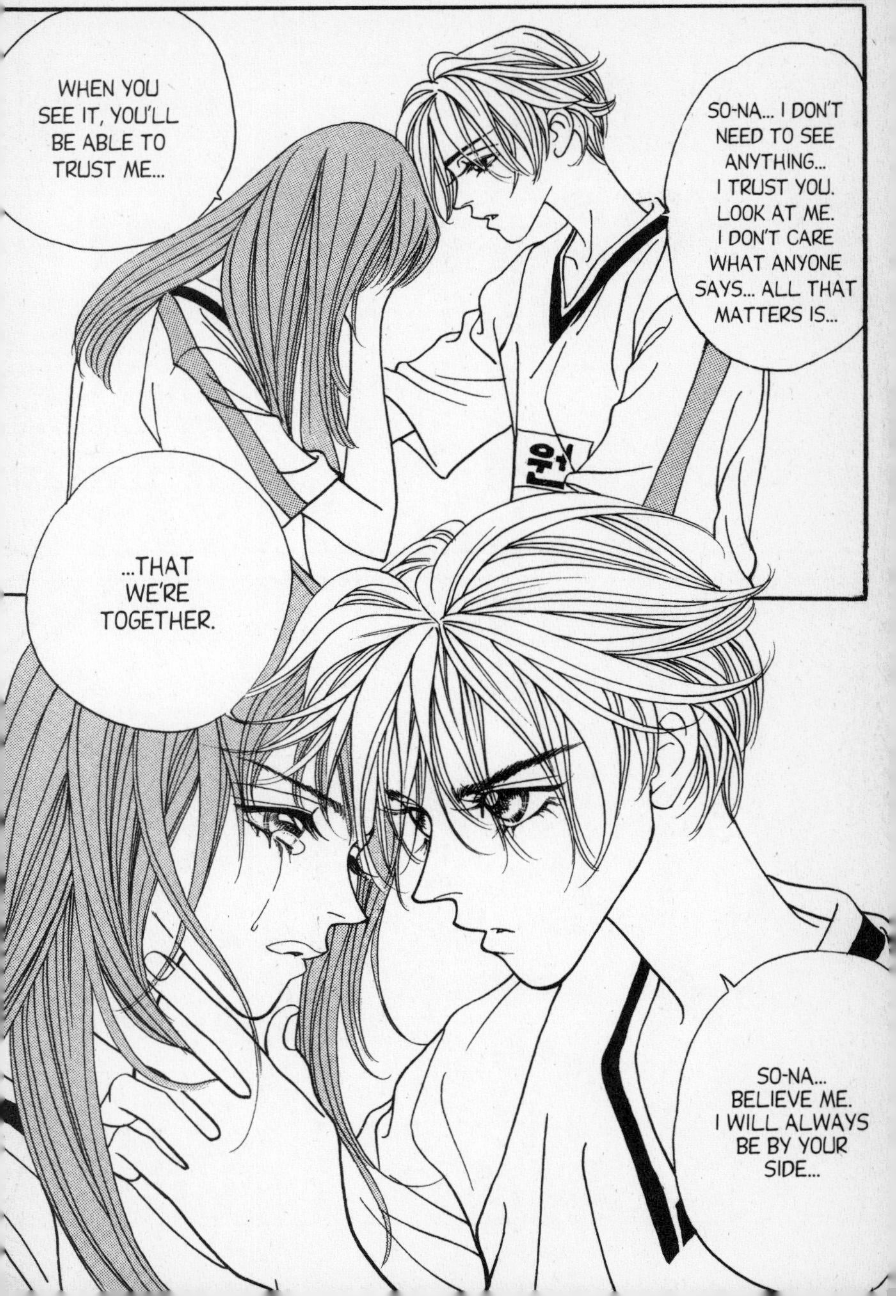
WHEN YOU SEE IT, YOU'LL BE ABLE TO TRUST ME...
SO-NA... I DON'T NEED TO SEE ANYTHING... I TRUST YOU. LOOK AT ME. I DON'T CARE WHAT ANYONE SAYS... ALL THAT MATTERS IS...
...THAT WE'RE TOGETHER.
SO-NA... BELIEVE ME. I WILL ALWAYS BE BY YOUR SIDE...

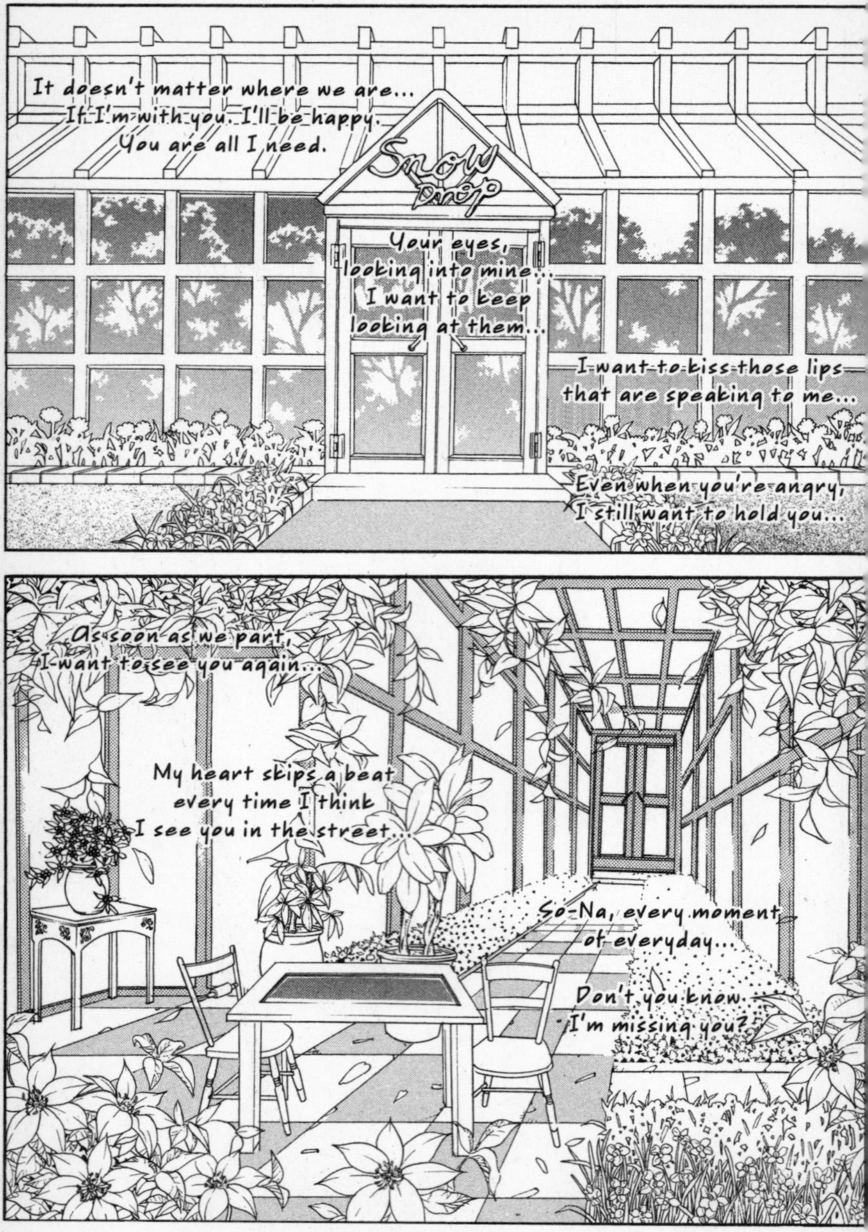
It doesn't matter where we are...
If I'm with you, I'll be happy.
You are all I need.
Snow Drop
Your eyes, looking into mine... I want to keep looking at them...
I want to kiss those lips that are speaking to me...
Even when you're angry, I still want to hold you...
As soon as we part, I want to see you again...
My heart skips a beat every time I think I see you in the street...
So-Na, every moment of everyday...
Don't you know I'm missing you?

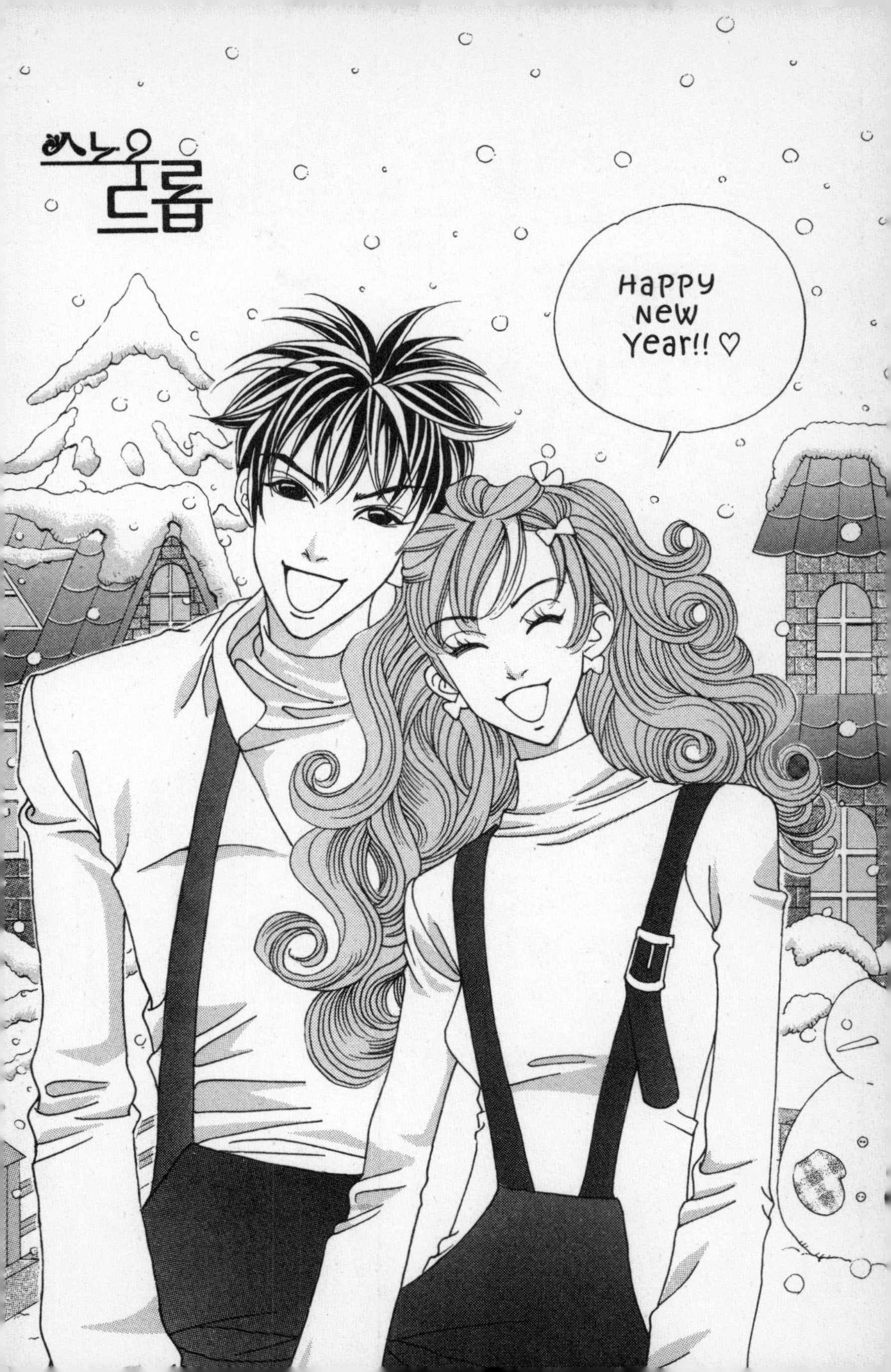
스노우 드롭
Happy New Year!! ♡

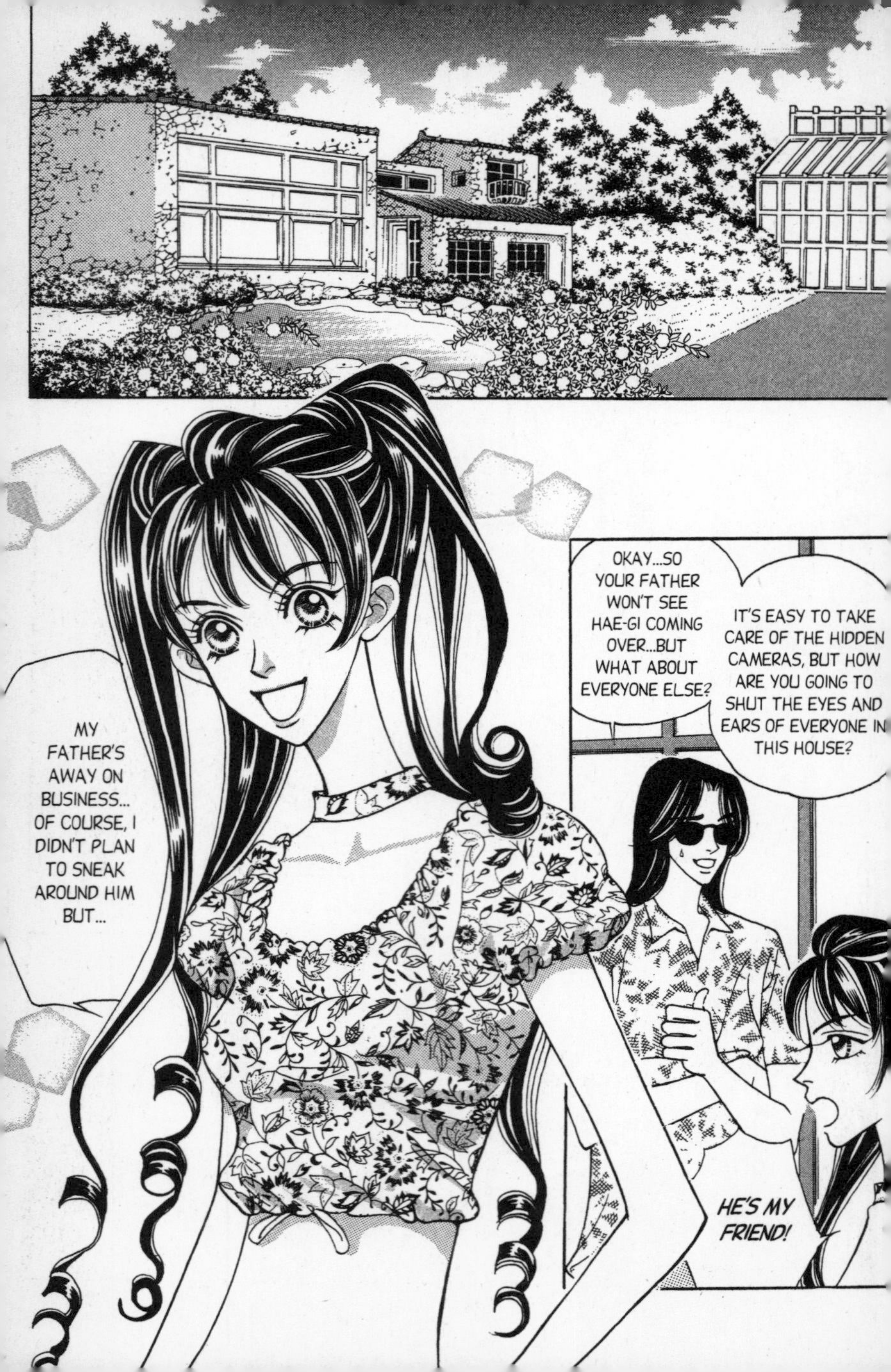
MY FATHER'S AWAY ON BUSINESS... OF COURSE, I DIDN'T PLAN TO SNEAK AROUND HIM BUT...
OKAY...SO YOUR FATHER WON'T SEE HAE-GI COMING OVER...BUT WHAT ABOUT EVERYONE ELSE?
IT'S EASY TO TAKE CARE OF THE HIDDEN CAMERAS, BUT HOW ARE YOU GOING TO SHUT THE EYES AND EARS OF EVERYONE IN THIS HOUSE?
HE'S MY FRIEND!

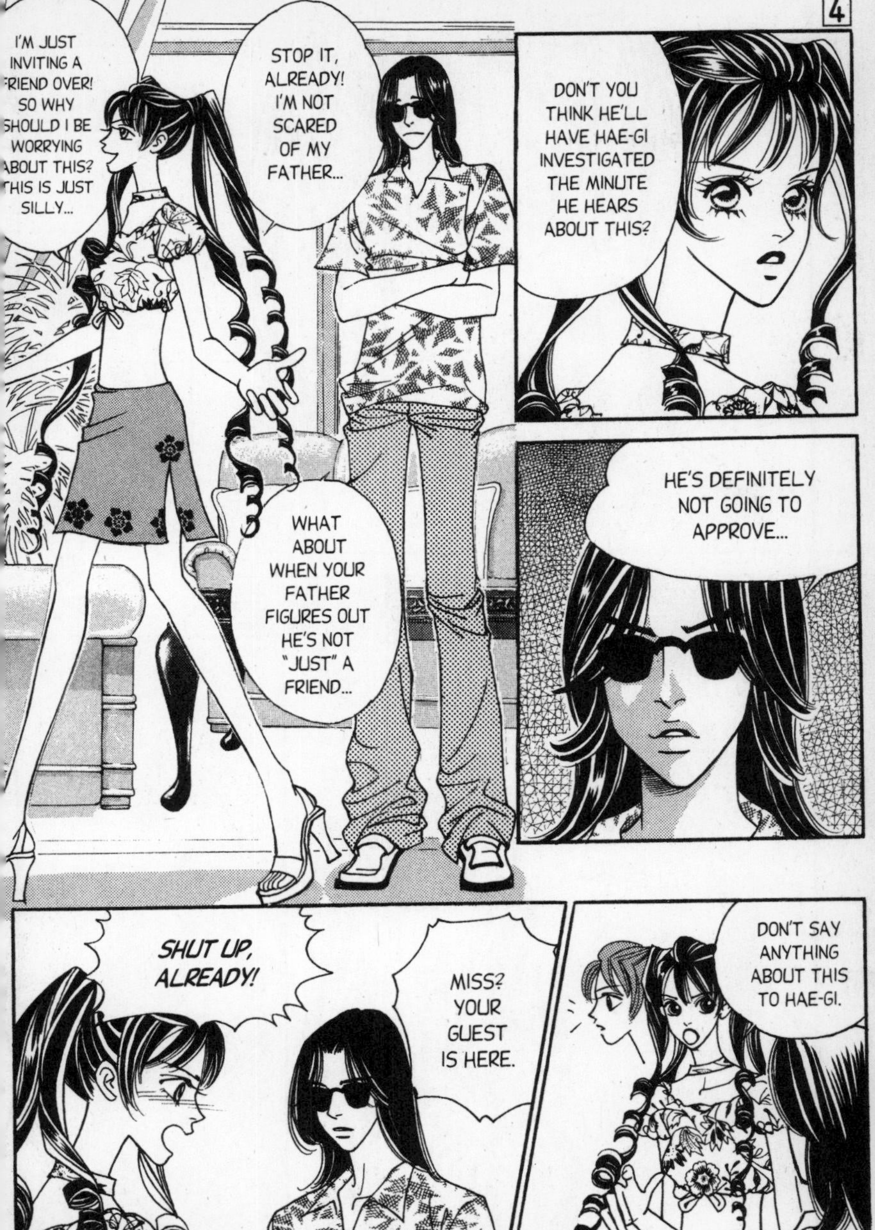

4
I'M JUST INVITING A FRIEND OVER! SO WHY SHOULD I BE WORRYING ABOUT THIS? THIS IS JUST SILLY...
STOP IT, ALREADY! I'M NOT SCARED OF MY FATHER...
WHAT ABOUT WHEN YOUR FATHER FIGURES OUT HE'S NOT "JUST" A FRIEND...
DON'T YOU THINK HE'LL HAVE HAE-GI INVESTIGATED THE MINUTE HE HEARS ABOUT THIS?
HE'S DEFINITELY NOT GOING TO APPROVE...
SHUT UP, ALREADY!
MISS? YOUR GUEST IS HERE.
DON'T SAY ANYTHING ABOUT THIS TO HAE-GI.

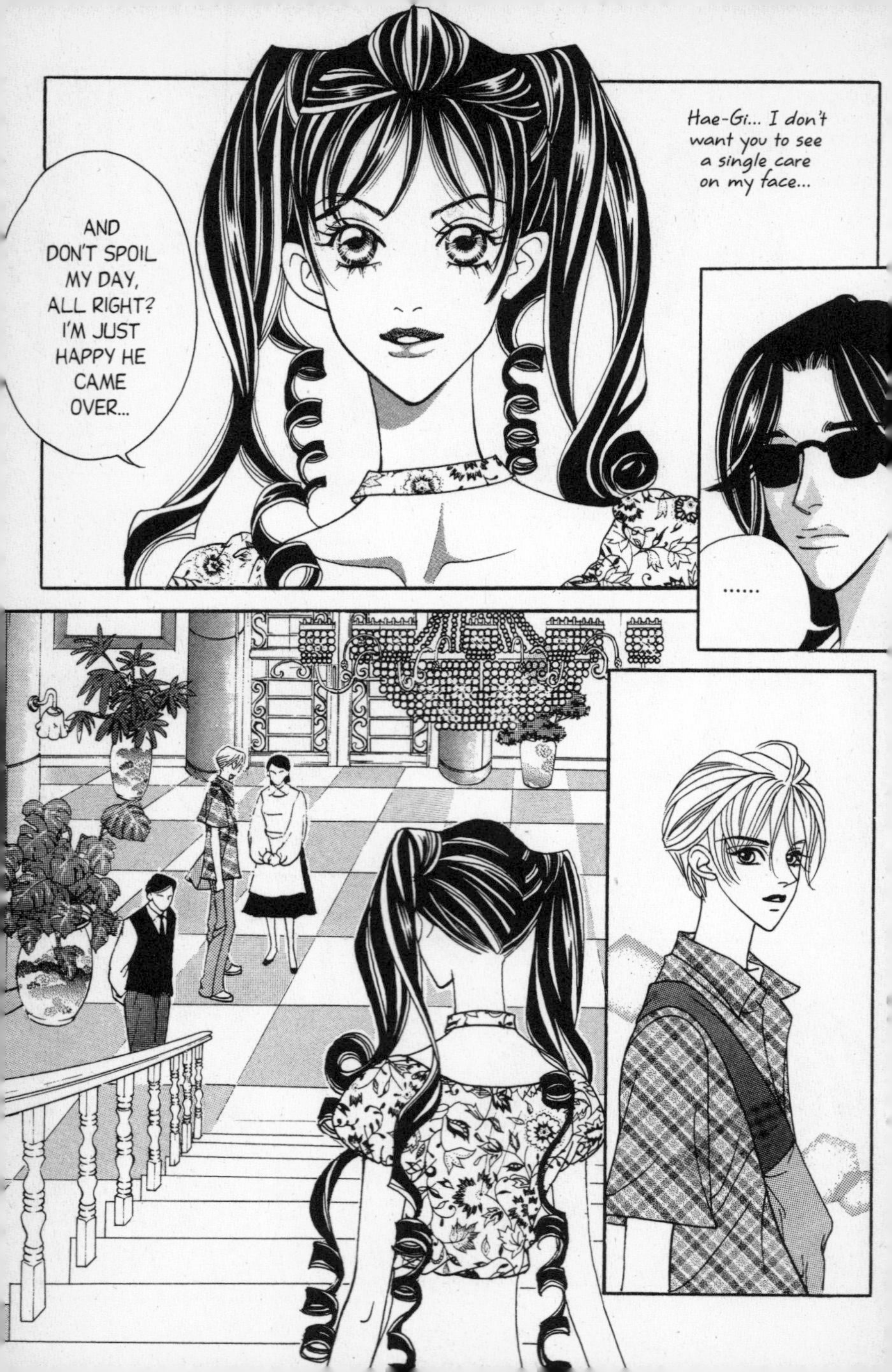
AND DON'T SPOIL MY DAY, ALL RIGHT? I'M JUST HAPPY HE CAME OVER...
Hae-Gi... I don't want you to see a single care on my face...
......

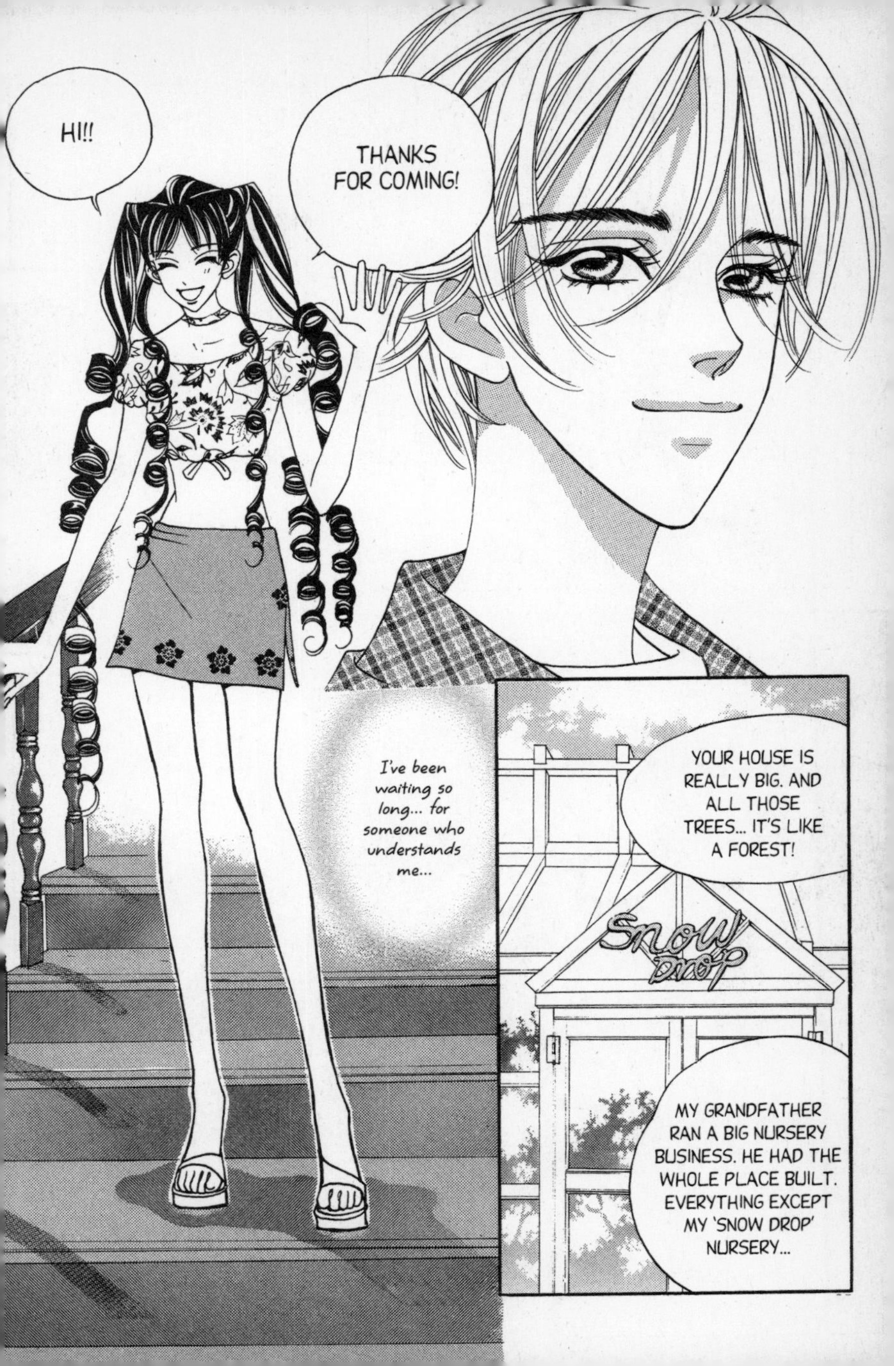
HI!!
THANKS FOR COMING!
I've been waiting so long... for someone who understands me...
YOUR HOUSE IS REALLY BIG. AND ALL THOSE TREES... IT'S LIKE A FOREST!
SNOW DROP
MY GRANDFATHER RAN A BIG NURSERY BUSINESS. HE HAD THE WHOLE PLACE BUILT. EVERYTHING EXCEPT MY 'SNOW DROP' NURSERY...

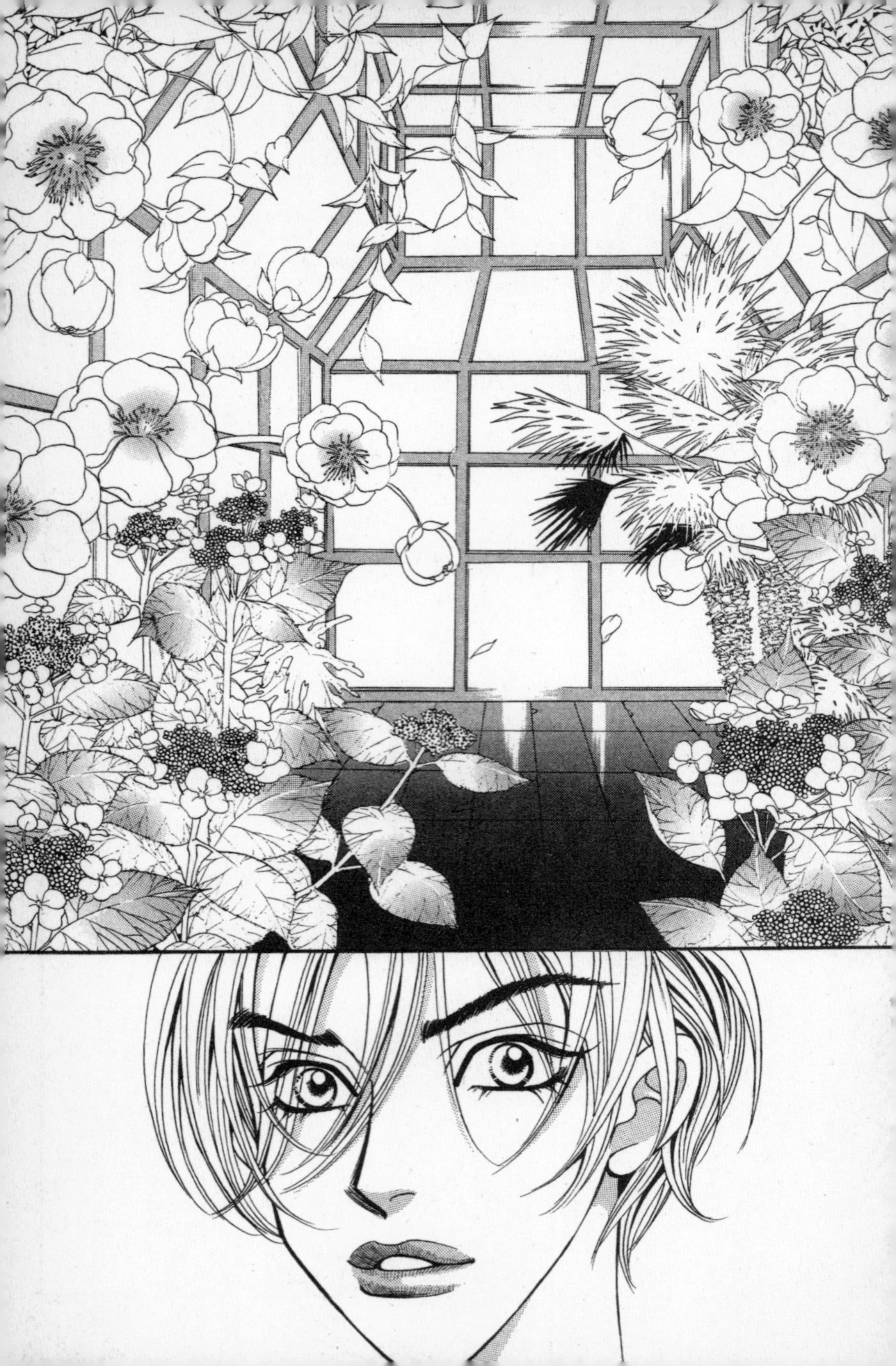

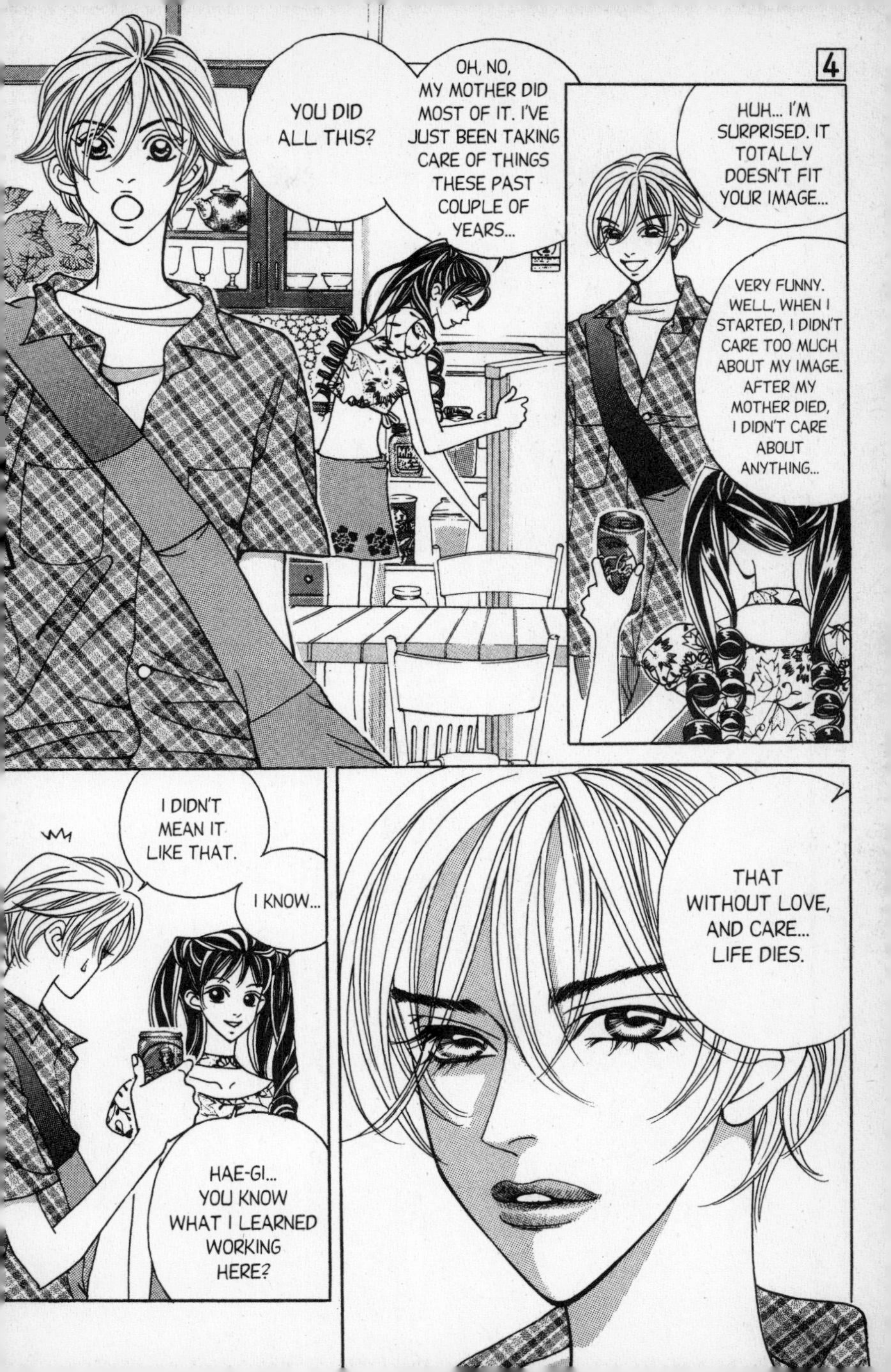
4
YOU DID ALL THIS?
OH, NO, MY MOTHER DID MOST OF IT. I'VE JUST BEEN TAKING CARE OF THINGS THESE PAST COUPLE OF YEARS...
HUH... I'M SURPRISED. IT TOTALLY DOESN'T FIT YOUR IMAGE...
VERY FUNNY. WELL, WHEN I STARTED, I DIDN'T CARE TOO MUCH ABOUT MY IMAGE. AFTER MY MOTHER DIED, I DIDN'T CARE ABOUT ANYTHING...
I DIDN'T MEAN IT LIKE THAT.
I KNOW...
HAE-GI... YOU KNOW WHAT I LEARNED WORKING HERE?
THAT WITHOUT LOVE, AND CARE... LIFE DIES.

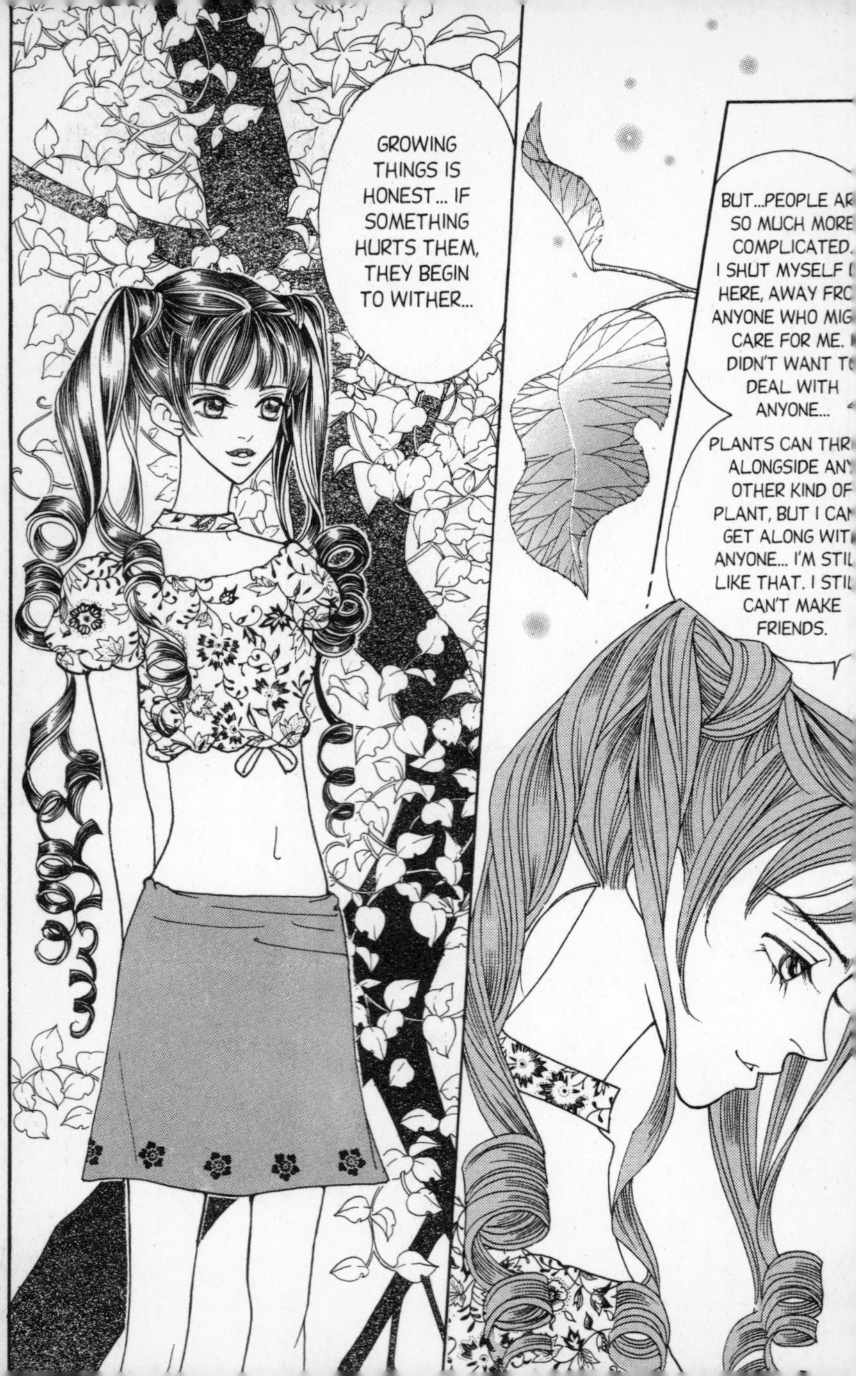
GROWING THINGS IS HONEST... IF SOMETHING HURTS THEM, THEY BEGIN TO WITHER...
BUT...PEOPLE AR SO MUCH MORE COMPLICATED. I SHUT MYSELF I HERE, AWAY FRO ANYONE WHO MIG CARE FOR ME. I DIDN'T WANT T DEAL WITH ANYONE...
PLANTS CAN THR ALONGSIDE AN OTHER KIND OF PLANT, BUT I CA GET ALONG WIT ANYONE... I'M STIL LIKE THAT. I STIL CAN'T MAKE FRIENDS.

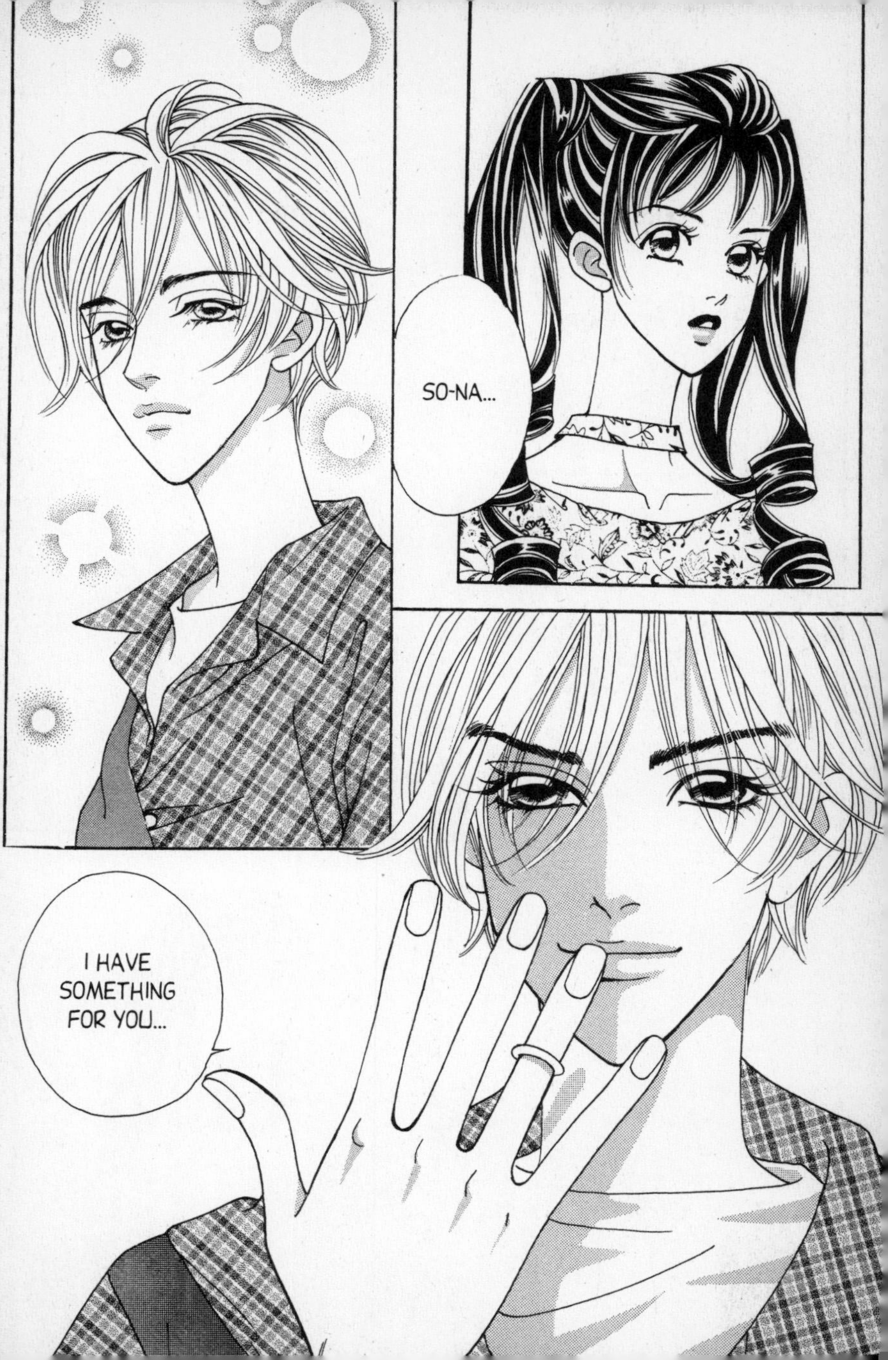
SO-NA...
I HAVE SOMETHING FOR YOU...

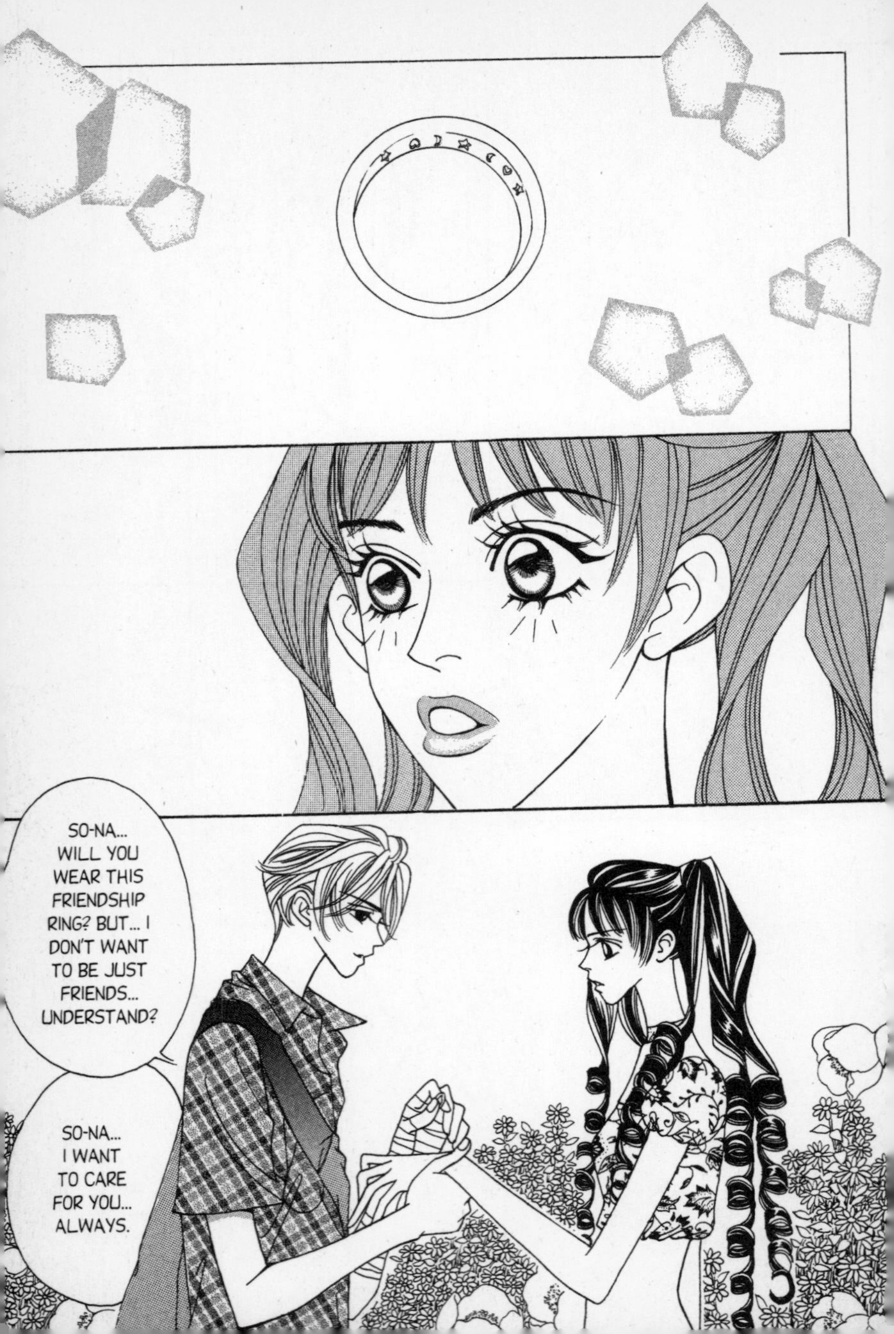
SO-NA... WILL YOU WEAR THIS FRIENDSHIP RING? BUT... I DON'T WANT TO BE JUST FRIENDS... UNDERSTAND?
SO-NA... I WANT TO CARE FOR YOU... ALWAYS.

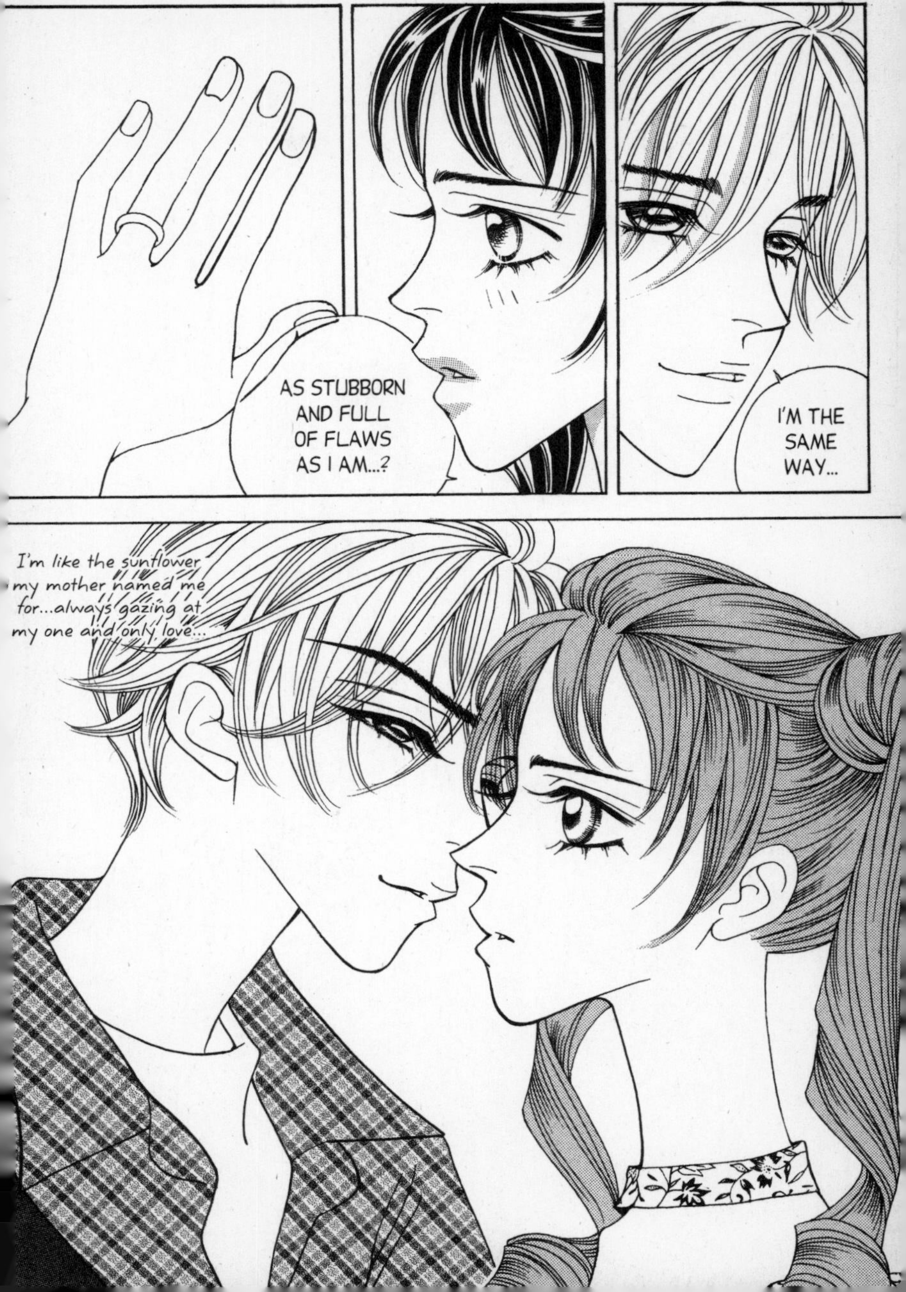
AS STUBBORN AND FULL OF FLAWS AS I AM...?
I'M THE SAME WAY...
I'm like the sunflower my mother named me for...always gazing at my one and only love...

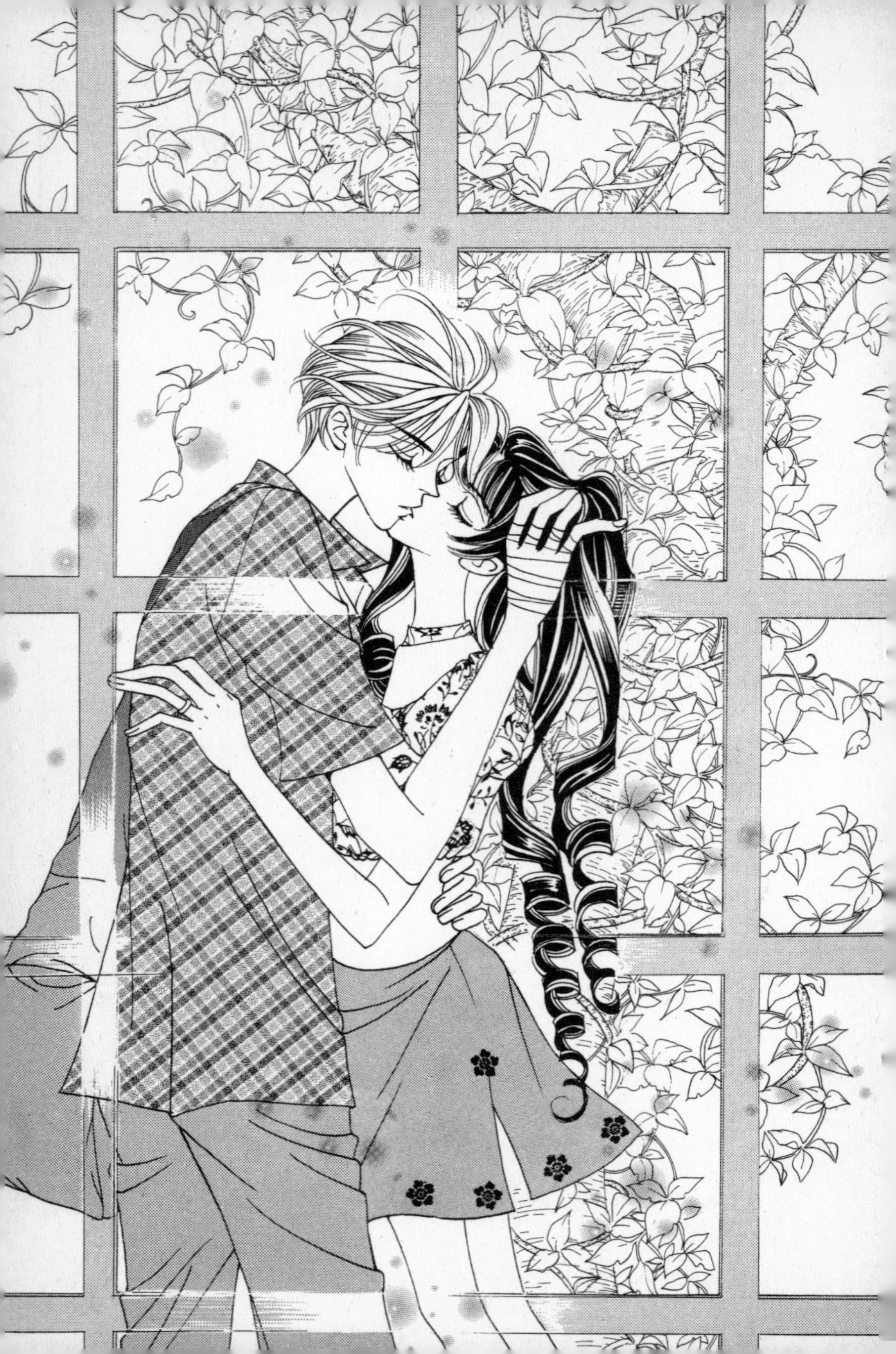

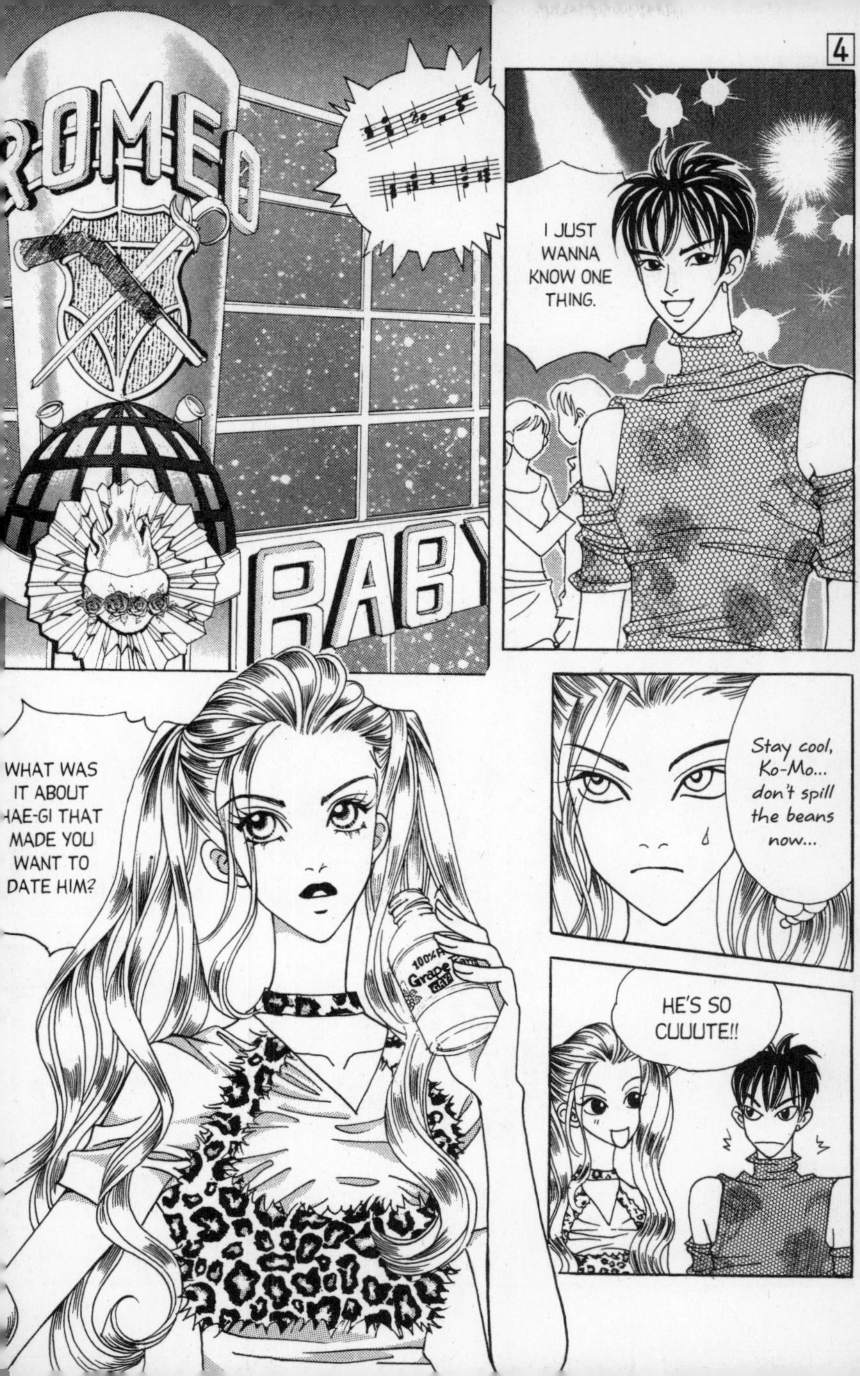
ROMEO
BABY
I JUST WANNA KNOW ONE THING.
WHAT WAS IT ABOUT HAE-GI THAT MADE YOU WANT TO DATE HIM?
Stay cool, Ko-Mo... don't spill the beans now...
HE'S SO CUUUTE!!

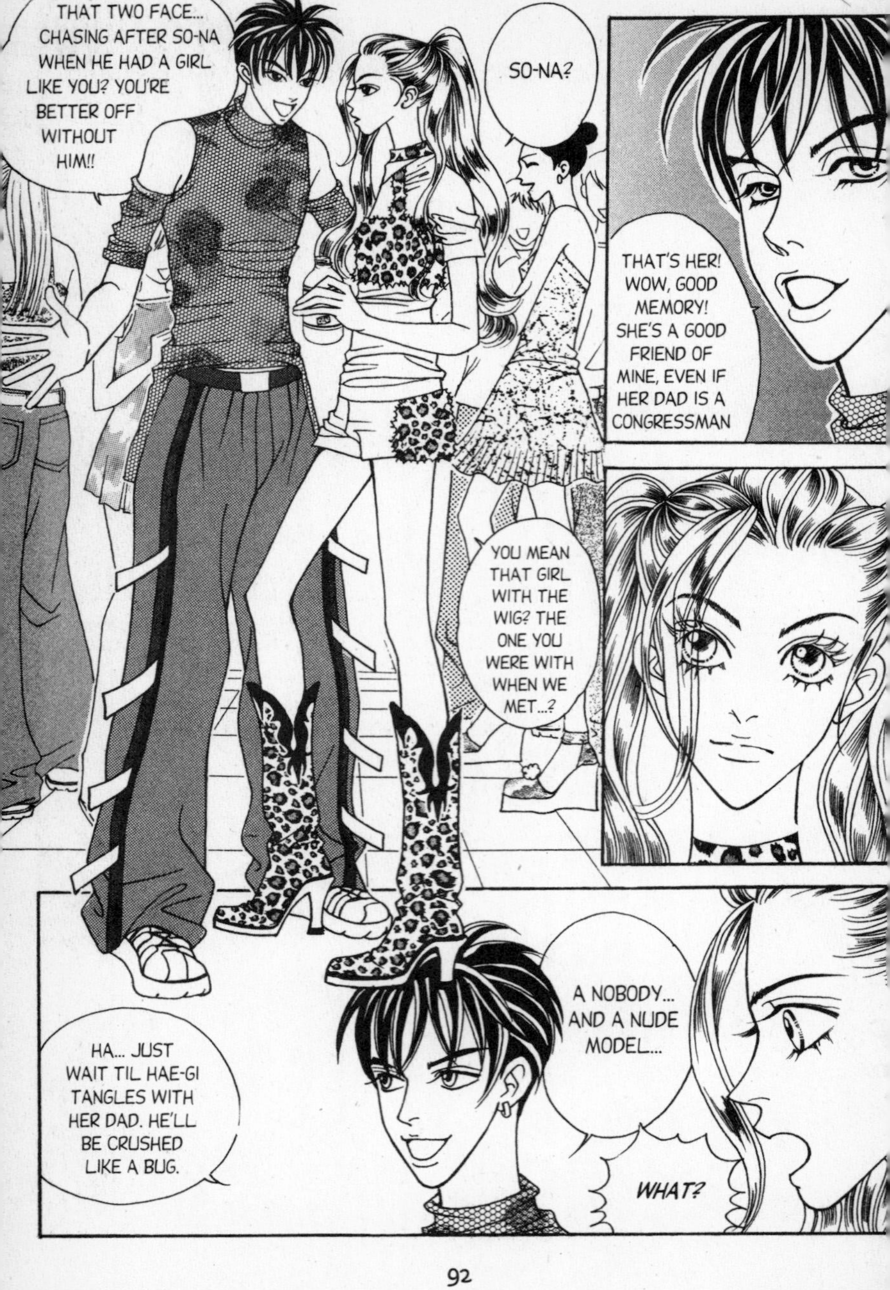
THAT TWO FACE... CHASING AFTER SO-NA WHEN HE HAD A GIRL LIKE YOU? YOU'RE BETTER OFF WITHOUT HIM!!
SO-NA?
THAT'S HER! WOW, GOOD MEMORY! SHE'S A GOOD FRIEND OF MINE, EVEN IF HER DAD IS A CONGRESSMAN
YOU MEAN THAT GIRL WITH THE WIG? THE ONE YOU WERE WITH WHEN WE MET...?
HA... JUST WAIT TIL HAE-GI TANGLES WITH HER DAD. HE'LL BE CRUSHED LIKE A BUG.
A NOBODY... AND A NUDE MODEL...
WHAT?

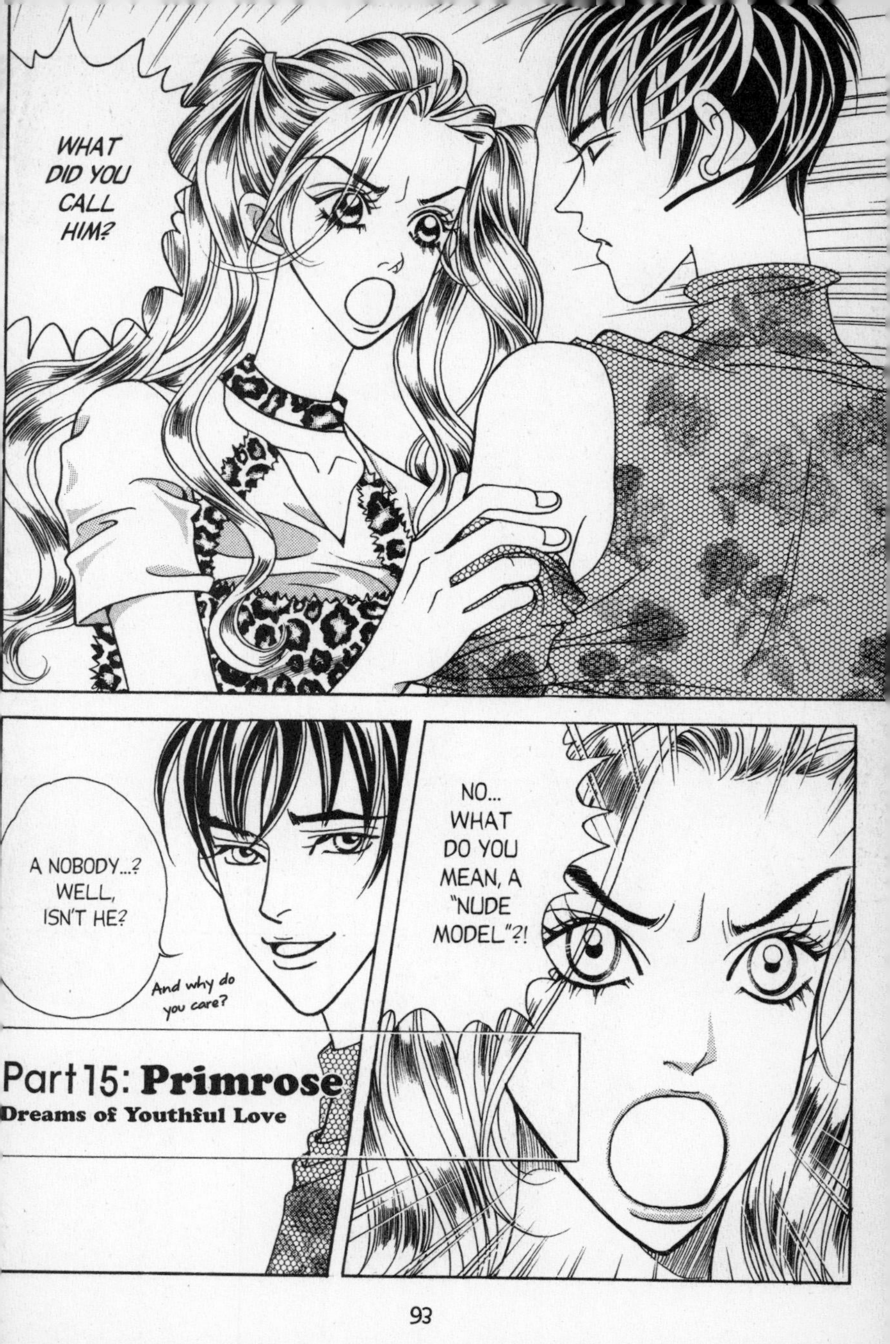
WHAT DID YOU CALL HIM?
A NOBODY...? WELL, ISN'T HE?
And why do you care?
Part 15: Primrose
Dreams of Youthful Love
NO... WHAT DO YOU MEAN, A "NUDE MODEL"?!

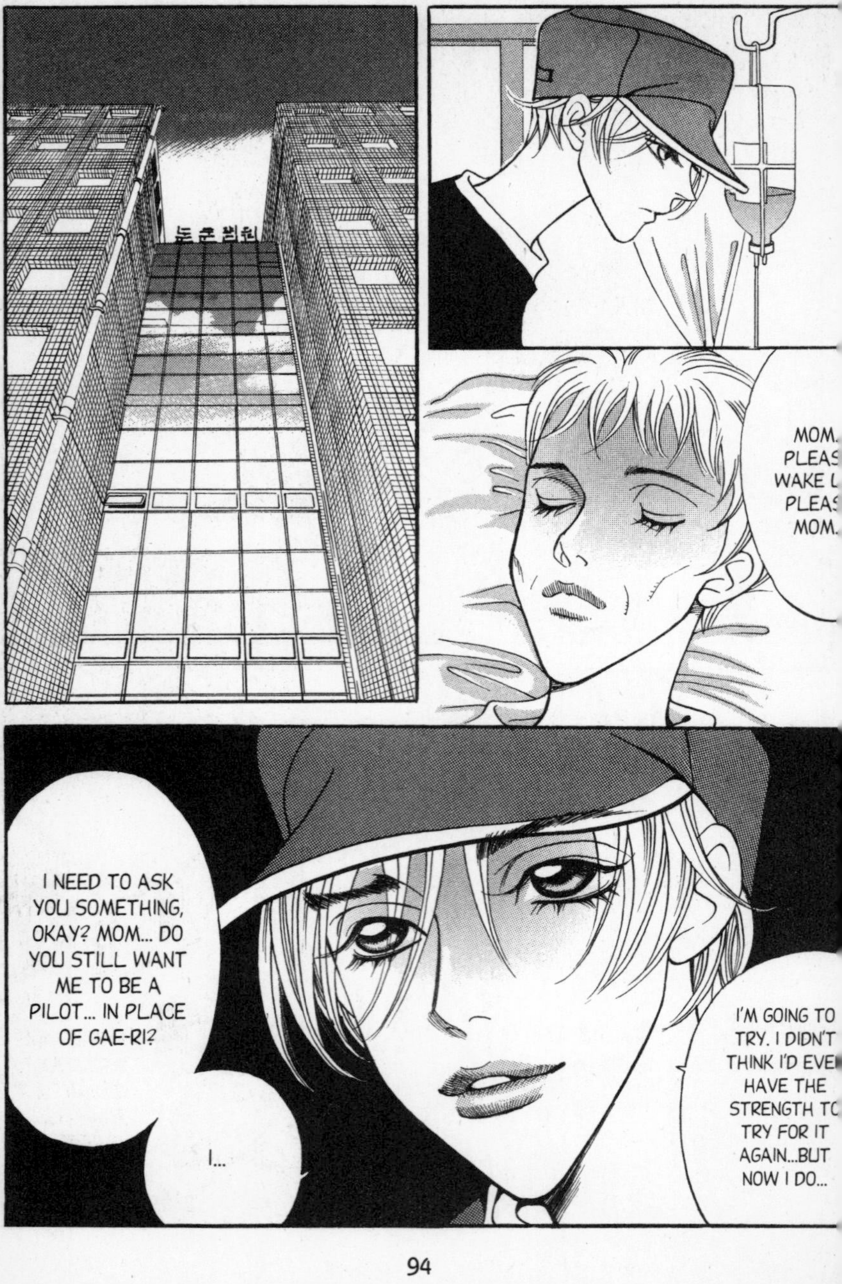
MOM. PLEAS WAKE U PLEAS MOM.
I NEED TO ASK YOU SOMETHING, OKAY? MOM... DO YOU STILL WANT ME TO BE A PILOT... IN PLACE OF GAE-RI?
I...
I'M GOING TO TRY. I DIDN'T THINK I'D EVE HAVE THE STRENGTH TO TRY FOR IT AGAIN...BUT NOW I DO...

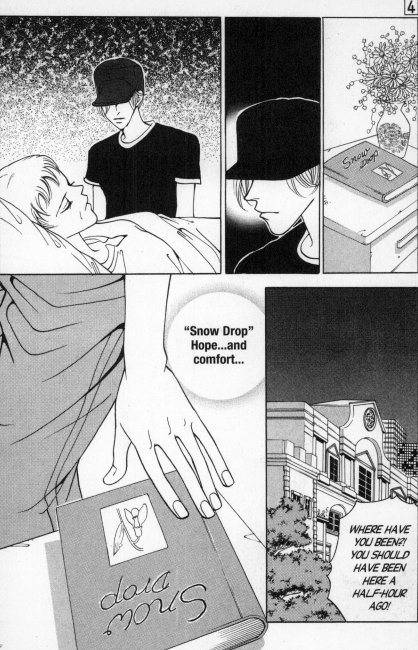

"Snow Drop" Hope...and comfort...

WHERE HAVE YOU BEEN?! YOU SHOULD HAVE BEEN HERE A HALF-HOUR AGO!

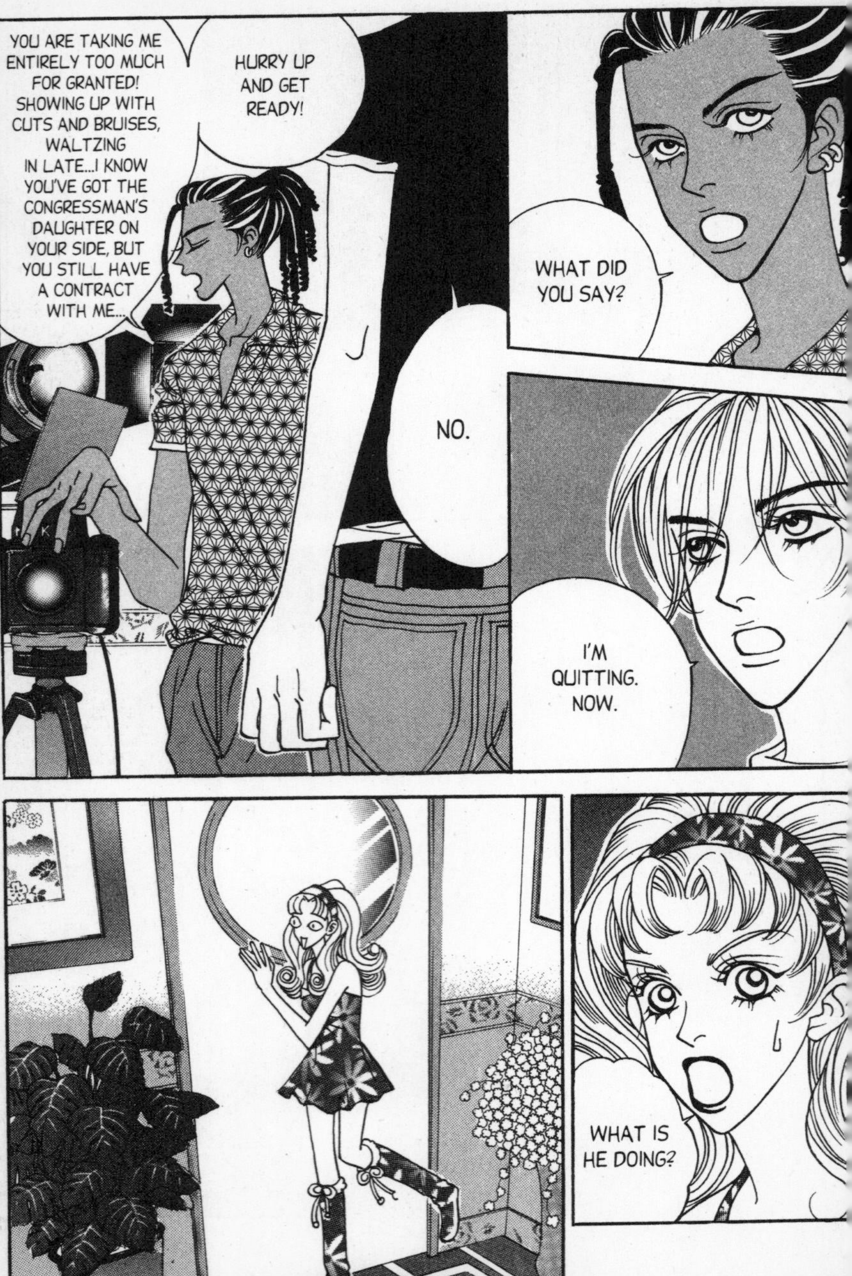
YOU ARE TAKING ME ENTIRELY TOO MUCH FOR GRANTED! SHOWING UP WITH CUTS AND BRUISES, WALTZING IN LATE...I KNOW YOU'VE GOT THE CONGRESSMAN'S DAUGHTER ON YOUR SIDE, BUT YOU STILL HAVE A CONTRACT WITH ME...
HURRY UP AND GET READY!
NO.
WHAT DID YOU SAY?
I'M QUITTING. NOW.
WHAT IS HE DOING?

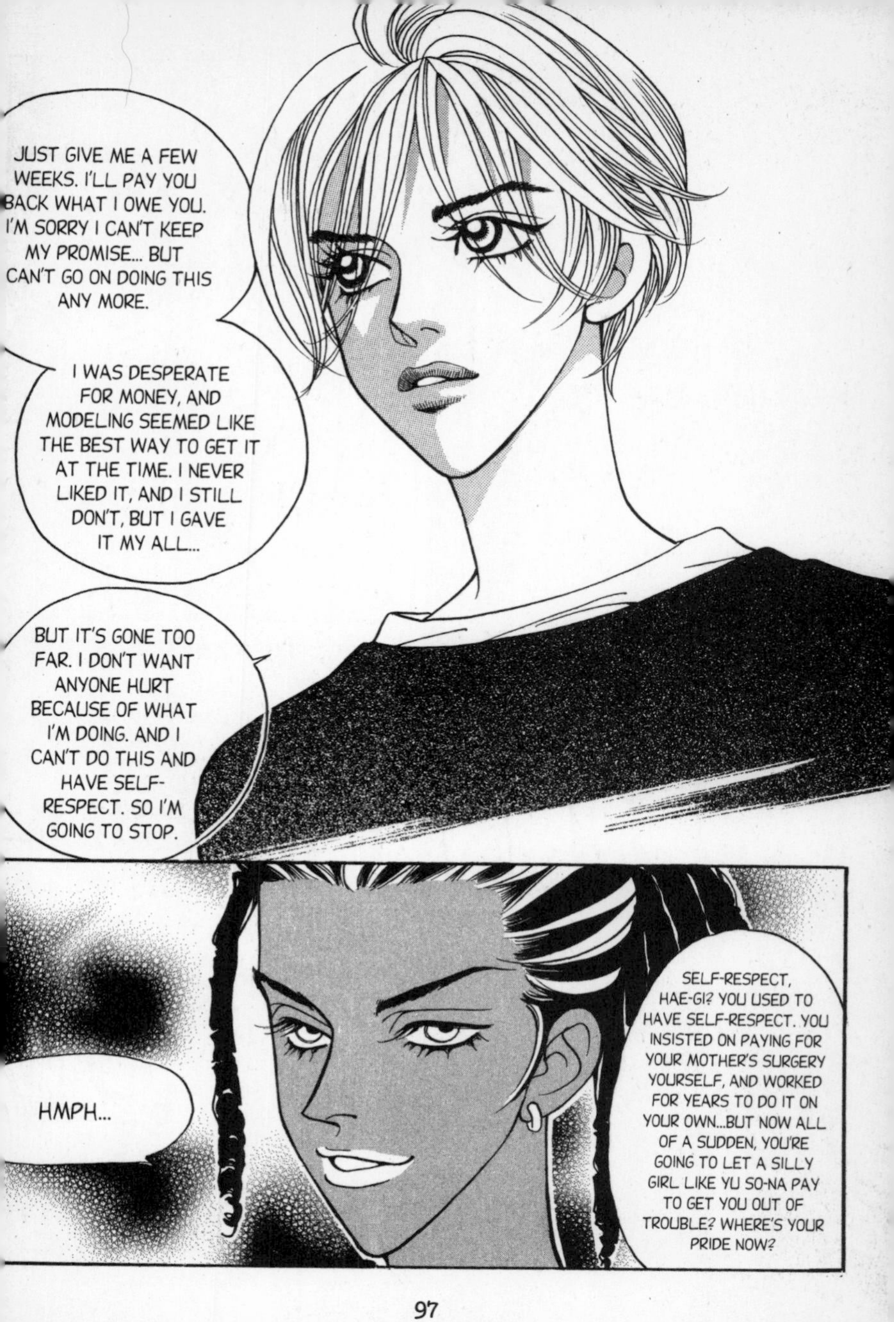
JUST GIVE ME A FEW WEEKS. I'LL PAY YOU BACK WHAT I OWE YOU. I'M SORRY I CAN'T KEEP MY PROMISE... BUT CAN'T GO ON DOING THIS ANY MORE.
I WAS DESPERATE FOR MONEY, AND MODELING SEEMED LIKE THE BEST WAY TO GET IT AT THE TIME. I NEVER LIKED IT, AND I STILL DON'T, BUT I GAVE IT MY ALL...
BUT IT'S GONE TOO FAR. I DON'T WANT ANYONE HURT BECAUSE OF WHAT I'M DOING. AND I CAN'T DO THIS AND HAVE SELF-RESPECT. SO I'M GOING TO STOP.
HMPH...
SELF-RESPECT, HAE-GI? YOU USED TO HAVE SELF-RESPECT. YOU INSISTED ON PAYING FOR YOUR MOTHER'S SURGERY YOURSELF, AND WORKED FOR YEARS TO DO IT ON YOUR OWN...BUT NOW ALL OF A SUDDEN, YOU'RE GOING TO LET A SILLY GIRL LIKE YU SO-NA PAY TO GET YOU OUT OF TROUBLE? WHERE'S YOUR PRIDE NOW?

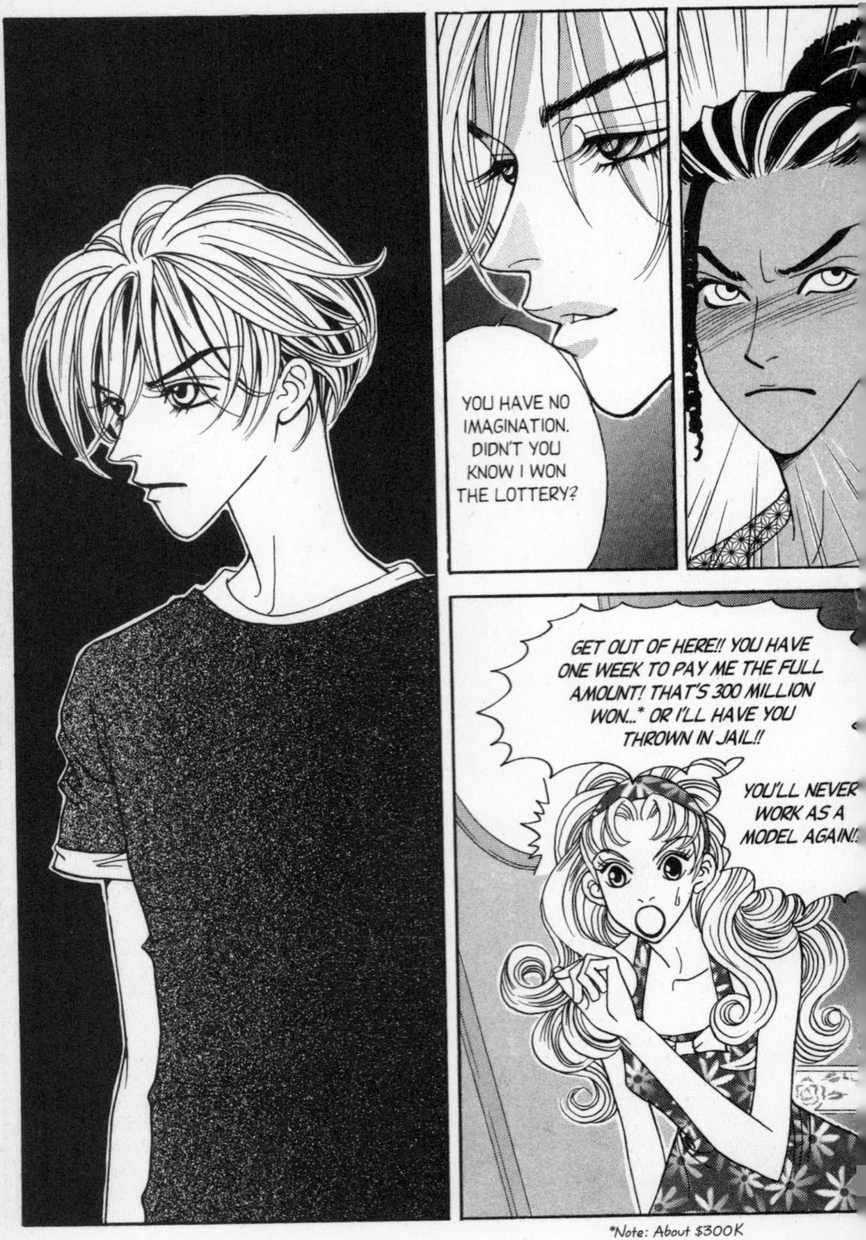
YOU HAVE NO IMAGINATION. DIDN'T YOU KNOW I WON THE LOTTERY?
GET OUT OF HERE!! YOU HAVE ONE WEEK TO PAY ME THE FULL AMOUNT! THAT'S 300 MILLION WON...* OR I'LL HAVE YOU THROWN IN JAIL!!
YOU'LL NEVER WORK AS A MODEL AGAIN!!

*Note: About $300K

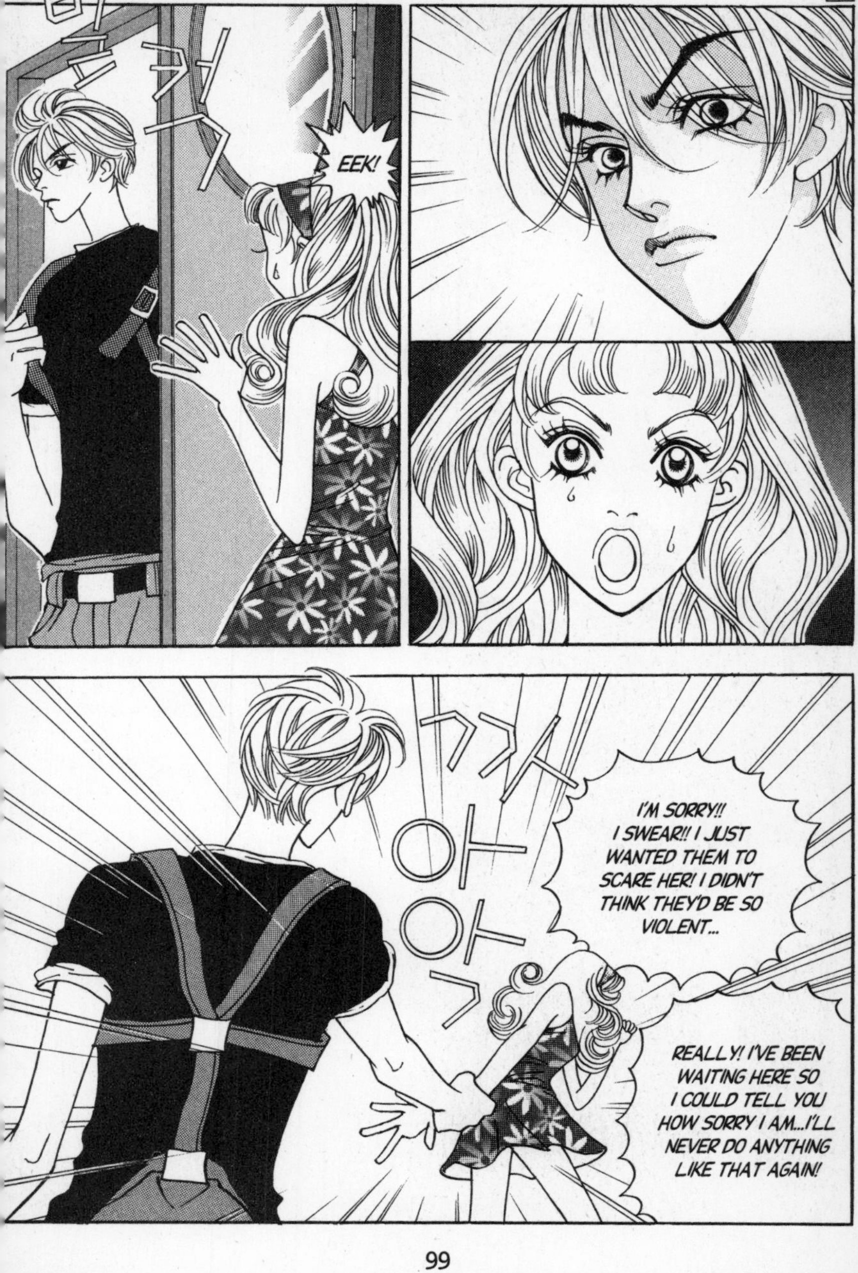
EEK!
I'M SORRY!! I SWEAR!! I JUST WANTED THEM TO SCARE HER! I DIDN'T THINK THEY'D BE SO VIOLENT...
REALLY! I'VE BEEN WAITING HERE SO I COULD TELL YOU HOW SORRY I AM...I'LL NEVER DO ANYTHING LIKE THAT AGAIN!

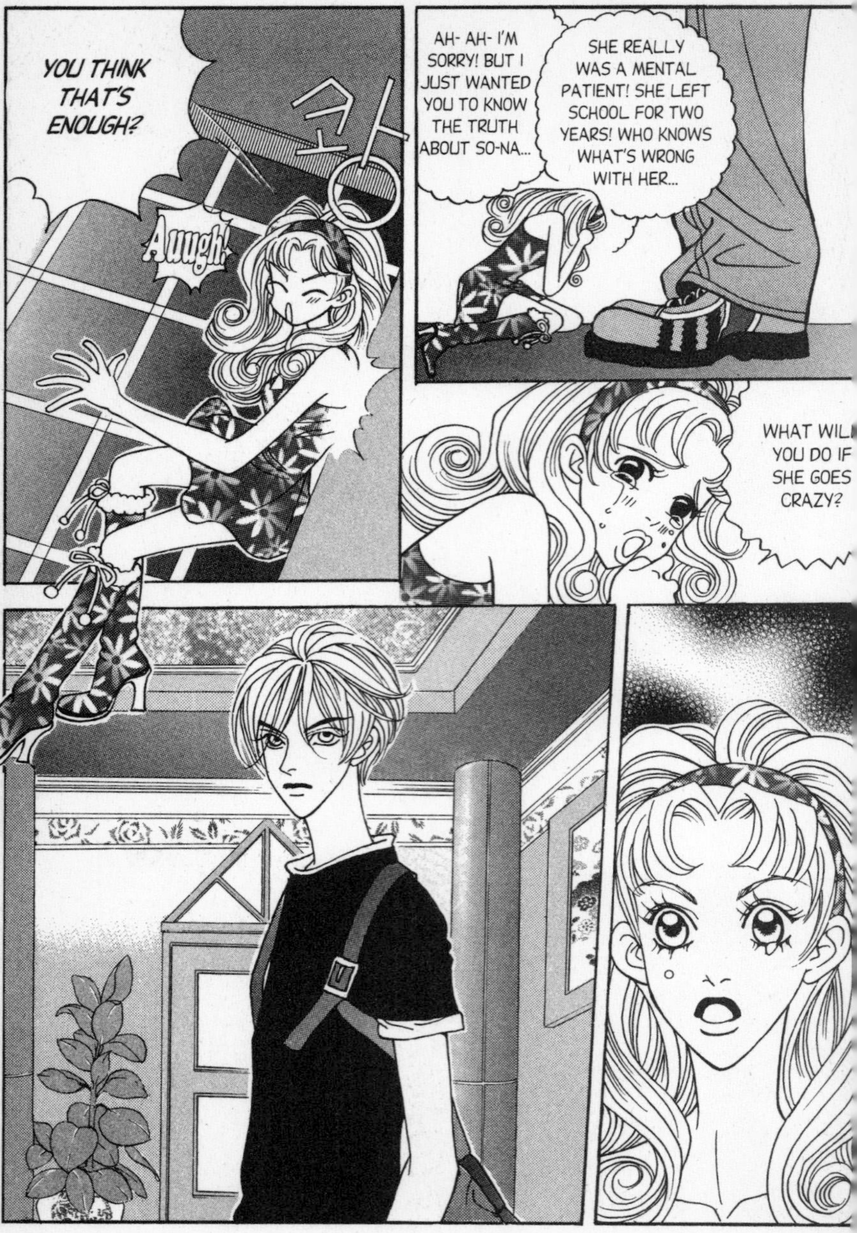
YOU THINK THAT'S ENOUGH?
Auugh!
AH- AH- I'M SORRY! BUT I JUST WANTED YOU TO KNOW THE TRUTH ABOUT SO-NA...
SHE REALLY WAS A MENTAL PATIENT! SHE LEFT SCHOOL FOR TWO YEARS! WHO KNOWS WHAT'S WRONG WITH HER...
WHAT WIL YOU DO IF SHE GOES CRAZY?

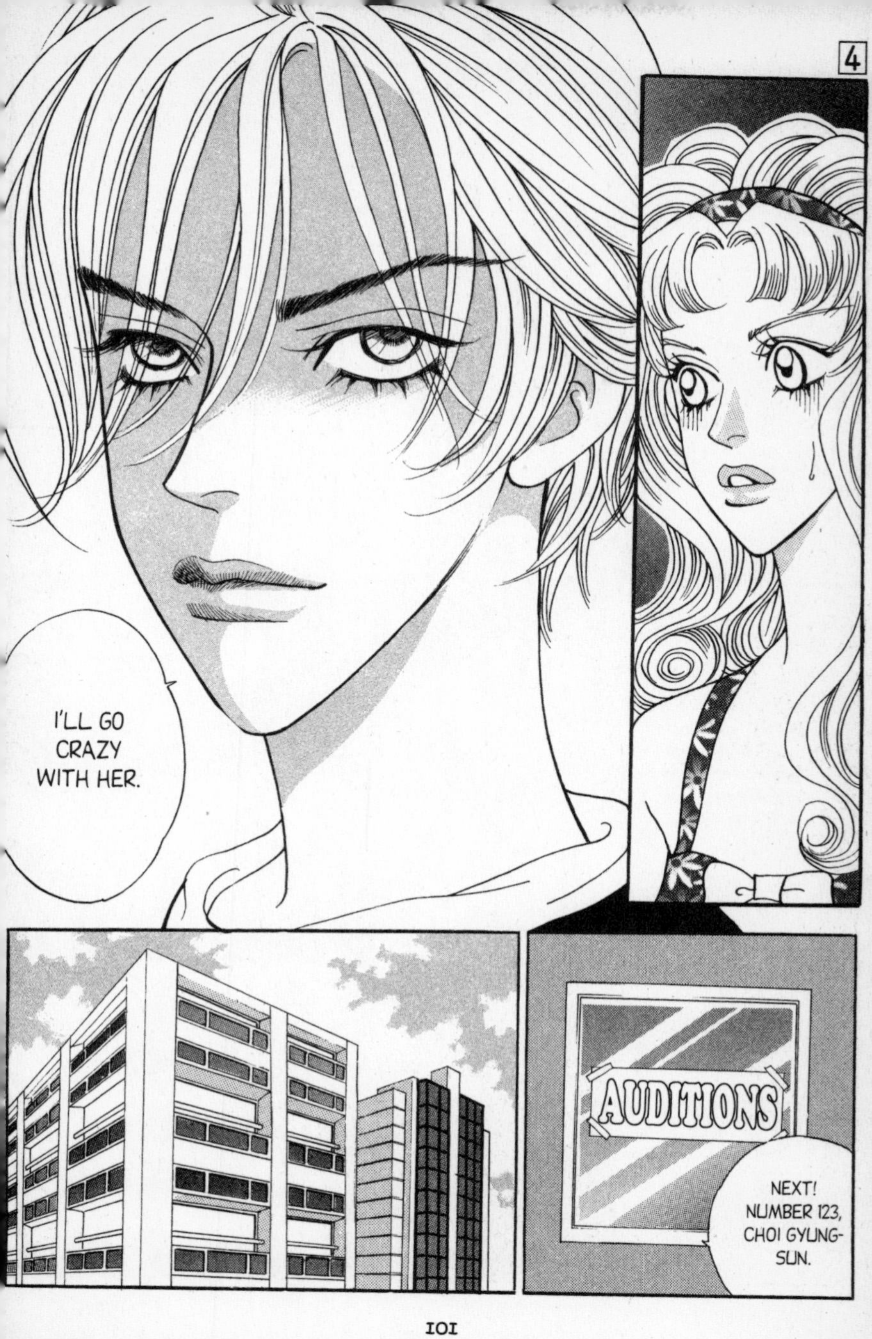
4
I'LL GO CRAZY WITH HER.
AUDITIONS
NEXT! NUMBER 123, CHOI GYUNG-SUN.

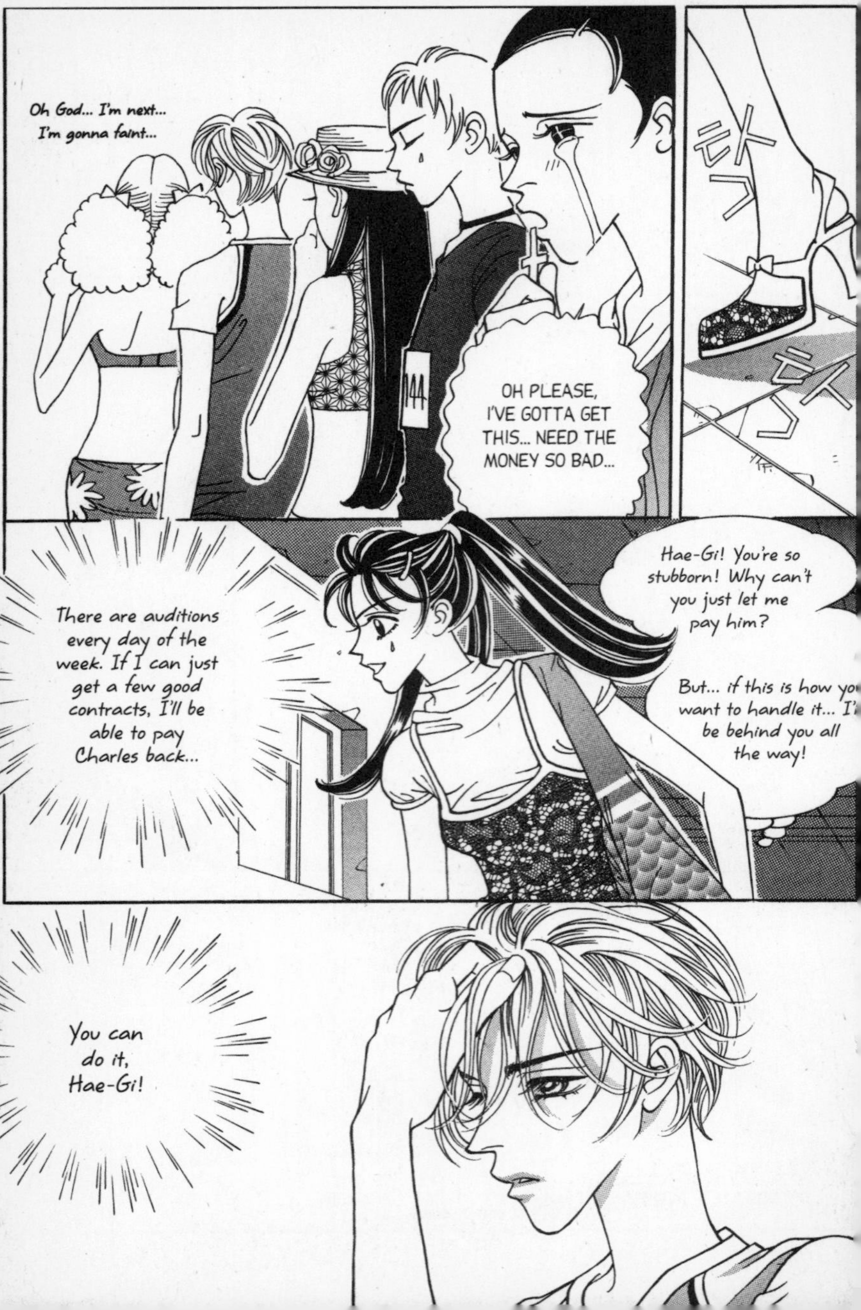
Oh God... I'm next... I'm gonna faint...
OH PLEASE, I'VE GOTTA GET THIS... NEED THE MONEY SO BAD...
There are auditions every day of the week. If I can just get a few good contracts, I'll be able to pay Charles back...
Hae-Gi! You're so stubborn! Why can't you just let me pay him?
But... if this is how yo want to handle it... I' be behind you all the way!
You can do it, Hae-Gi!

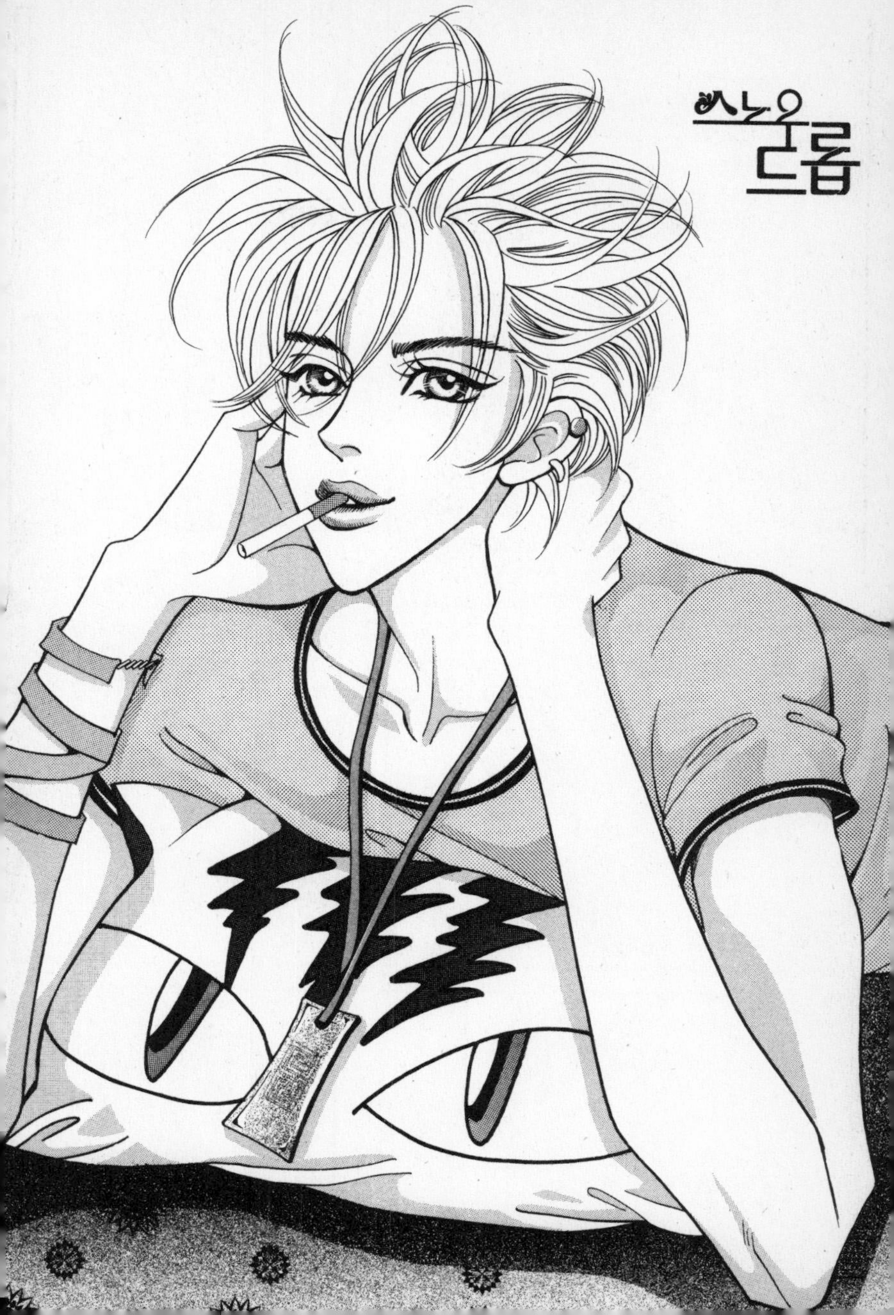
스노우 드롭

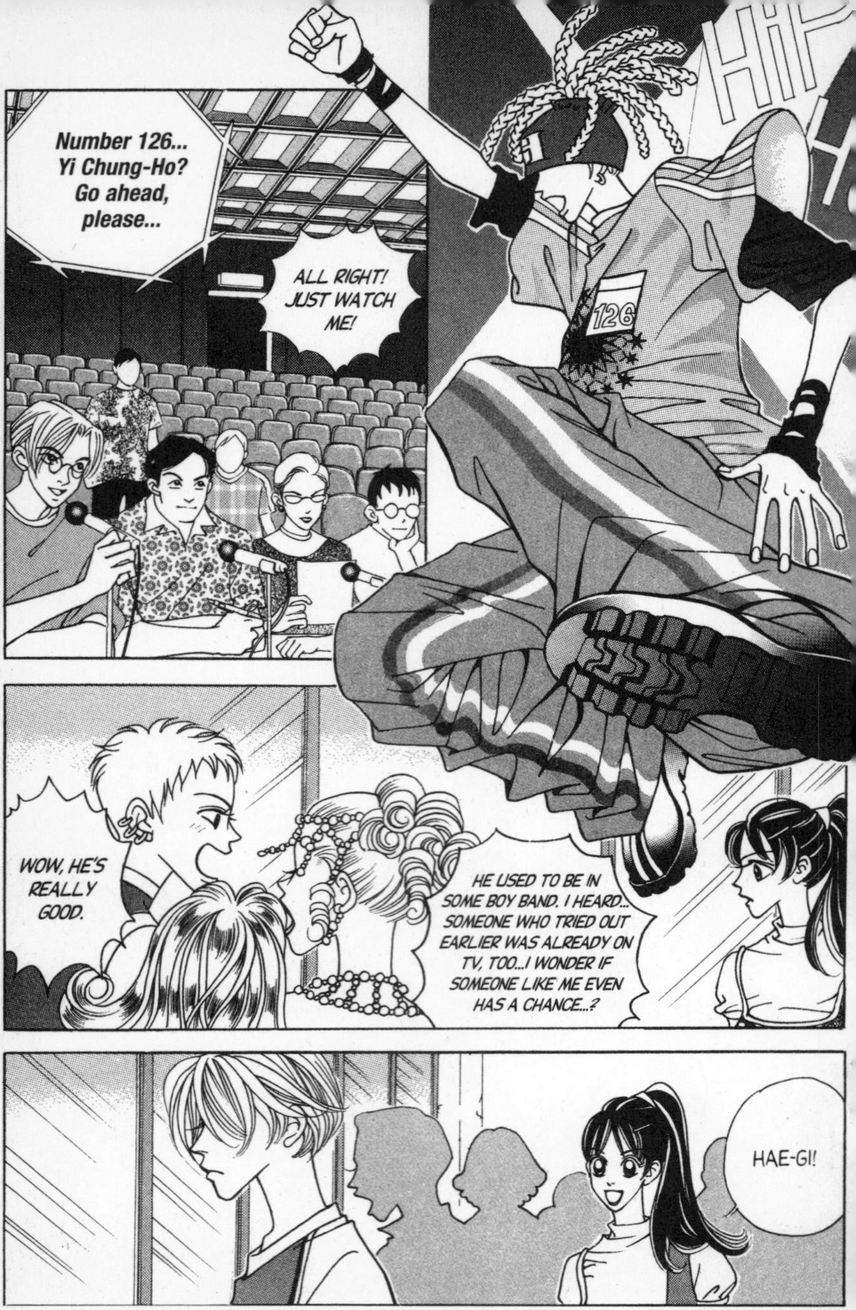
Number 126... Yi Chung-Ho? Go ahead, please...
ALL RIGHT! JUST WATCH ME!
WOW, HE'S REALLY GOOD.
HE USED TO BE IN SOME BOY BAND. I HEARD... SOMEONE WHO TRIED OUT EARLIER WAS ALREADY ON TV, TOO...I WONDER IF SOMEONE LIKE ME EVEN HAS A CHANCE...?
HAE-GI!

SO-NA! HOW...

I KNOW, I KNOW...YOU TOLD ME NOT TO COME. BUT I WANT TO CHEER YOU ON! AND I'VE ALWAYS WANTED TO SEE WHAT AN AUDITION IS LIKE! YOU DIDN'T GO YET, DID YOU?

WOW! LOOK AT THAT GUY!!

SO DO THEY REALLY GIVE A CASH PRIZE TO THE WINNER? LIKE THE AD SAID...?

YEAH. YOU GET 1 MILLION WON*, AND A YEARLONG CONTRACT WITH THEM...

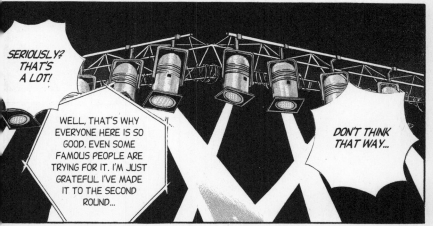

SERIOUSLY? THAT'S A LOT!

WELL, THAT'S WHY EVERYONE HERE IS SO GOOD. EVEN SOME FAMOUS PEOPLE ARE TRYING FOR IT. I'M JUST GRATEFUL I'VE MADE IT TO THE SECOND ROUND...

DON'T THINK THAT WAY...

*Note: About $850

105

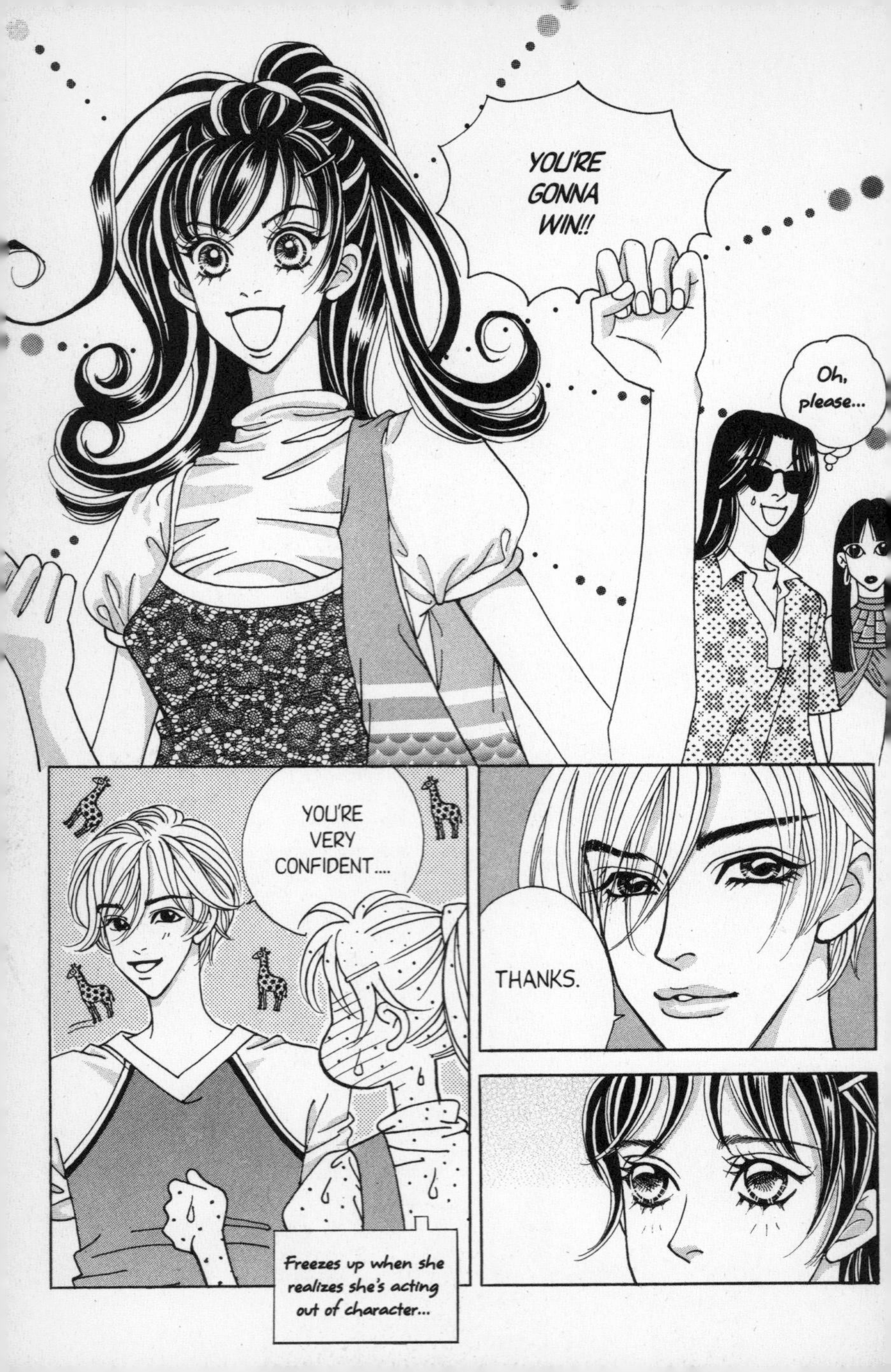
YOU'RE GONNA WIN!!
Oh, please...
YOU'RE VERY CONFIDENT....
Freezes up when she realizes she's acting out of character...
THANKS.

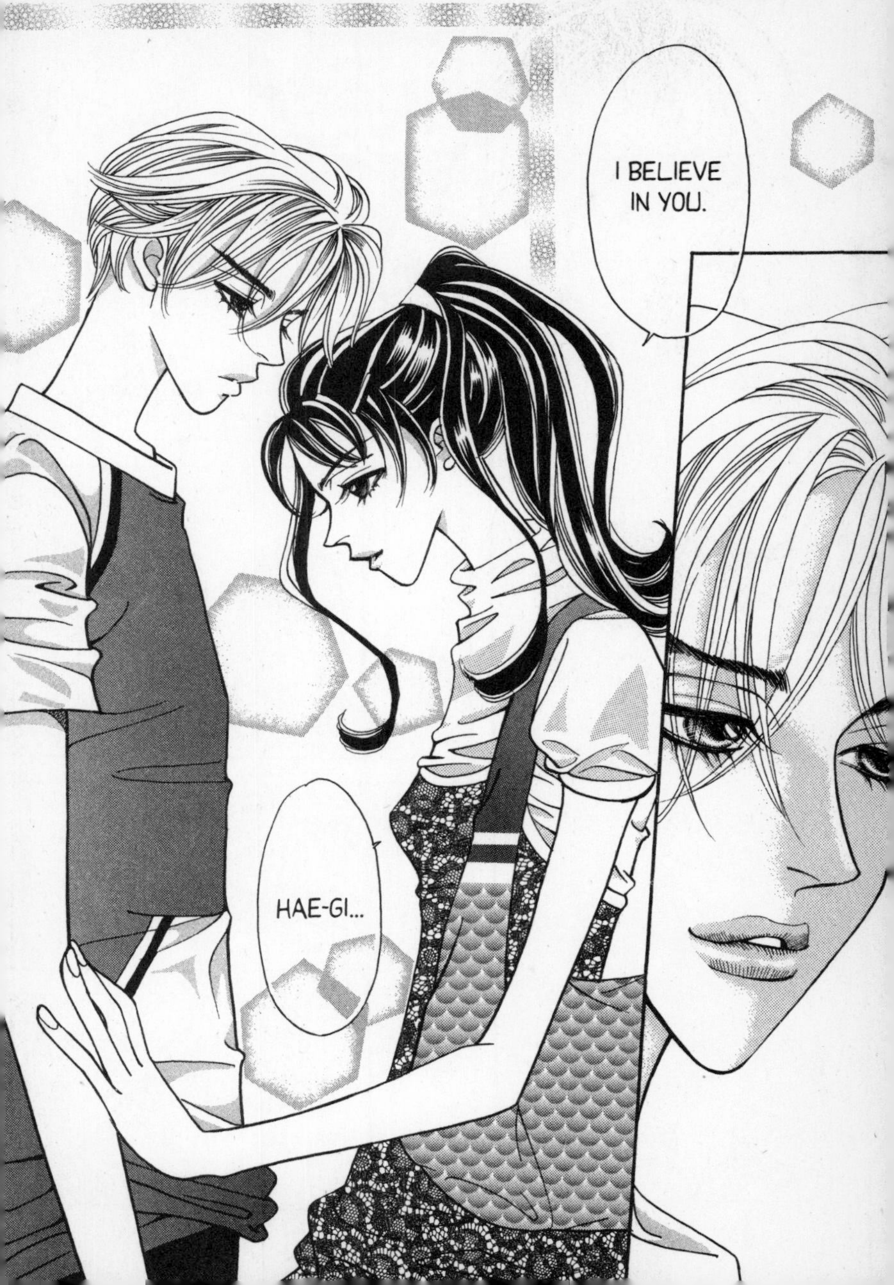
I BELIEVE IN YOU.
HAE-GI...

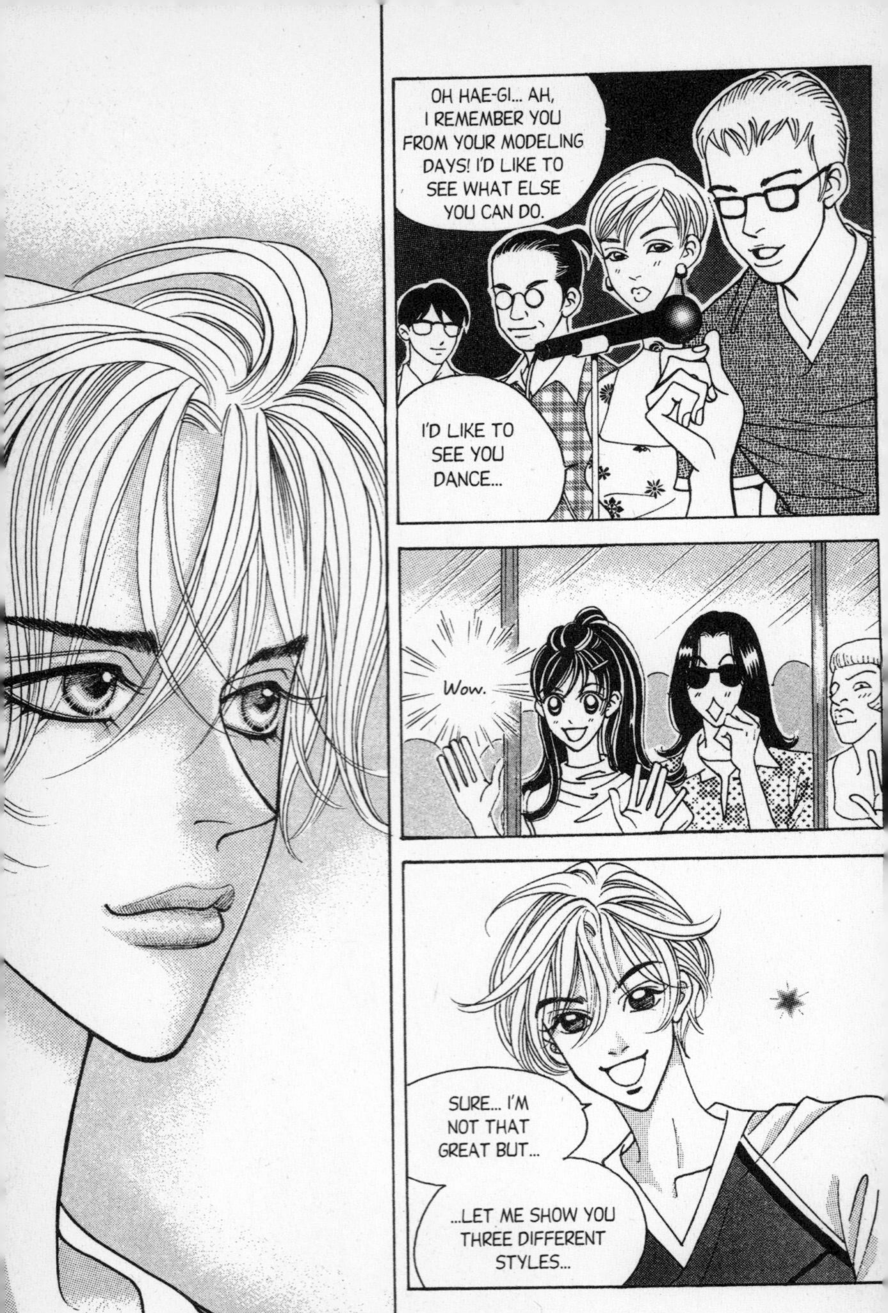
OH HAE-GI... AH, I REMEMBER YOU FROM YOUR MODELING DAYS! I'D LIKE TO SEE WHAT ELSE YOU CAN DO.
I'D LIKE TO SEE YOU DANCE...
Wow.
SURE... I'M NOT THAT GREAT BUT...
...LET ME SHOW YOU THREE DIFFERENT STYLES...

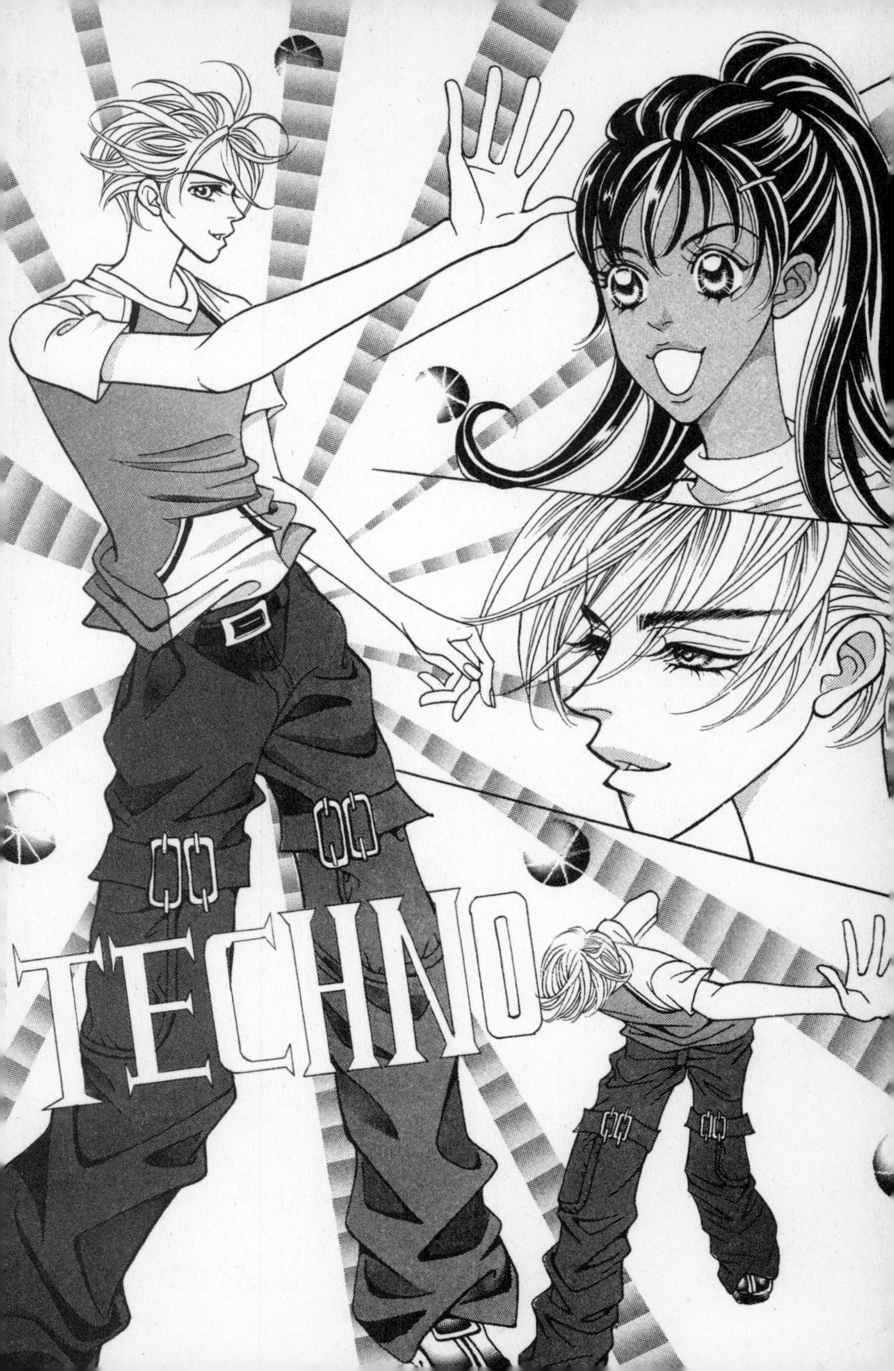
TECHNO

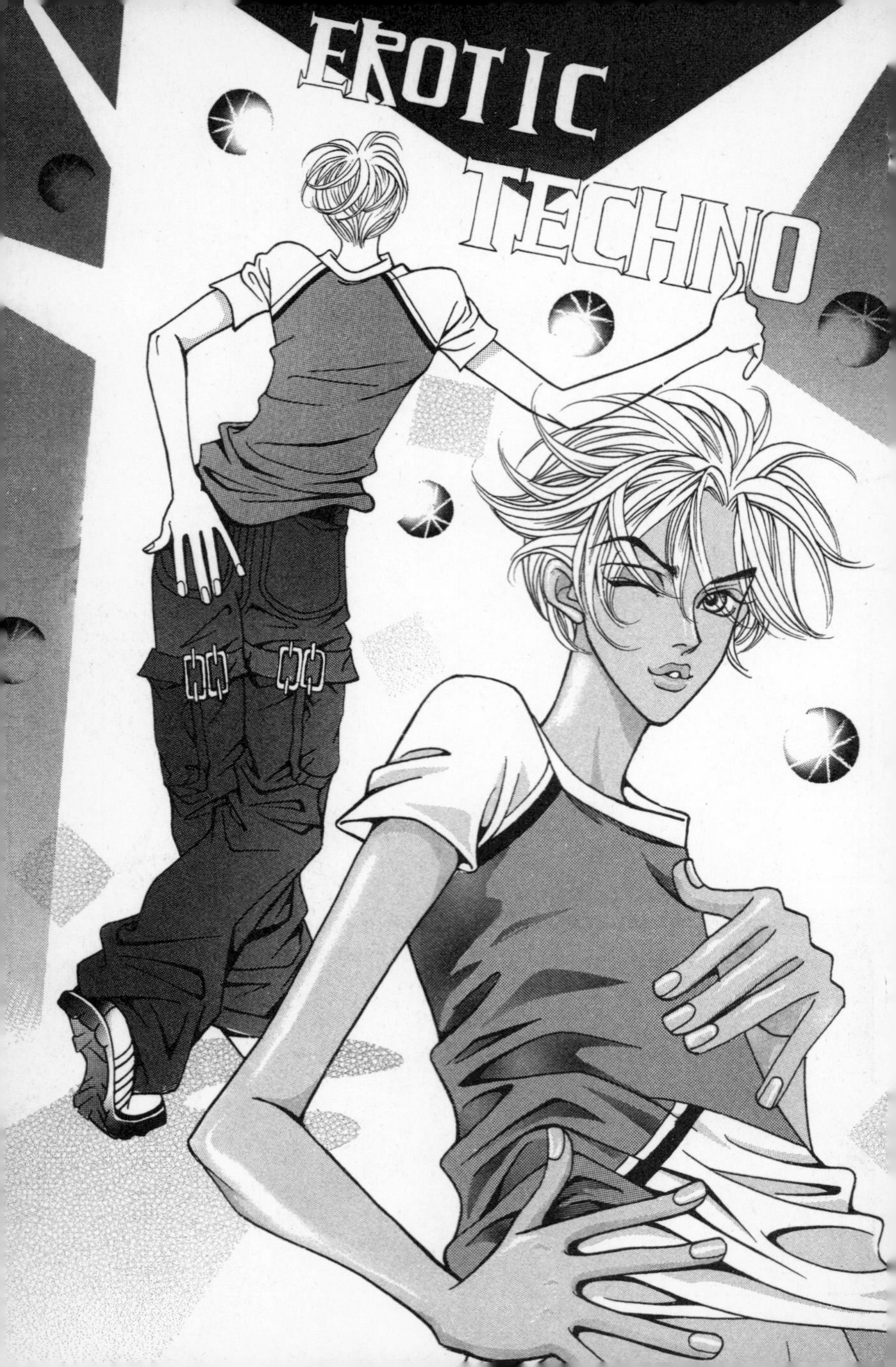
EROTIC
TECHNO

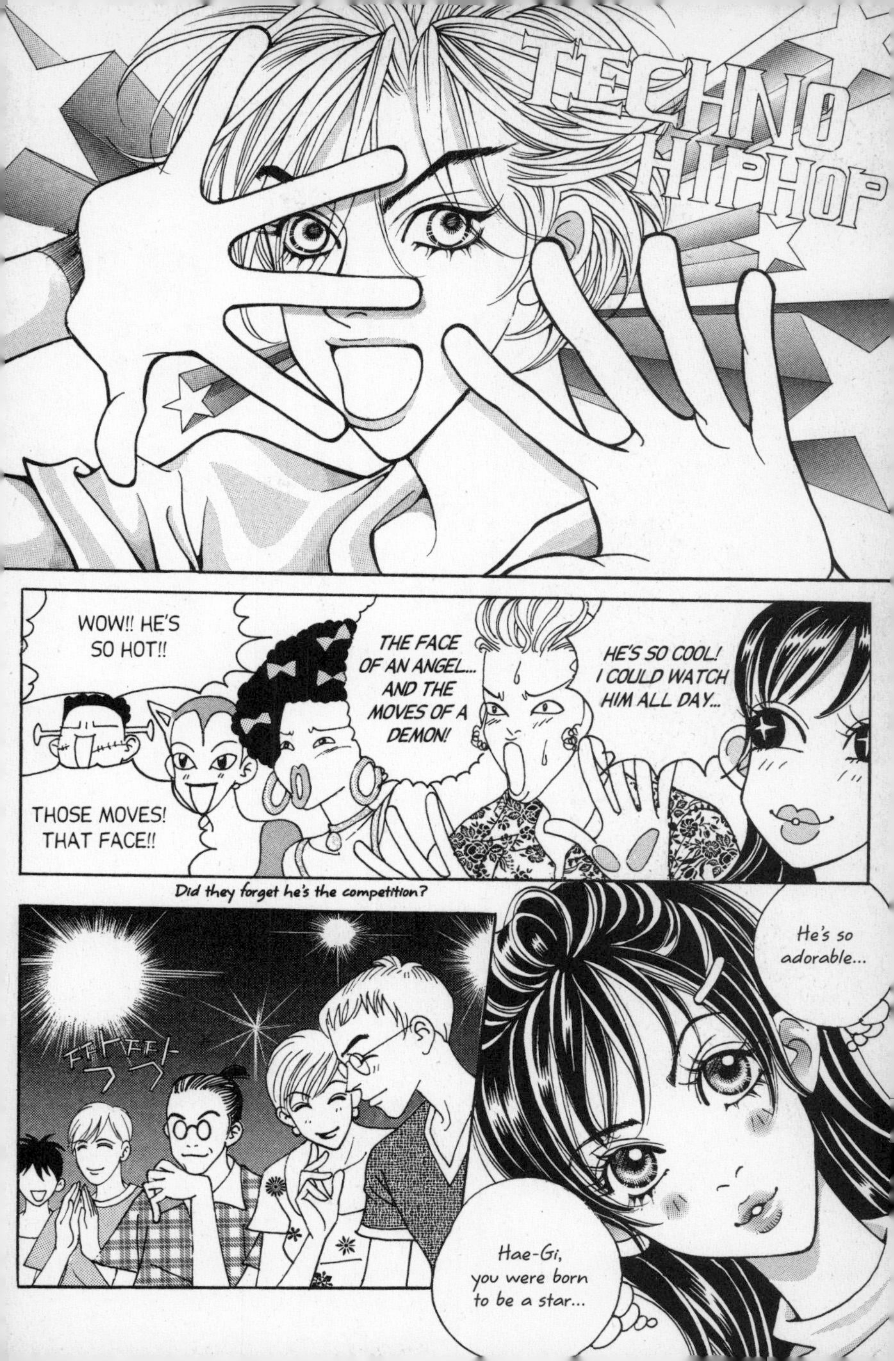
TECHNO HIPHOP
WOW!! HE'S SO HOT!!
THOSE MOVES! THAT FACE!!
THE FACE OF AN ANGEL... AND THE MOVES OF A DEMON!
HE'S SO COOL! I COULD WATCH HIM ALL DAY...
Did they forget he's the competition?
He's so adorable...
Hae-Gi, you were born to be a star...

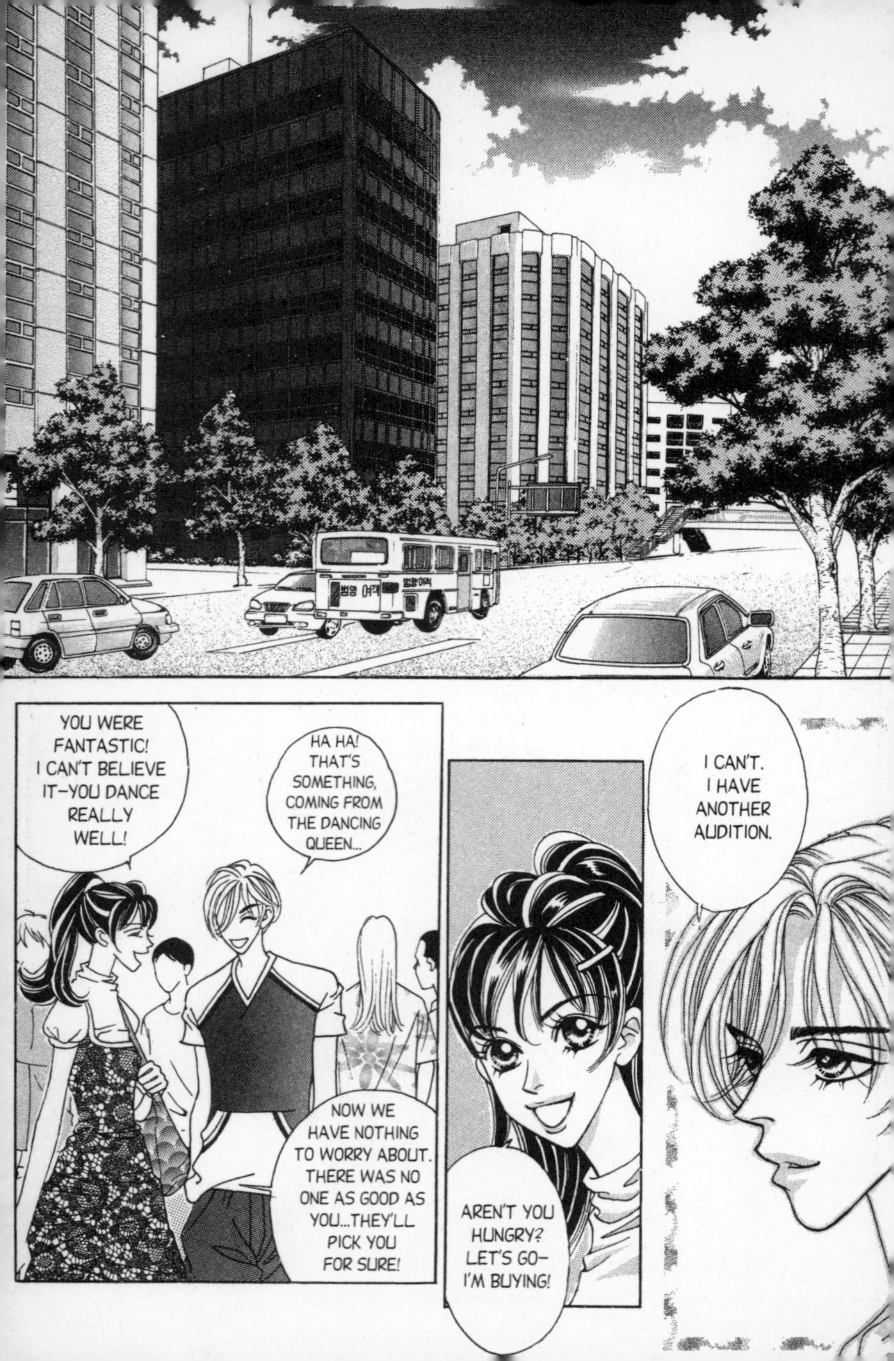
YOU WERE FANTASTIC! I CAN'T BELIEVE IT—YOU DANCE REALLY WELL!
HA HA! THAT'S SOMETHING, COMING FROM THE DANCING QUEEN...
NOW WE HAVE NOTHING TO WORRY ABOUT. THERE WAS NO ONE AS GOOD AS YOU...THEY'LL PICK YOU FOR SURE!
AREN'T YOU HUNGRY? LET'S GO—I'M BUYING!
I CAN'T. I HAVE ANOTHER AUDITION.

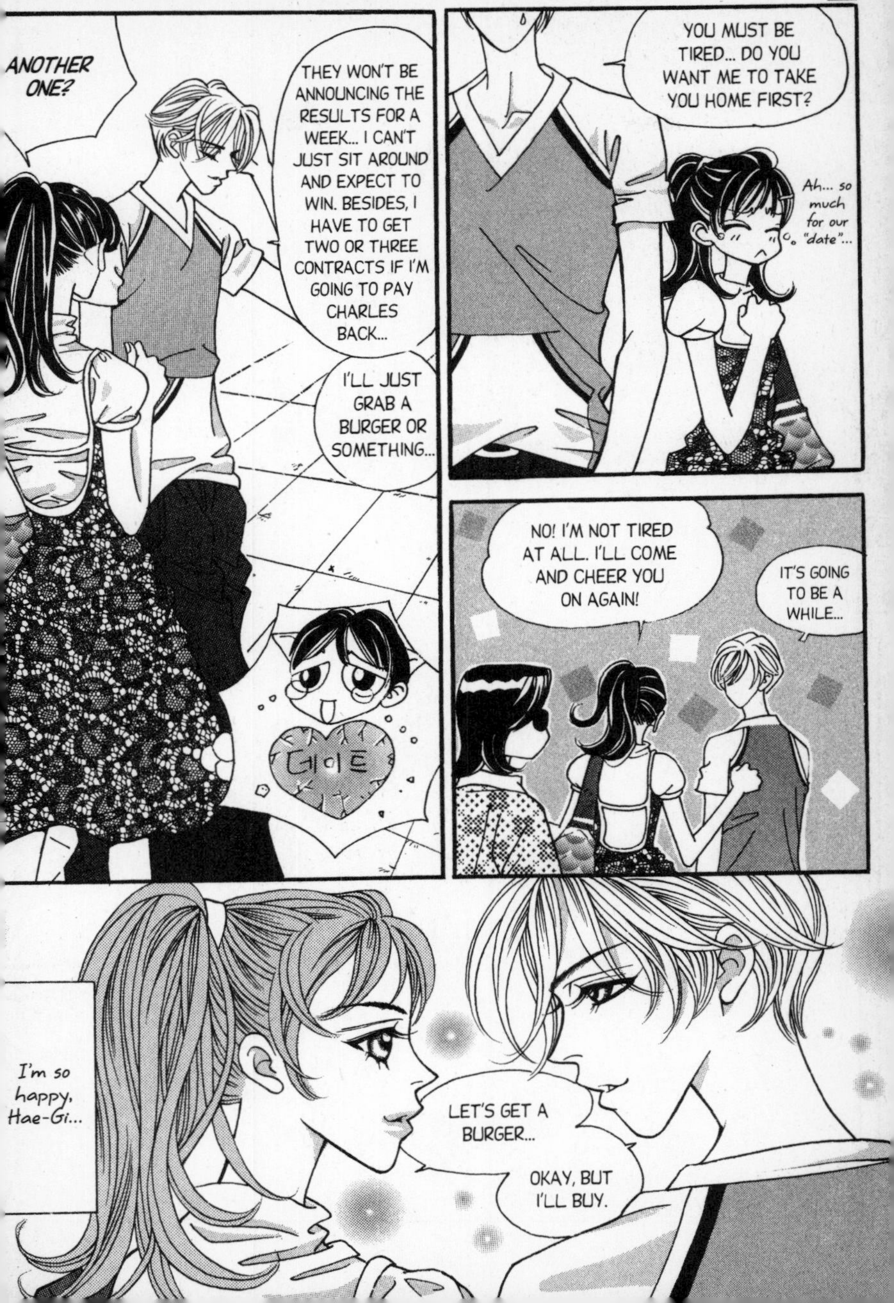
ANOTHER ONE?
THEY WON'T BE ANNOUNCING THE RESULTS FOR A WEEK... I CAN'T JUST SIT AROUND AND EXPECT TO WIN. BESIDES, I HAVE TO GET TWO OR THREE CONTRACTS IF I'M GOING TO PAY CHARLES BACK...
I'LL JUST GRAB A BURGER OR SOMETHING...
YOU MUST BE TIRED... DO YOU WANT ME TO TAKE YOU HOME FIRST?
Ah... so much for our "date"...
NO! I'M NOT TIRED AT ALL. I'LL COME AND CHEER YOU ON AGAIN!
IT'S GOING TO BE A WHILE...
I'm so happy, Hae-Gi...
LET'S GET A BURGER...
OKAY, BUT I'LL BUY.

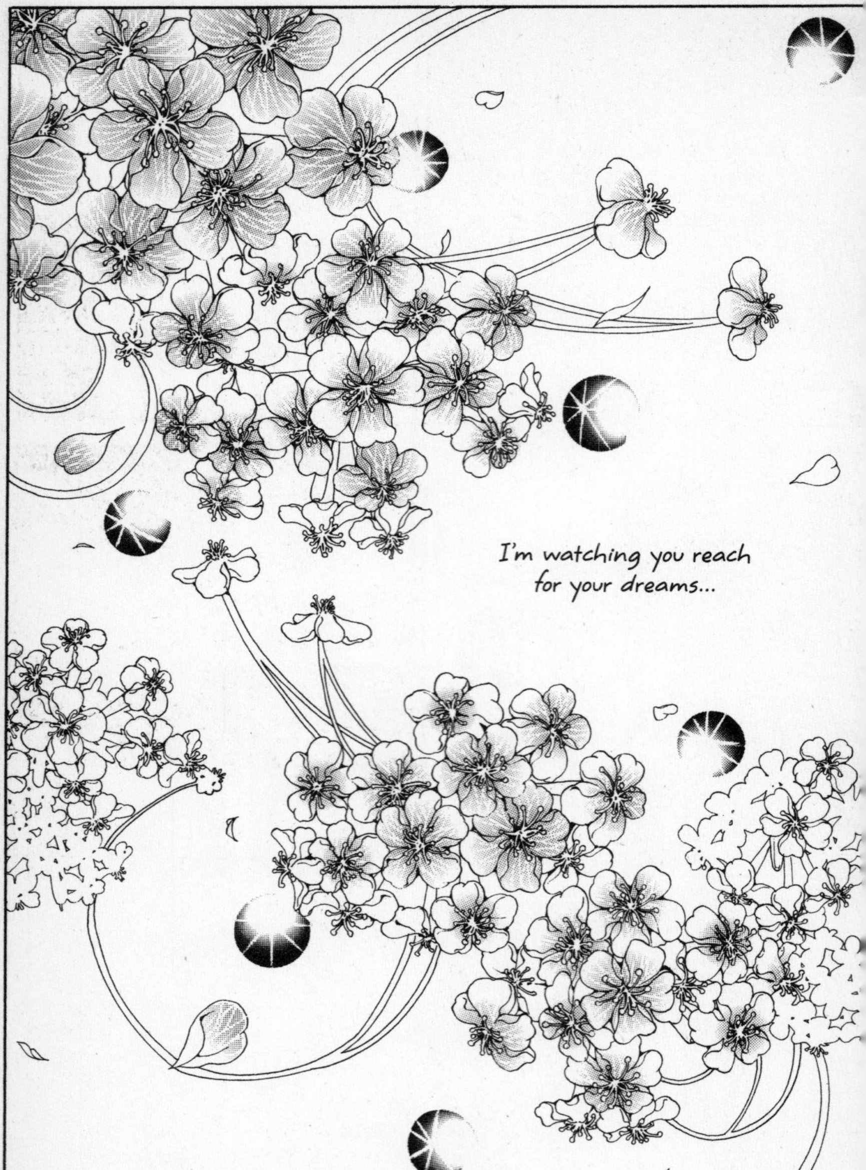
I'm watching you reach for your dreams...

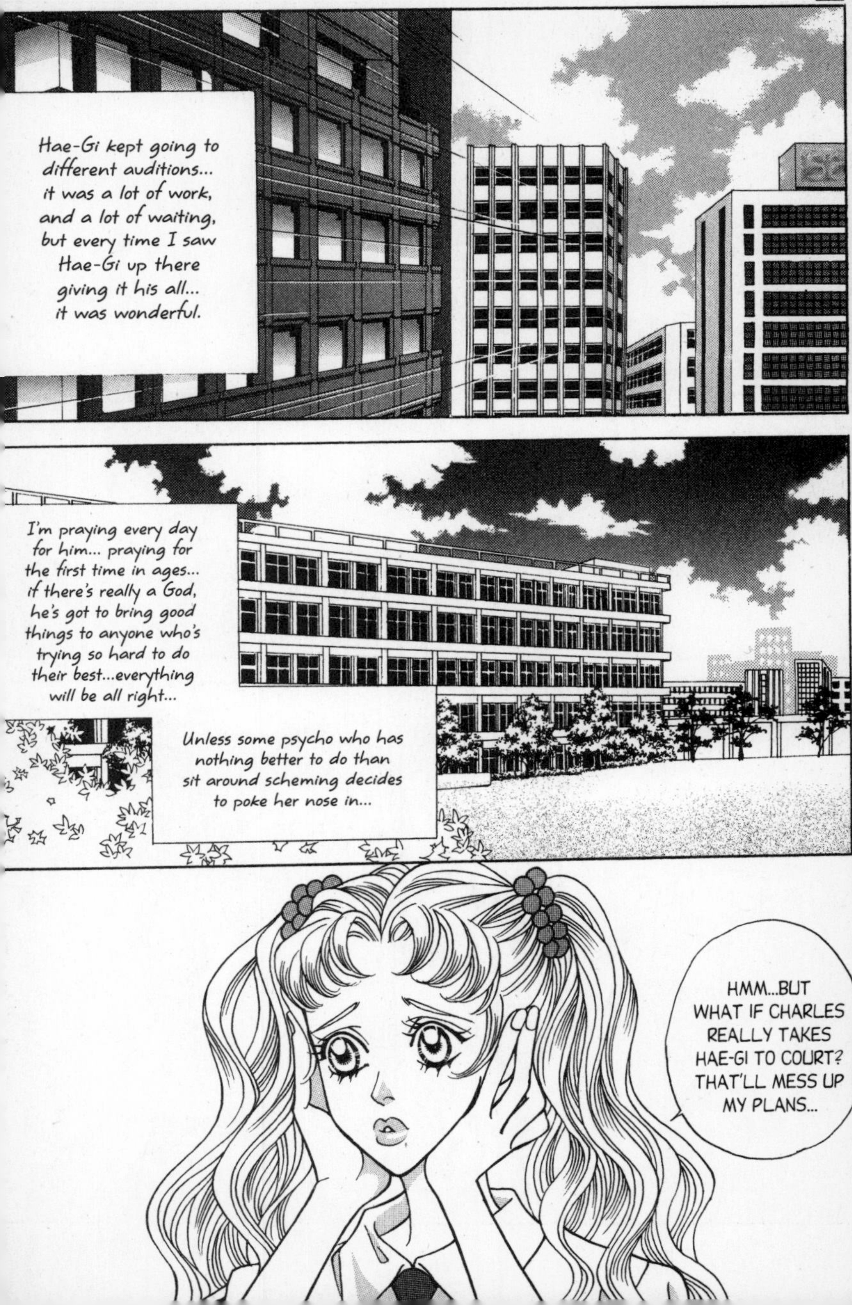
Hae-Gi kept going to different auditions... it was a lot of work, and a lot of waiting, but every time I saw Hae-Gi up there giving it his all... it was wonderful.
I'm praying every day for him... praying for the first time in ages... if there's really a God, he's got to bring good things to anyone who's trying so hard to do their best...everything will be all right...
Unless some psycho who has nothing better to do than sit around scheming decides to poke her nose in...
HMM...BUT WHAT IF CHARLES REALLY TAKES HAE-GI TO COURT? THAT'LL MESS UP MY PLANS...

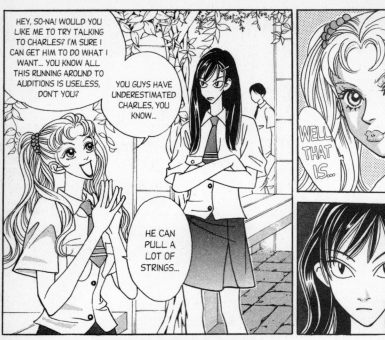

HEY, SO-NA! WOULD YOU LIKE ME TO TRY TALKING TO CHARLES? I'M SURE I CAN GET HIM TO DO WHAT I WANT... YOU KNOW ALL THIS RUNNING AROUND TO AUDITIONS IS USELESS, DON'T YOU?

YOU GUYS HAVE UNDERESTIMATED CHARLES, YOU KNOW...

WELL THAT IS...

HE CAN PULL A LOT OF STRINGS...

HEY, I'M JUST TRYING TO MAKE UP FOR WHAT I DID, OKAY...?

MAKE UP FOR IT?

ARE YOU CRAZY?

116

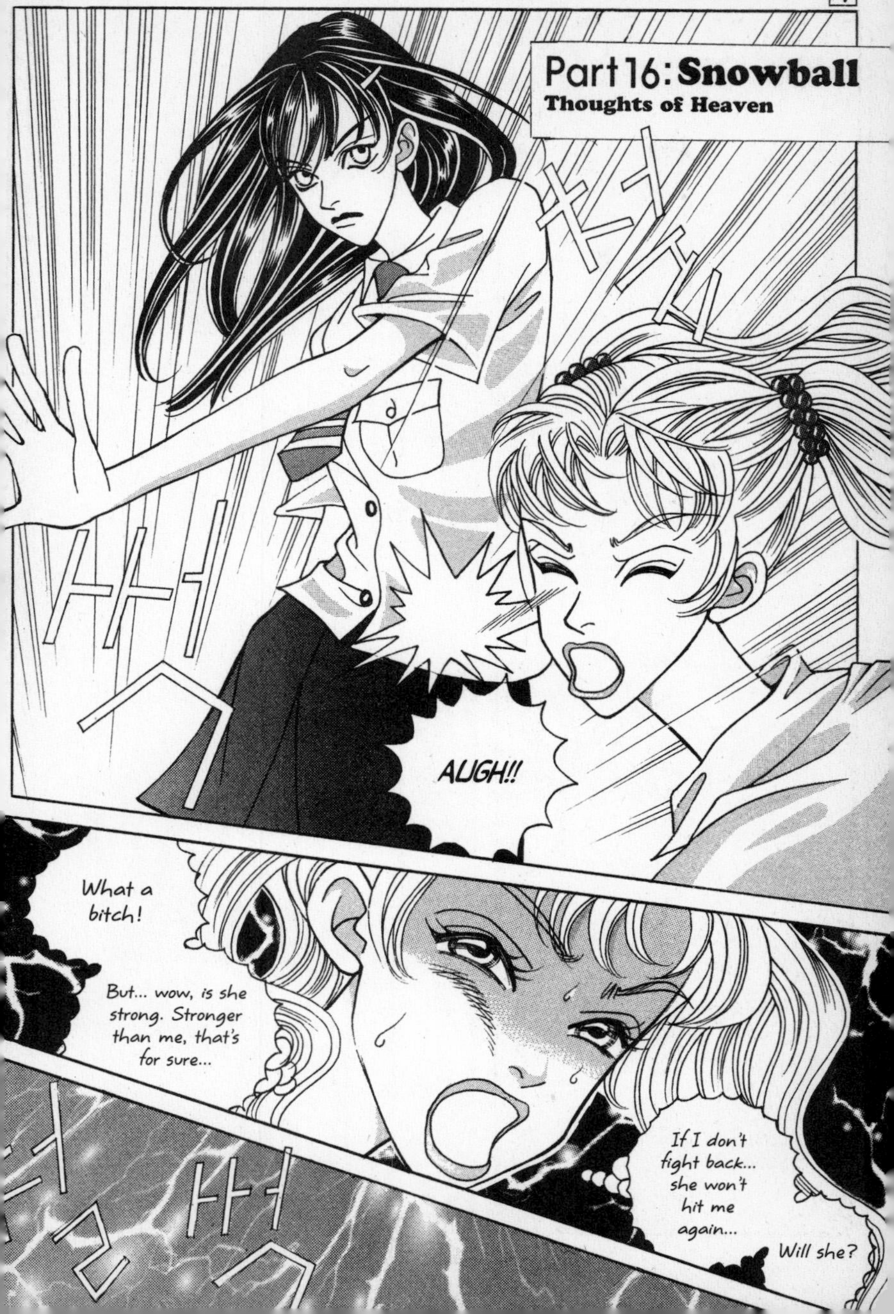
Part 16: Snowball
Thoughts of Heaven
AUGH!!
What a bitch!
But... wow, is she strong. Stronger than me, that's for sure...
If I don't fight back... she won't hit me again...
Will she?

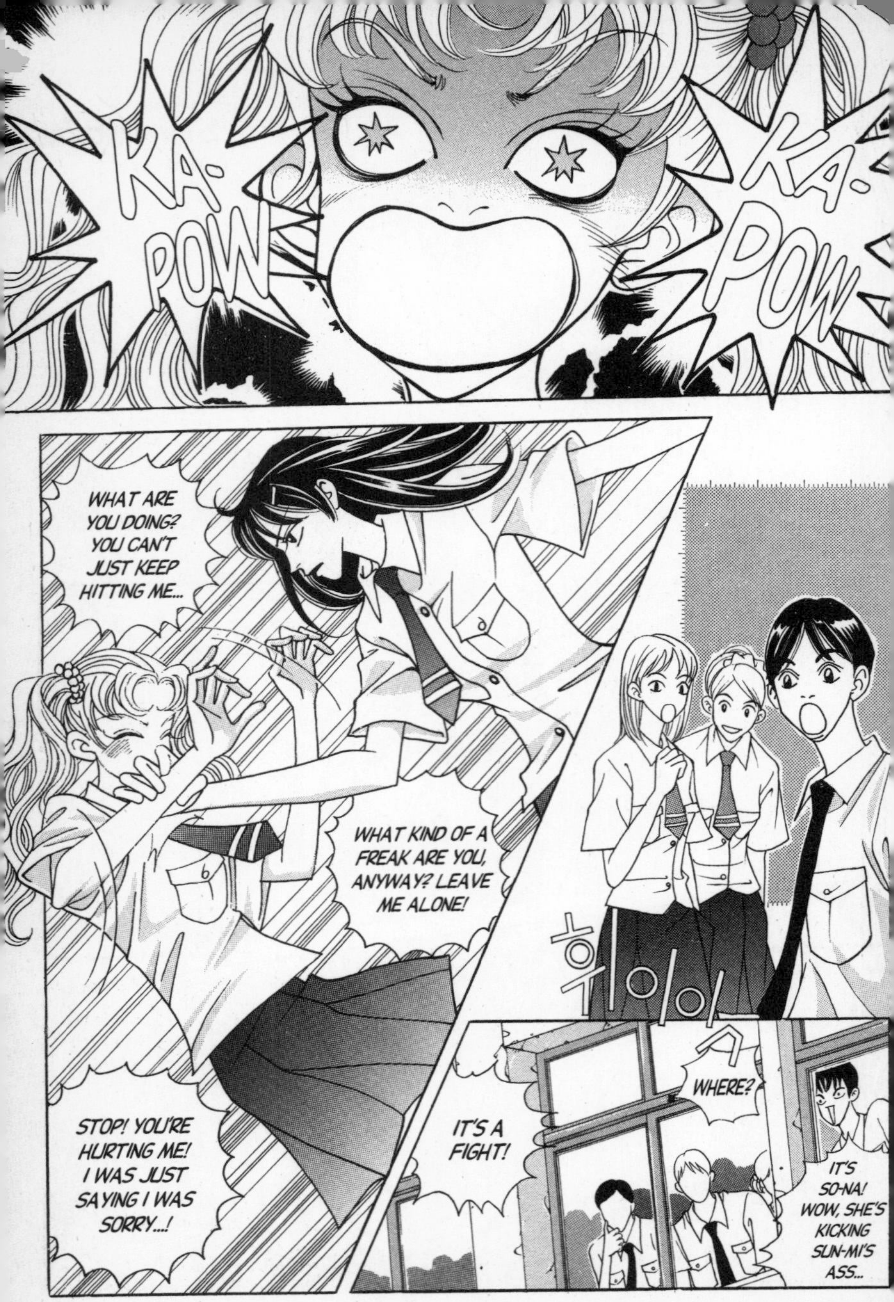
KA-POW
KA-POW
WHAT ARE YOU DOING? YOU CAN'T JUST KEEP HITTING ME...
WHAT KIND OF A FREAK ARE YOU, ANYWAY? LEAVE ME ALONE!
STOP! YOU'RE HURTING ME! I WAS JUST SAYING I WAS SORRY...!
IT'S A FIGHT!
WHERE?
IT'S SO-NA! WOW, SHE'S KICKING SUN-MI'S ASS...

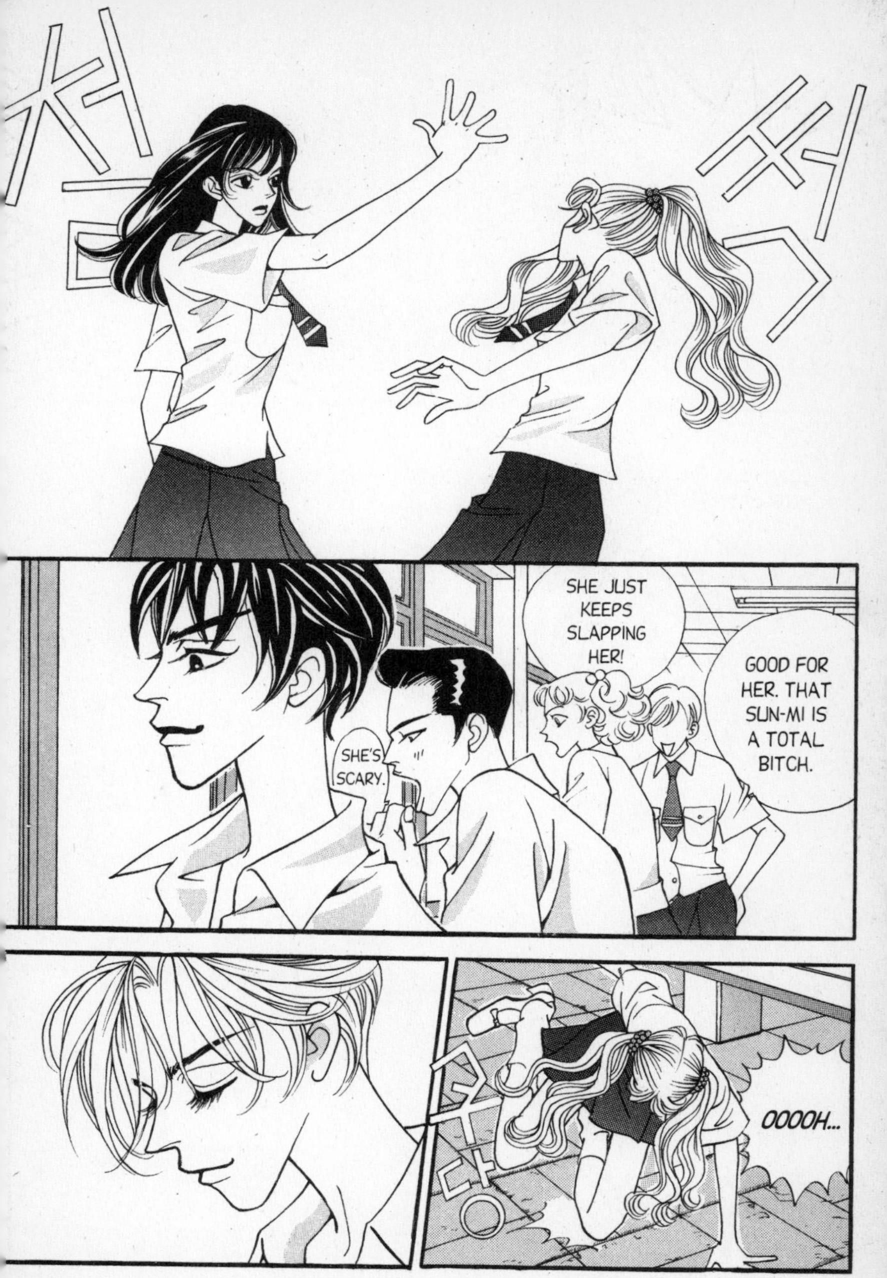
SHE'S SCARY.
SHE JUST KEEPS SLAPPING HER!
GOOD FOR HER. THAT SUN-MI IS A TOTAL BITCH.
OOOOH...

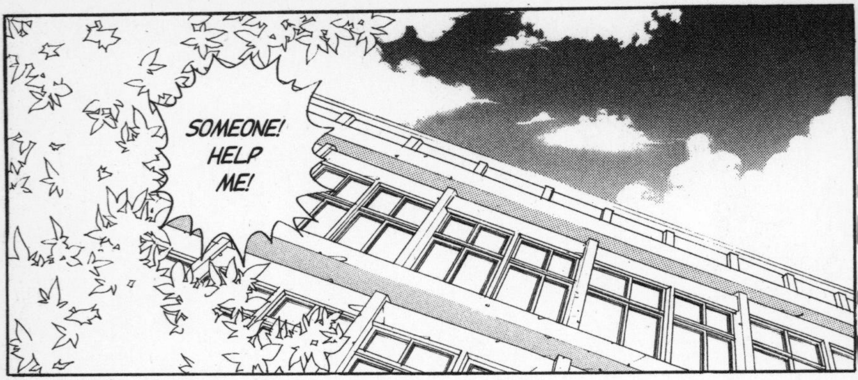
SOMEONE! HELP ME!
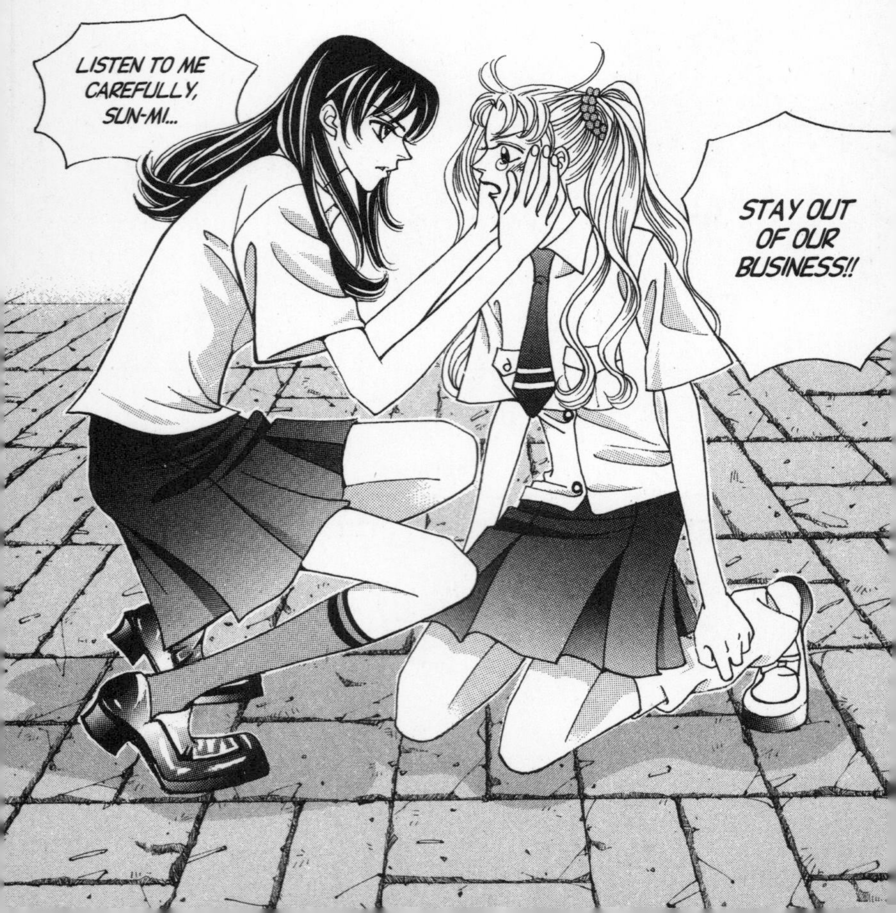
LISTEN TO ME CAREFULLY, SUN-MI...
STAY OUT OF OUR BUSINESS!!

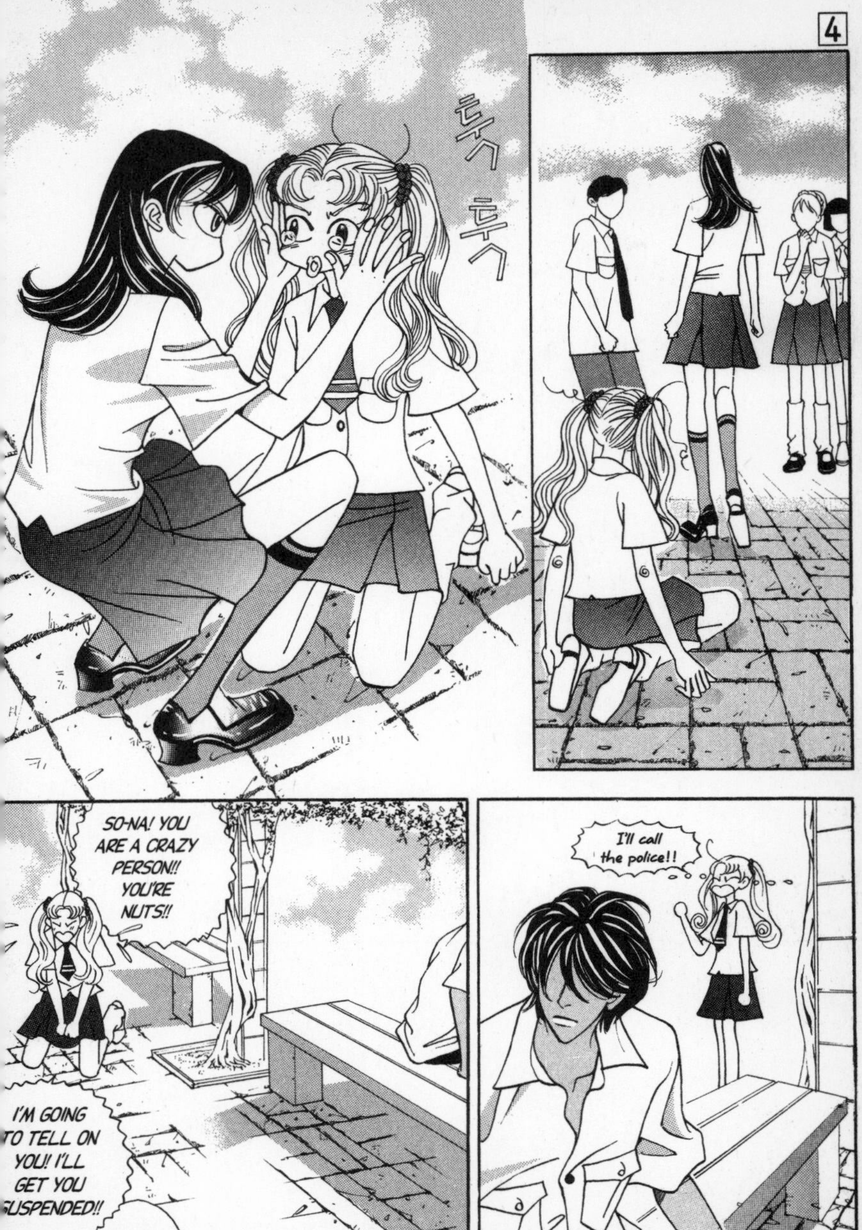
4
SO-NA! YOU ARE A CRAZY PERSON!! YOU'RE NUTS!!
I'M GOING TO TELL ON YOU! I'LL GET YOU SUSPENDED!!
But school is almost over...
I'll call the police!!

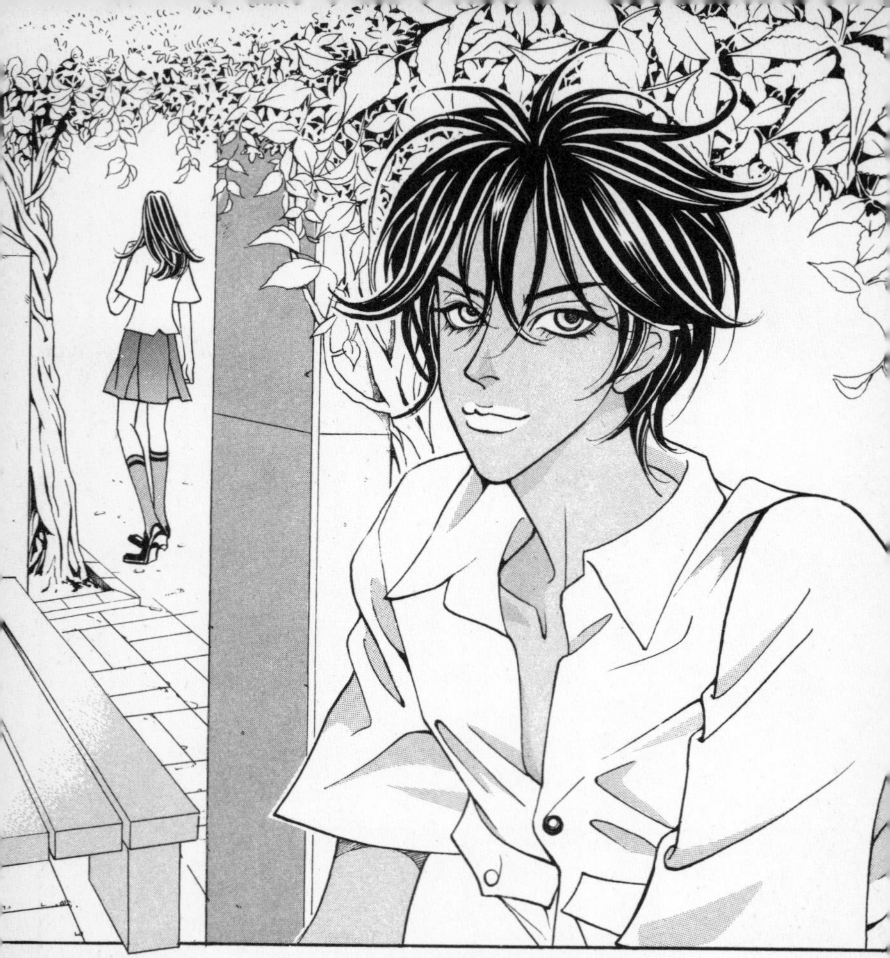

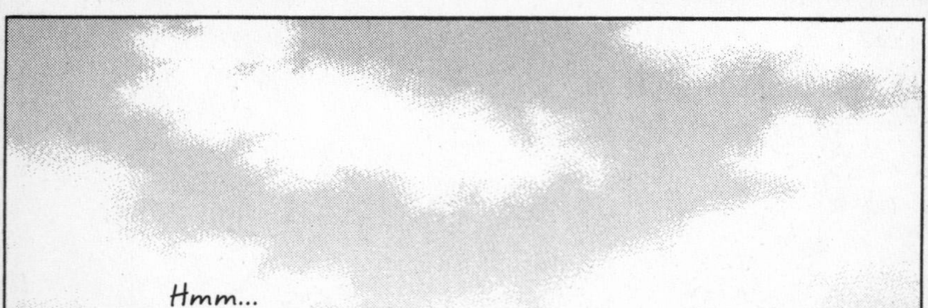
Hmm...
impressive.

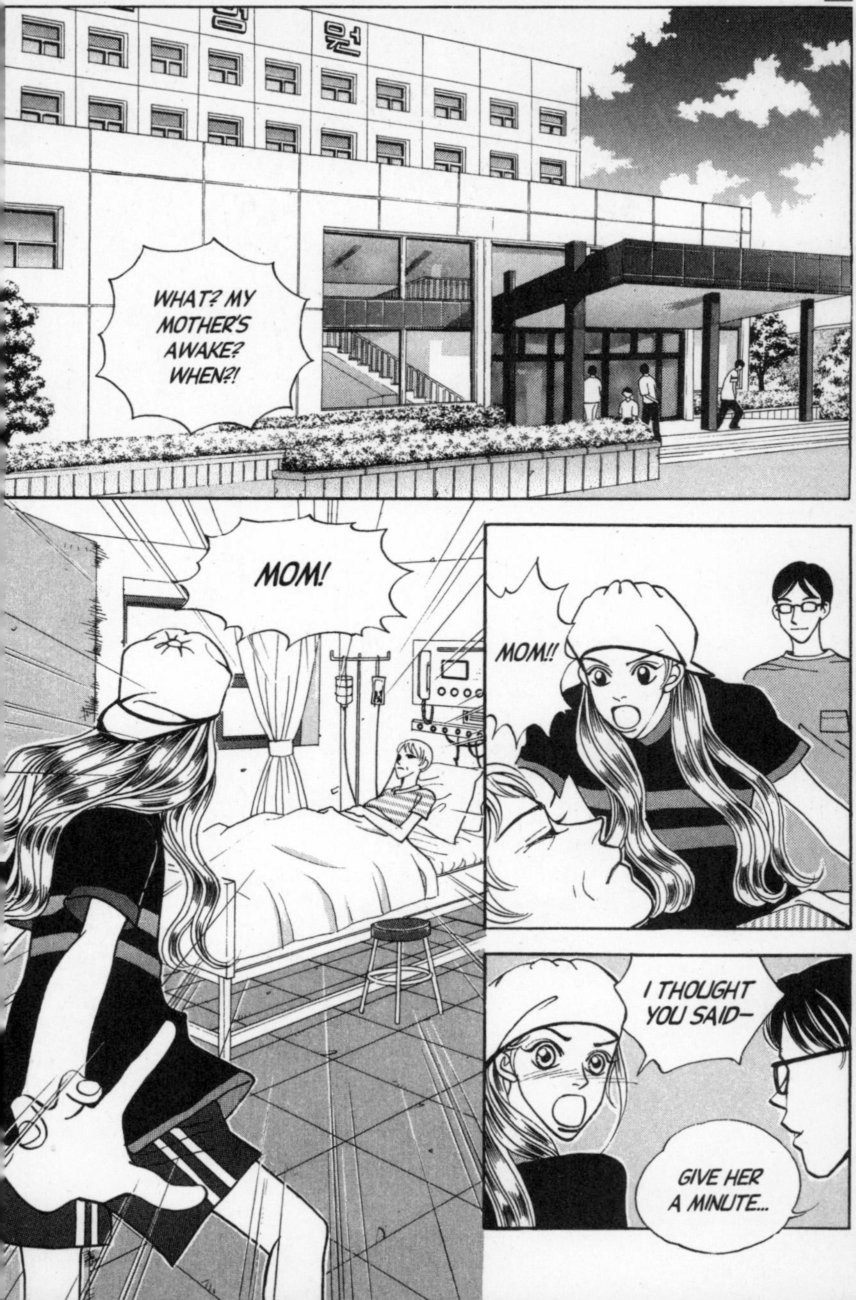
WHAT? MY MOTHER'S AWAKE? WHEN?!
MOM!
MOM!!
I THOUGHT YOU SAID—
GIVE HER A MINUTE...

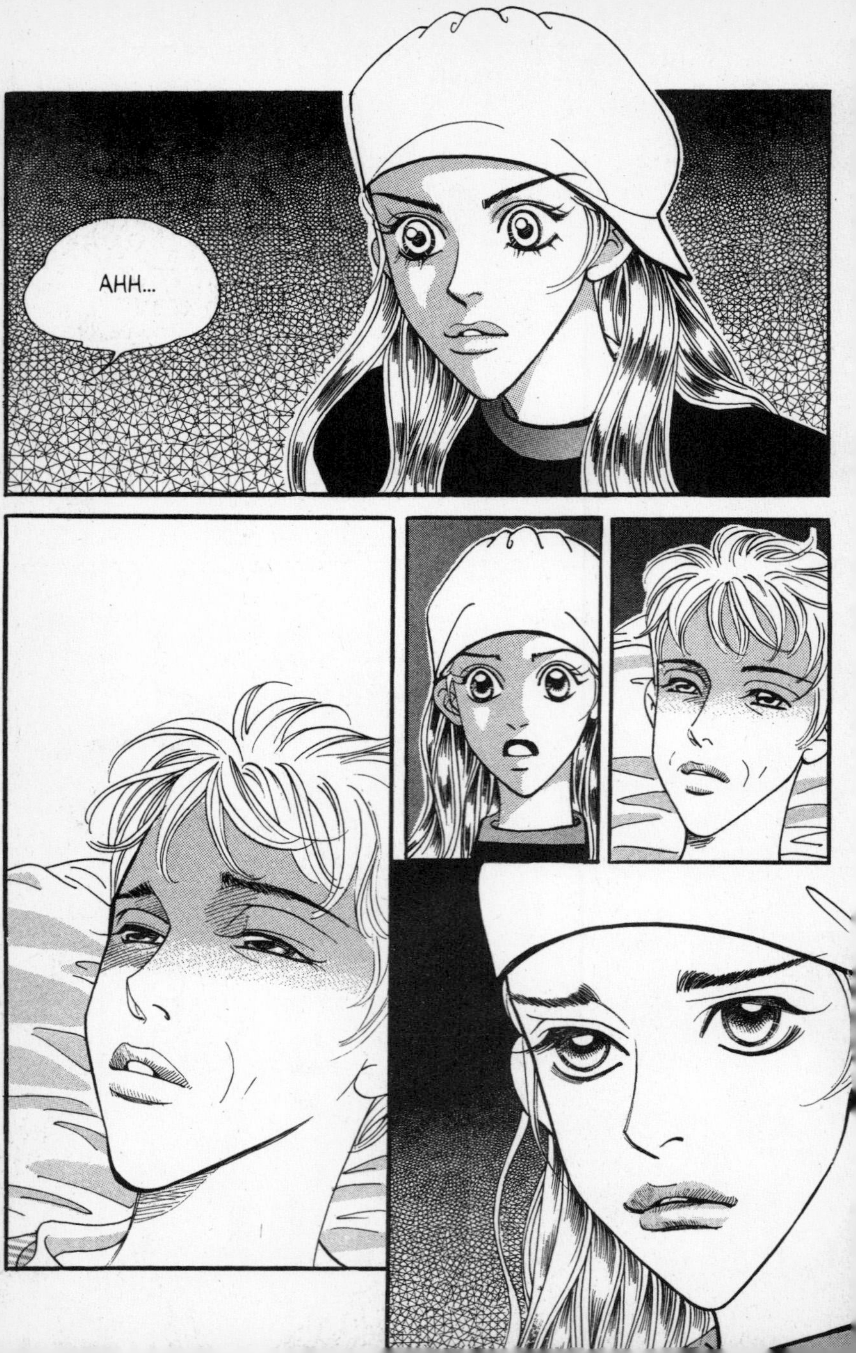
AHH...

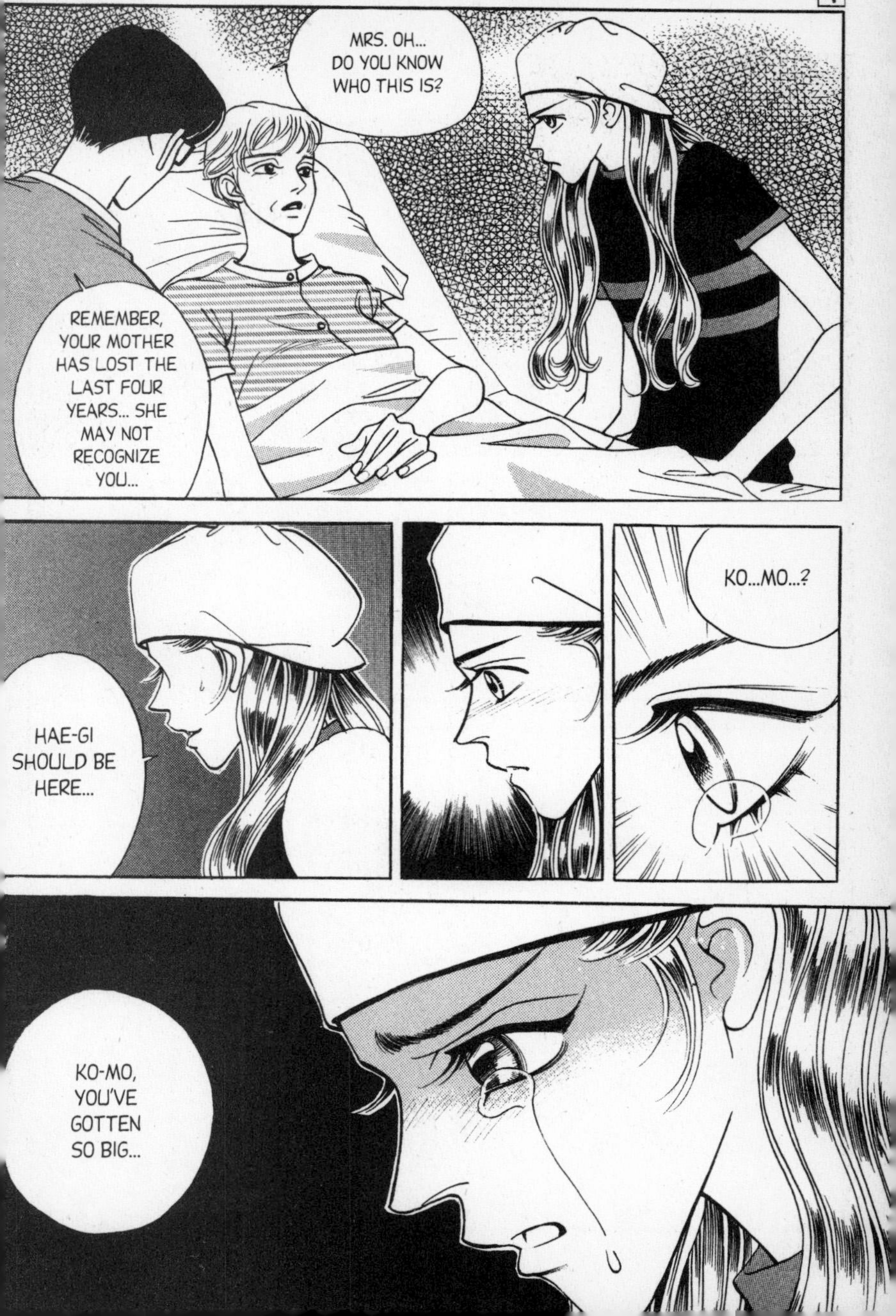
MRS. OH... DO YOU KNOW WHO THIS IS?
REMEMBER, YOUR MOTHER HAS LOST THE LAST FOUR YEARS... SHE MAY NOT RECOGNIZE YOU...
HAE-GI SHOULD BE HERE...
KO...MO...?
KO-MO, YOU'VE GOTTEN SO BIG...

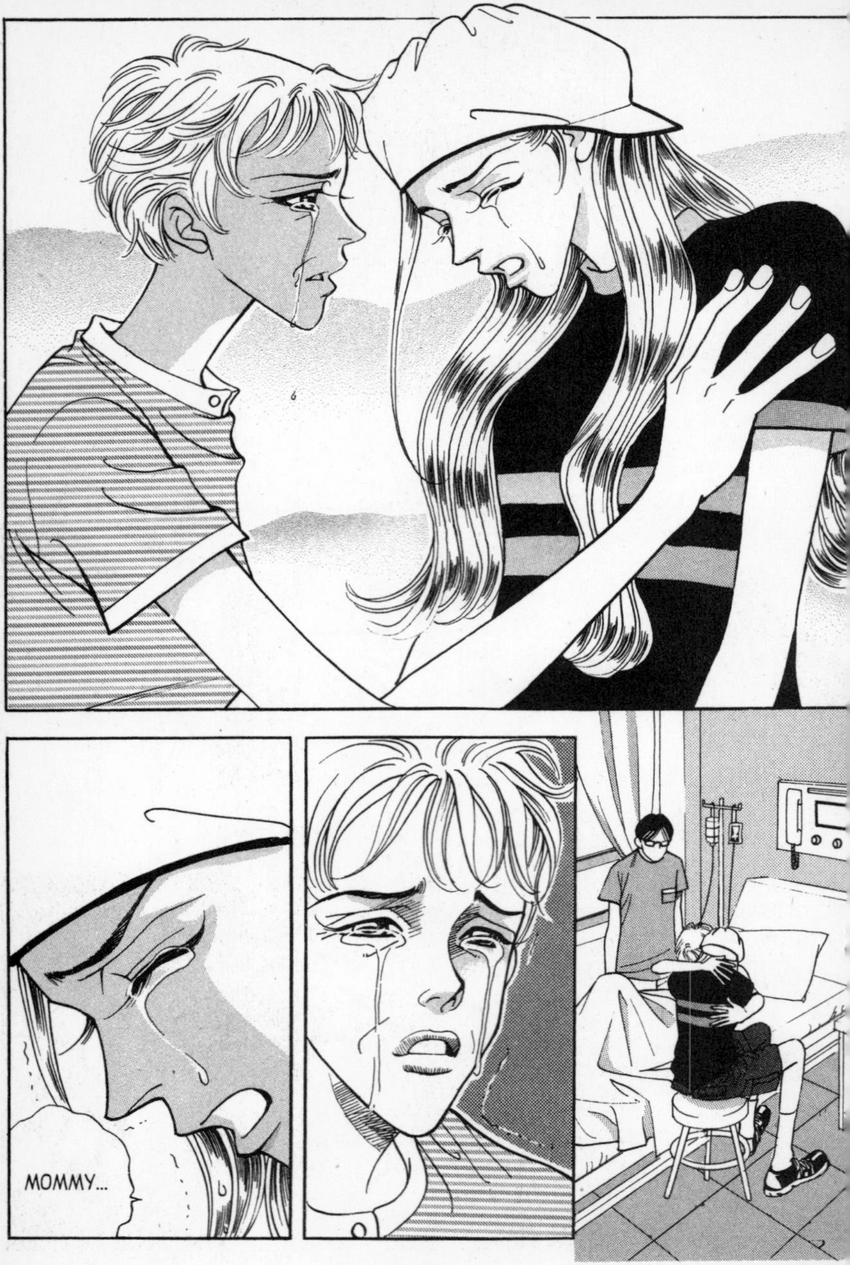
MOMMY...

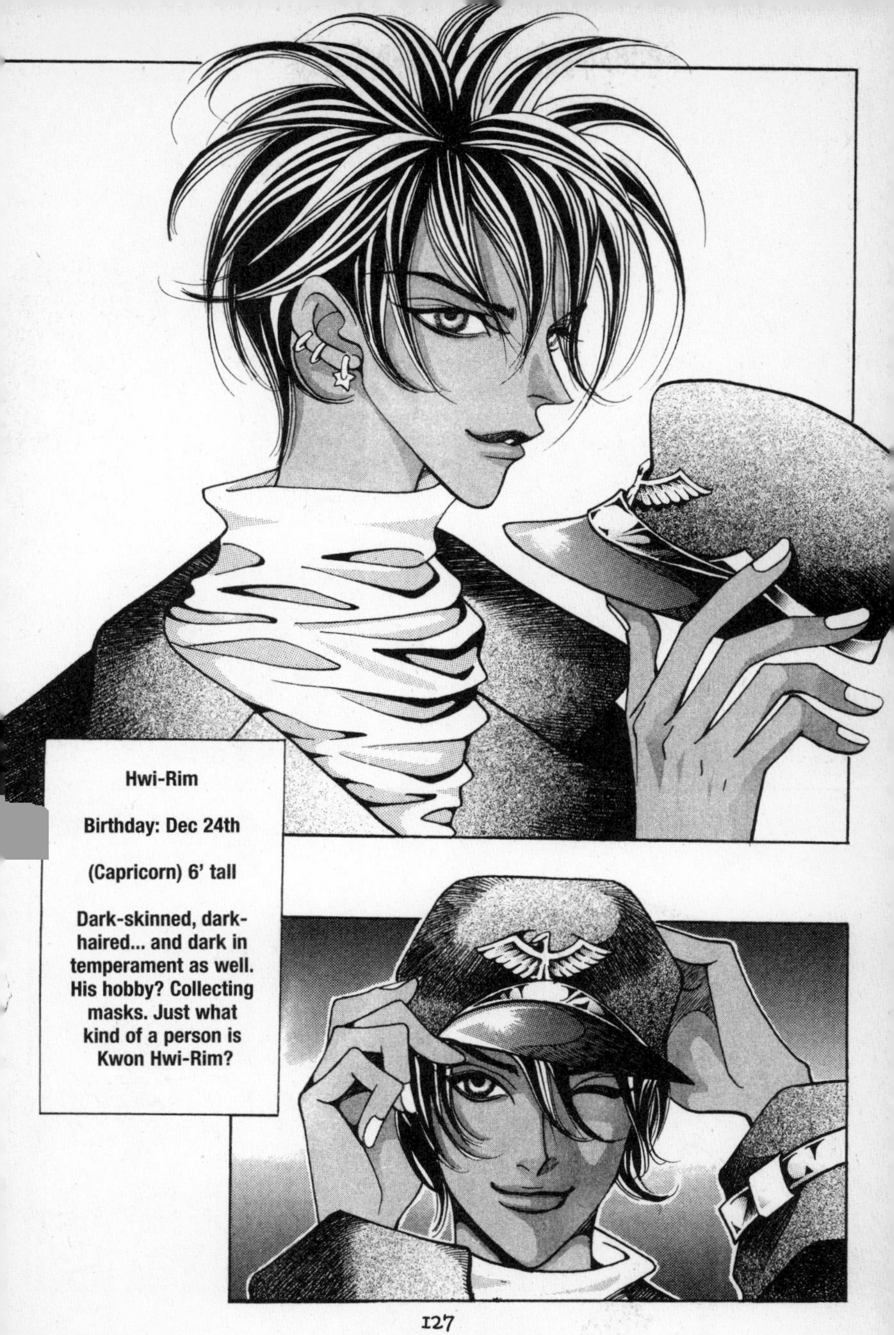
Hwi-Rim
Birthday: Dec 24th
(Capricorn) 6' tall
Dark-skinned, dark-haired... and dark in temperament as well. His hobby? Collecting masks. Just what kind of a person is Kwon Hwi-Rim?

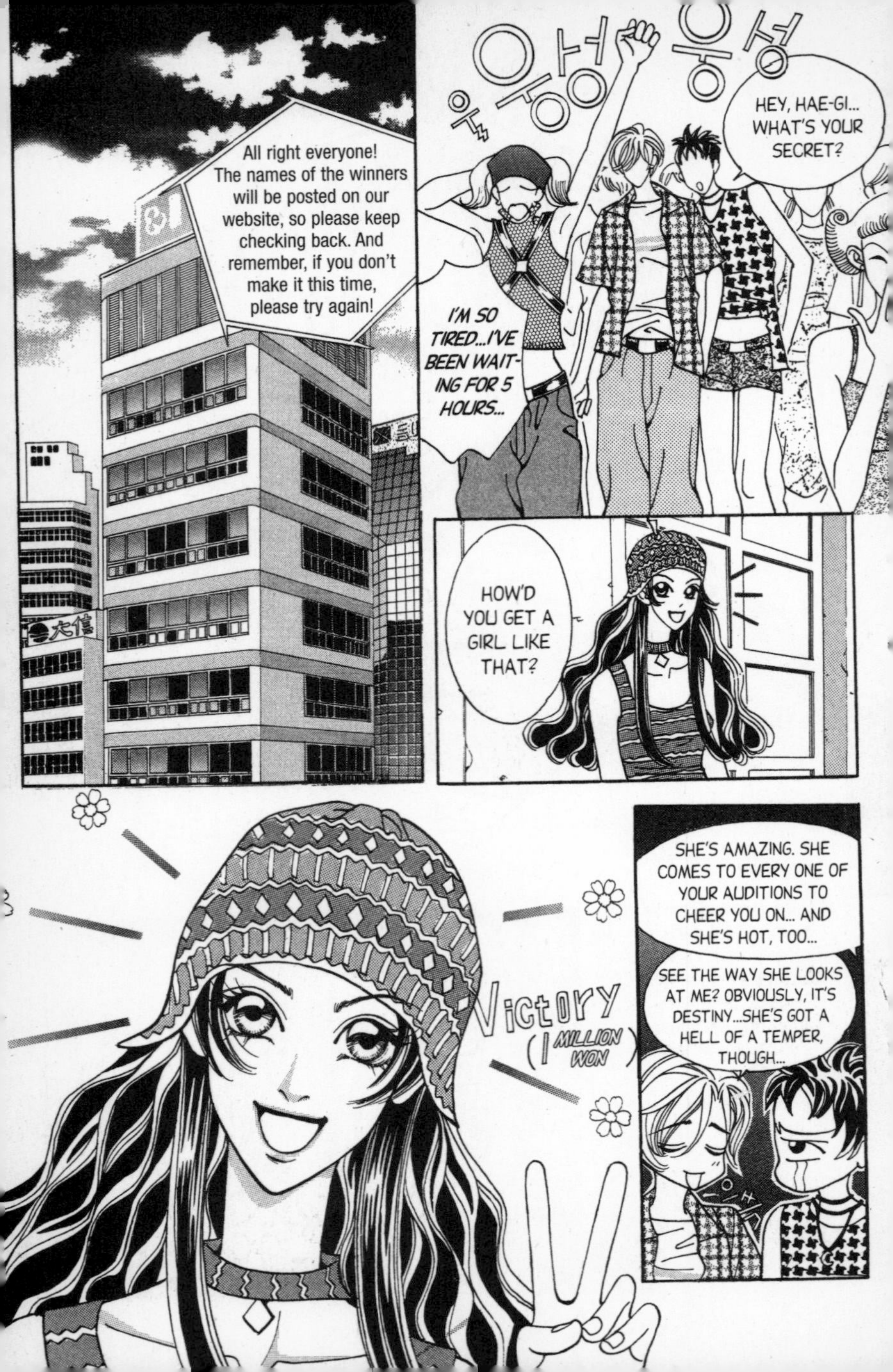
All right everyone! The names of the winners will be posted on our website, so please keep checking back. And remember, if you don't make it this time, please try again!
I'M SO TIRED...I'VE BEEN WAIT-ING FOR 5 HOURS...
HEY, HAE-GI... WHAT'S YOUR SECRET?
HOW'D YOU GET A GIRL LIKE THAT?
Victory (1 MILLION WON)
SHE'S AMAZING. SHE COMES TO EVERY ONE OF YOUR AUDITIONS TO CHEER YOU ON... AND SHE'S HOT, TOO...
SEE THE WAY SHE LOOKS AT ME? OBVIOUSLY, IT'S DESTINY...SHE'S GOT A HELL OF A TEMPER, THOUGH...

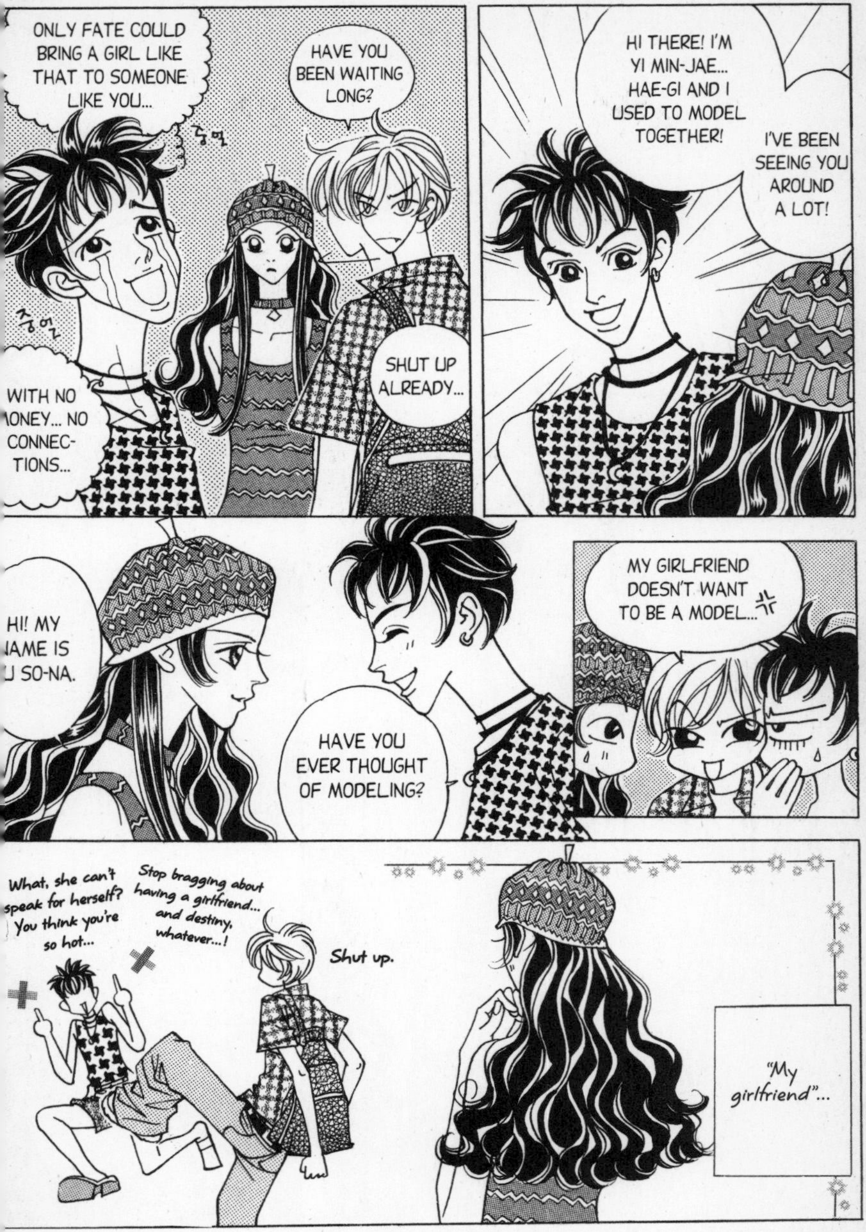
ONLY FATE COULD BRING A GIRL LIKE THAT TO SOMEONE LIKE YOU...
HAVE YOU BEEN WAITING LONG?
WITH NO ONEY... NO CONNEC-TIONS...
SHUT UP ALREADY...
HI THERE! I'M YI MIN-JAE... HAE-GI AND I USED TO MODEL TOGETHER!
I'VE BEEN SEEING YOU AROUND A LOT!
HI! MY AME IS U SO-NA.
HAVE YOU EVER THOUGHT OF MODELING?
MY GIRLFRIEND DOESN'T WANT TO BE A MODEL...
What, she can't speak for herself? You think you're so hot...
Stop bragging about having a girlfriend... and destiny, whatever...!
Shut up.
"My girlfriend"...

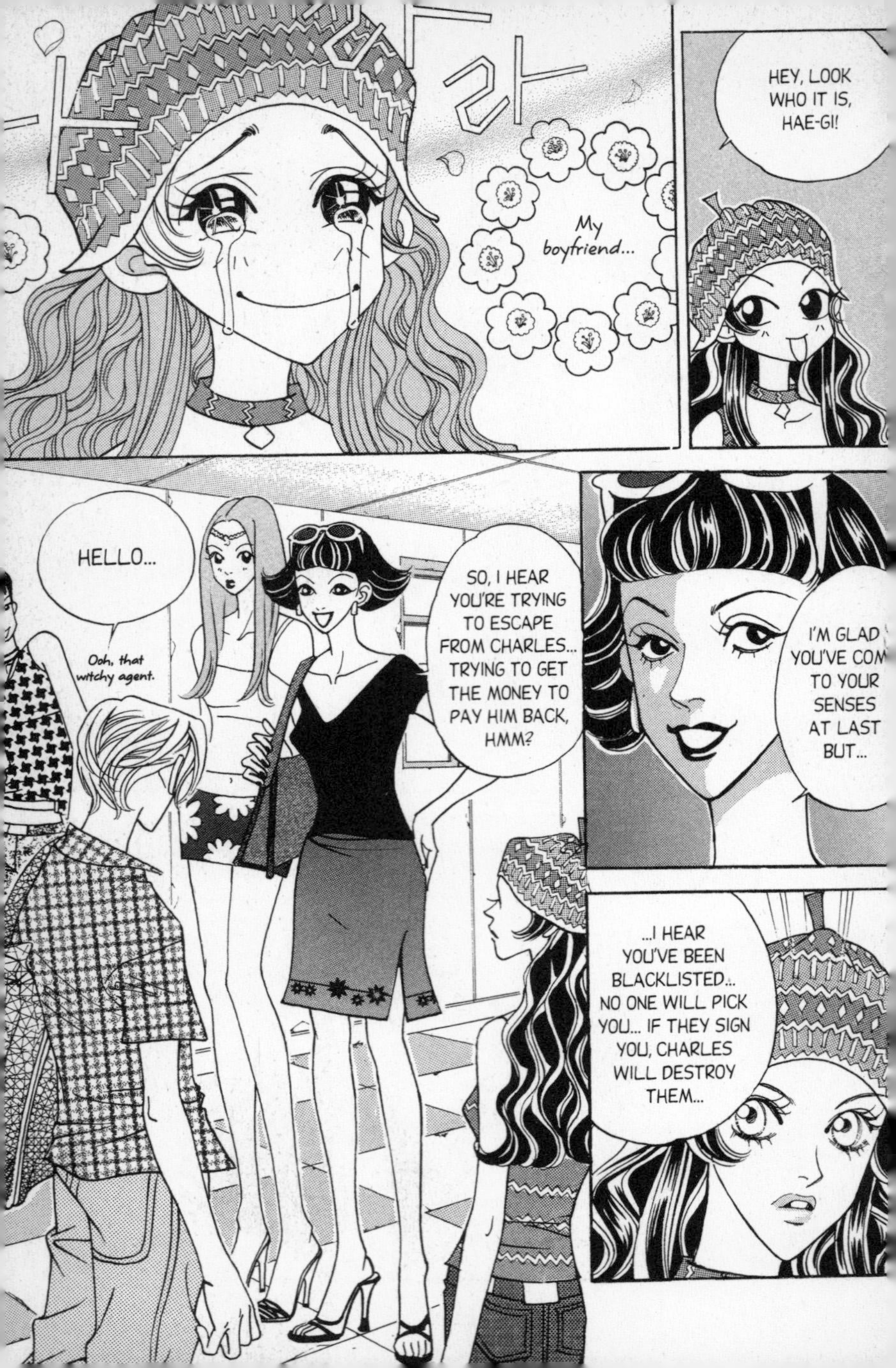

My boyfriend...
HEY, LOOK WHO IT IS, HAE-GI!
HELLO...
Ooh, that witchy agent.
SO, I HEAR YOU'RE TRYING TO ESCAPE FROM CHARLES... TRYING TO GET THE MONEY TO PAY HIM BACK, HMM?
I'M GLAD YOU'VE COM TO YOUR SENSES AT LAST BUT...
...I HEAR YOU'VE BEEN BLACKLISTED... NO ONE WILL PICK YOU... IF THEY SIGN YOU, CHARLES WILL DESTROY THEM...

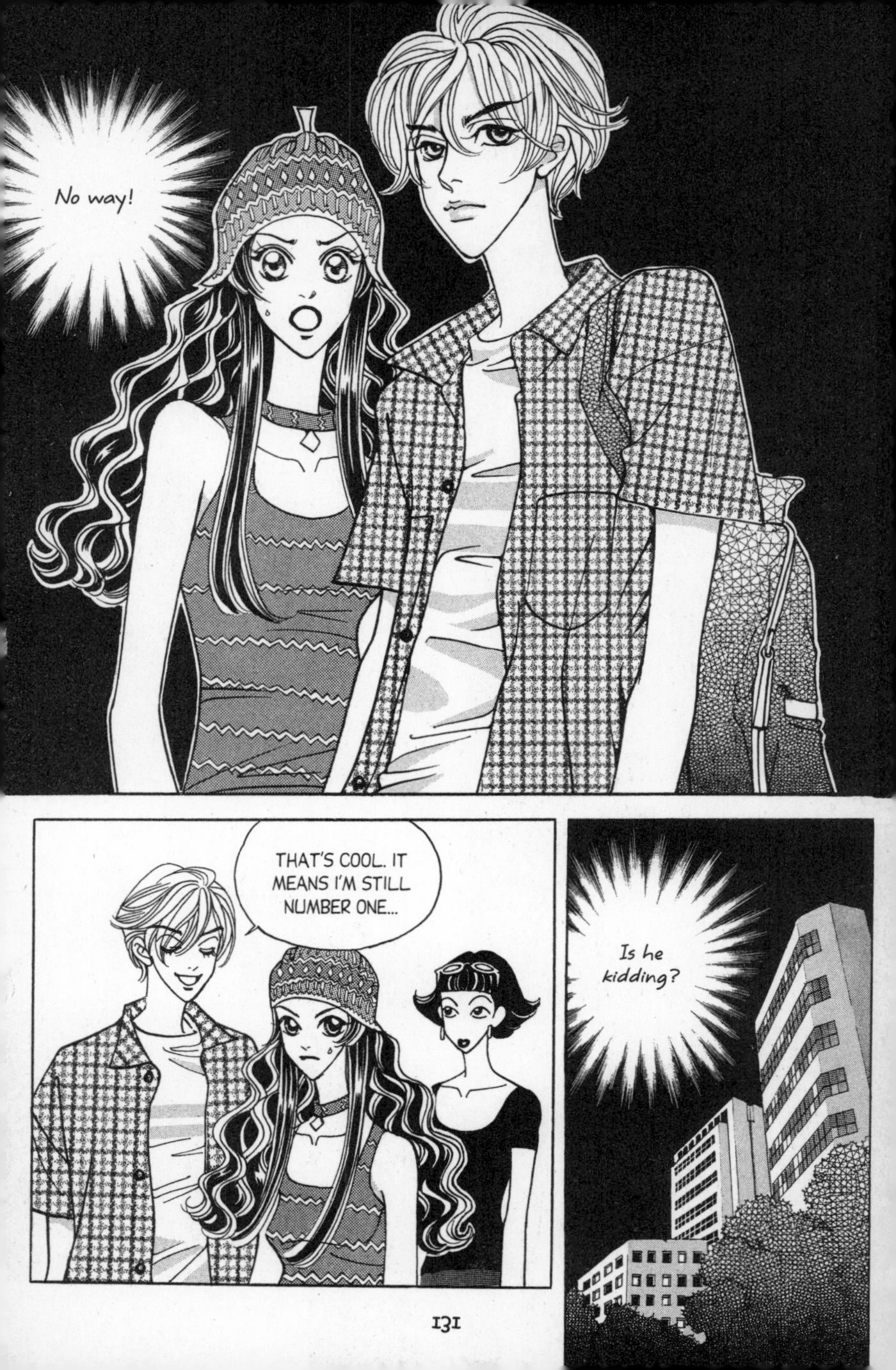
No way!
THAT'S COOL. IT MEANS I'M STILL NUMBER ONE...
Is he kidding?

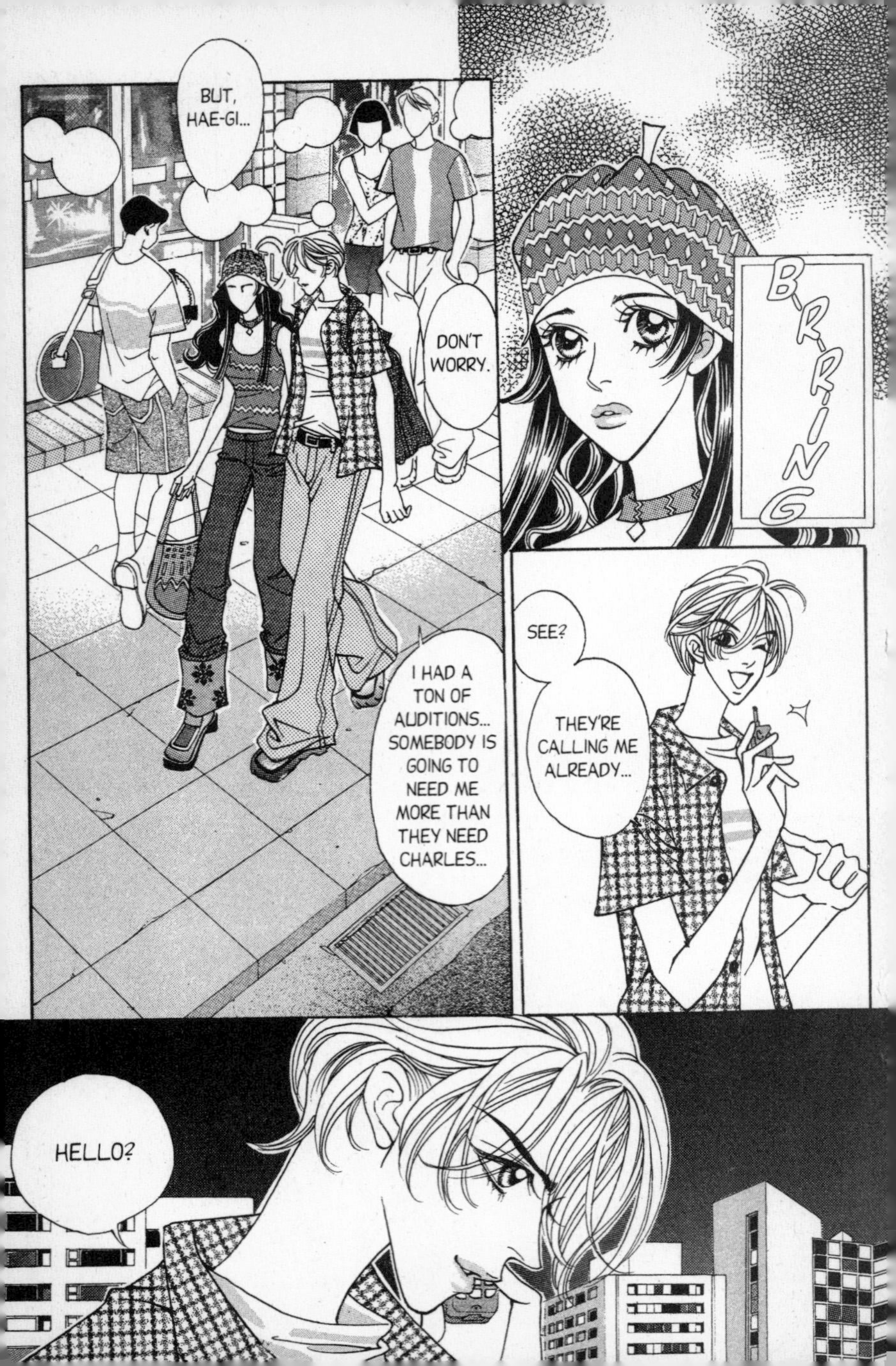
BUT, HAE-GI...
DON'T WORRY.
I HAD A TON OF AUDITIONS... SOMEBODY IS GOING TO NEED ME MORE THAN THEY NEED CHARLES...
B-R-R-I-N-G
SEE?
THEY'RE CALLING ME ALREADY...
HELLO?

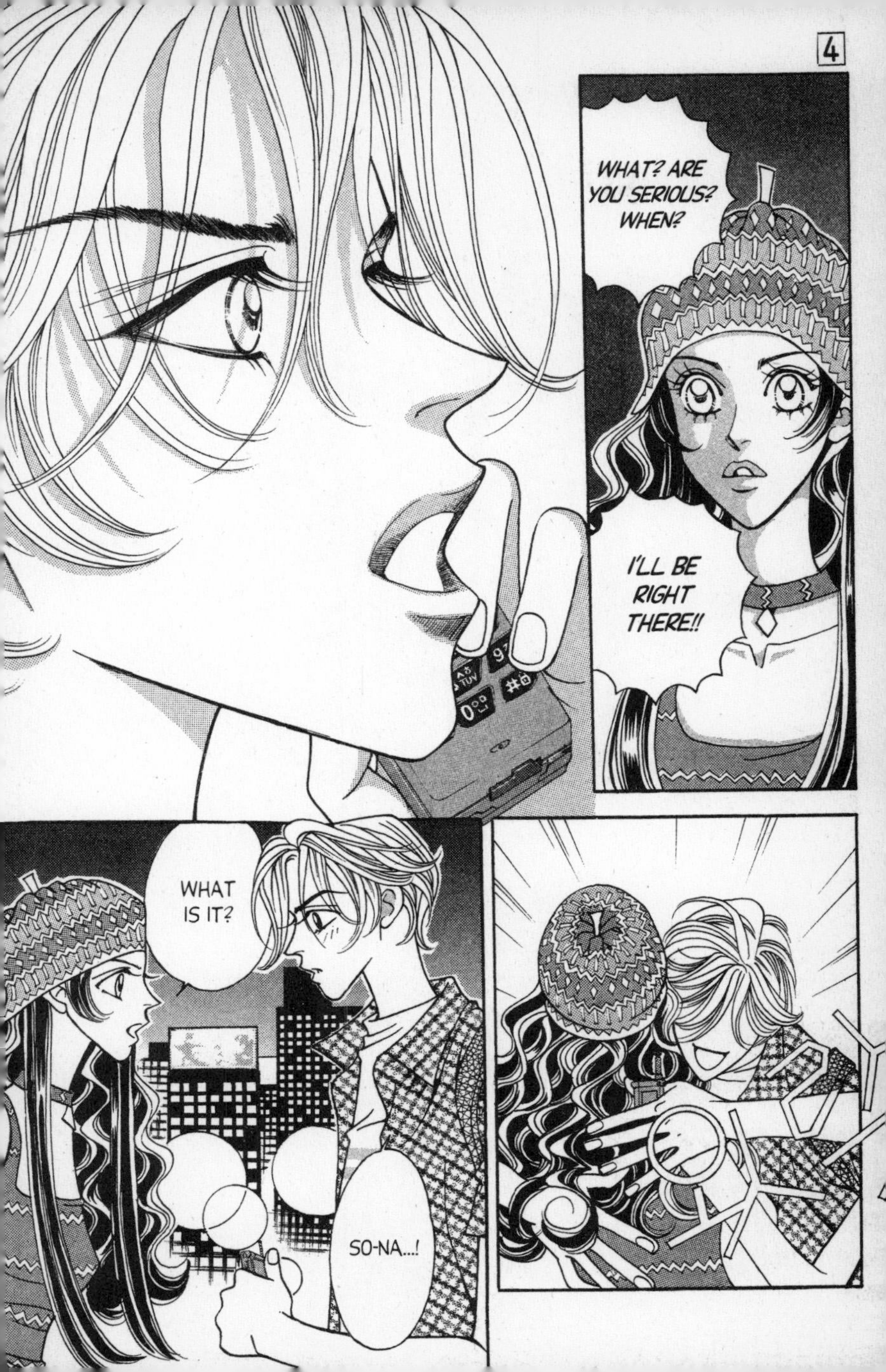
WHAT? ARE YOU SERIOUS? WHEN?
I'LL BE RIGHT THERE!!
WHAT IS IT?
SO-NA...!

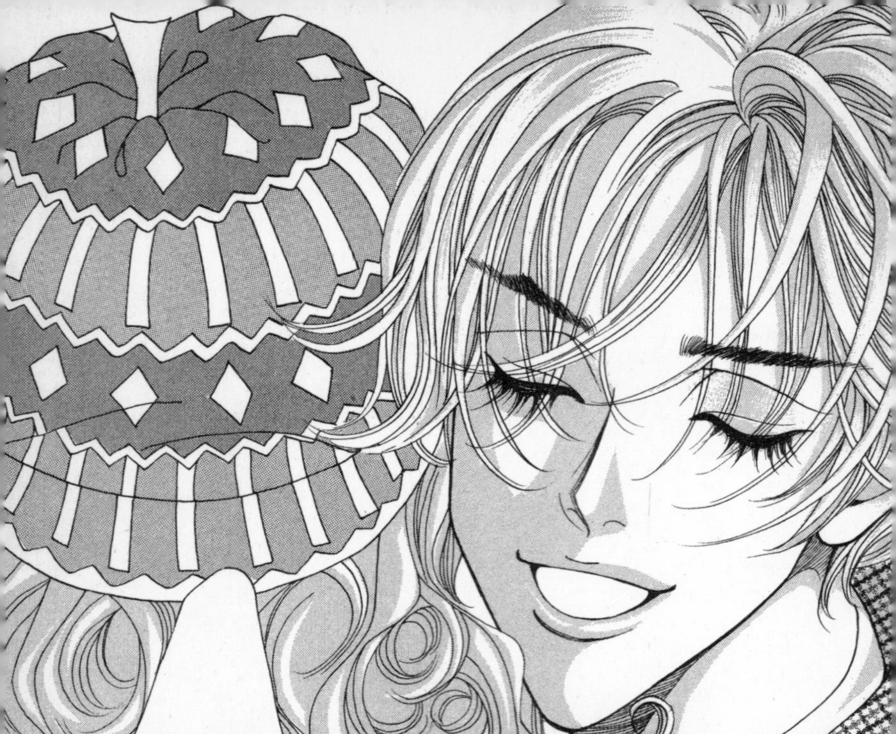
FINALLY...
I CAN'T
BELIEVE IT...
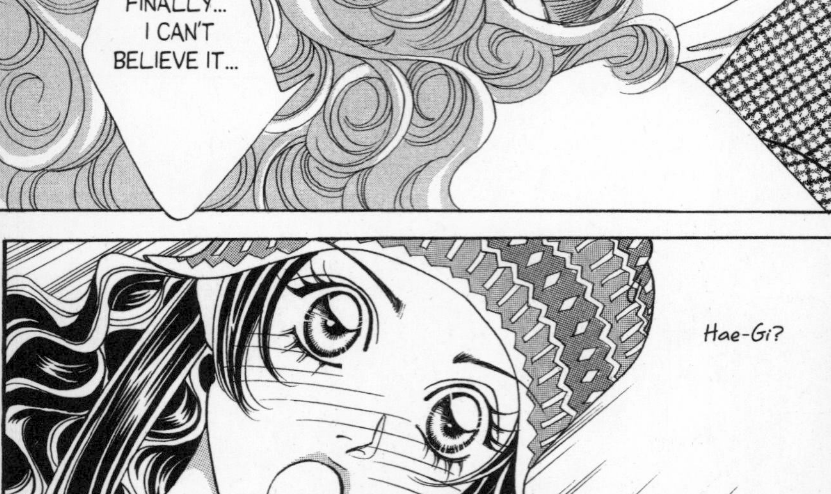
Hae-Gi?

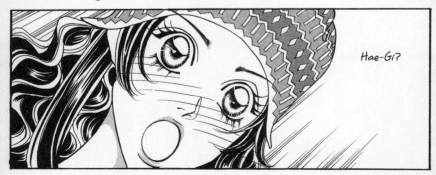

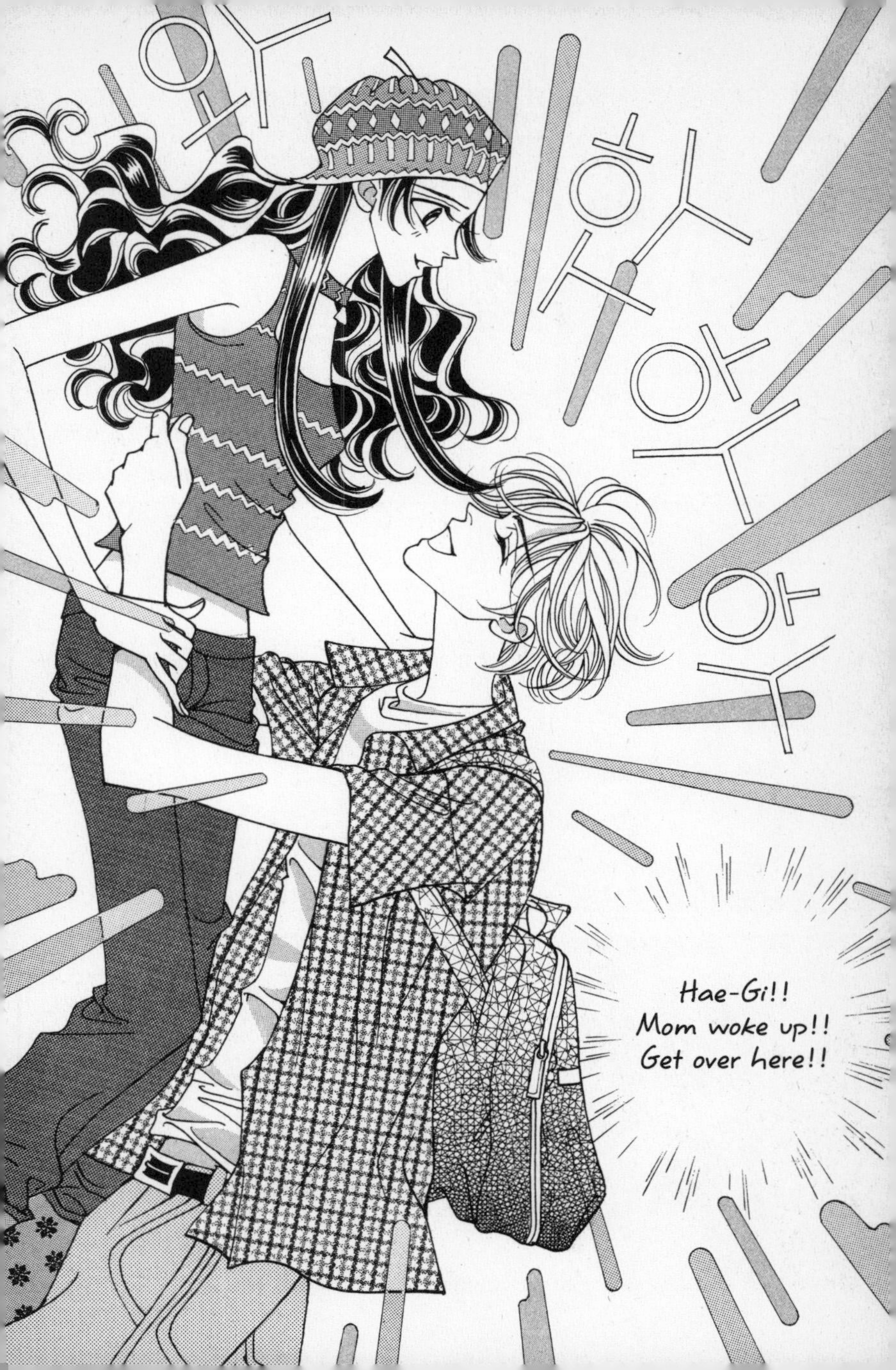
Hae-Gi!!
Mom woke up!!
Get over here!!

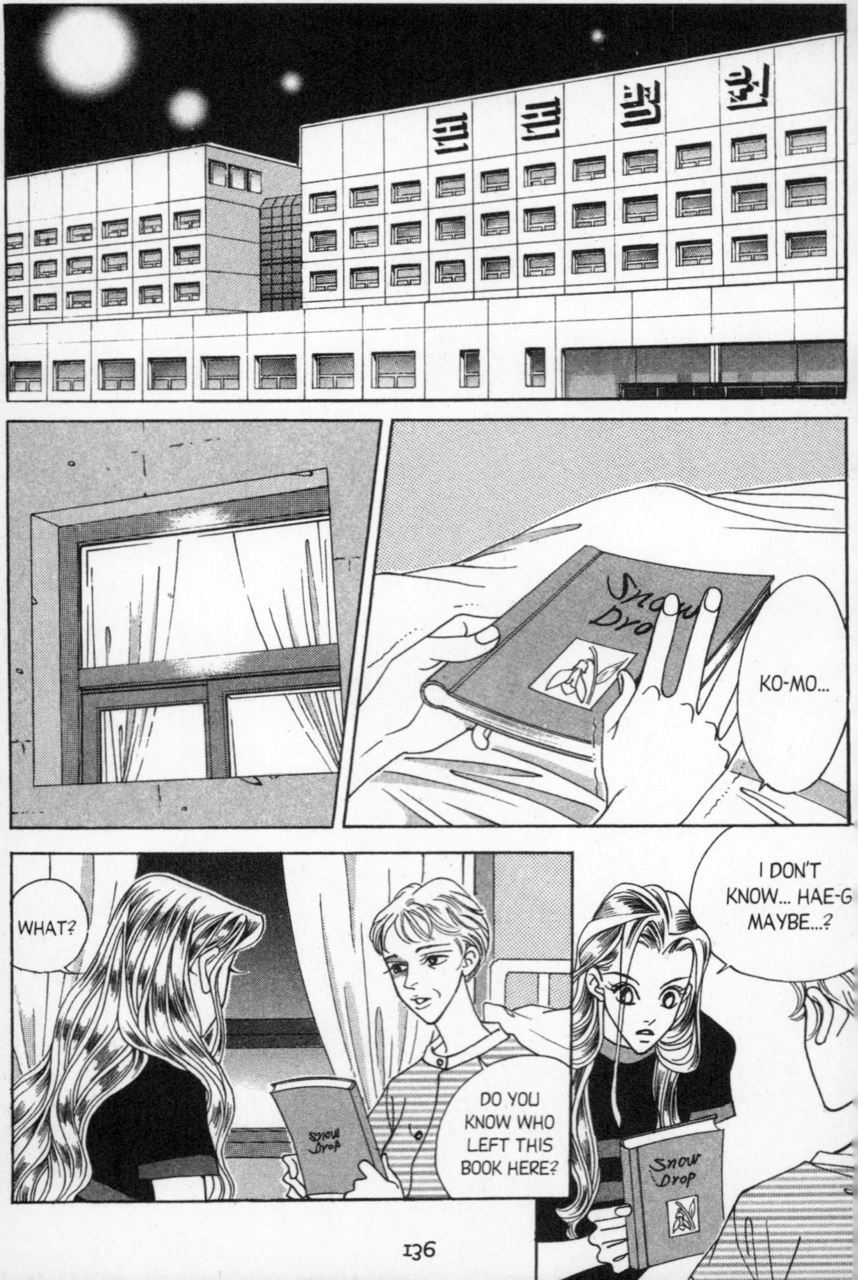
KO-MO...
WHAT?
DO YOU KNOW WHO LEFT THIS BOOK HERE?
I DON'T KNOW... HAE-G MAYBE...?
Snow Drop

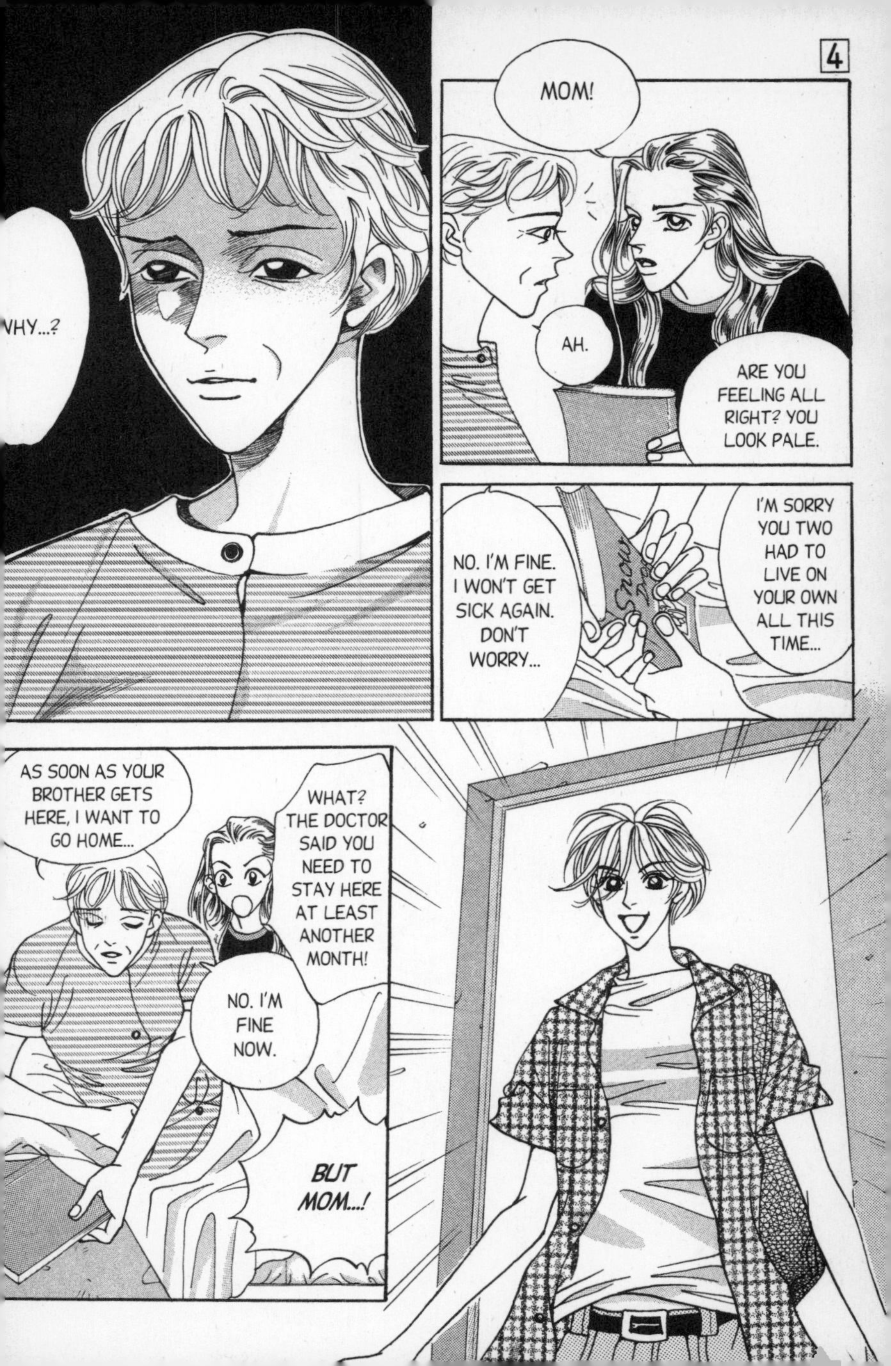
WHY...?
MOM!
AH.
ARE YOU FEELING ALL RIGHT? YOU LOOK PALE.
NO. I'M FINE. I WON'T GET SICK AGAIN. DON'T WORRY...
I'M SORRY YOU TWO HAD TO LIVE ON YOUR OWN ALL THIS TIME...
AS SOON AS YOUR BROTHER GETS HERE, I WANT TO GO HOME...
WHAT? THE DOCTOR SAID YOU NEED TO STAY HERE AT LEAST ANOTHER MONTH!
NO. I'M FINE NOW.
BUT MOM...!

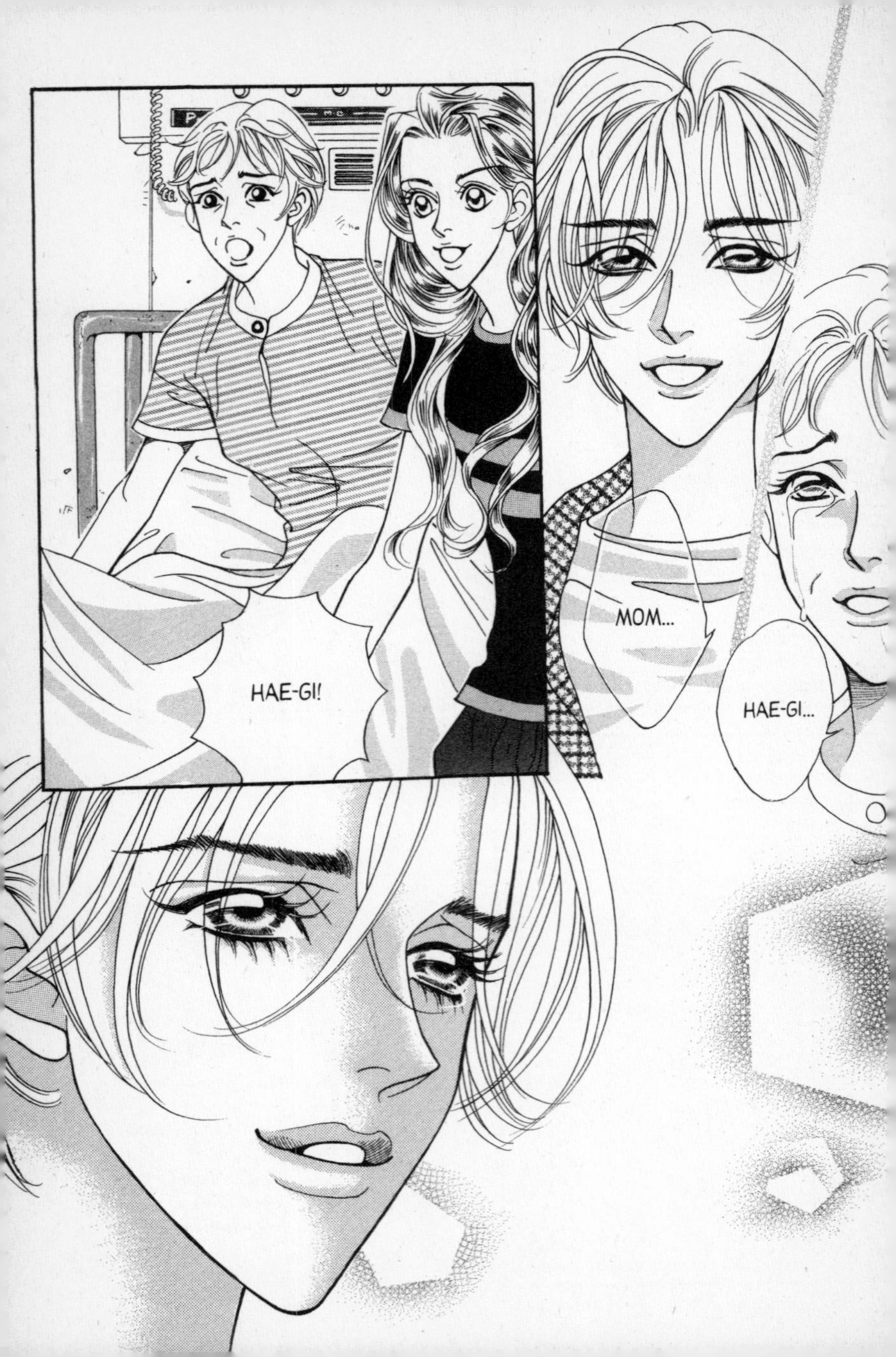
HAE-GI!
MOM...
HAE-GI...

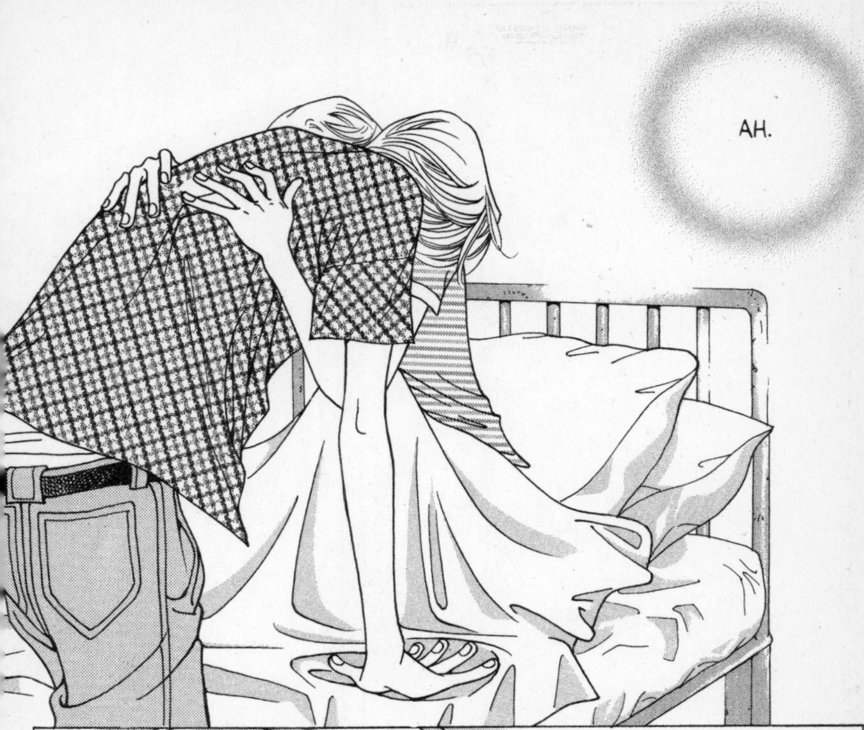
AH.

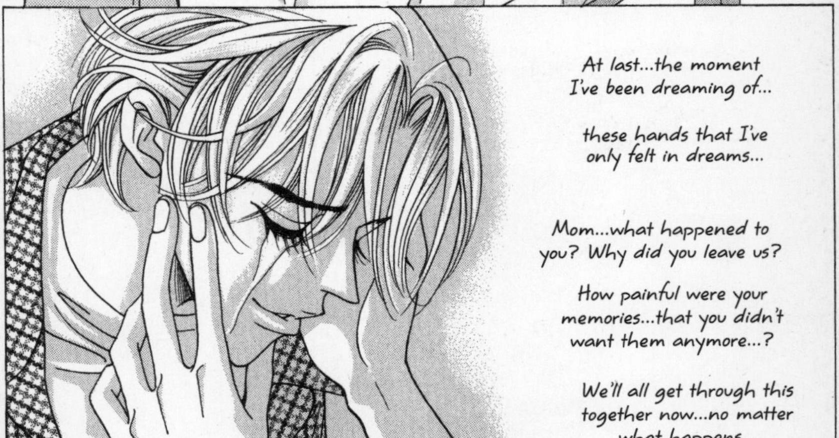
At last...the moment I've been dreaming of...
these hands that I've only felt in dreams...
Mom...what happened to you? Why did you leave us?
How painful were your memories...that you didn't want them anymore...?
We'll all get through this together now...no matter what happens...

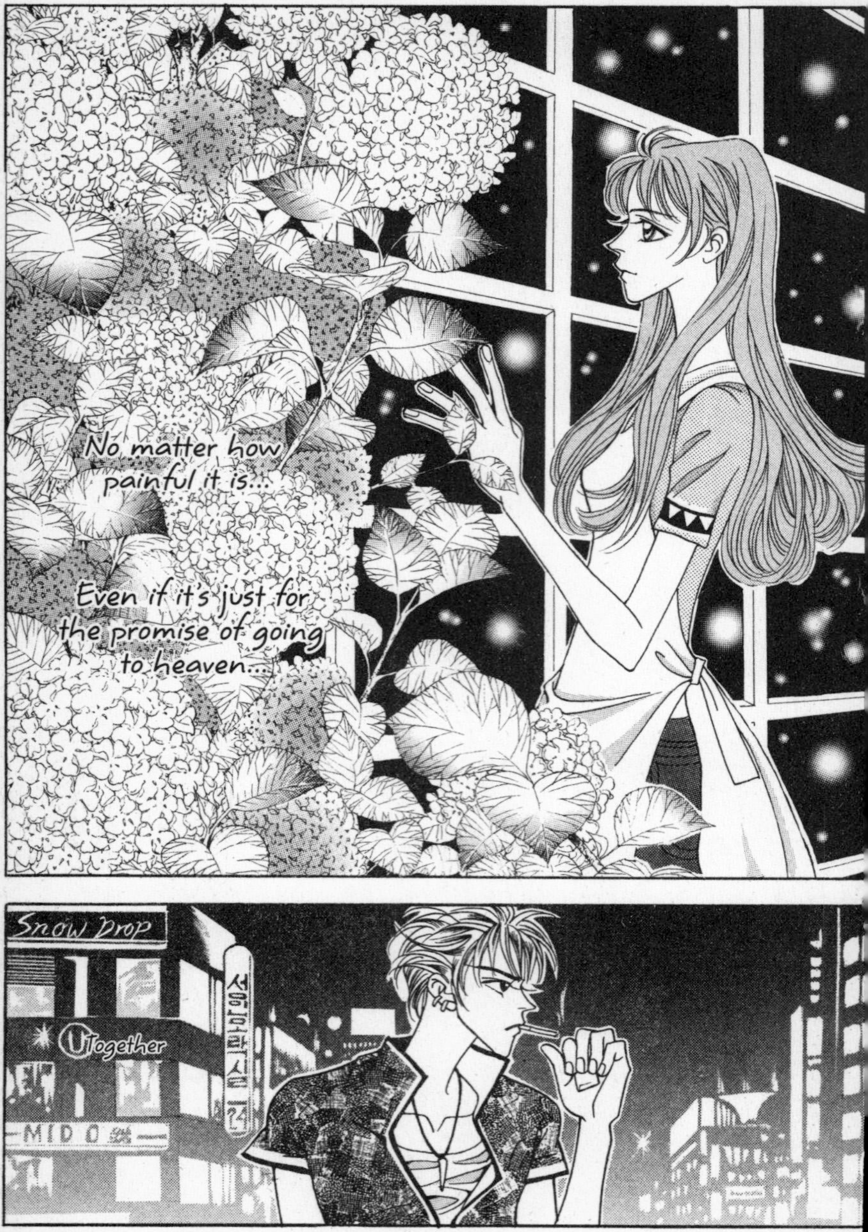
No matter how painful it is...
Even if it's just for the promise of going to heaven...
Snow Drop
Together
성인오락실 24
MIDO

Part 17: Rose
A Passionate Person

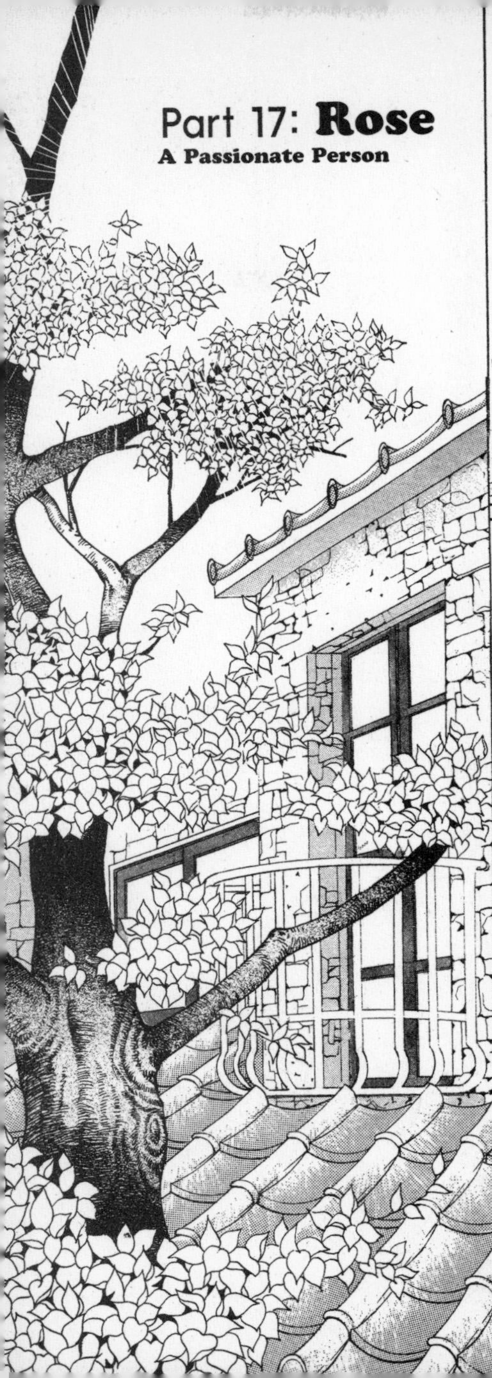

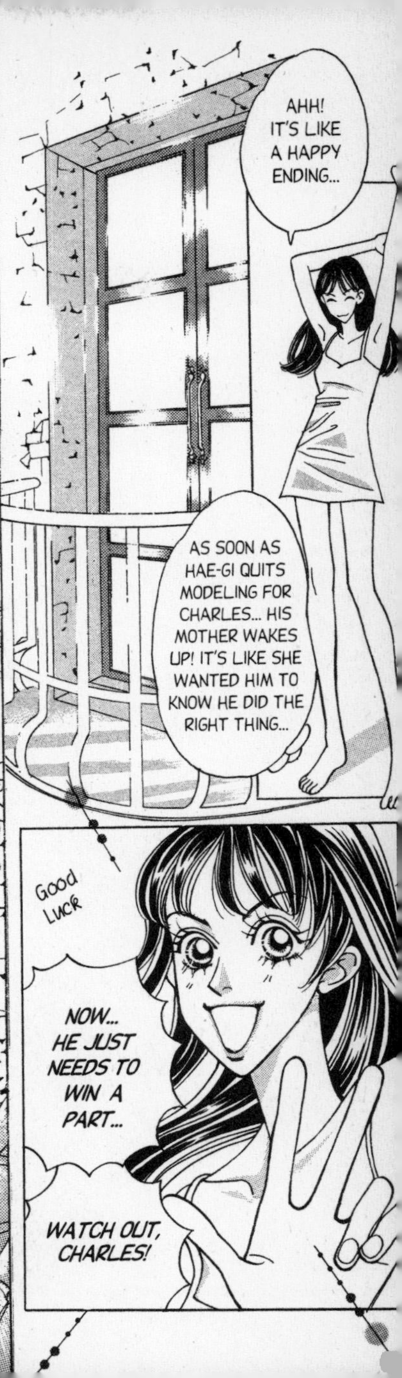
AHH! IT'S LIKE A HAPPY ENDING...
AS SOON AS HAE-GI QUITS MODELING FOR CHARLES... HIS MOTHER WAKES UP! IT'S LIKE SHE WANTED HIM TO KNOW HE DID THE RIGHT THING...
Good Luck
NOW... HE JUST NEEDS TO WIN A PART...
WATCH OUT, CHARLES!

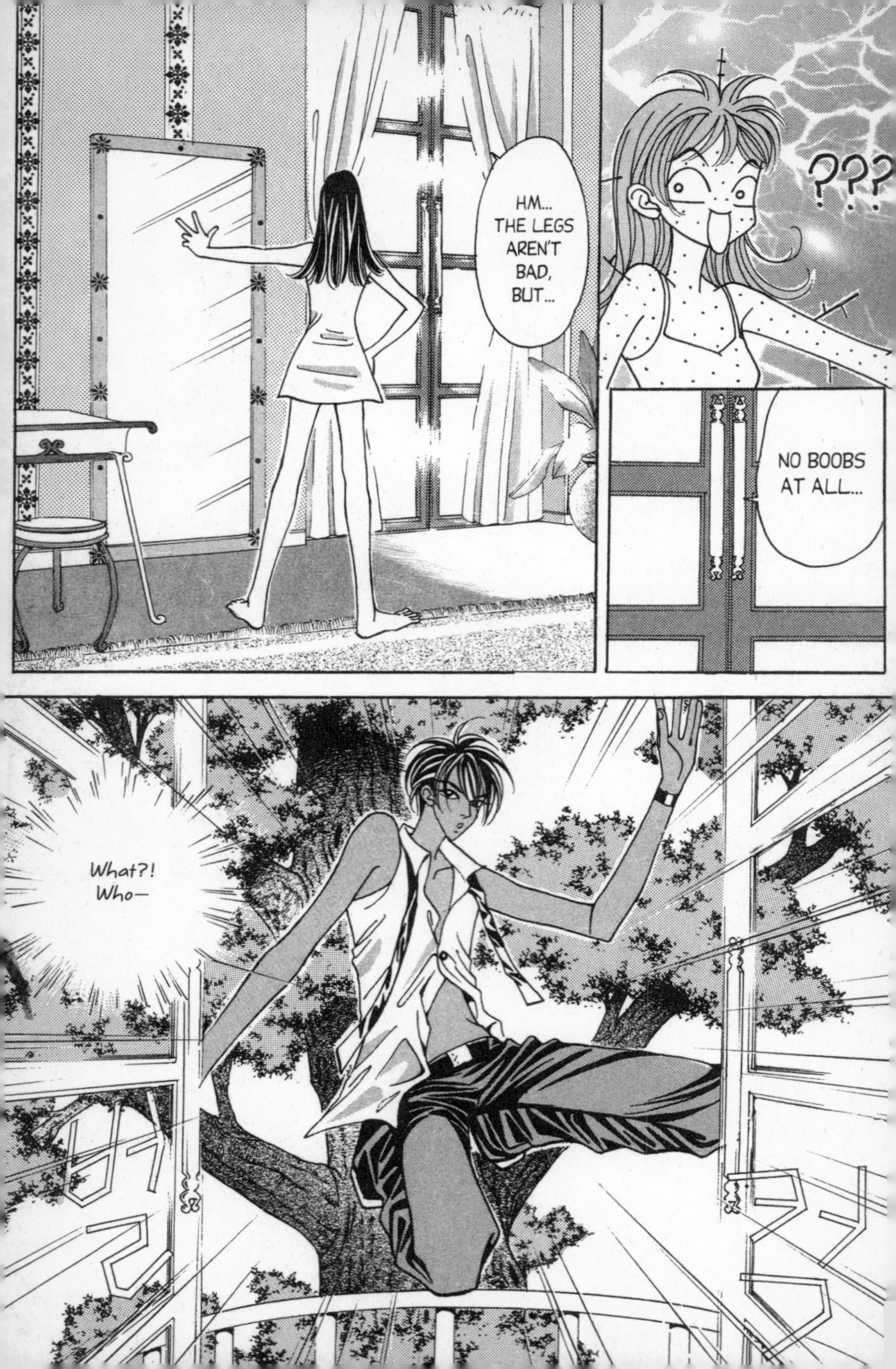
HM... THE LEGS AREN'T BAD, BUT...
???
NO BOOBS AT ALL...
What?! Who-

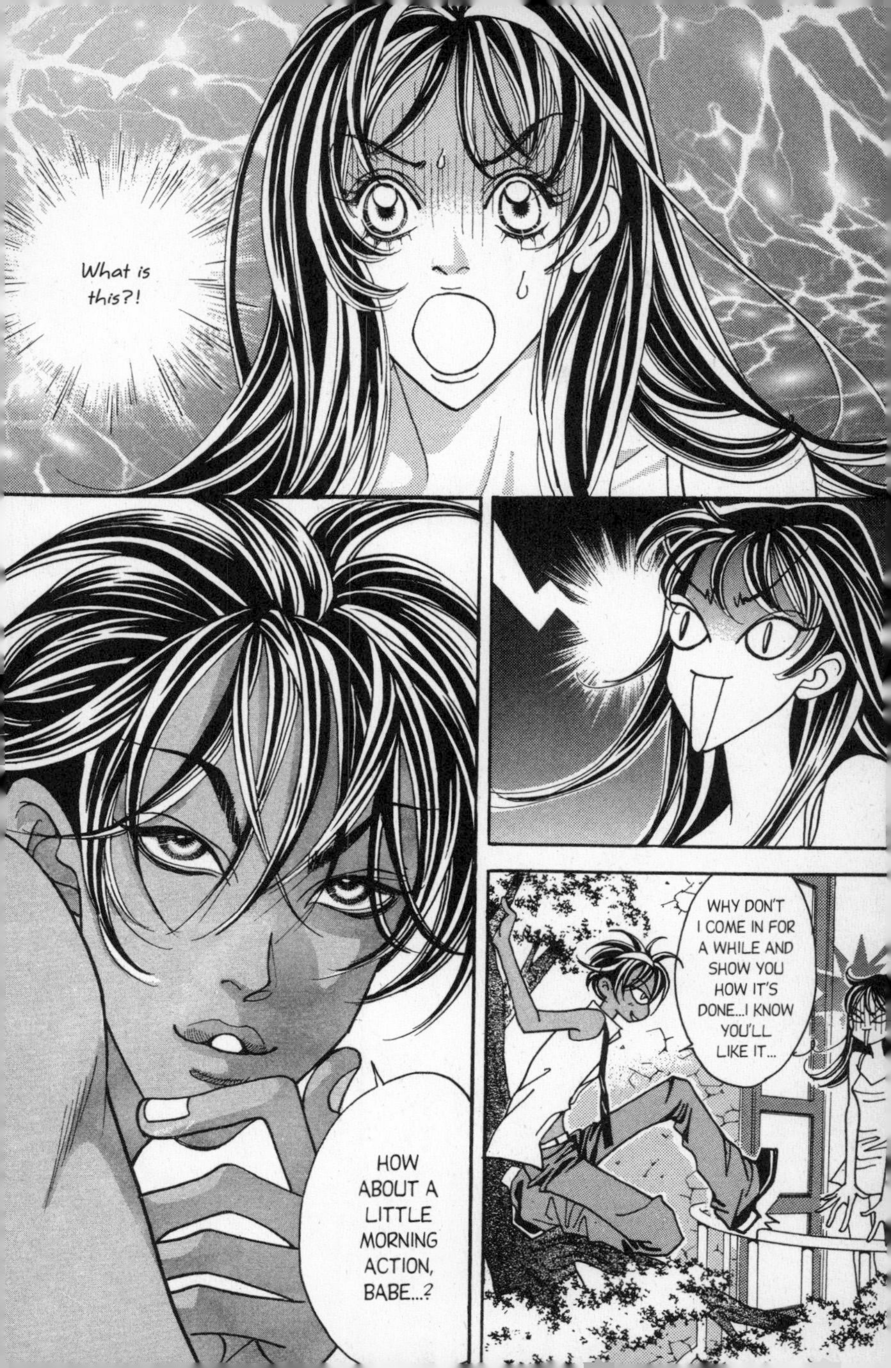
What is this?!
HOW ABOUT A LITTLE MORNING ACTION, BABE...?
WHY DON'T I COME IN FOR A WHILE AND SHOW YOU HOW IT'S DONE...I KNOW YOU'LL LIKE IT...

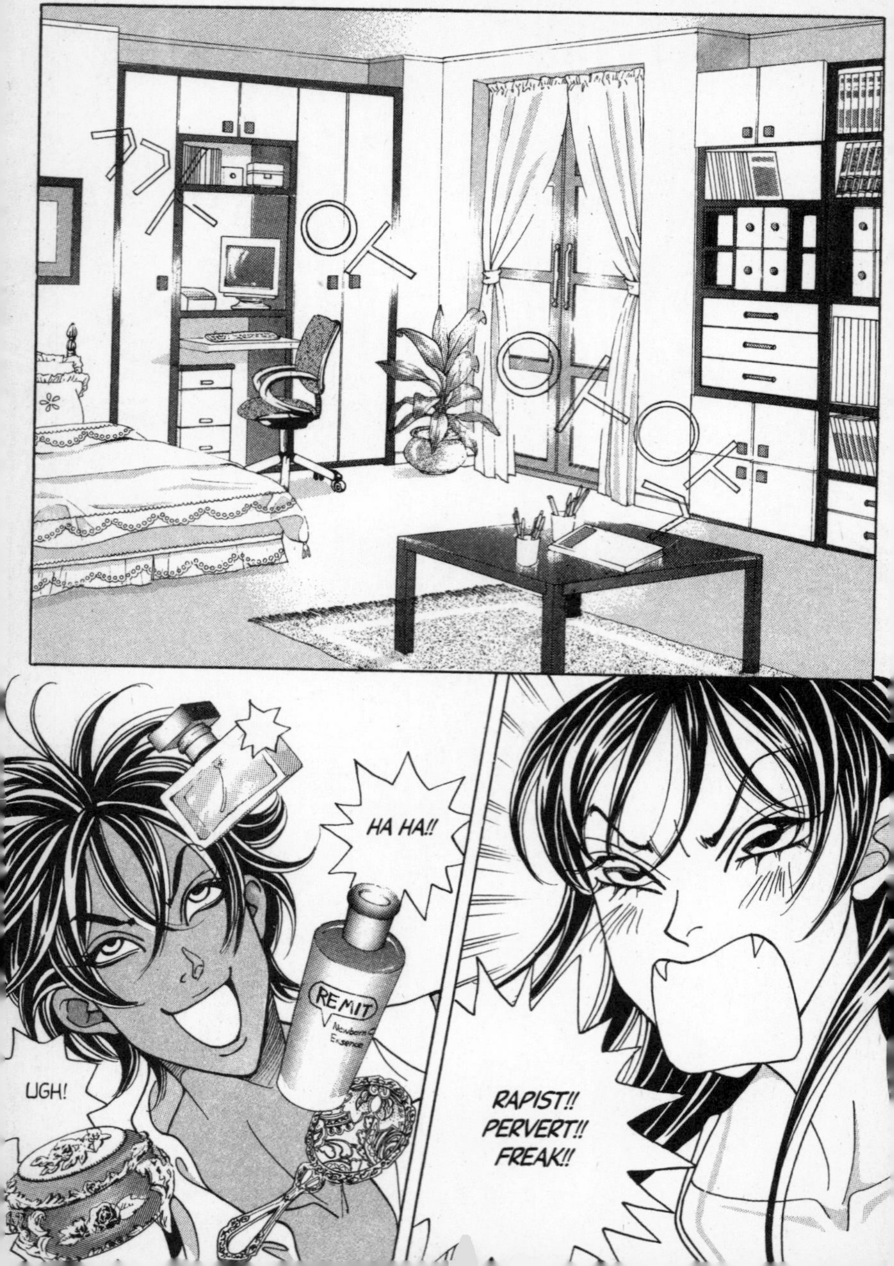
HA HA!!
REMIT
UGH!
RAPIST!!
PERVERT!!
FREAK!!

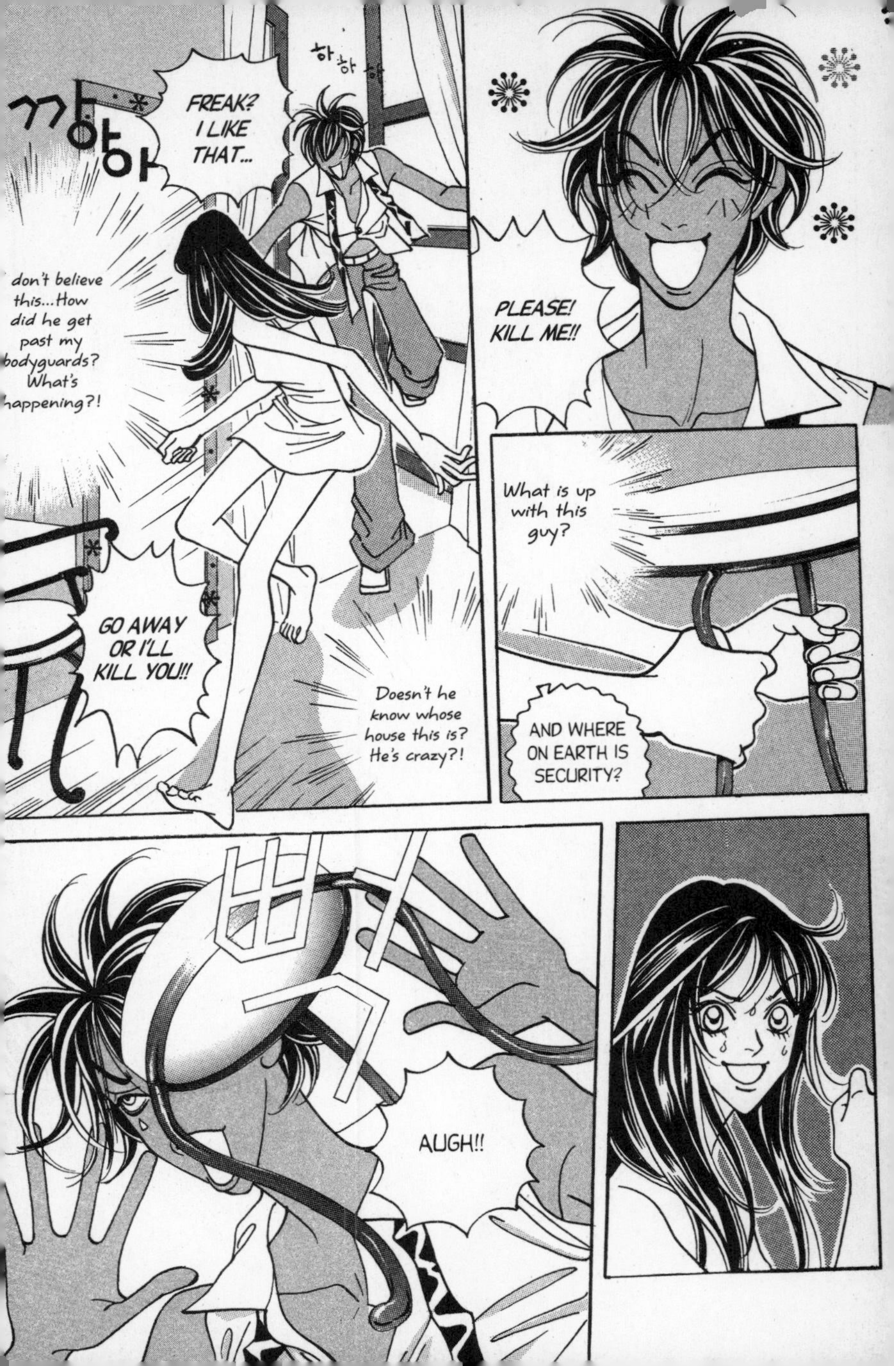
꺄아아
하하하
FREAK? I LIKE THAT...
don't believe this...How did he get past my bodyguards? What's happening?!
GO AWAY OR I'LL KILL YOU!!
Doesn't he know whose house this is? He's crazy?!
PLEASE! KILL ME!!
What is up with this guy?
AND WHERE ON EARTH IS SECURITY?
빡
AUGH!!

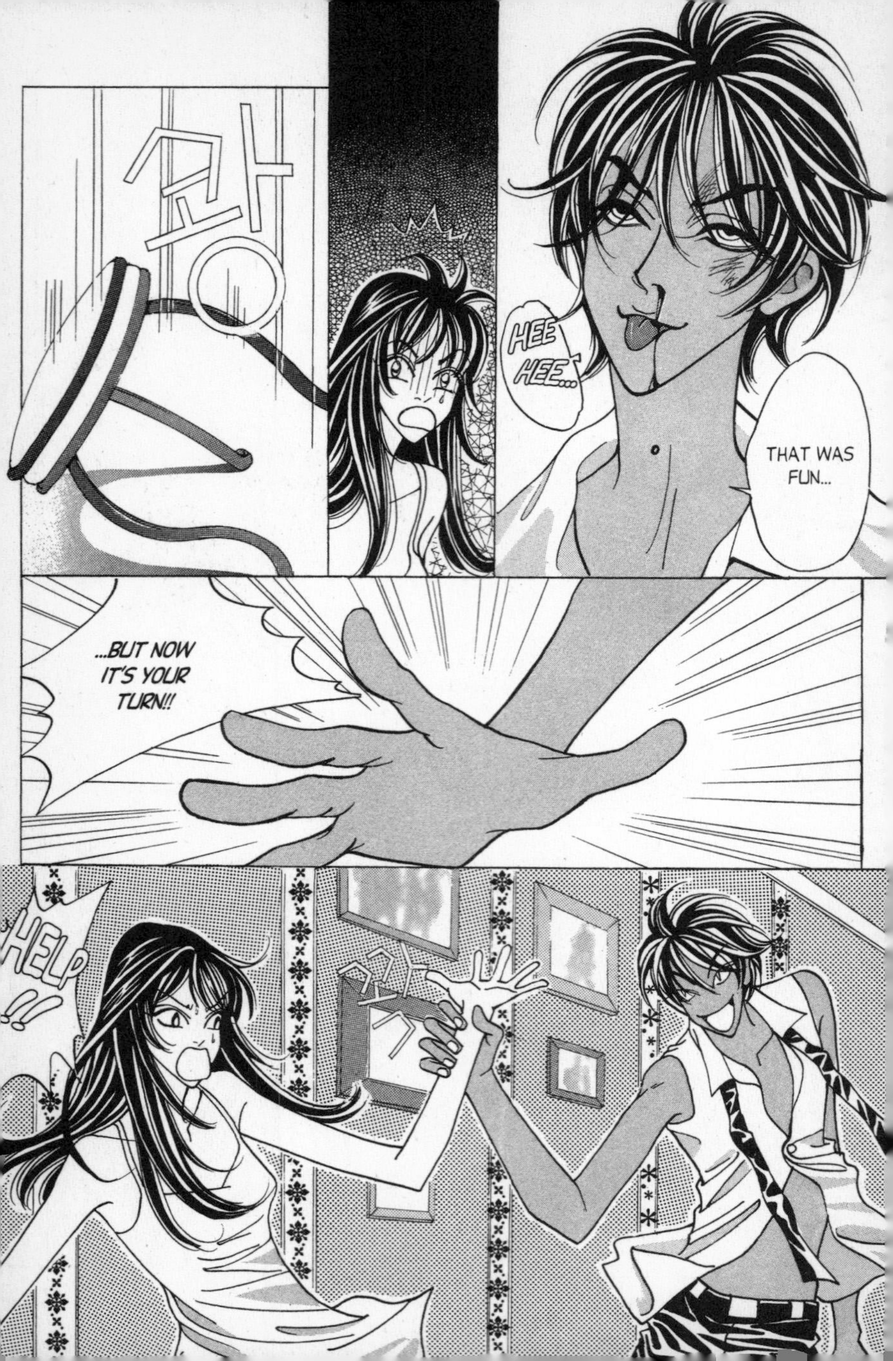
HEE HEE...
THAT WAS FUN...
...BUT NOW IT'S YOUR TURN!!
HELP!!!

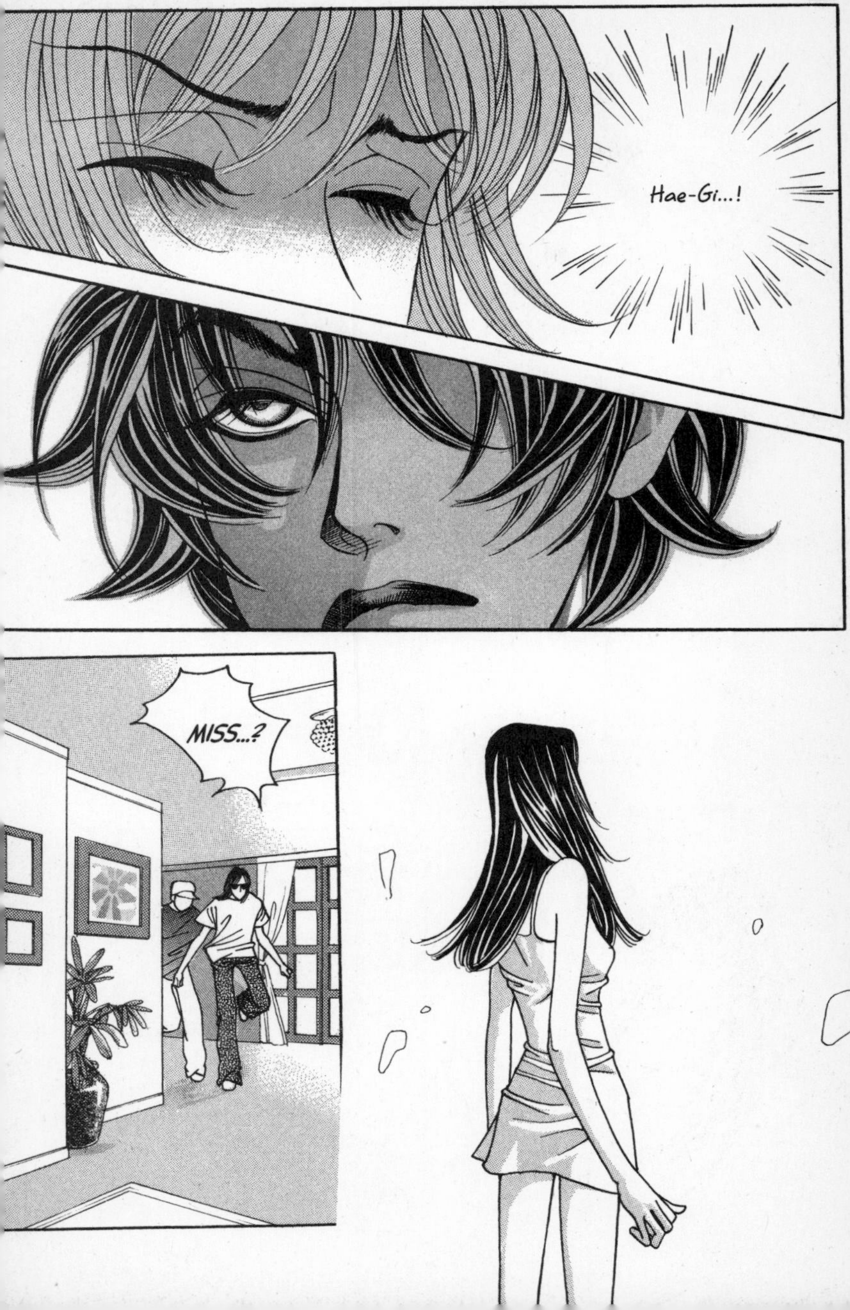
Hae-Gi...!
MISS...?
!

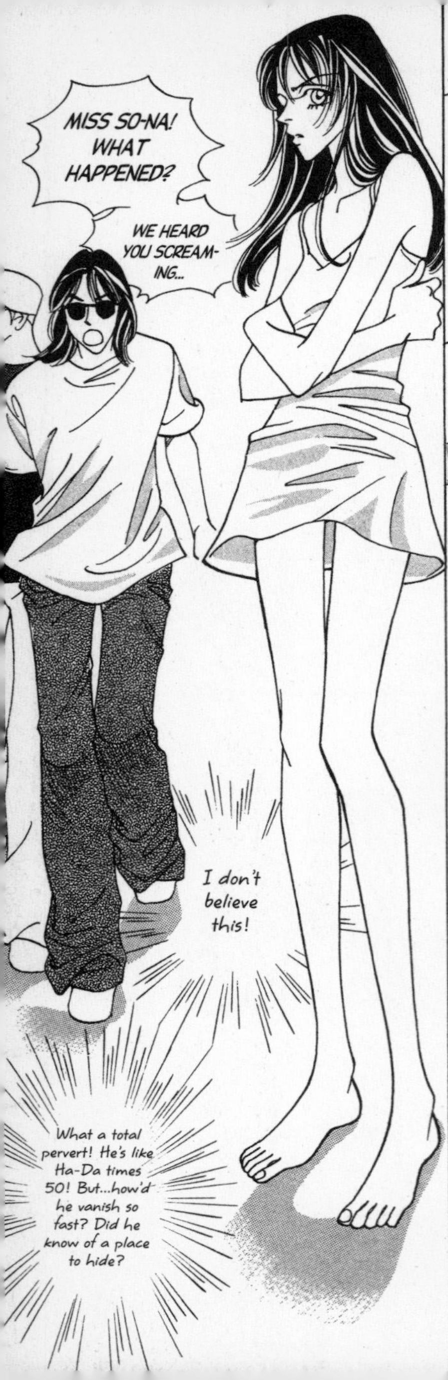
MISS SO-NA! WHAT HAPPENED?
WE HEARD YOU SCREAMING...
I don't believe this!
What a total pervert! He's like Ha-Da times 50! But...how'd he vanish so fast? Did he know of a place to hide?

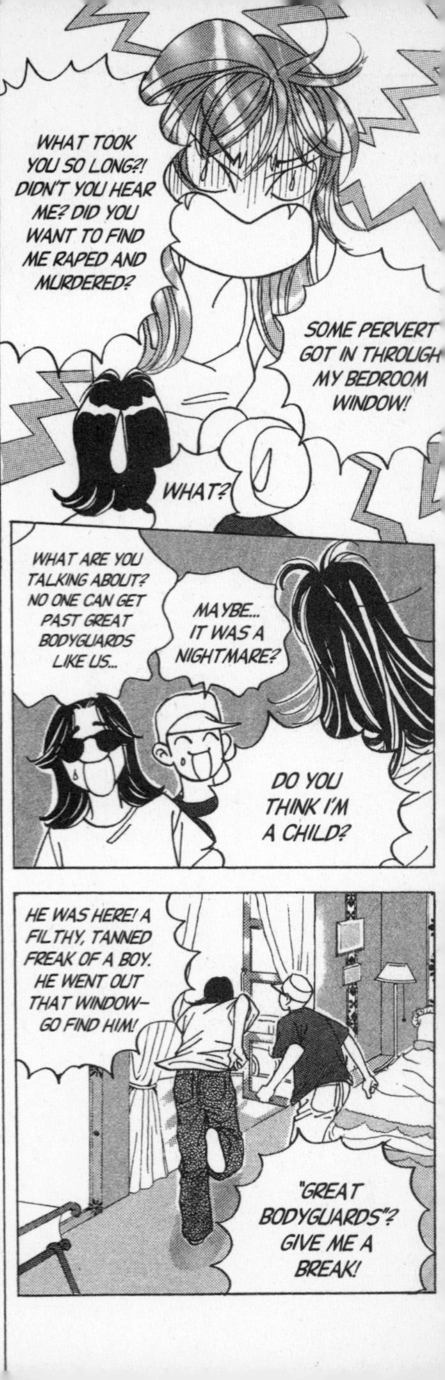
WHAT TOOK YOU SO LONG?! DIDN'T YOU HEAR ME? DID YOU WANT TO FIND ME RAPED AND MURDERED?
SOME PERVERT GOT IN THROUGH MY BEDROOM WINDOW!
WHAT?
WHAT ARE YOU TALKING ABOUT? NO ONE CAN GET PAST GREAT BODYGUARDS LIKE US...
MAYBE... IT WAS A NIGHTMARE?
DO YOU THINK I'M A CHILD?
HE WAS HERE! A FILTHY, TANNED FREAK OF A BOY. HE WENT OUT THAT WINDOW— GO FIND HIM!
"GREAT BODYGUARDS"? GIVE ME A BREAK!

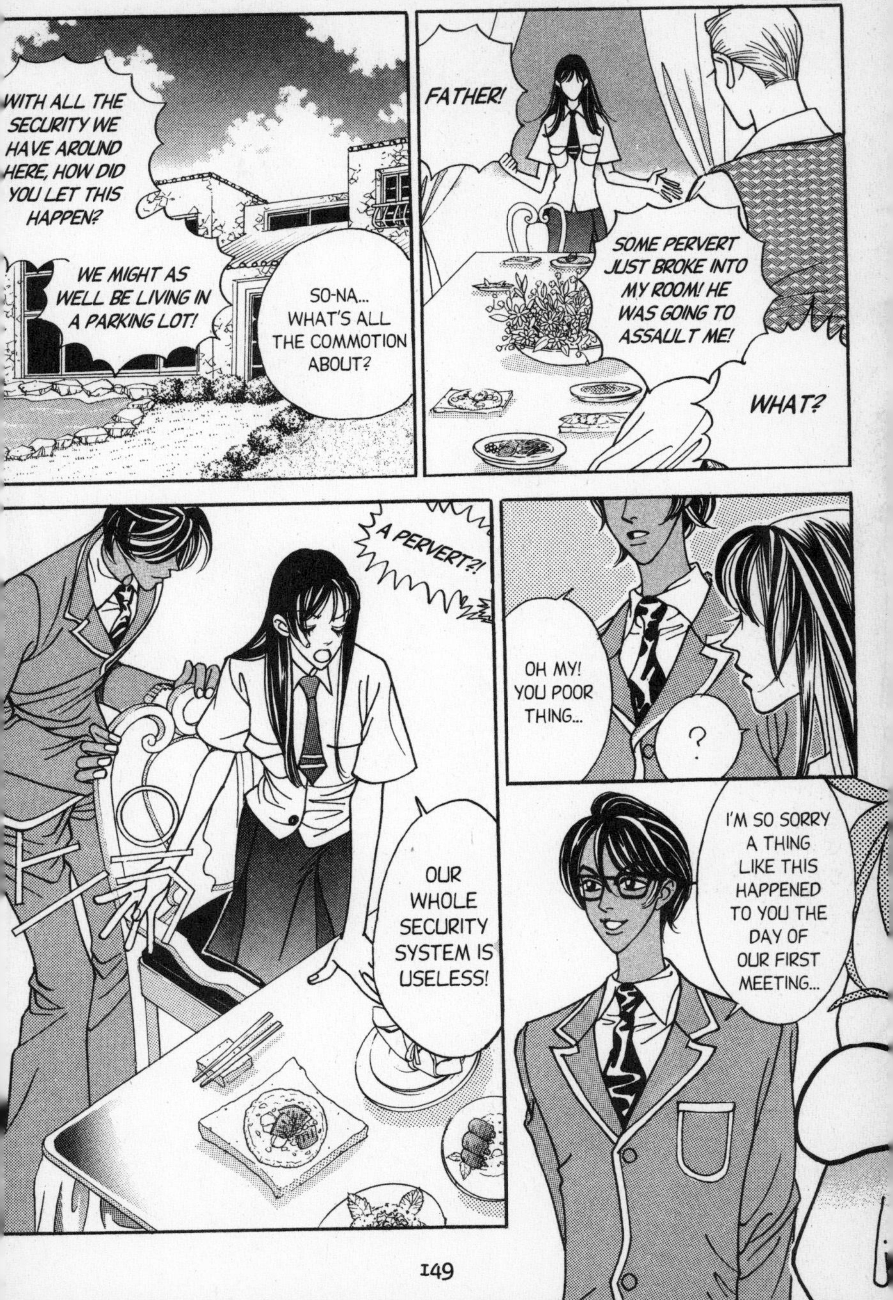
WITH ALL THE SECURITY WE HAVE AROUND HERE, HOW DID YOU LET THIS HAPPEN?
WE MIGHT AS WELL BE LIVING IN A PARKING LOT!
SO-NA... WHAT'S ALL THE COMMOTION ABOUT?
FATHER!
SOME PERVERT JUST BROKE INTO MY ROOM! HE WAS GOING TO ASSAULT ME!
WHAT?
A PERVERT?!
OUR WHOLE SECURITY SYSTEM IS USELESS!
OH MY! YOU POOR THING...
?
I'M SO SORRY A THING LIKE THIS HAPPENED TO YOU THE DAY OF OUR FIRST MEETING...

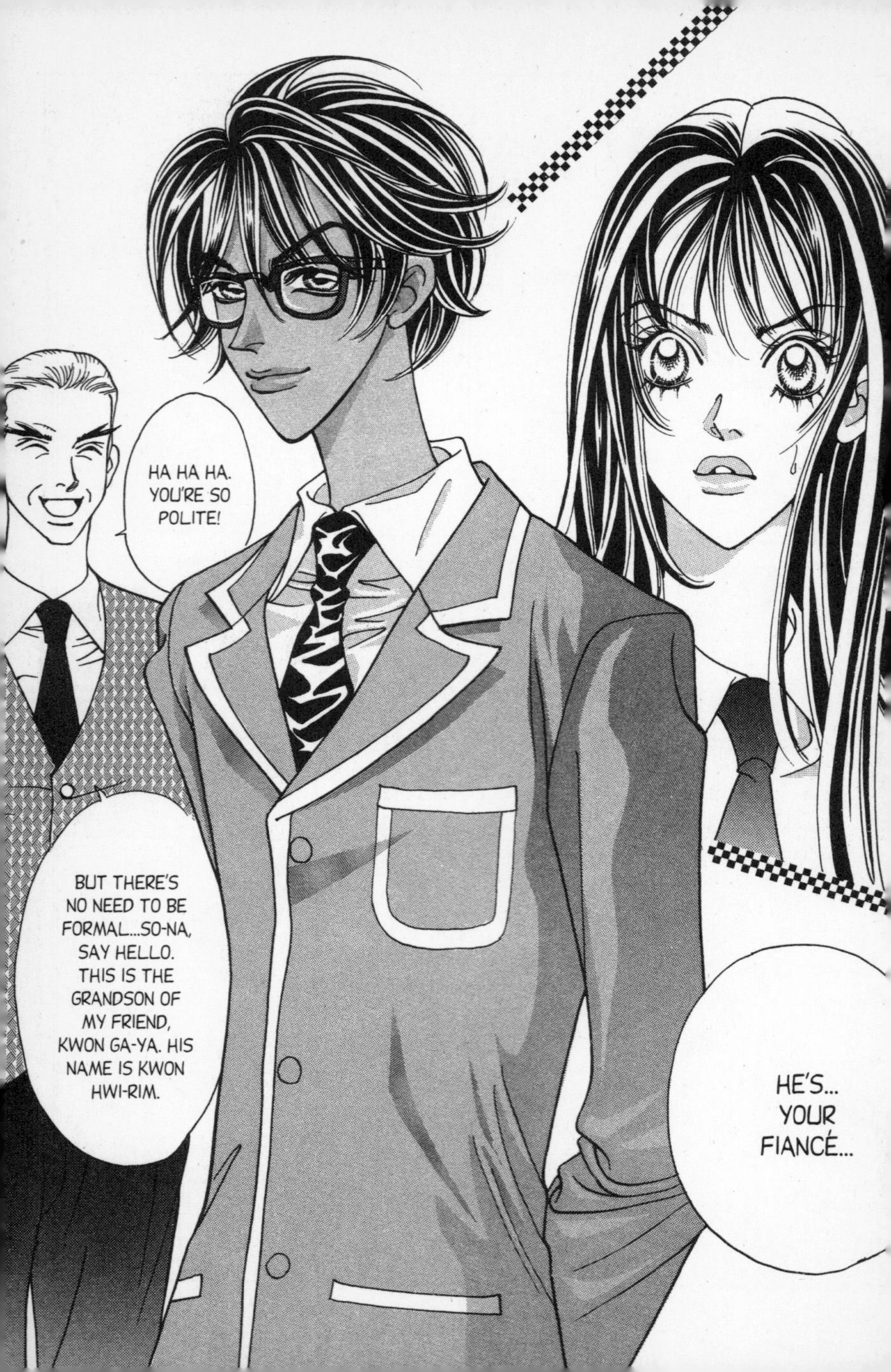
HA HA HA. YOU'RE SO POLITE!
BUT THERE'S NO NEED TO BE FORMAL...SO-NA, SAY HELLO. THIS IS THE GRANDSON OF MY FRIEND, KWON GA-YA. HIS NAME IS KWON HWI-RIM.
HE'S... YOUR FIANCÉ...

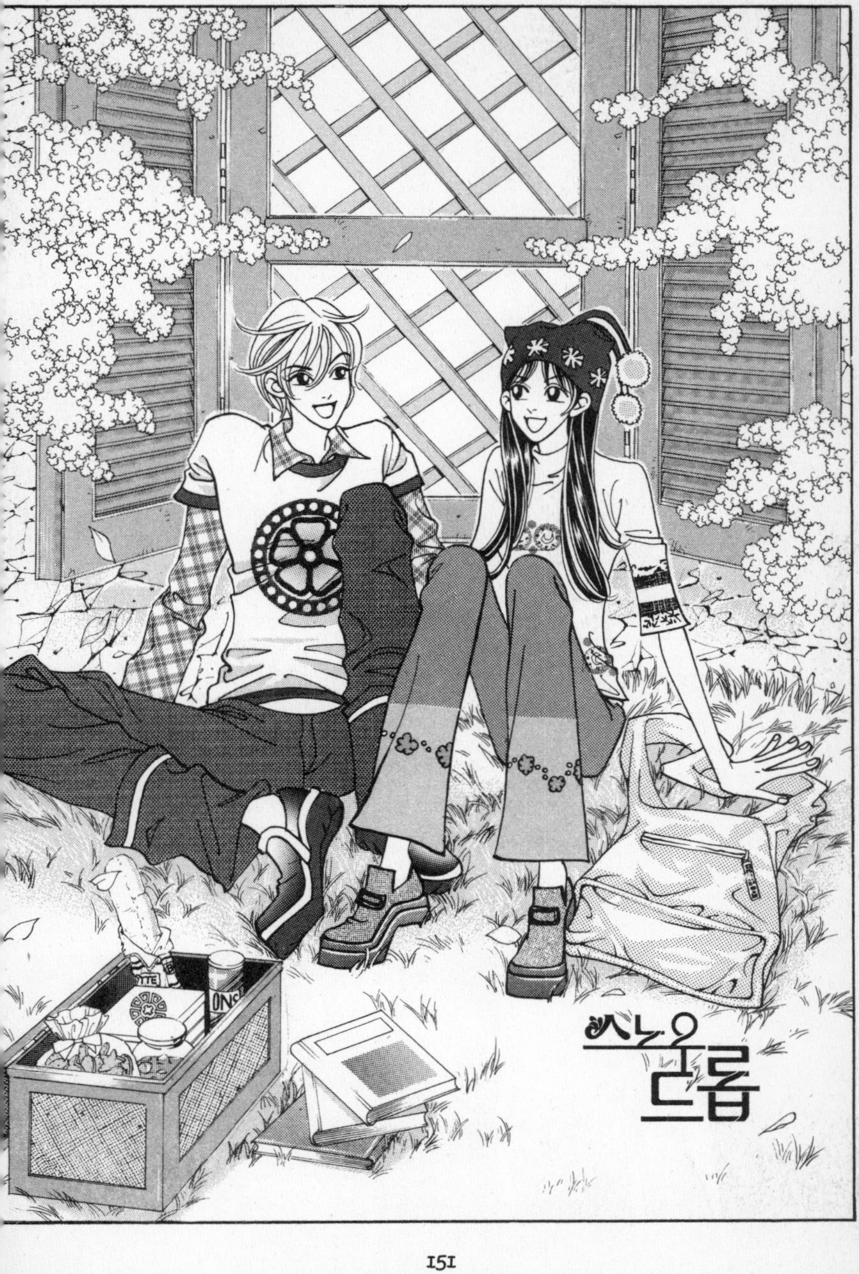
스노우 드롭

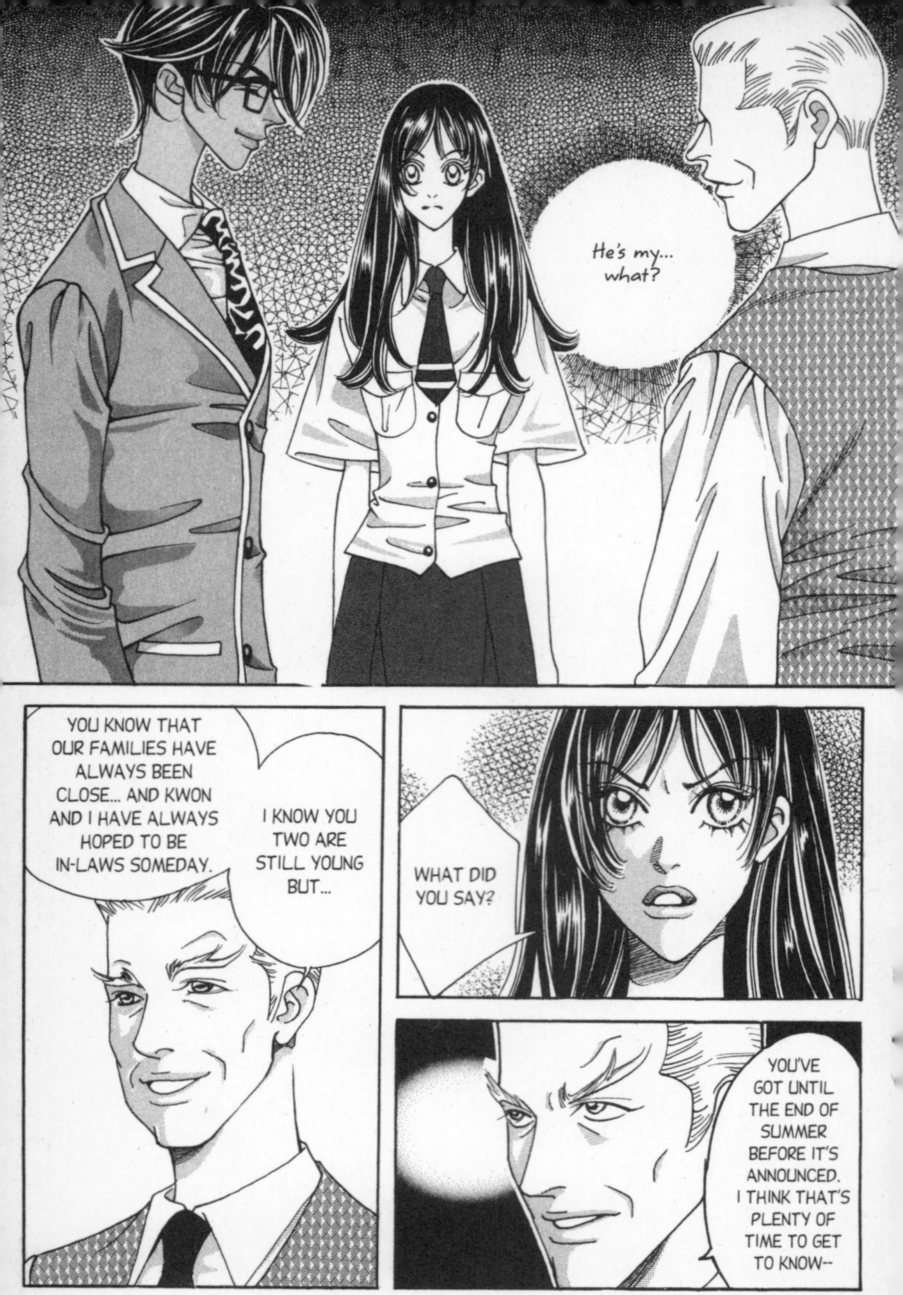
He's my... what?
YOU KNOW THAT OUR FAMILIES HAVE ALWAYS BEEN CLOSE... AND KWON AND I HAVE ALWAYS HOPED TO BE IN-LAWS SOMEDAY.
I KNOW YOU TWO ARE STILL YOUNG BUT...
WHAT DID YOU SAY?
YOU'VE GOT UNTIL THE END OF SUMMER BEFORE IT'S ANNOUNCED. I THINK THAT'S PLENTY OF TIME TO GET TO KNOW--

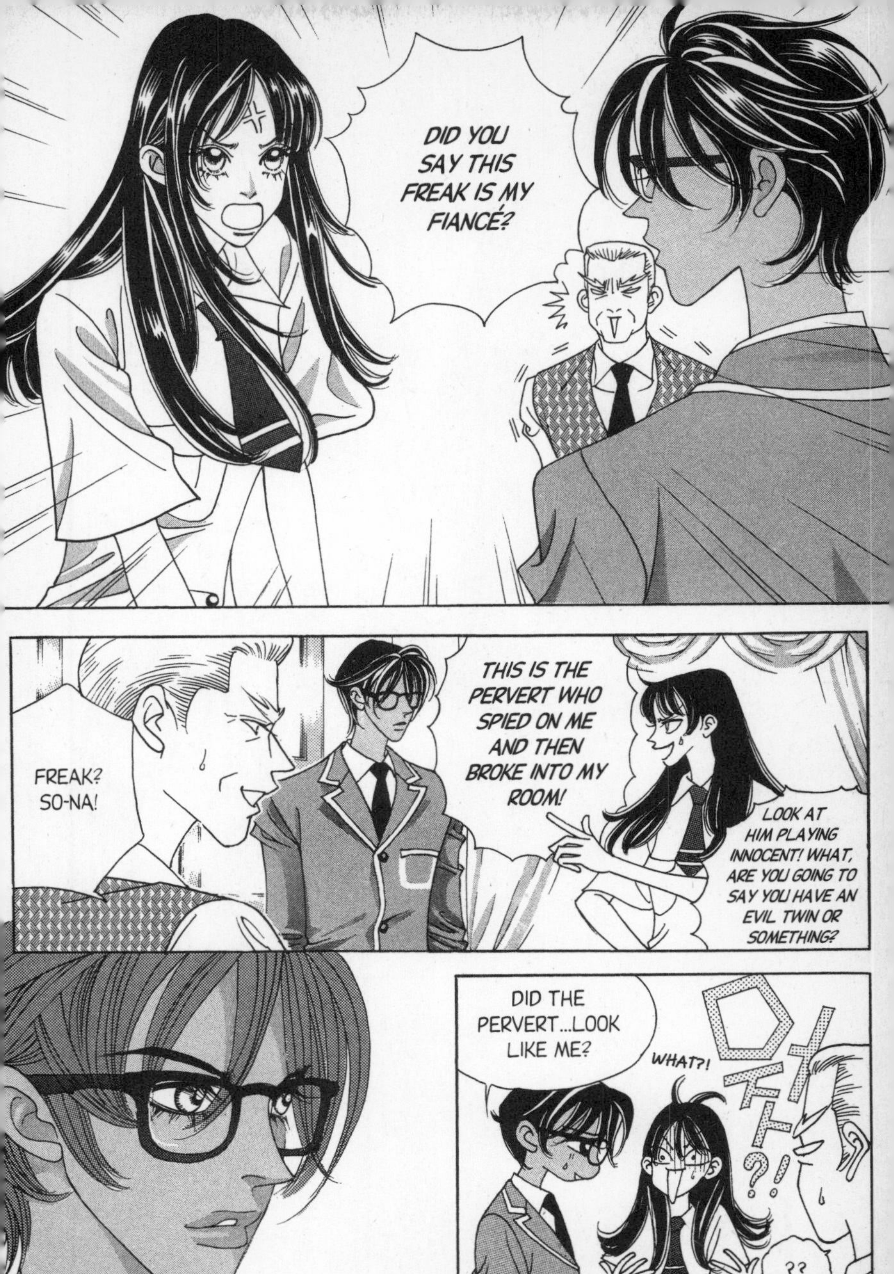
DID YOU SAY THIS FREAK IS MY FIANCÉ?
FREAK? SO-NA!
THIS IS THE PERVERT WHO SPIED ON ME AND THEN BROKE INTO MY ROOM!
LOOK AT HIM PLAYING INNOCENT! WHAT, ARE YOU GOING TO SAY YOU HAVE AN EVIL TWIN OR SOMETHING?
DID THE PERVERT...LOOK LIKE ME?
WHAT?!
?!
??

He didn't look like you, he IS you!

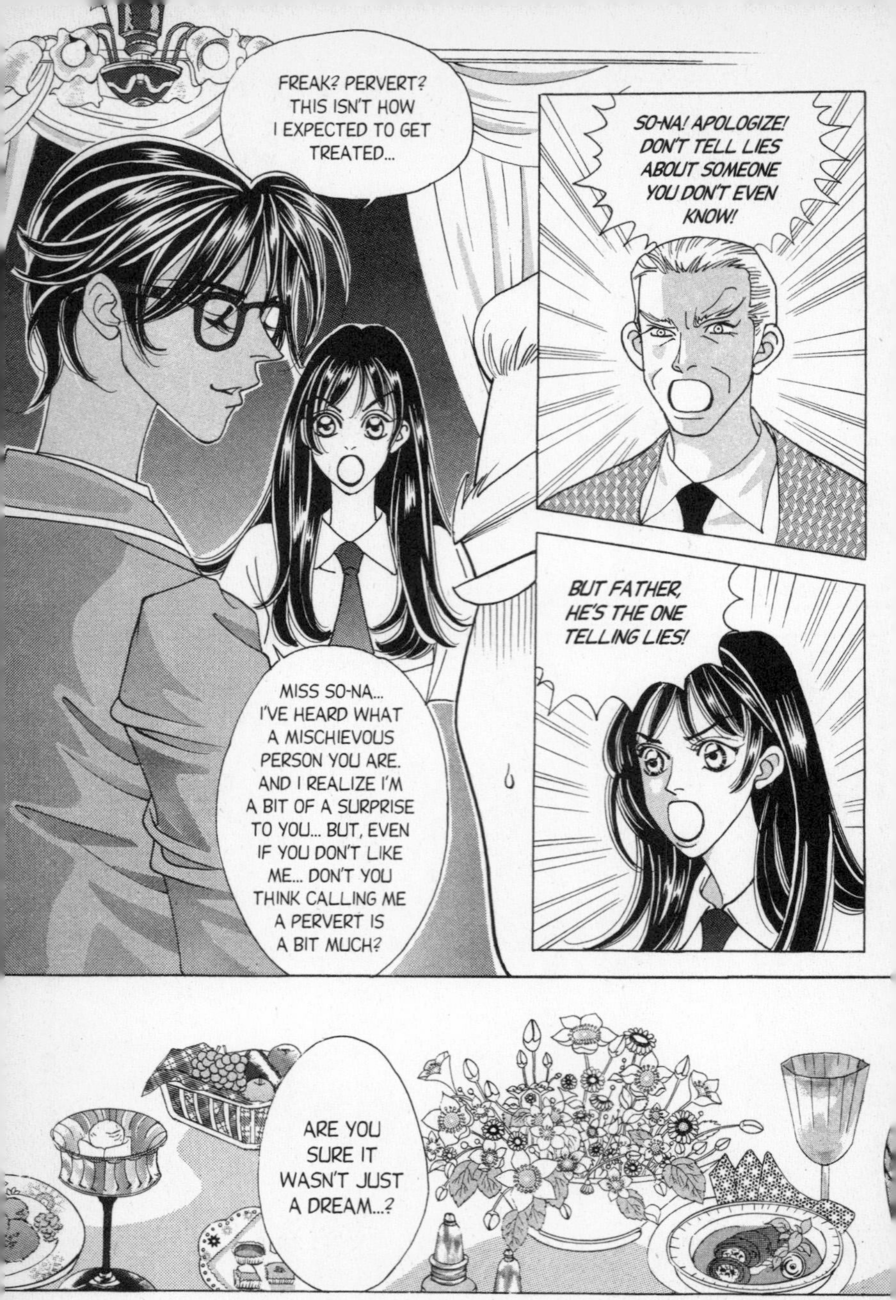
FREAK? PERVERT? THIS ISN'T HOW I EXPECTED TO GET TREATED...
MISS SO-NA... I'VE HEARD WHAT A MISCHIEVOUS PERSON YOU ARE. AND I REALIZE I'M A BIT OF A SURPRISE TO YOU... BUT, EVEN IF YOU DON'T LIKE ME... DON'T YOU THINK CALLING ME A PERVERT IS A BIT MUCH?
SO-NA! APOLOGIZE! DON'T TELL LIES ABOUT SOMEONE YOU DON'T EVEN KNOW!
BUT FATHER, HE'S THE ONE TELLING LIES!
ARE YOU SURE IT WASN'T JUST A DREAM...?

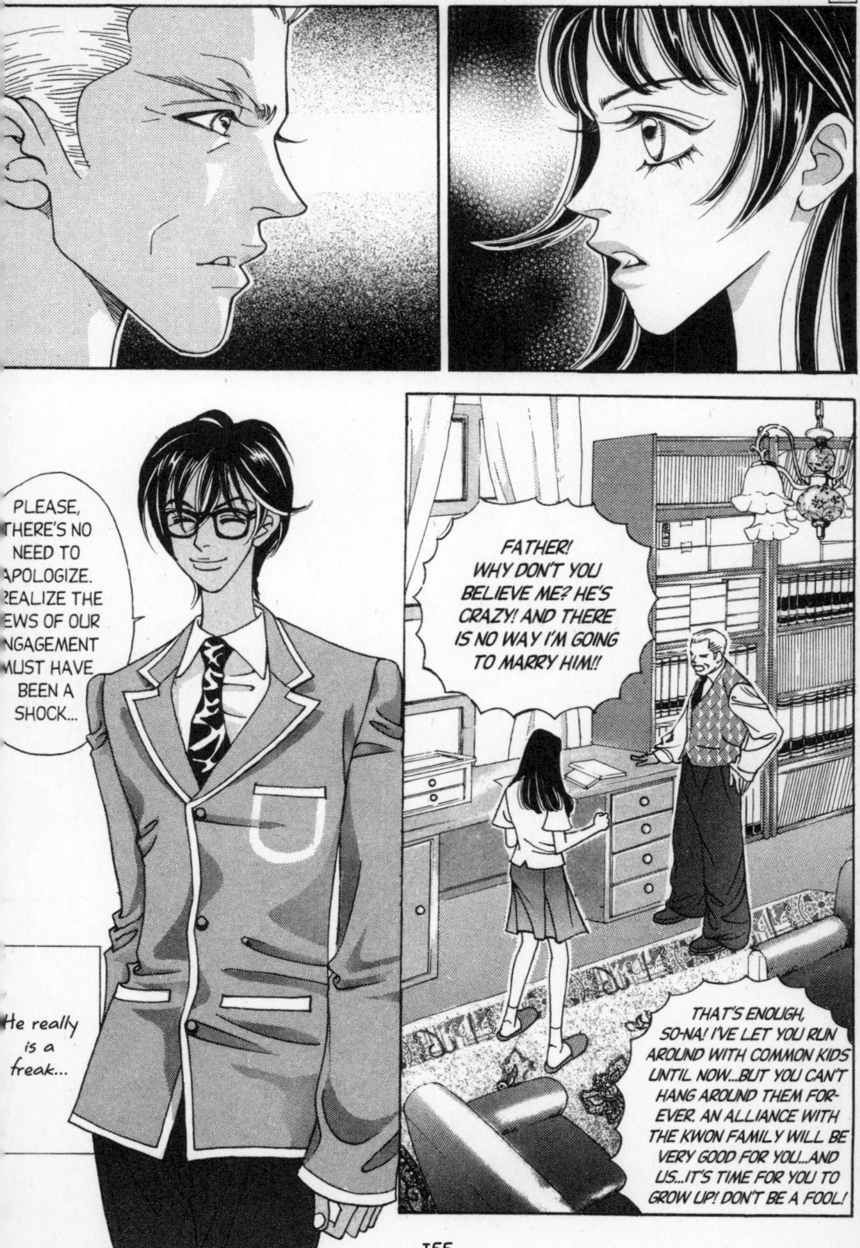
PLEASE, THERE'S NO NEED TO APOLOGIZE. REALIZE THE EWS OF OUR NGAGEMENT MUST HAVE BEEN A SHOCK...
He really is a freak...
FATHER! WHY DON'T YOU BELIEVE ME? HE'S CRAZY! AND THERE IS NO WAY I'M GOING TO MARRY HIM!!
THAT'S ENOUGH, SO-NA! I'VE LET YOU RUN AROUND WITH COMMON KIDS UNTIL NOW...BUT YOU CAN'T HANG AROUND THEM FOR-EVER. AN ALLIANCE WITH THE KWON FAMILY WILL BE VERY GOOD FOR YOU...AND US...IT'S TIME FOR YOU TO GROW UP! DON'T BE A FOOL!

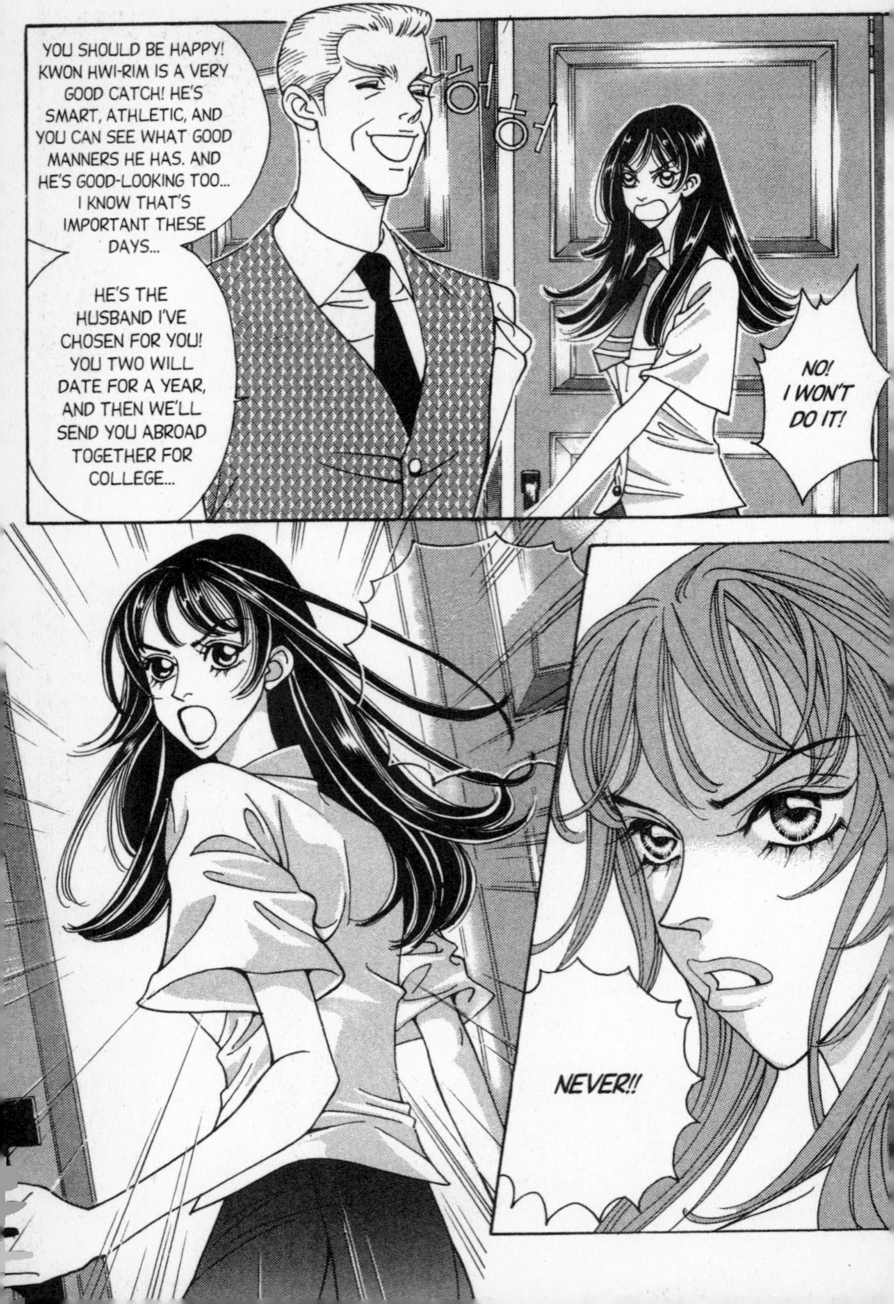
YOU SHOULD BE HAPPY! KWON HWI-RIM IS A VERY GOOD CATCH! HE'S SMART, ATHLETIC, AND YOU CAN SEE WHAT GOOD MANNERS HE HAS. AND HE'S GOOD-LOOKING TOO... I KNOW THAT'S IMPORTANT THESE DAYS...
HE'S THE HUSBAND I'VE CHOSEN FOR YOU! YOU TWO WILL DATE FOR A YEAR, AND THEN WE'LL SEND YOU ABROAD TOGETHER FOR COLLEGE...
헤헤
NO! I WON'T DO IT!
NEVER!!

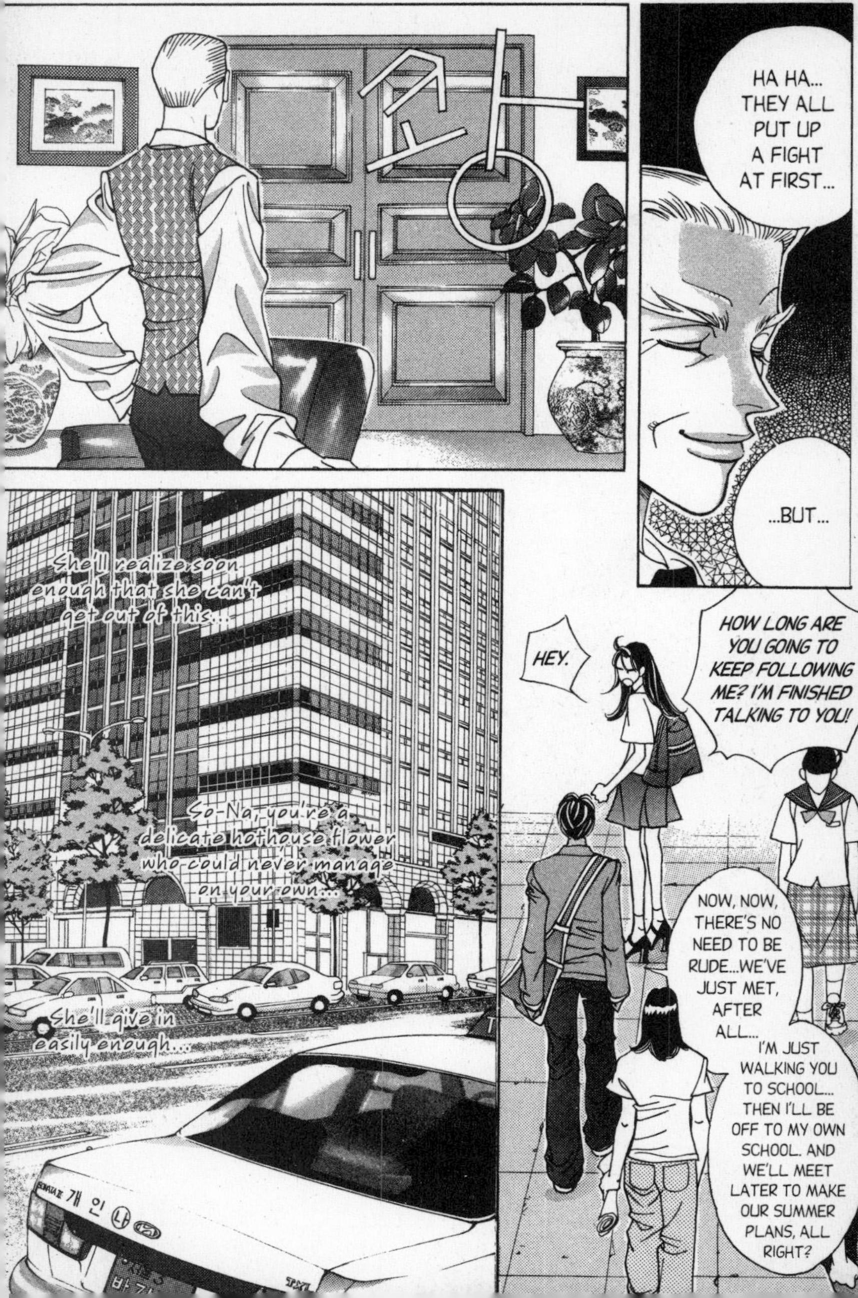
쾅
HA HA... THEY ALL PUT UP A FIGHT AT FIRST...
...BUT...
She'll realize soon enough that she can't get out of this...
So-Na, you're a delicate hothouse flower who could never manage on your own...
She'll give in easily enough...
HEY.
HOW LONG ARE YOU GOING TO KEEP FOLLOWING ME? I'M FINISHED TALKING TO YOU!
NOW, NOW, THERE'S NO NEED TO BE RUDE...WE'VE JUST MET, AFTER ALL...
I'M JUST WALKING YOU TO SCHOOL... THEN I'LL BE OFF TO MY OWN SCHOOL. AND WE'LL MEET LATER TO MAKE OUR SUMMER PLANS, ALL RIGHT?

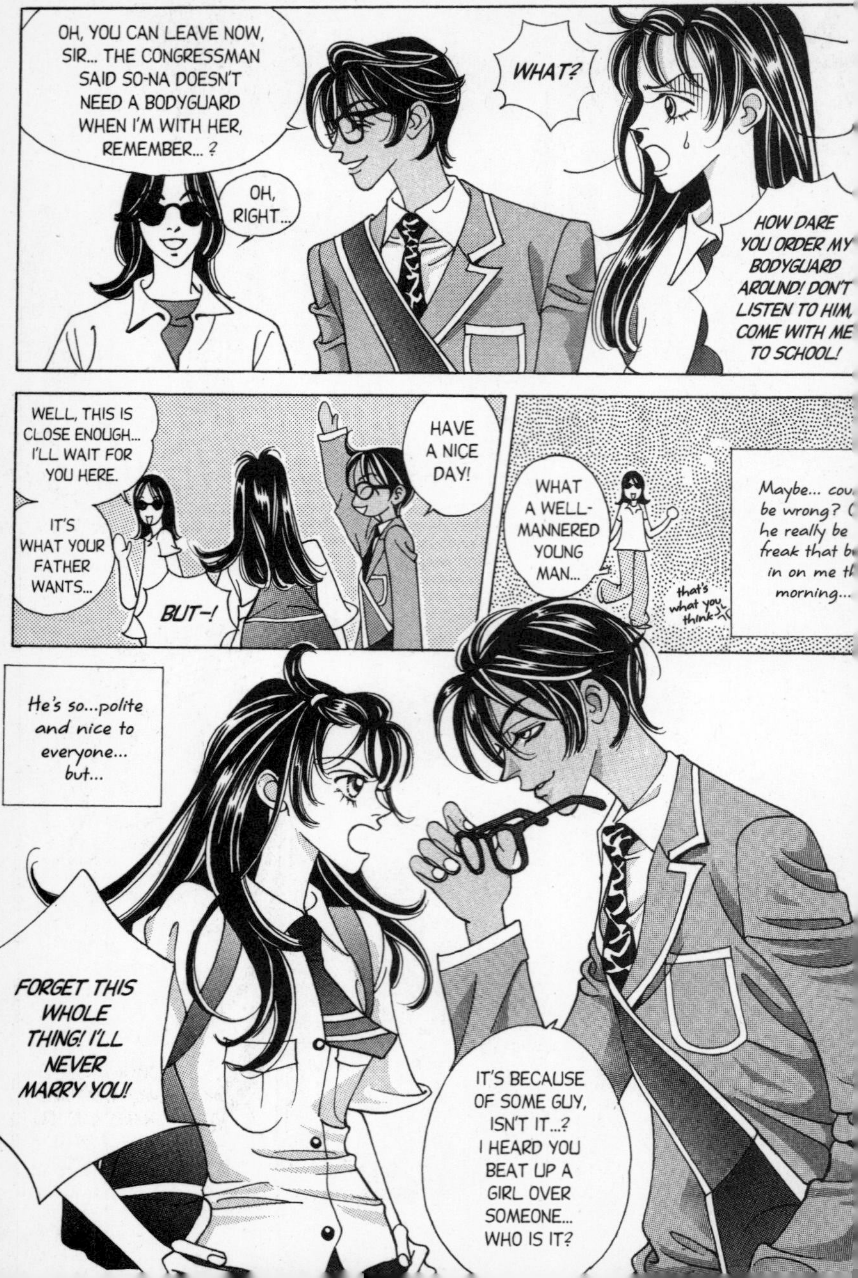
OH, YOU CAN LEAVE NOW, SIR... THE CONGRESSMAN SAID SO-NA DOESN'T NEED A BODYGUARD WHEN I'M WITH HER, REMEMBER...?
OH, RIGHT...
WHAT?
HOW DARE YOU ORDER MY BODYGUARD AROUND! DON'T LISTEN TO HIM, COME WITH ME TO SCHOOL!
WELL, THIS IS CLOSE ENOUGH... I'LL WAIT FOR YOU HERE.
IT'S WHAT YOUR FATHER WANTS...
BUT-!
HAVE A NICE DAY!
WHAT A WELL-MANNERED YOUNG MAN...
that's what you think
Maybe... cou be wrong? C he really be freak that b in on me th morning...
He's so...polite and nice to everyone... but...
FORGET THIS WHOLE THING! I'LL NEVER MARRY YOU!
IT'S BECAUSE OF SOME GUY, ISN'T IT...? I HEARD YOU BEAT UP A GIRL OVER SOMEONE... WHO IS IT?

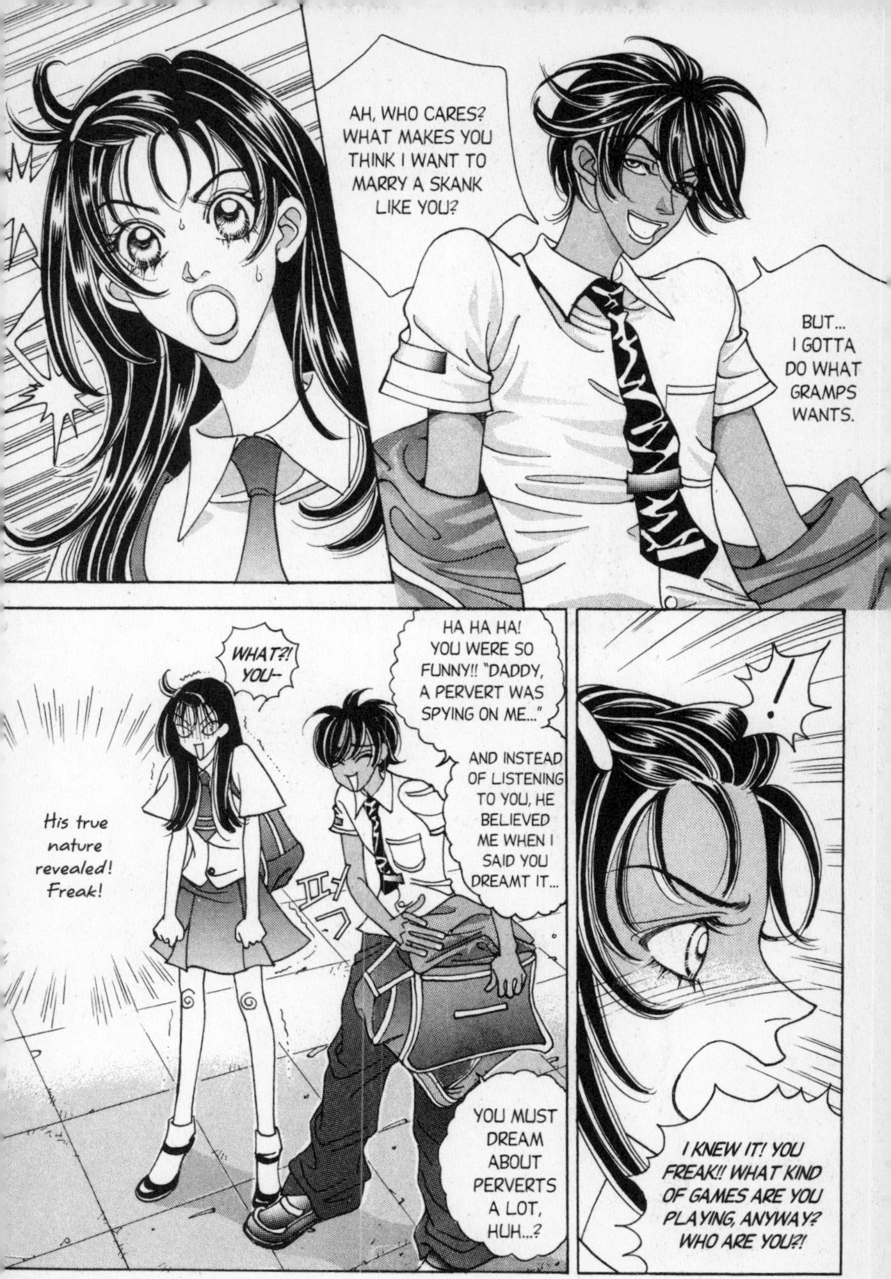
AH, WHO CARES? WHAT MAKES YOU THINK I WANT TO MARRY A SKANK LIKE YOU?
BUT... I GOTTA DO WHAT GRAMPS WANTS.
WHAT?! YOU--
His true nature revealed! Freak!
HA HA HA! YOU WERE SO FUNNY!! "DADDY, A PERVERT WAS SPYING ON ME..."
AND INSTEAD OF LISTENING TO YOU, HE BELIEVED ME WHEN I SAID YOU DREAMT IT...
YOU MUST DREAM ABOUT PERVERTS A LOT, HUH...?
!
I KNEW IT! YOU FREAK!! WHAT KIND OF GAMES ARE YOU PLAYING, ANYWAY? WHO ARE YOU?!

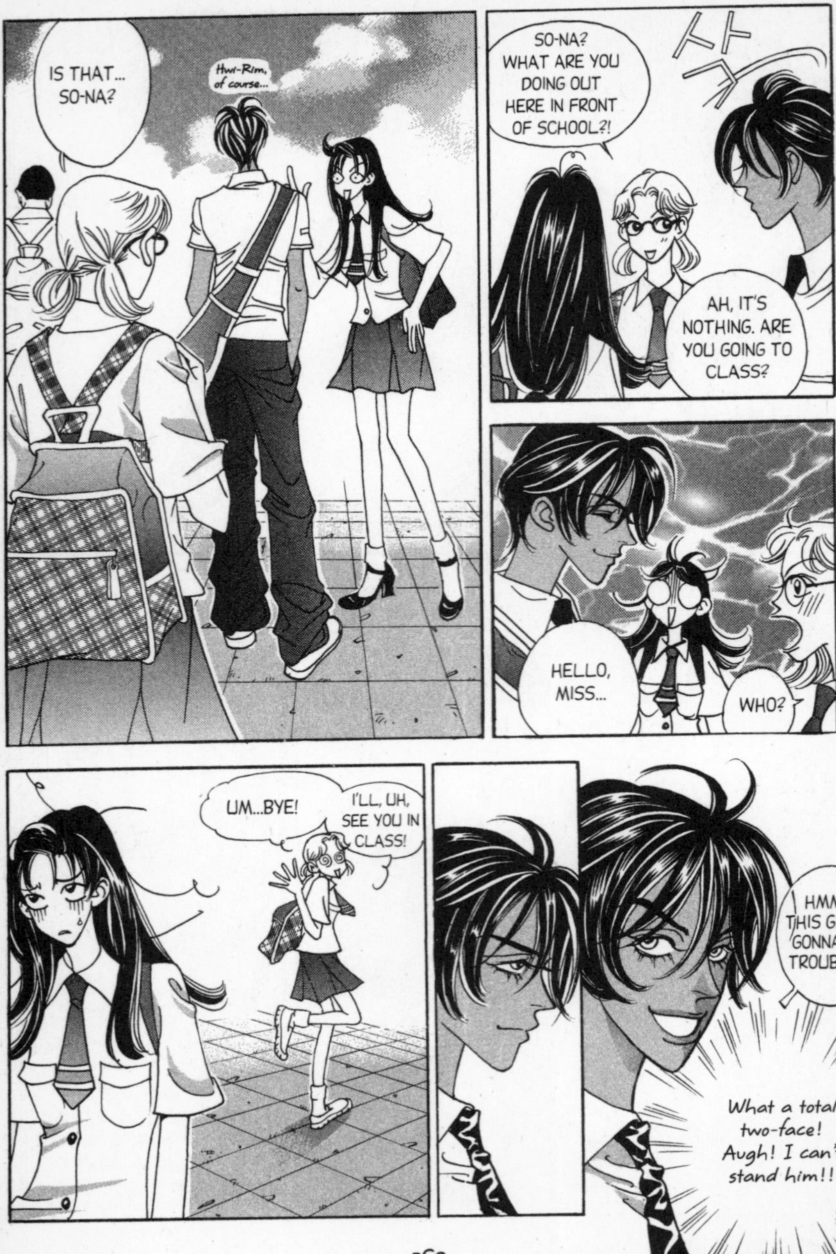
IS THAT... SO-NA?
Hwi-Rim, of course...
SO-NA? WHAT ARE YOU DOING OUT HERE IN FRONT OF SCHOOL?!
AH, IT'S NOTHING. ARE YOU GOING TO CLASS?
HELLO, MISS...
WHO?
UM...BYE!
I'LL, UH, SEE YOU IN CLASS!
HMM... THIS GIRL GONNA B TROUBLE
What a total two-face! Augh! I can't stand him!!

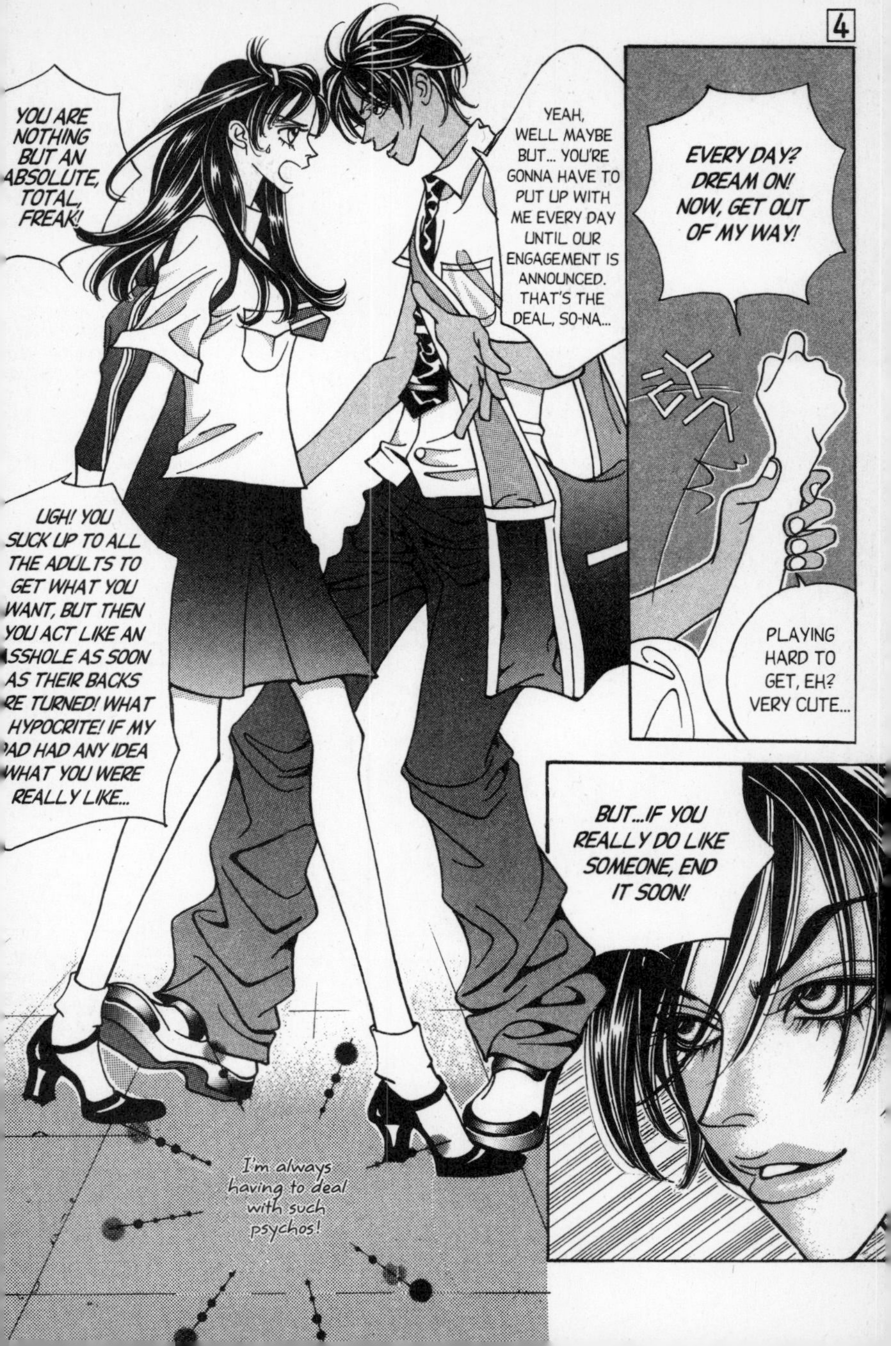
YOU ARE NOTHING BUT AN ABSOLUTE, TOTAL, FREAK!
YEAH, WELL MAYBE BUT... YOU'RE GONNA HAVE TO PUT UP WITH ME EVERY DAY UNTIL OUR ENGAGEMENT IS ANNOUNCED. THAT'S THE DEAL, SO-NA...
UGH! YOU SUCK UP TO ALL THE ADULTS TO GET WHAT YOU WANT, BUT THEN YOU ACT LIKE AN SSHOLE AS SOON AS THEIR BACKS RE TURNED! WHAT HYPOCRITE! IF MY AD HAD ANY IDEA WHAT YOU WERE REALLY LIKE...
I'm always having to deal with such psychos!
EVERY DAY? DREAM ON! NOW, GET OUT OF MY WAY!
PLAYING HARD TO GET, EH? VERY CUTE...
BUT...IF YOU REALLY DO LIKE SOMEONE, END IT SOON!

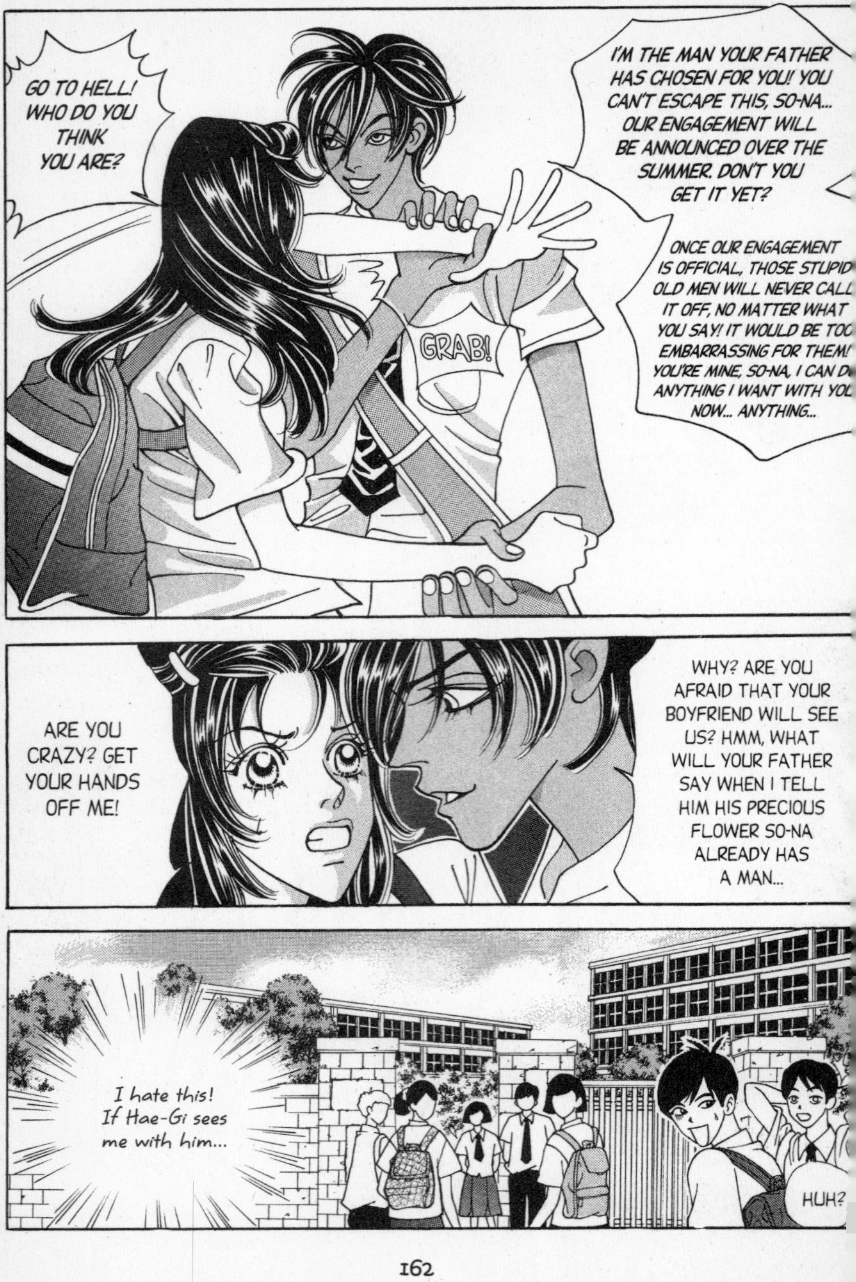
GO TO HELL! WHO DO YOU THINK YOU ARE?
I'M THE MAN YOUR FATHER HAS CHOSEN FOR YOU! YOU CAN'T ESCAPE THIS, SO-NA... OUR ENGAGEMENT WILL BE ANNOUNCED OVER THE SUMMER. DON'T YOU GET IT YET?
ONCE OUR ENGAGEMENT IS OFFICIAL, THOSE STUPID OLD MEN WILL NEVER CALL IT OFF, NO MATTER WHAT YOU SAY! IT WOULD BE TOO EMBARRASSING FOR THEM! YOU'RE MINE, SO-NA, I CAN D ANYTHING I WANT WITH YO NOW... ANYTHING...
GRAB!
ARE YOU CRAZY? GET YOUR HANDS OFF ME!
WHY? ARE YOU AFRAID THAT YOUR BOYFRIEND WILL SEE US? HMM, WHAT WILL YOUR FATHER SAY WHEN I TELL HIM HIS PRECIOUS FLOWER SO-NA ALREADY HAS A MAN...
I hate this! If Hae-Gi sees me with him...
HUH?

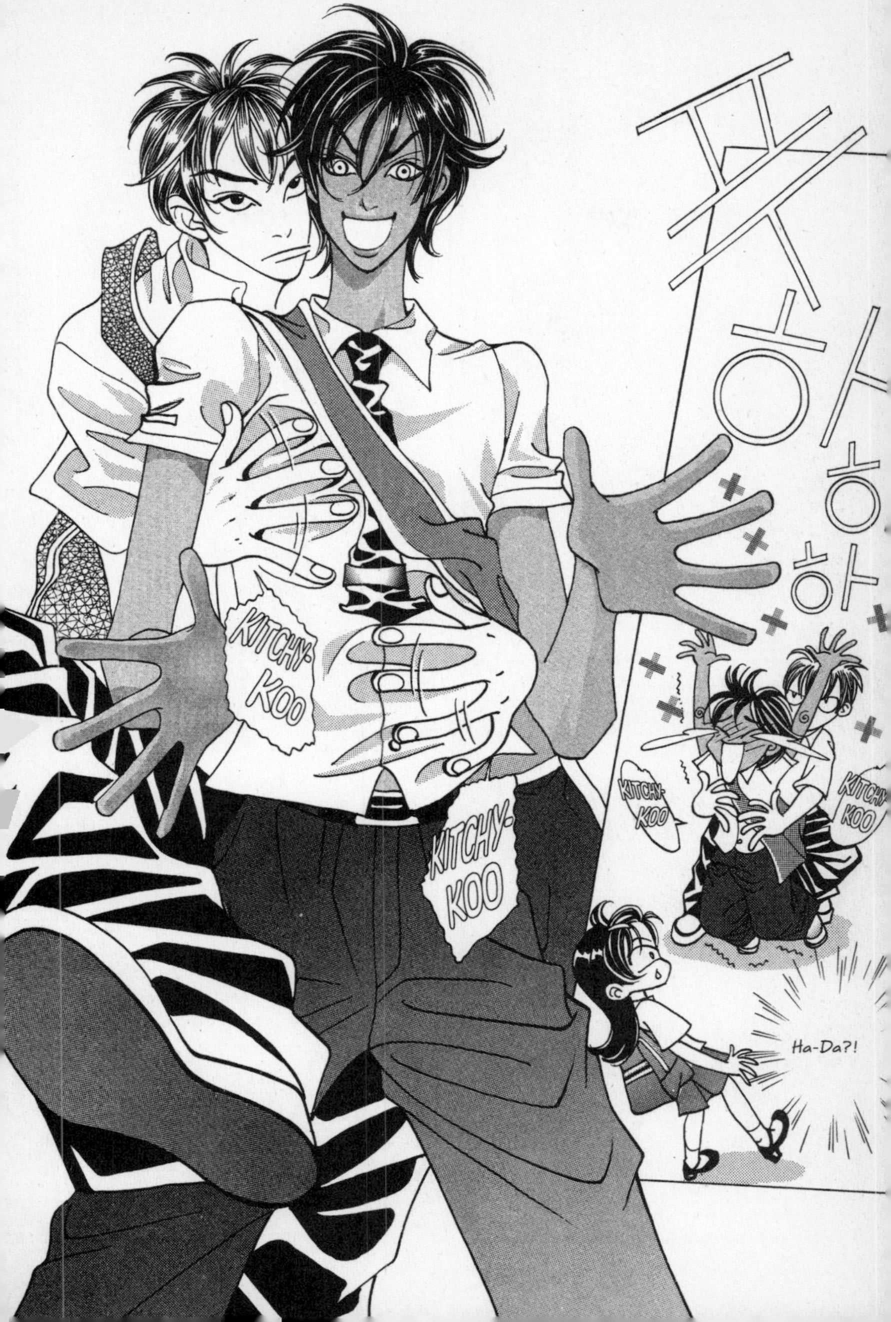
KITCHY-KOO
KITCHY-KOO
하하하
KITCHY-KOO
KITCHY-KOO
Ha-Da?!

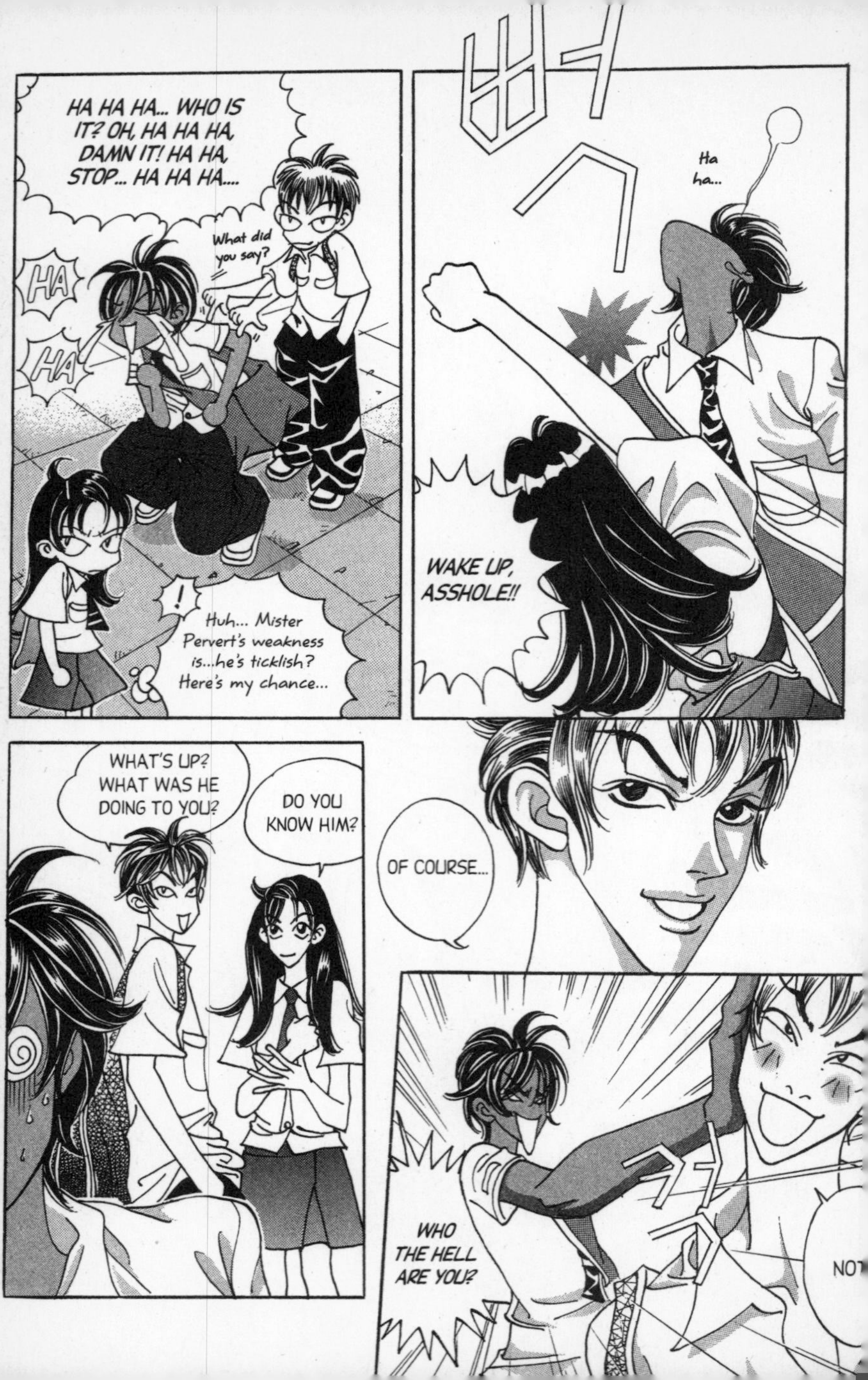
HA HA HA... WHO IS IT? OH, HA HA HA, DAMN IT! HA HA, STOP... HA HA HA....
What did you say?
HA
HA
!
Huh... Mister Pervert's weakness is...he's ticklish? Here's my chance...
Ha ha...
WAKE UP, ASSHOLE!!
WHAT'S UP? WHAT WAS HE DOING TO YOU?
DO YOU KNOW HIM?
OF COURSE...
WHO THE HELL ARE YOU?
NOT

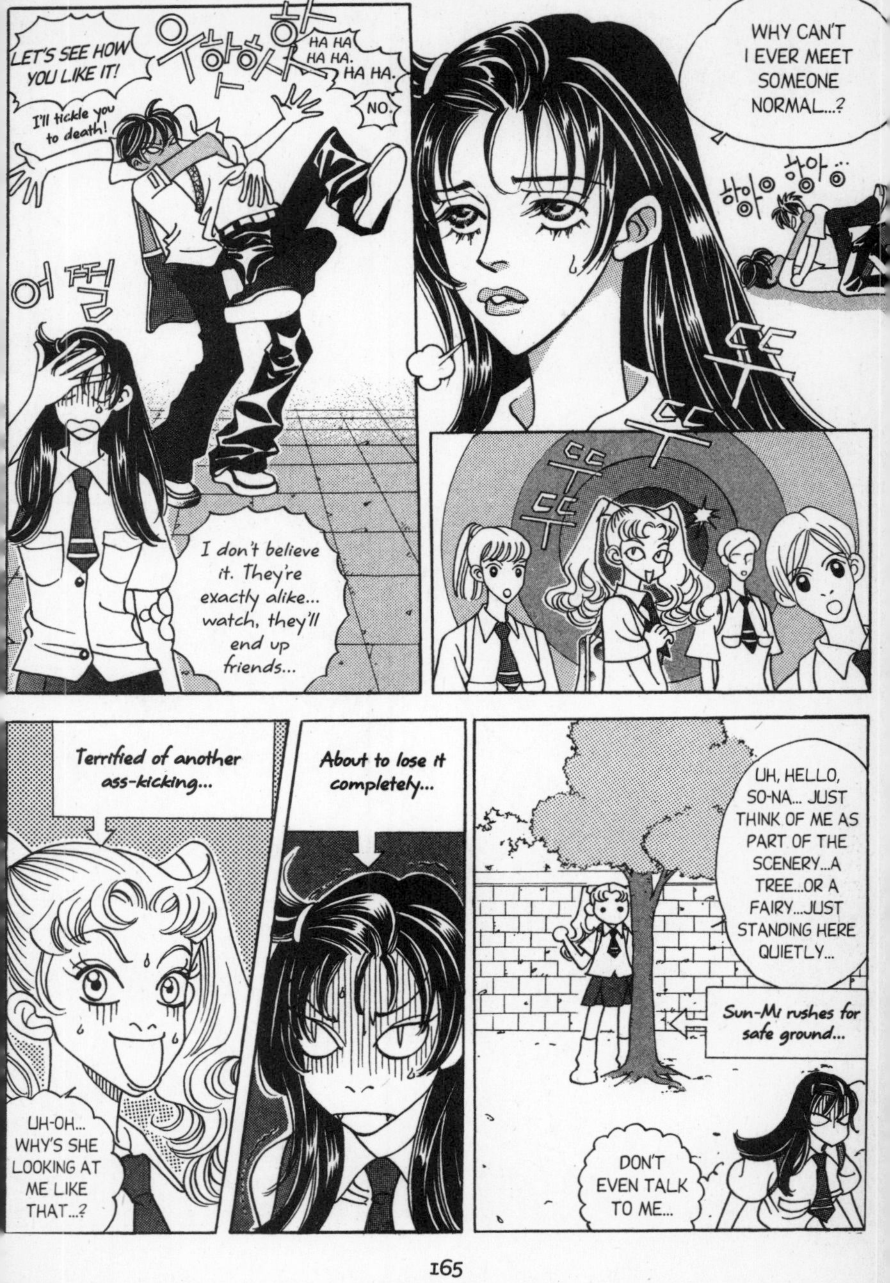
LET'S SEE HOW YOU LIKE IT!
우하하핫
HA HA HA HA. HA HA.
NO.
I'll tickle you to death!
어쩔
I don't believe it. They're exactly alike... watch, they'll end up friends...
WHY CAN'T I EVER MEET SOMEONE NORMAL...?
항아 항아...
뚜
뚜
뚜
뚜
Terrified of another ass-kicking...
UH-OH... WHY'S SHE LOOKING AT ME LIKE THAT...?
About to lose it completely...
UH, HELLO, SO-NA... JUST THINK OF ME AS PART OF THE SCENERY...A TREE...OR A FAIRY...JUST STANDING HERE QUIETLY...
Sun-Mi rushes for safe ground...
DON'T EVEN TALK TO ME...

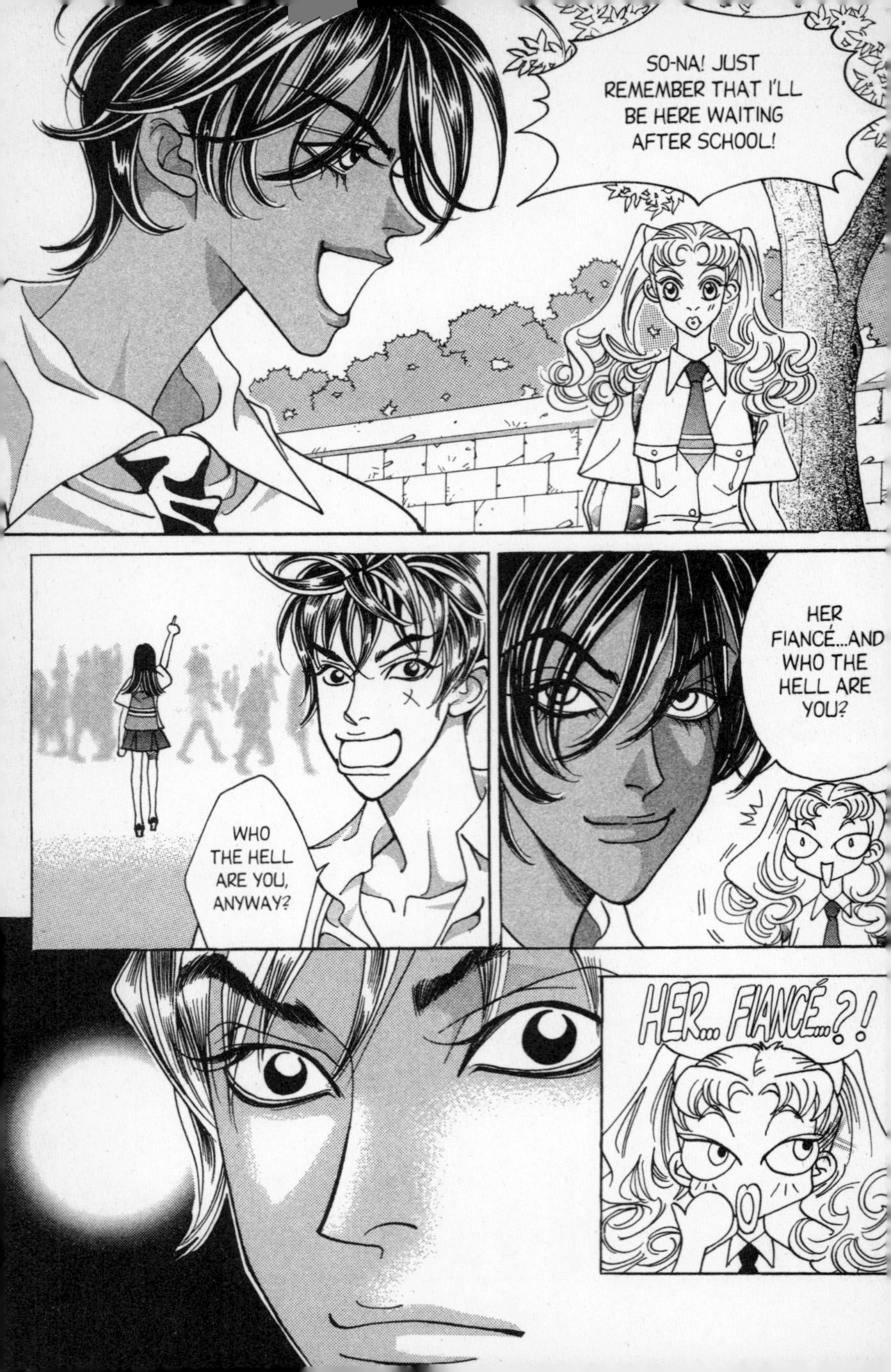
SO-NA! JUST REMEMBER THAT I'LL BE HERE WAITING AFTER SCHOOL!
WHO THE HELL ARE YOU, ANYWAY?
HER FIANCÉ...AND WHO THE HELL ARE YOU?
HER... FIANCÉ...?!

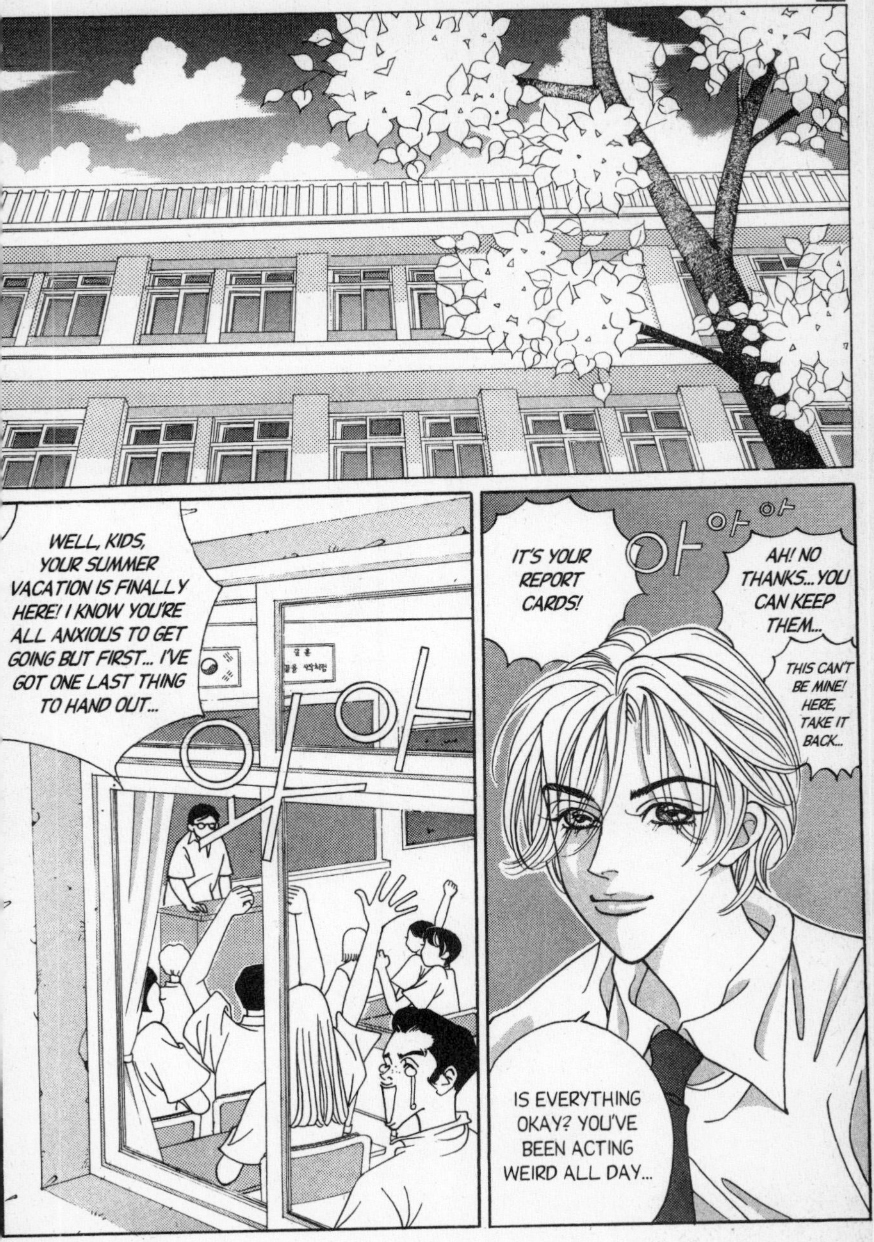
WELL, KIDS, YOUR SUMMER VACATION IS FINALLY HERE! I KNOW YOU'RE ALL ANXIOUS TO GET GOING BUT FIRST... I'VE GOT ONE LAST THING TO HAND OUT...
아 아
IT'S YOUR REPORT CARDS!
아 아 아
AH! NO THANKS...YOU CAN KEEP THEM...
THIS CAN'T BE MINE! HERE, TAKE IT BACK...
IS EVERYTHING OKAY? YOU'VE BEEN ACTING WEIRD ALL DAY...

I can't tell him the truth...
that in this day and age,
I have an arranged marriage...

I'm going to fight it but...
I don't know how yet...

Hae-Gi...I can't cause any more
worry for you after all that
you've been through...

You still have so much
on your shoulders...

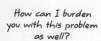

IT'S
NOTHING...

How can I burden
you with this problem
as well?

...and I just wanted to
spend the summer
with you... going to
the beach...and...

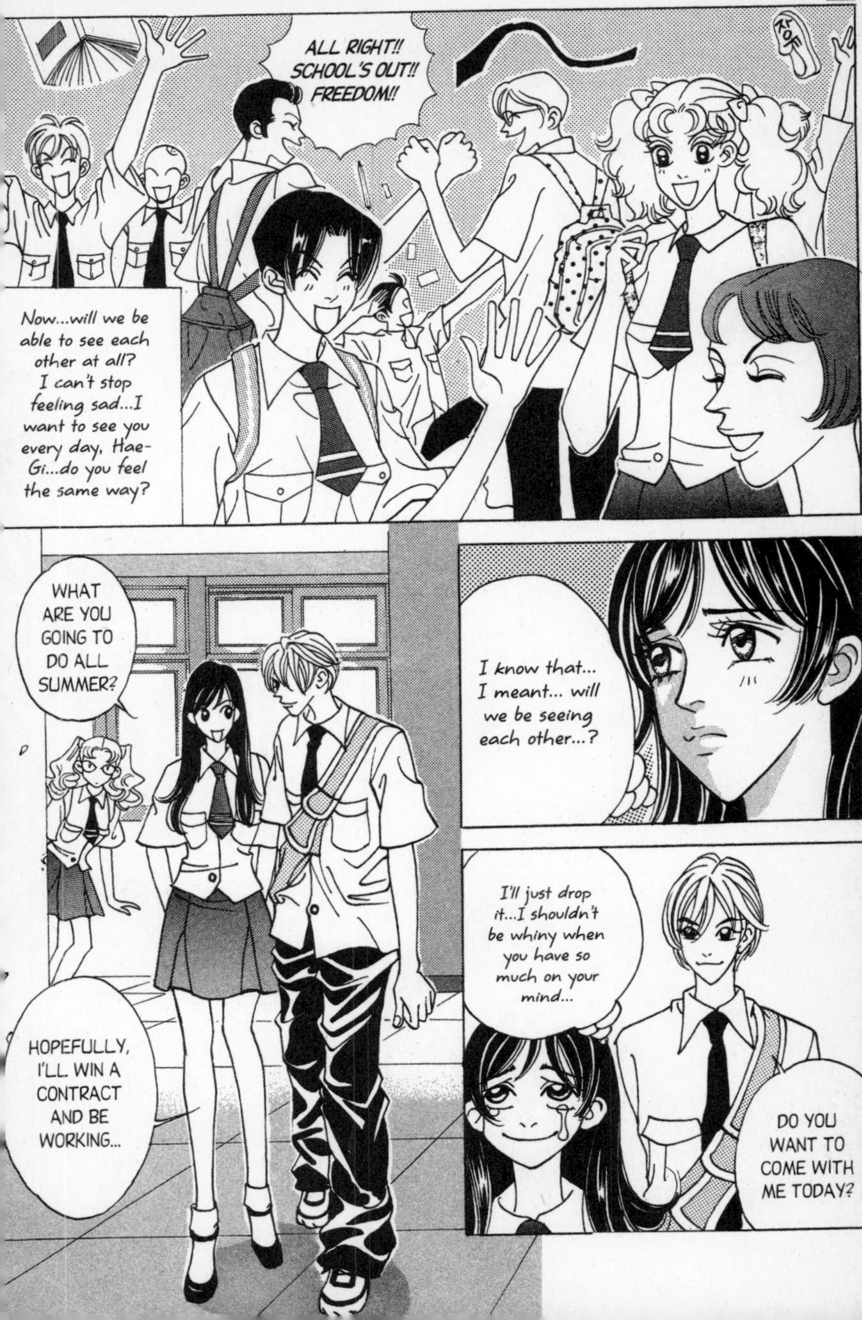
ALL RIGHT!! SCHOOL'S OUT!! FREEDOM!!
자유
Now...will we be able to see each other at all? I can't stop feeling sad...I want to see you every day, Hae-Gi...do you feel the same way?
WHAT ARE YOU GOING TO DO ALL SUMMER?
HOPEFULLY, I'LL WIN A CONTRACT AND BE WORKING...
I know that... I meant... will we be seeing each other...?
I'll just drop it...I shouldn't be whiny when you have so much on your mind...
DO YOU WANT TO COME WITH ME TODAY?

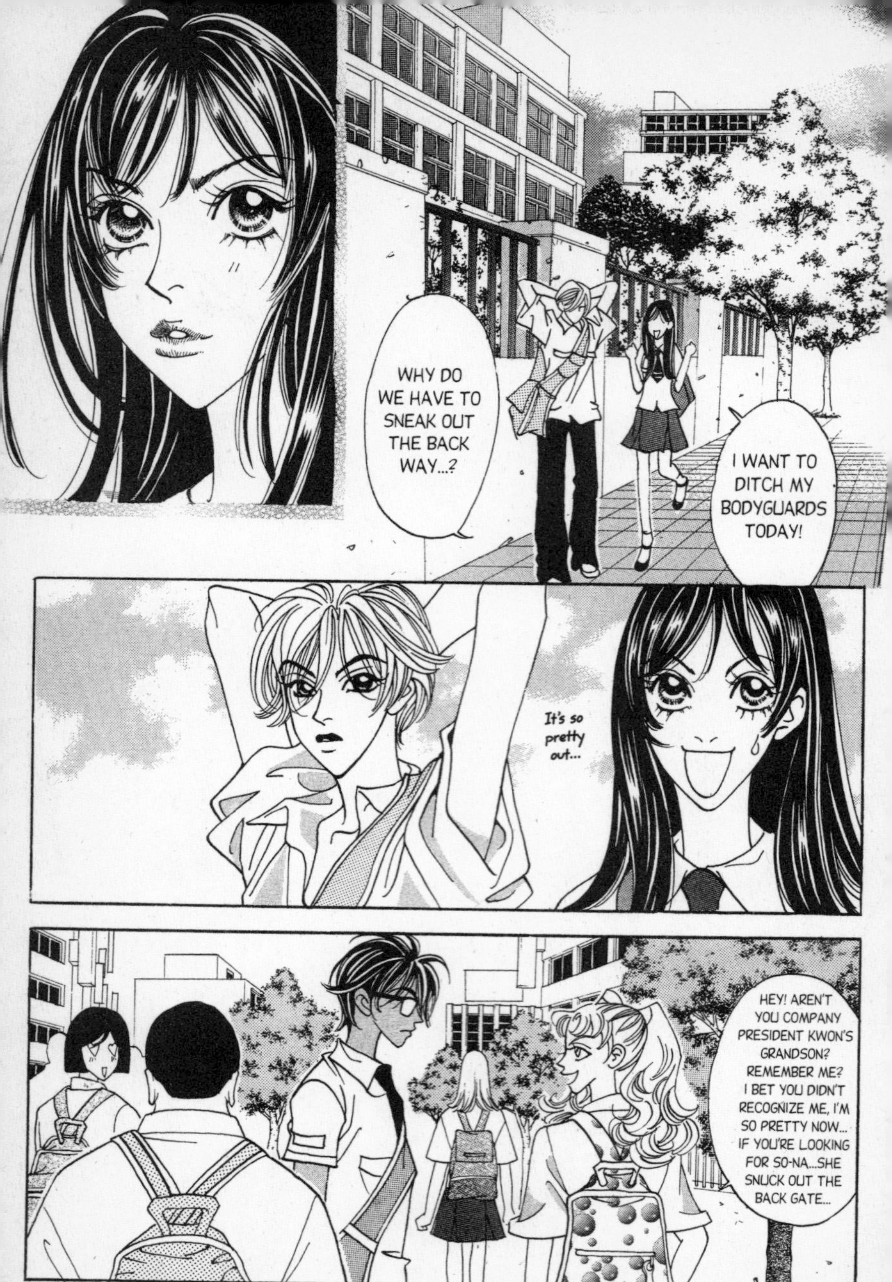
WHY DO WE HAVE TO SNEAK OUT THE BACK WAY...?
I WANT TO DITCH MY BODYGUARDS TODAY!
It's so pretty out...
HEY! AREN'T YOU COMPANY PRESIDENT KWON'S GRANDSON? REMEMBER ME? I BET YOU DIDN'T RECOGNIZE ME, I'M SO PRETTY NOW... IF YOU'RE LOOKING FOR SO-NA...SHE SNUCK OUT THE BACK GATE...

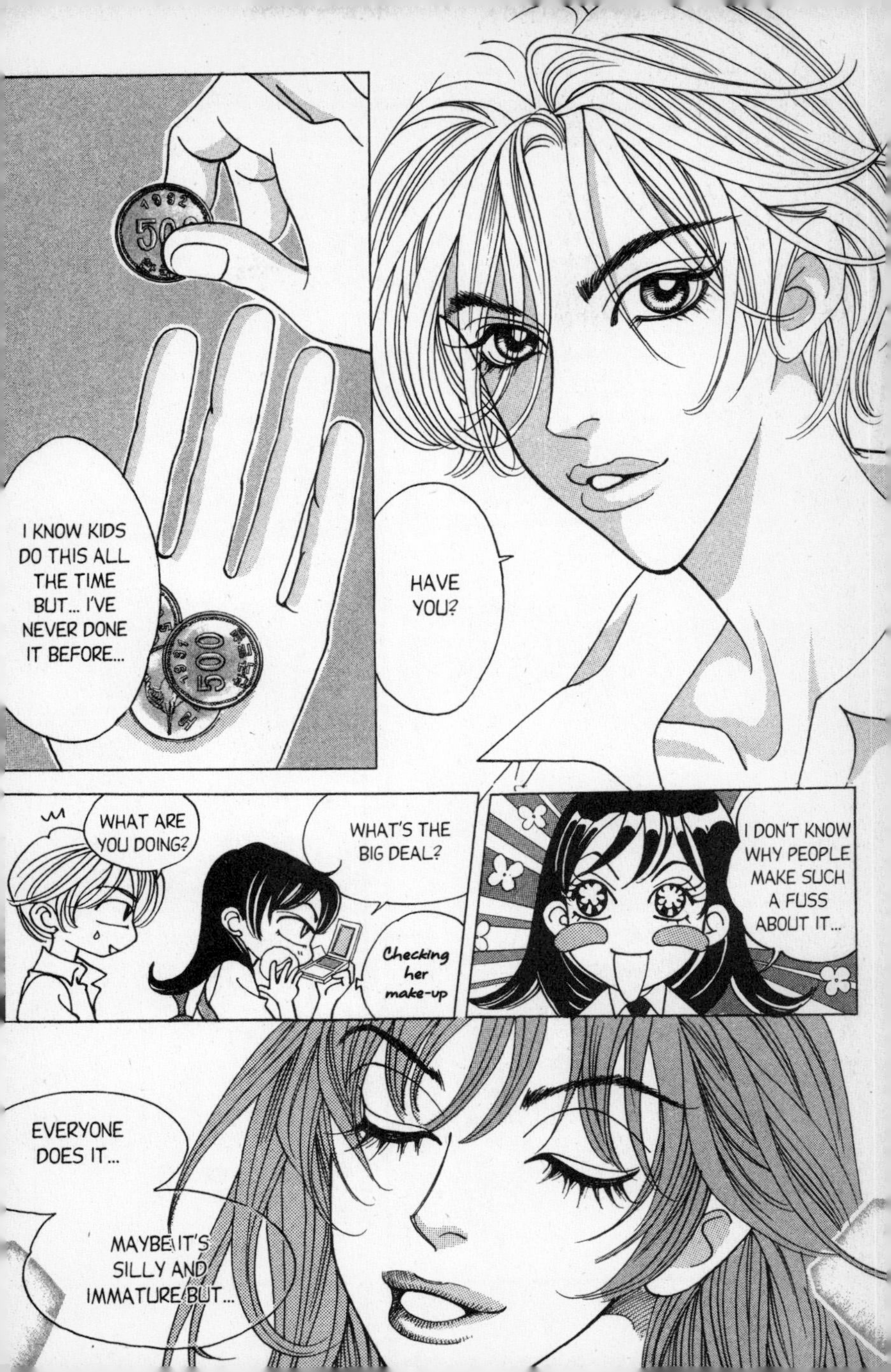
I KNOW KIDS DO THIS ALL THE TIME BUT... I'VE NEVER DONE IT BEFORE...
HAVE YOU?
WHAT ARE YOU DOING?
WHAT'S THE BIG DEAL?
Checking her make-up
I DON'T KNOW WHY PEOPLE MAKE SUCH A FUSS ABOUT IT...
EVERYONE DOES IT...
MAYBE IT'S SILLY AND IMMATURE BUT...

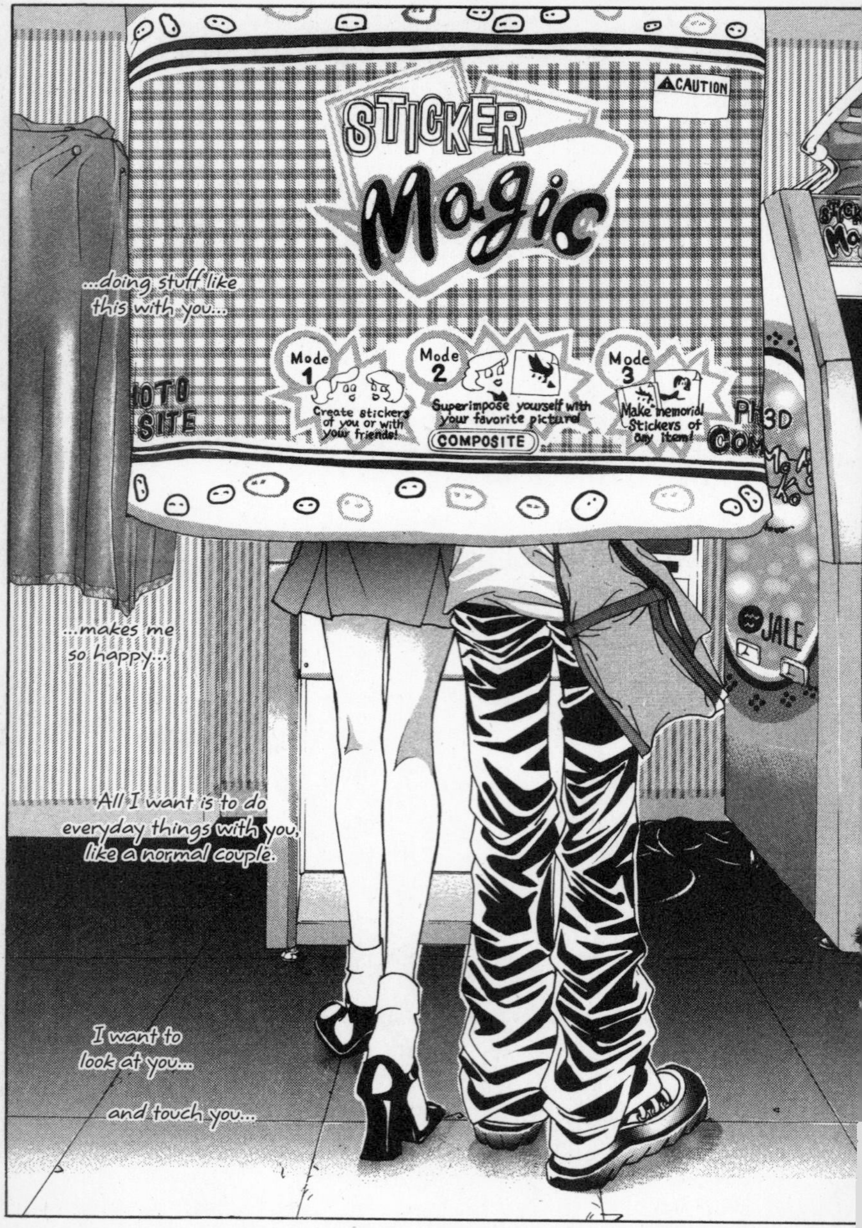
STICKER
Magic
CAUTION
...doing stuff like this with you...
Mode 1
Create stickers of you or with your friends!
Mode 2
Superimpose yourself with your favorite picture!
COMPOSITE
Mode 3
Make memorial Stickers of any item!
...makes me so happy...
All I want is to do everyday things with you, like a normal couple.
I want to look at you...
and touch you...

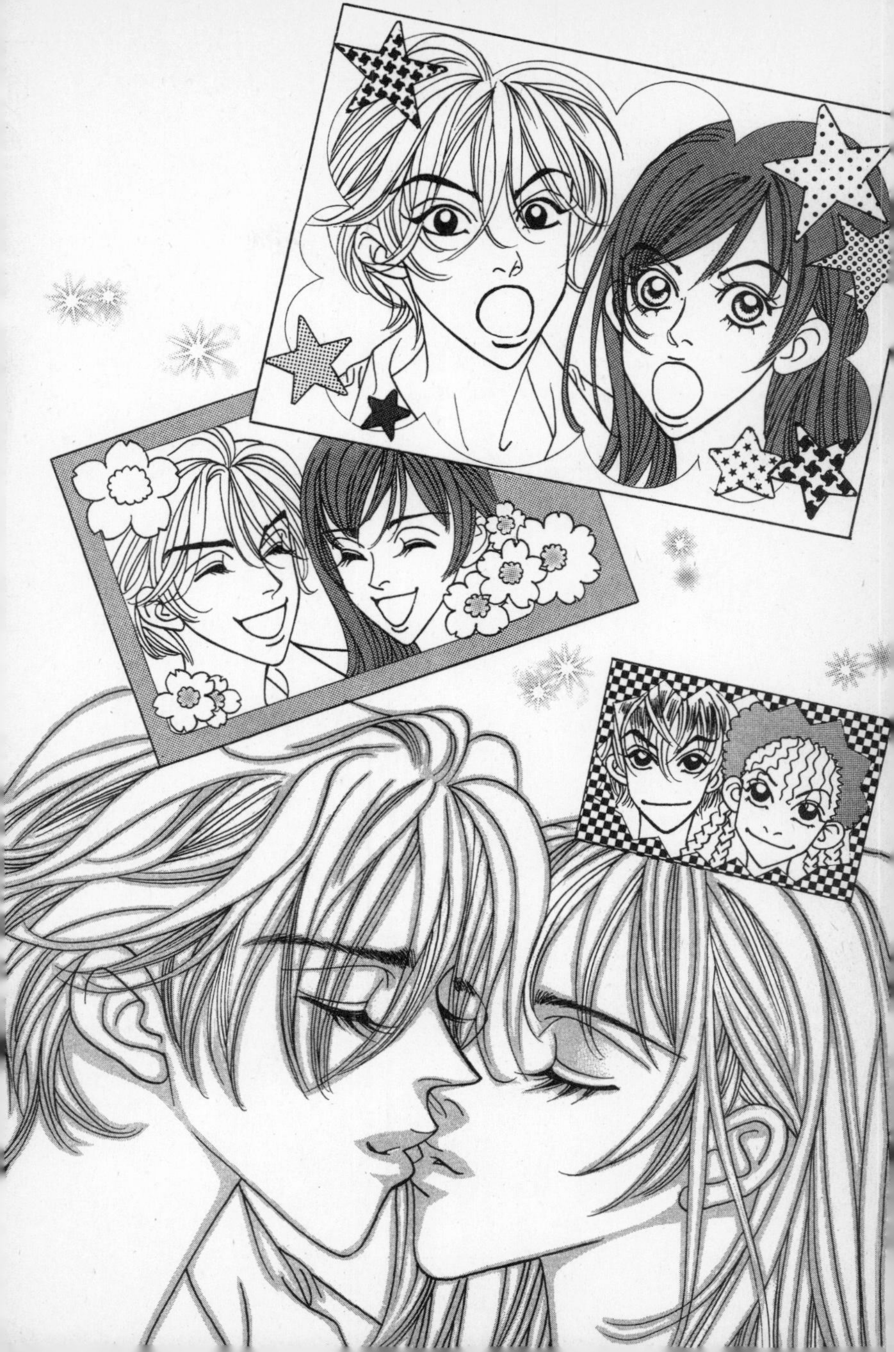

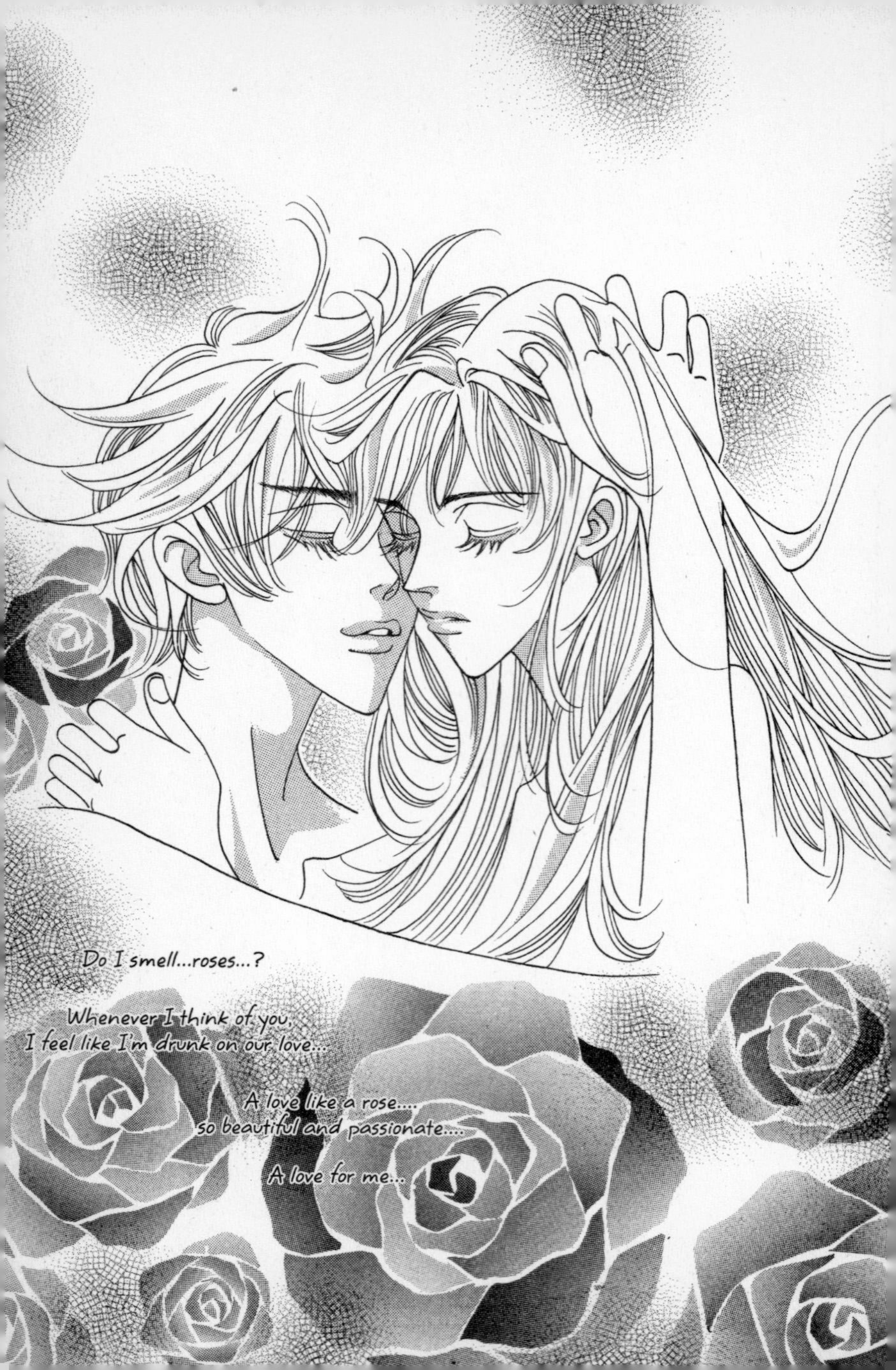
Do I smell...roses...?
Whenever I think of you,
I feel like I'm drunk on our love...
A love like a rose....
so beautiful and passionate....
A love for me...

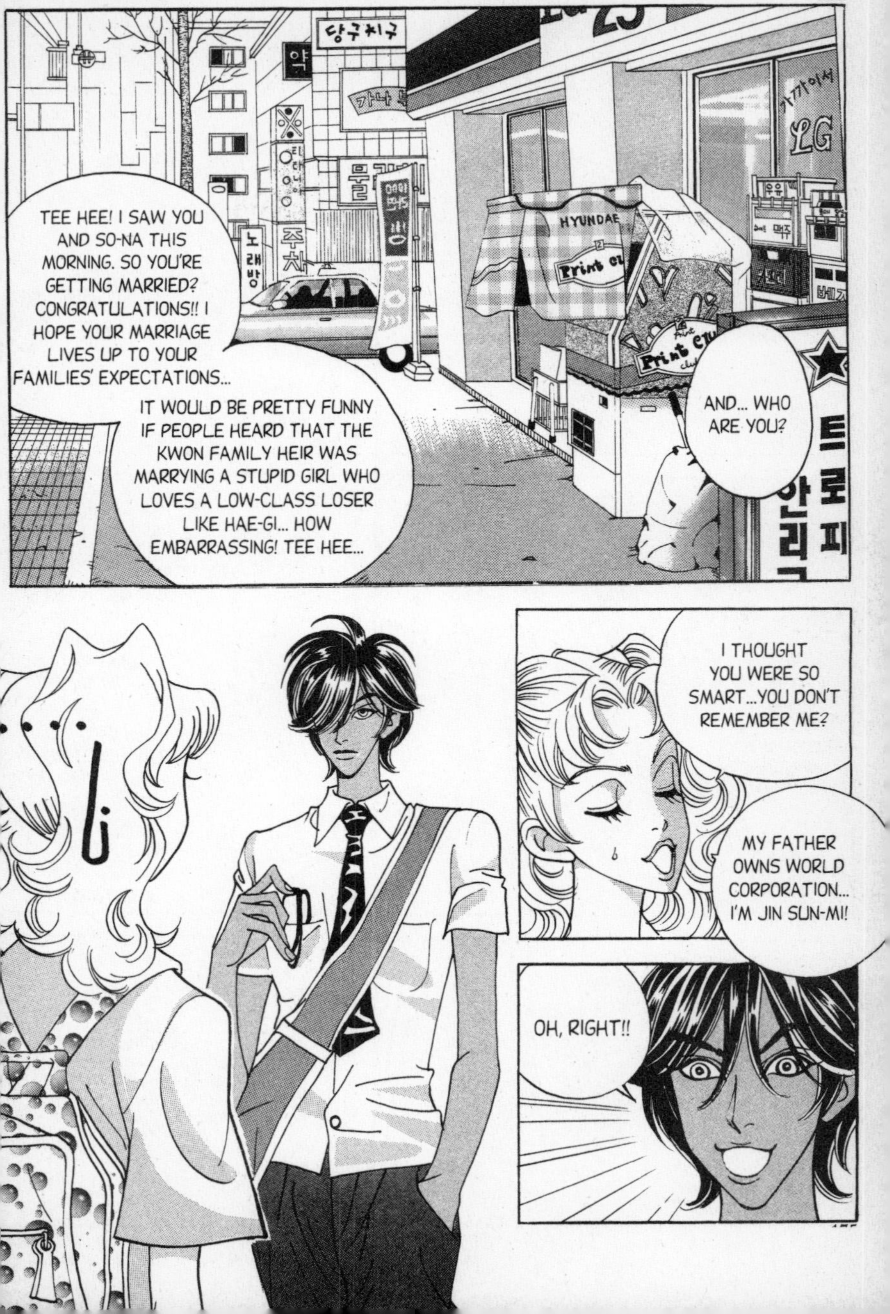
TEE HEE! I SAW YOU AND SO-NA THIS MORNING. SO YOU'RE GETTING MARRIED? CONGRATULATIONS!! I HOPE YOUR MARRIAGE LIVES UP TO YOUR FAMILIES' EXPECTATIONS...
IT WOULD BE PRETTY FUNNY IF PEOPLE HEARD THAT THE KWON FAMILY HEIR WAS MARRYING A STUPID GIRL WHO LOVES A LOW-CLASS LOSER LIKE HAE-GI... HOW EMBARRASSING! TEE HEE...
HYUNDAE
LG
AND... WHO ARE YOU?
...!
I THOUGHT YOU WERE SO SMART...YOU DON'T REMEMBER ME?
MY FATHER OWNS WORLD CORPORATION... I'M JIN SUN-MI!
OH, RIGHT!!

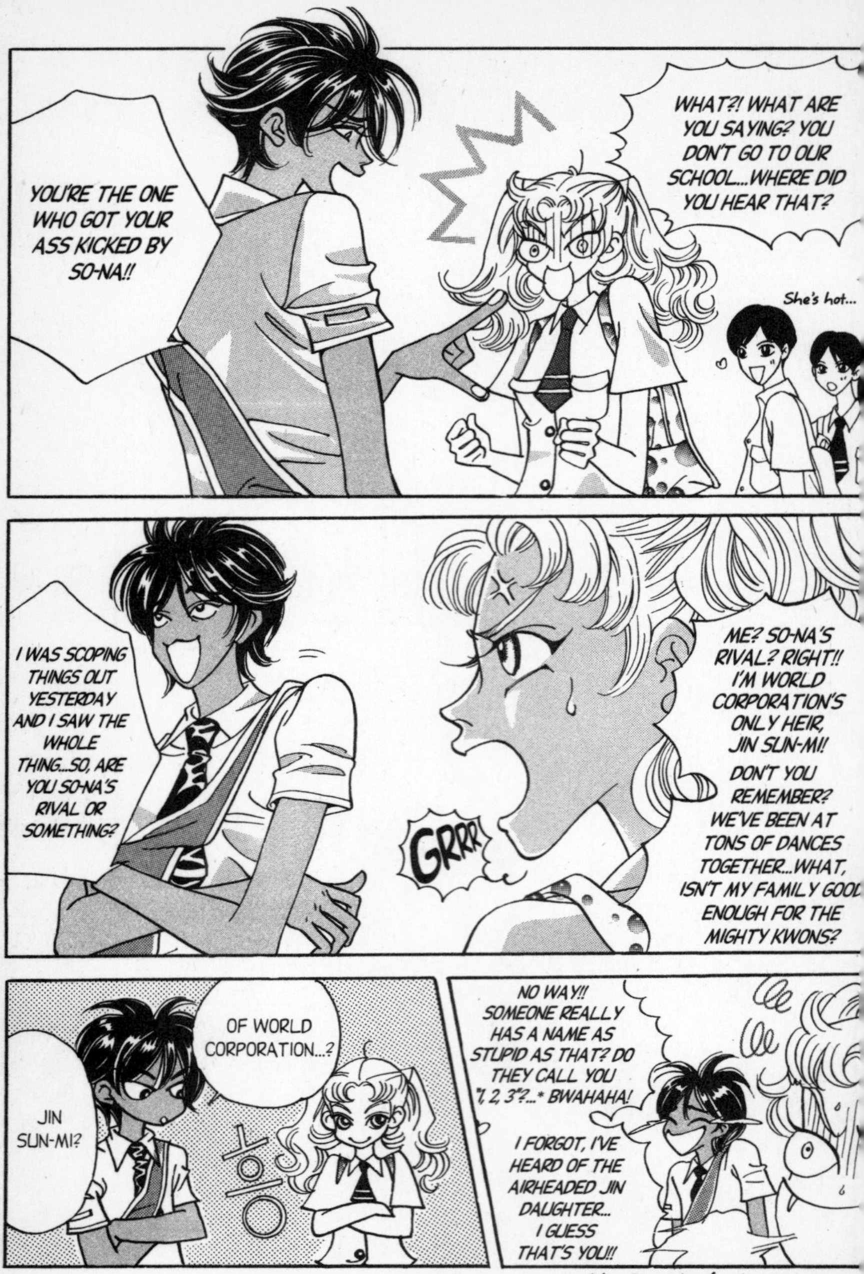
YOU'RE THE ONE WHO GOT YOUR ASS KICKED BY SO-NA!!
WHAT?! WHAT ARE YOU SAYING? YOU DON'T GO TO OUR SCHOOL...WHERE DID YOU HEAR THAT?
She's hot...
I WAS SCOPING THINGS OUT YESTERDAY AND I SAW THE WHOLE THING...SO, ARE YOU SO-NA'S RIVAL OR SOMETHING?
ME? SO-NA'S RIVAL? RIGHT!! I'M WORLD CORPORATION'S ONLY HEIR, JIN SUN-MI!
DON'T YOU REMEMBER? WE'VE BEEN AT TONS OF DANCES TOGETHER...WHAT, ISN'T MY FAMILY GOOD ENOUGH FOR THE MIGHTY KWONS?
GRRR
JIN SUN-MI?
OF WORLD CORPORATION...?
NO WAY!! SOMEONE REALLY HAS A NAME AS STUPID AS THAT? DO THEY CALL YOU "1, 2, 3"?...* BWAHAHA!
I FORGOT, I'VE HEARD OF THE AIRHEADED JIN DAUGHTER... I GUESS THAT'S YOU!!

*Note: Remember, from book 2? "Jin Sun Mi" means "1st, 2nd, and 3rd"...

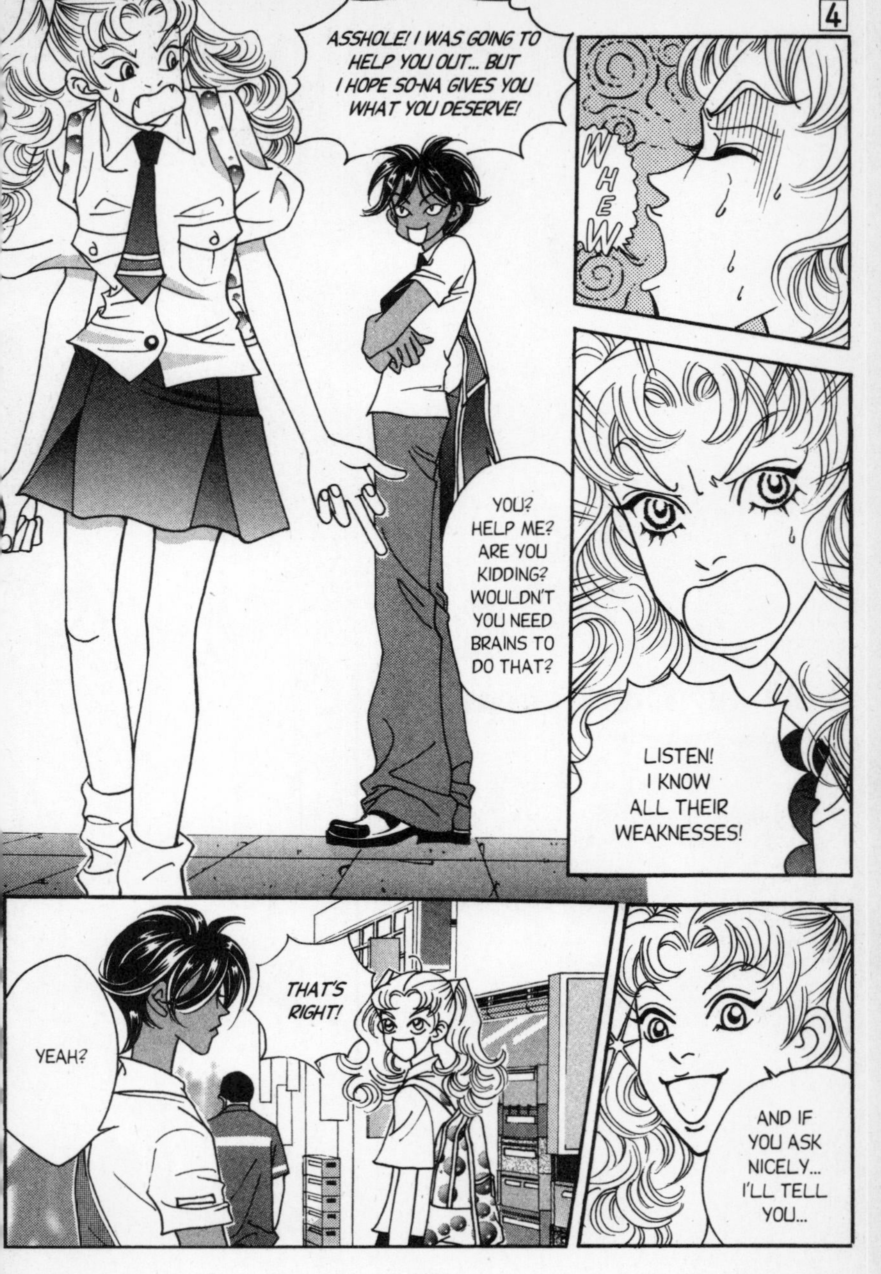
4
ASSHOLE! I WAS GOING TO HELP YOU OUT... BUT I HOPE SO-NA GIVES YOU WHAT YOU DESERVE!
YOU? HELP ME? ARE YOU KIDDING? WOULDN'T YOU NEED BRAINS TO DO THAT?
WHEW
LISTEN! I KNOW ALL THEIR WEAKNESSES!
YEAH?
THAT'S RIGHT!
AND IF YOU ASK NICELY... I'LL TELL YOU...

Part 18: **Cockscomb**

Bragging Competition

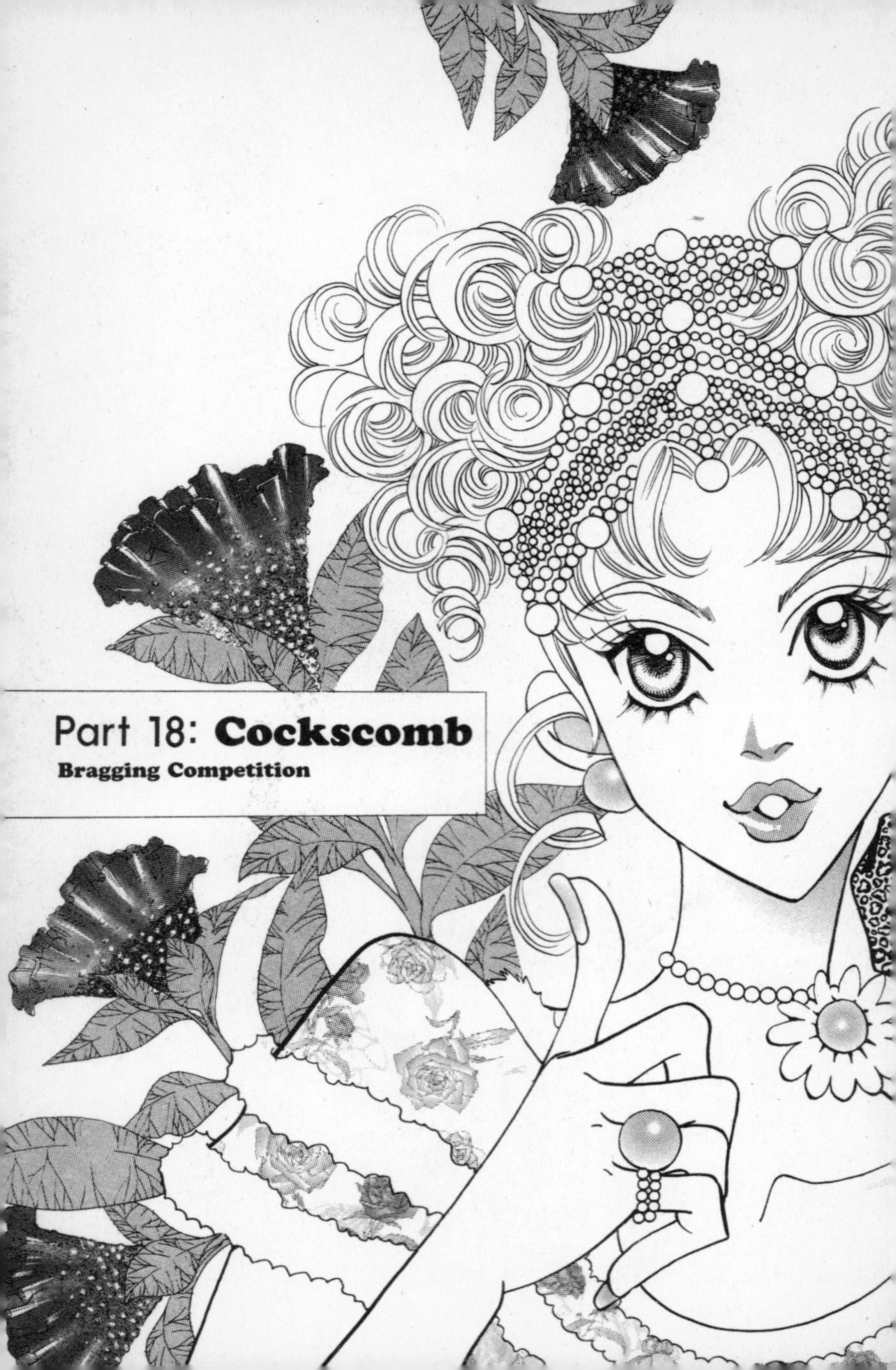

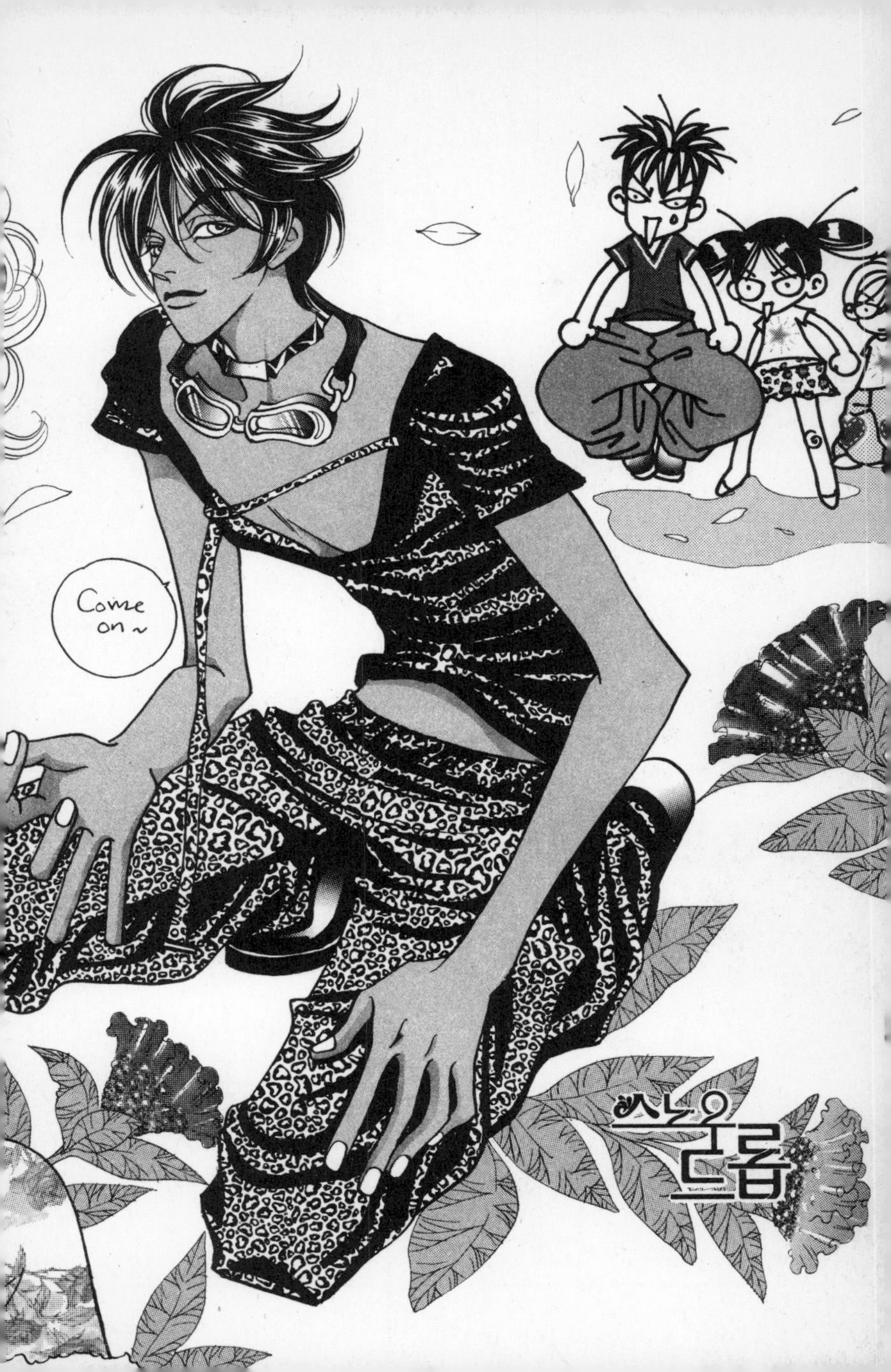
Come on~
스노우 드롭

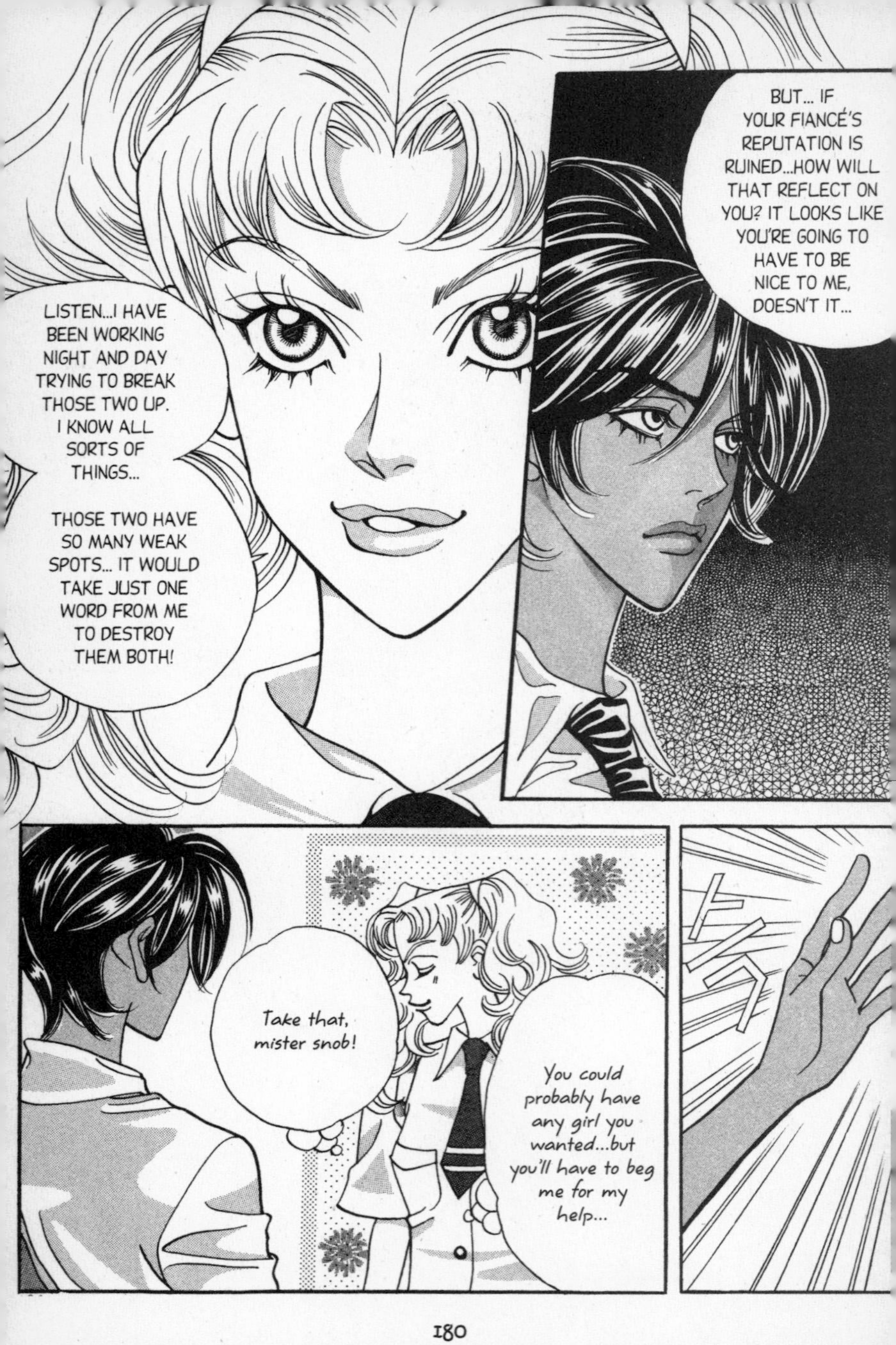
LISTEN...I HAVE BEEN WORKING NIGHT AND DAY TRYING TO BREAK THOSE TWO UP. I KNOW ALL SORTS OF THINGS...
THOSE TWO HAVE SO MANY WEAK SPOTS... IT WOULD TAKE JUST ONE WORD FROM ME TO DESTROY THEM BOTH!
BUT... IF YOUR FIANCÉ'S REPUTATION IS RUINED...HOW WILL THAT REFLECT ON YOU? IT LOOKS LIKE YOU'RE GOING TO HAVE TO BE NICE TO ME, DOESN'T IT...
Take that, mister snob!
You could probably have any girl you wanted...but you'll have to beg me for my help...

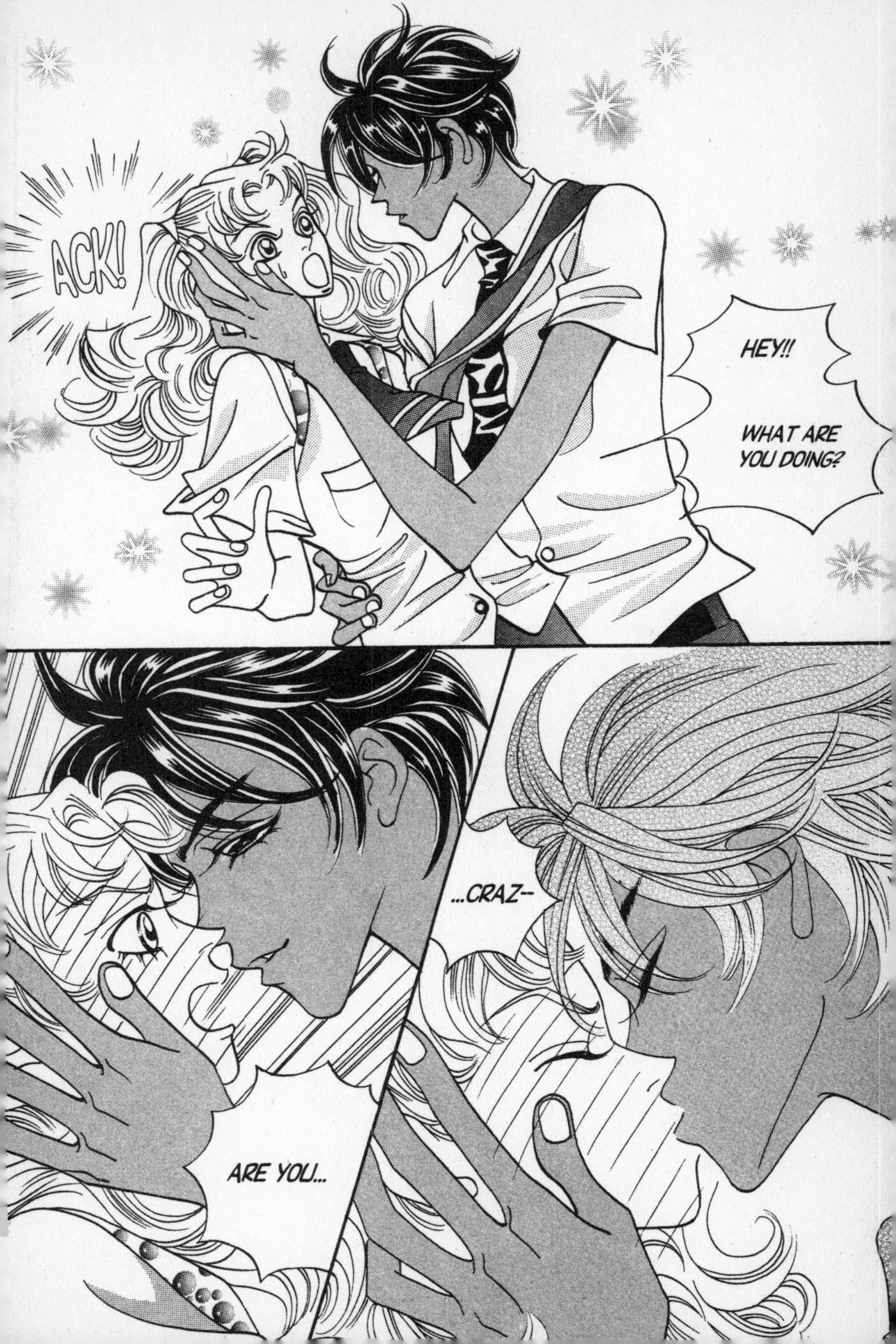
ACK!
HEY!!
WHAT ARE YOU DOING?
ARE YOU...
...CRAZ--

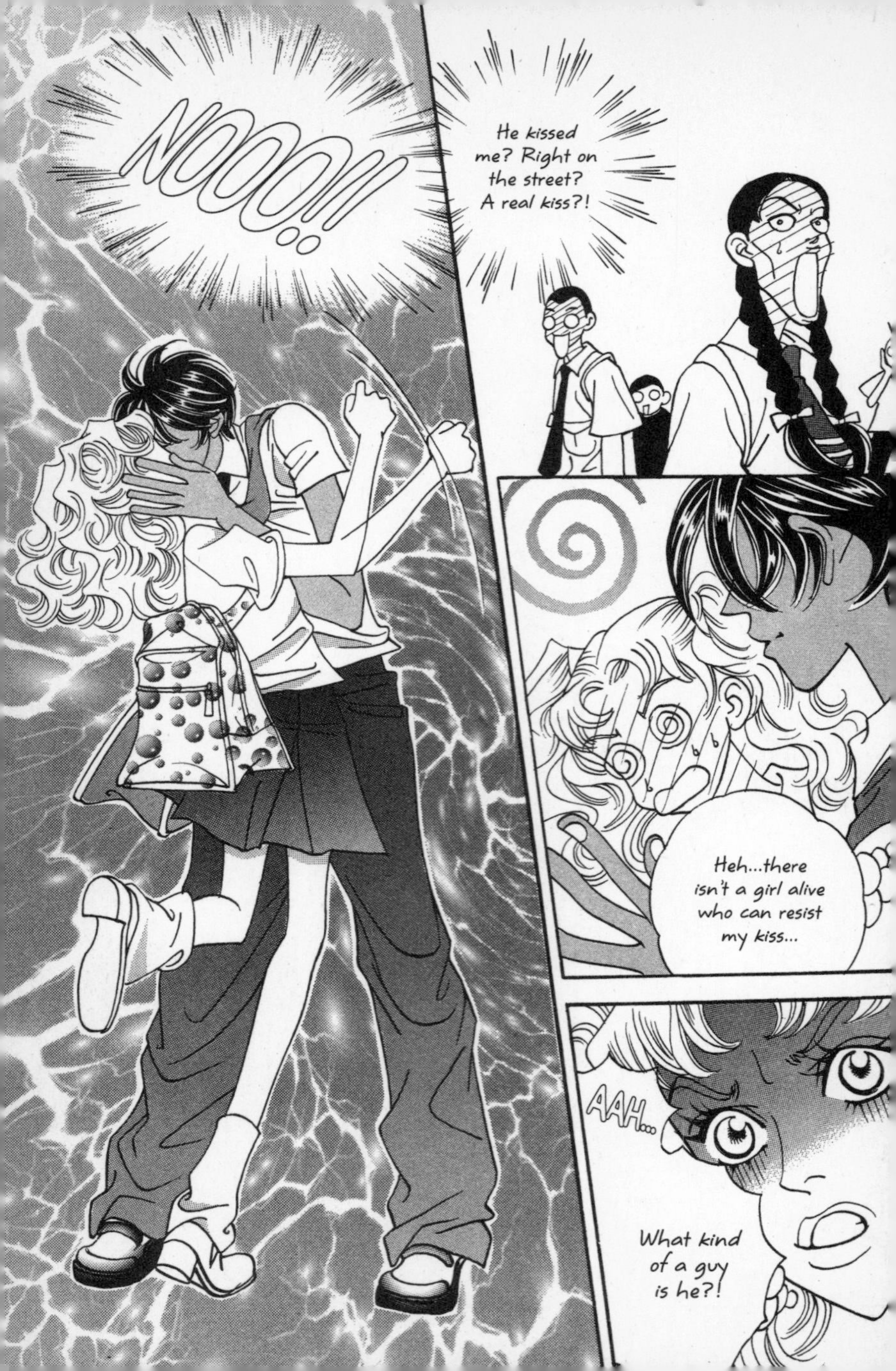
NOOOO!!
He kissed me? Right on the street? A real kiss?!
Heh...there isn't a girl alive who can resist my kiss...
AAH...
What kind of a guy is he?!

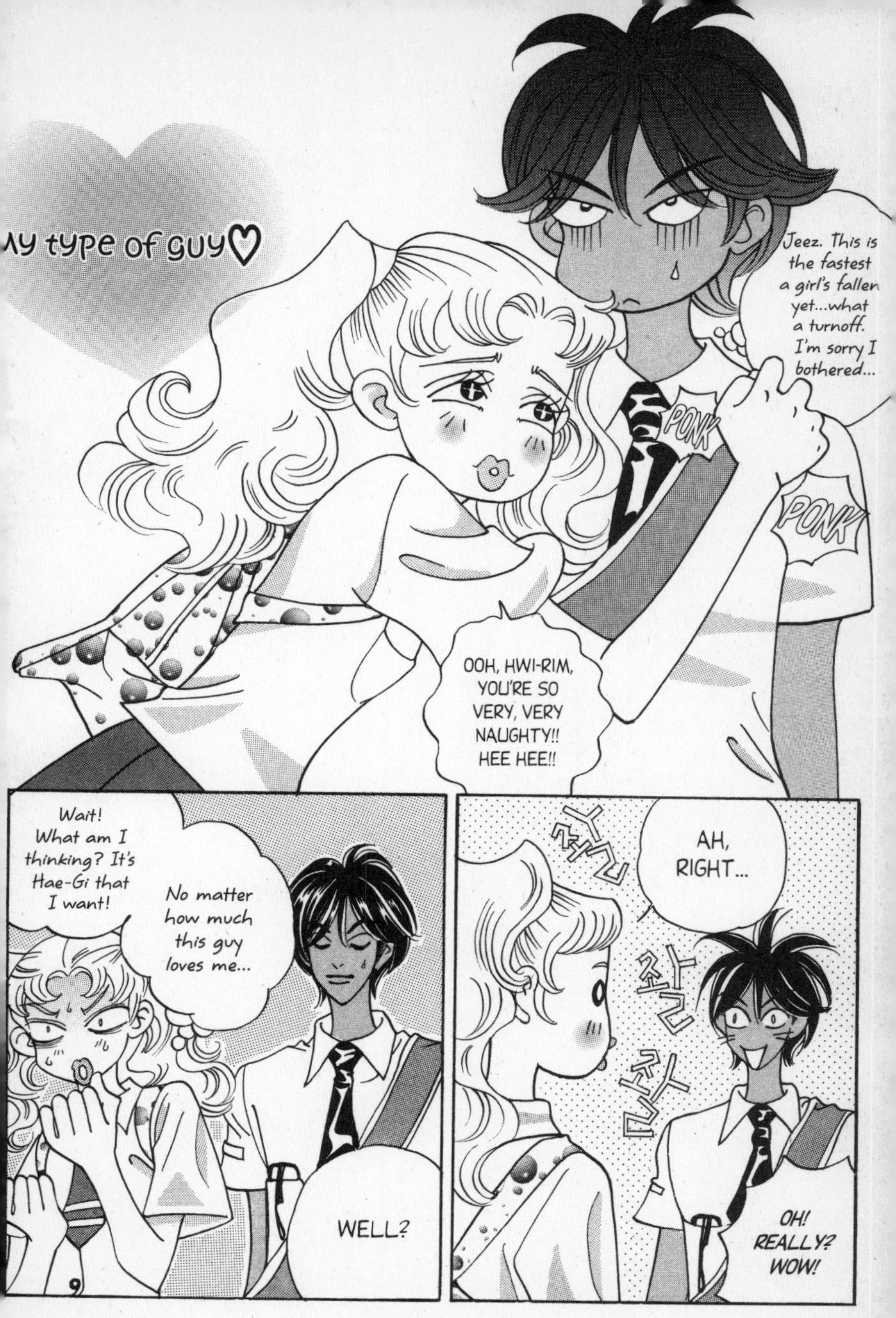
my type of guy♡
Jeez. This is the fastest a girl's fallen yet...what a turnoff. I'm sorry I bothered...
PONK
PONK
OOH, HWI-RIM, YOU'RE SO VERY, VERY NAUGHTY!! HEE HEE!!
Wait! What am I thinking? It's Hae-Gi that I want!
No matter how much this guy loves me...
WELL?
AH, RIGHT...
OH! REALLY? WOW!

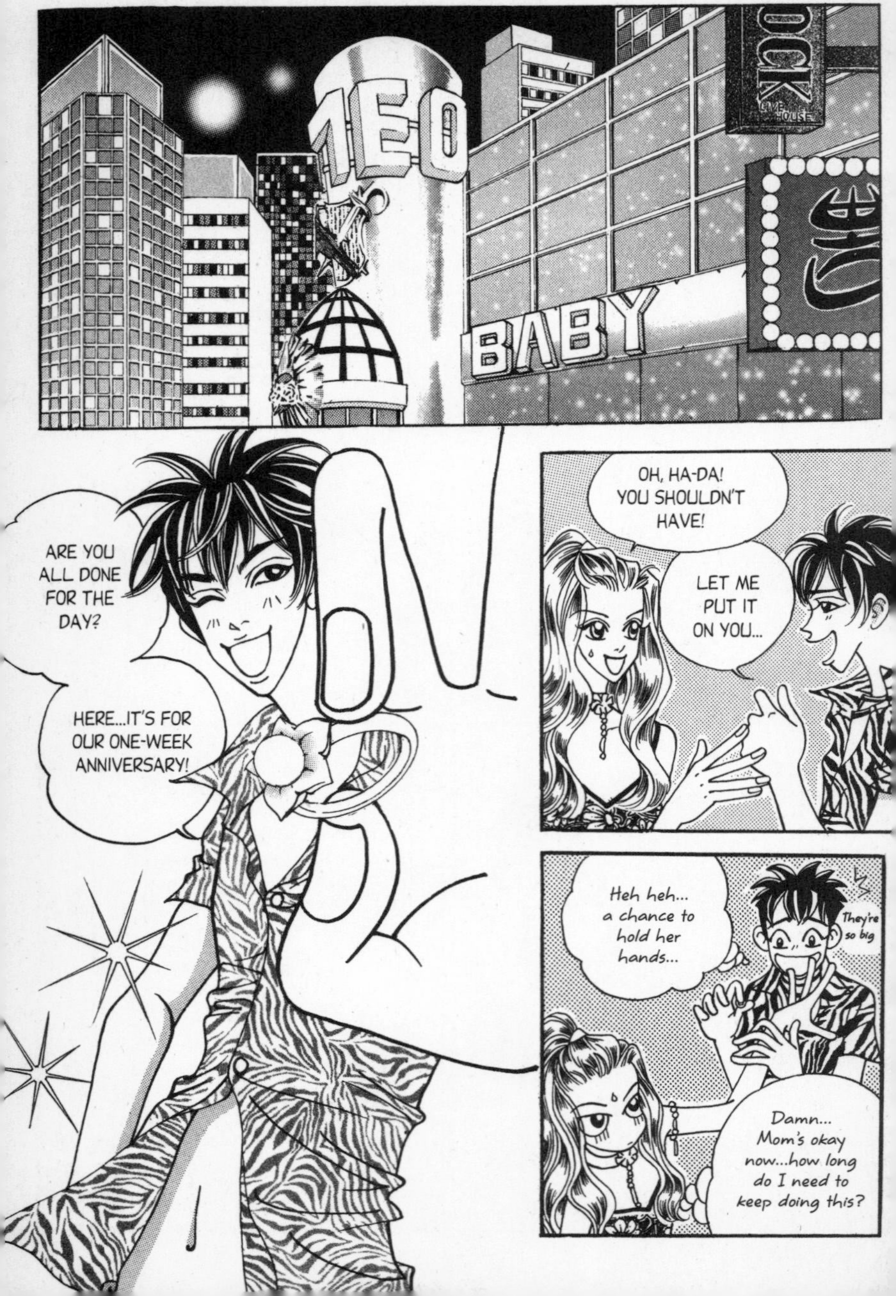
BABY
ARE YOU ALL DONE FOR THE DAY?
HERE...IT'S FOR OUR ONE-WEEK ANNIVERSARY!
OH, HA-DA! YOU SHOULDN'T HAVE!
LET ME PUT IT ON YOU...
Heh heh... a chance to hold her hands...
They're so big
Damn... Mom's okay now...how long do I need to keep doing this?

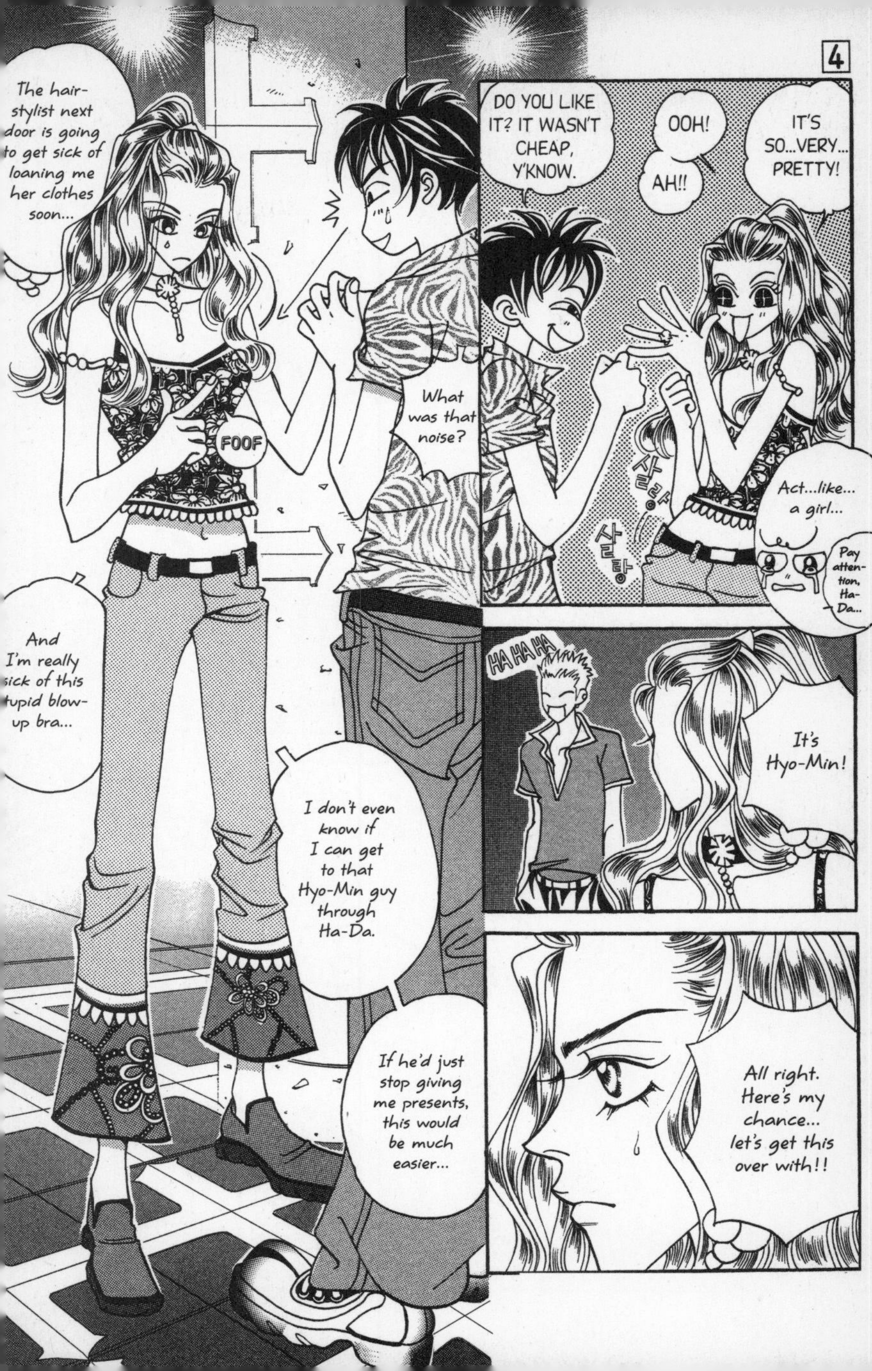
The hair-stylist next door is going to get sick of loaning me her clothes soon...
FOOF
What was that noise?
And I'm really sick of this stupid blow-up bra...
I don't even know if I can get to that Hyo-Min guy through Ha-Da.
If he'd just stop giving me presents, this would be much easier...
DO YOU LIKE IT? IT WASN'T CHEAP, Y'KNOW.
OOH!
AH!!
IT'S SO...VERY... PRETTY!
살랑
살랑
Act...like... a girl...
Pay attention, Ha-Da...
HA HA HA
It's Hyo-Min!
All right. Here's my chance... let's get this over with!!

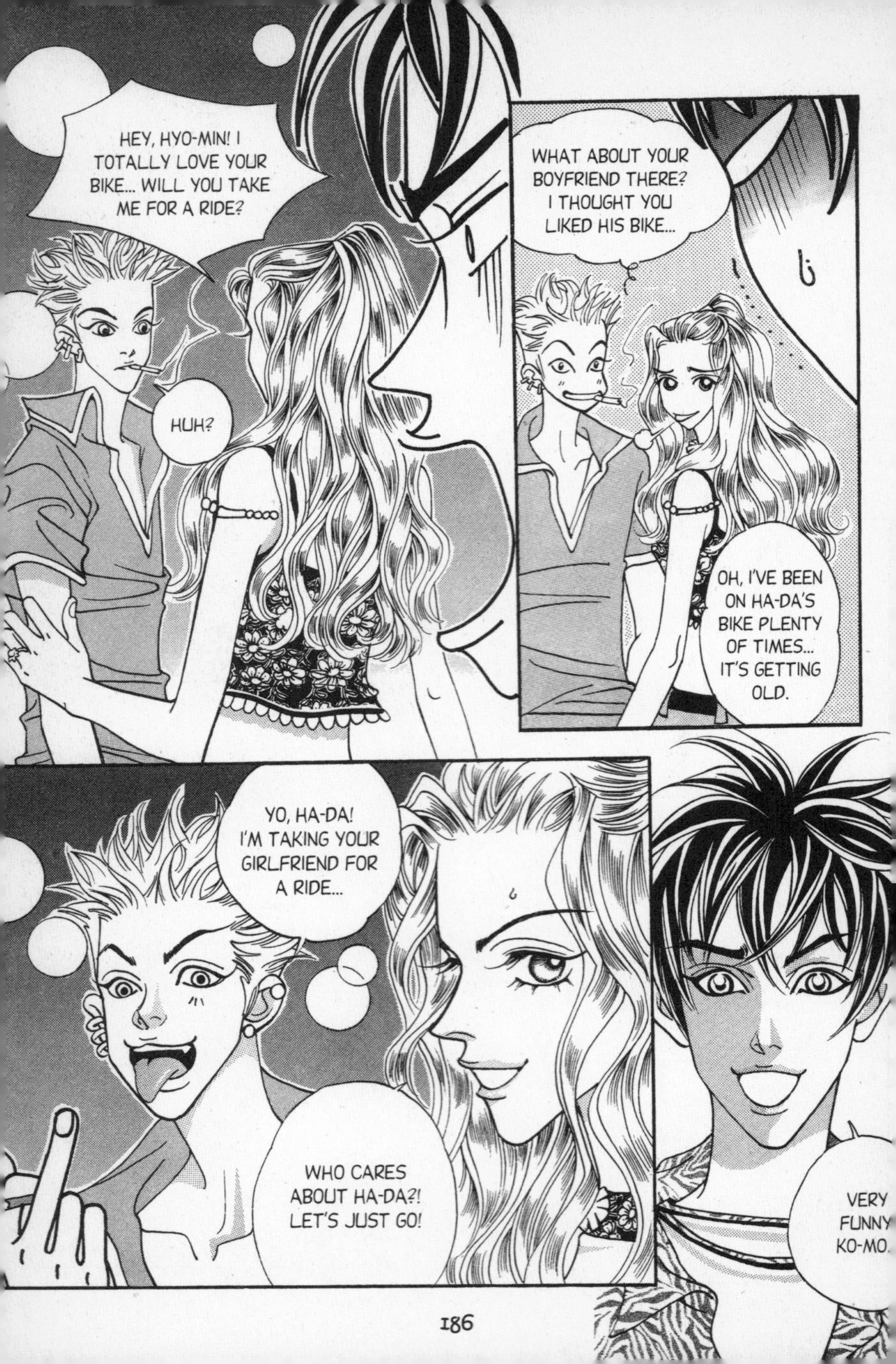
HEY, HYO-MIN! I TOTALLY LOVE YOUR BIKE... WILL YOU TAKE ME FOR A RIDE?
HUH?
WHAT ABOUT YOUR BOYFRIEND THERE? I THOUGHT YOU LIKED HIS BIKE...
OH, I'VE BEEN ON HA-DA'S BIKE PLENTY OF TIMES... IT'S GETTING OLD.
YO, HA-DA! I'M TAKING YOUR GIRLFRIEND FOR A RIDE...
WHO CARES ABOUT HA-DA?! LET'S JUST GO!
VERY FUNNY KO-MO.

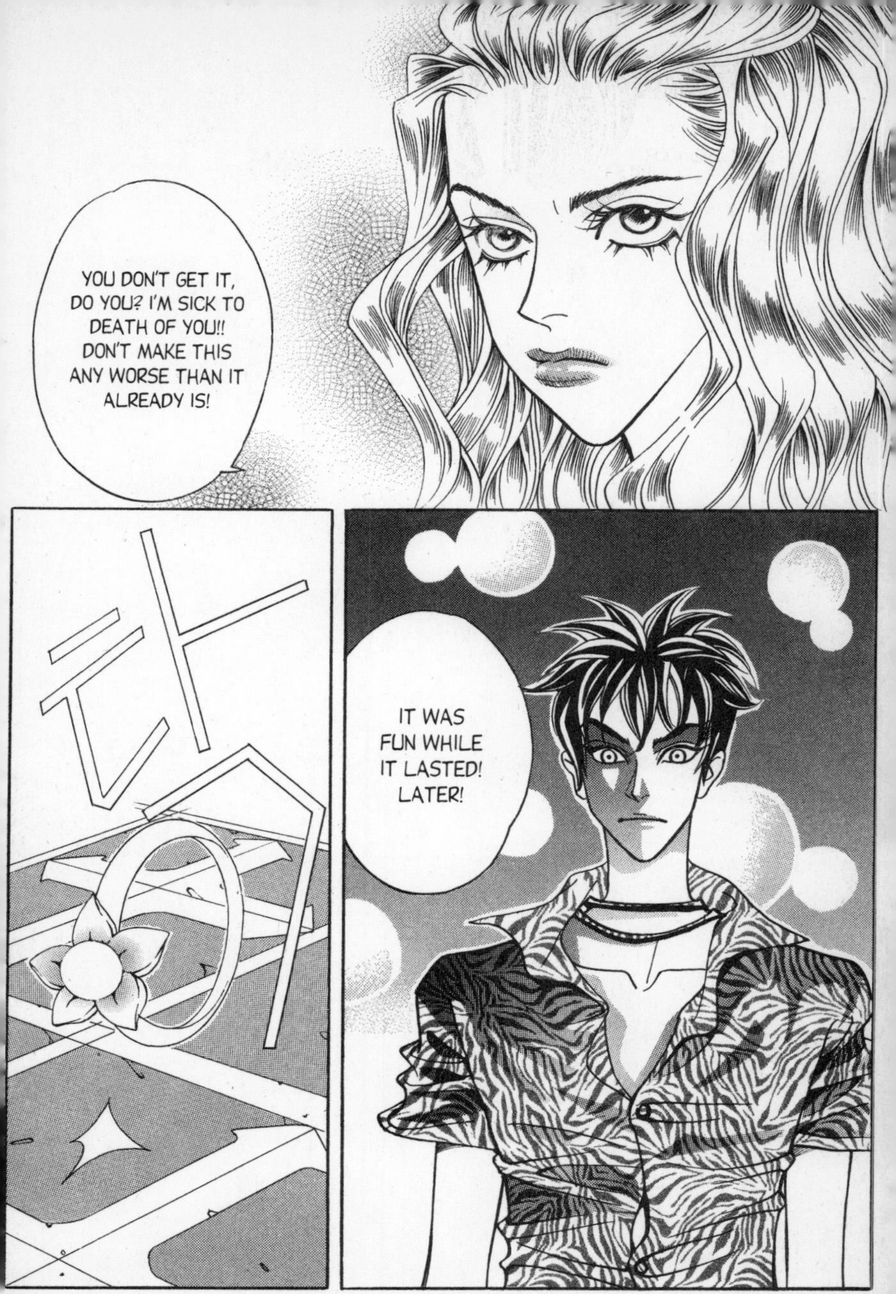
YOU DON'T GET IT, DO YOU? I'M SICK TO DEATH OF YOU!! DON'T MAKE THIS ANY WORSE THAN IT ALREADY IS!
IT WAS FUN WHILE IT LASTED! LATER!

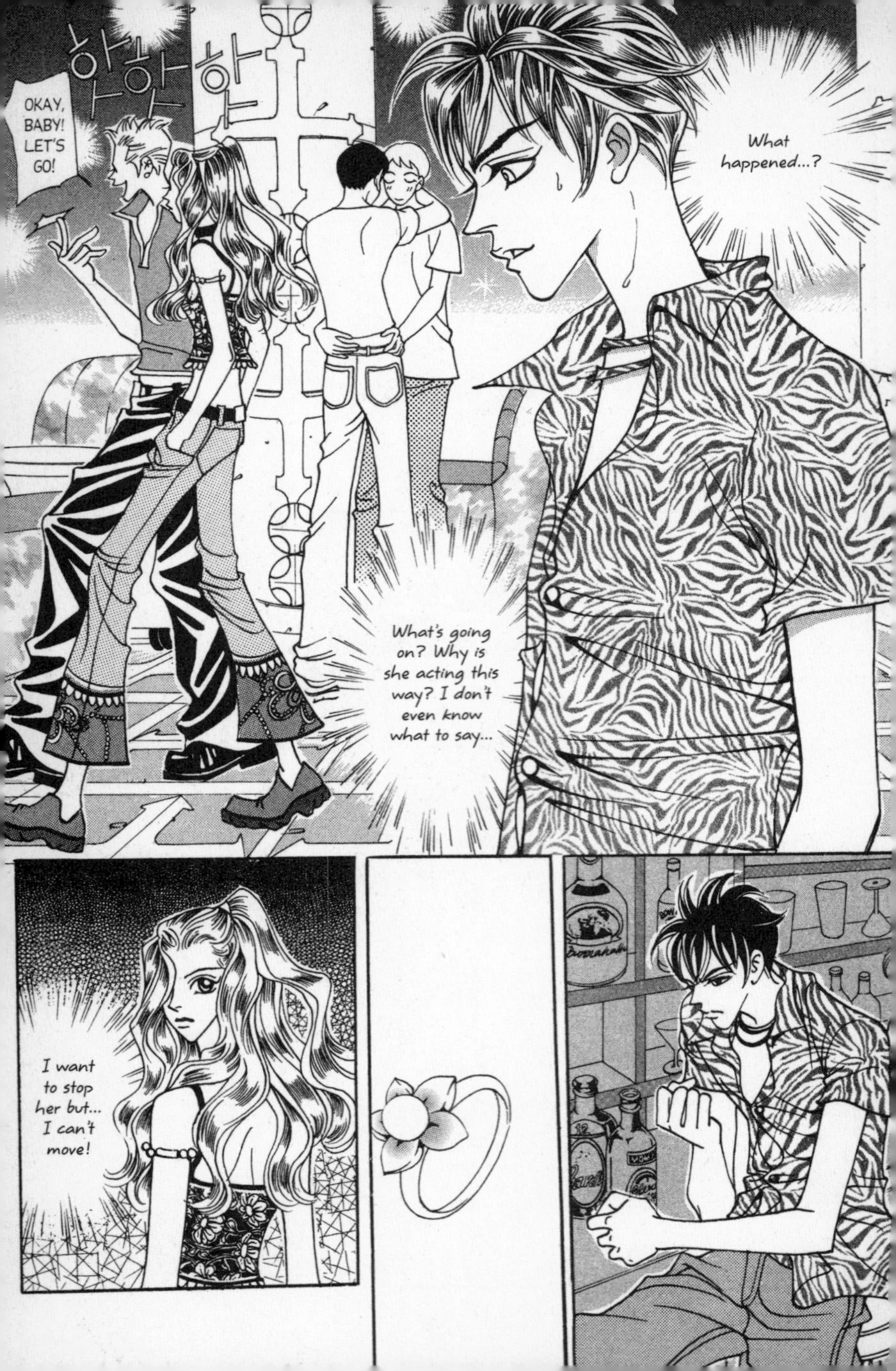
하하하
OKAY, BABY! LET'S GO!
What happened...?
What's going on? Why is she acting this way? I don't even know what to say...
I want to stop her but... I can't move!

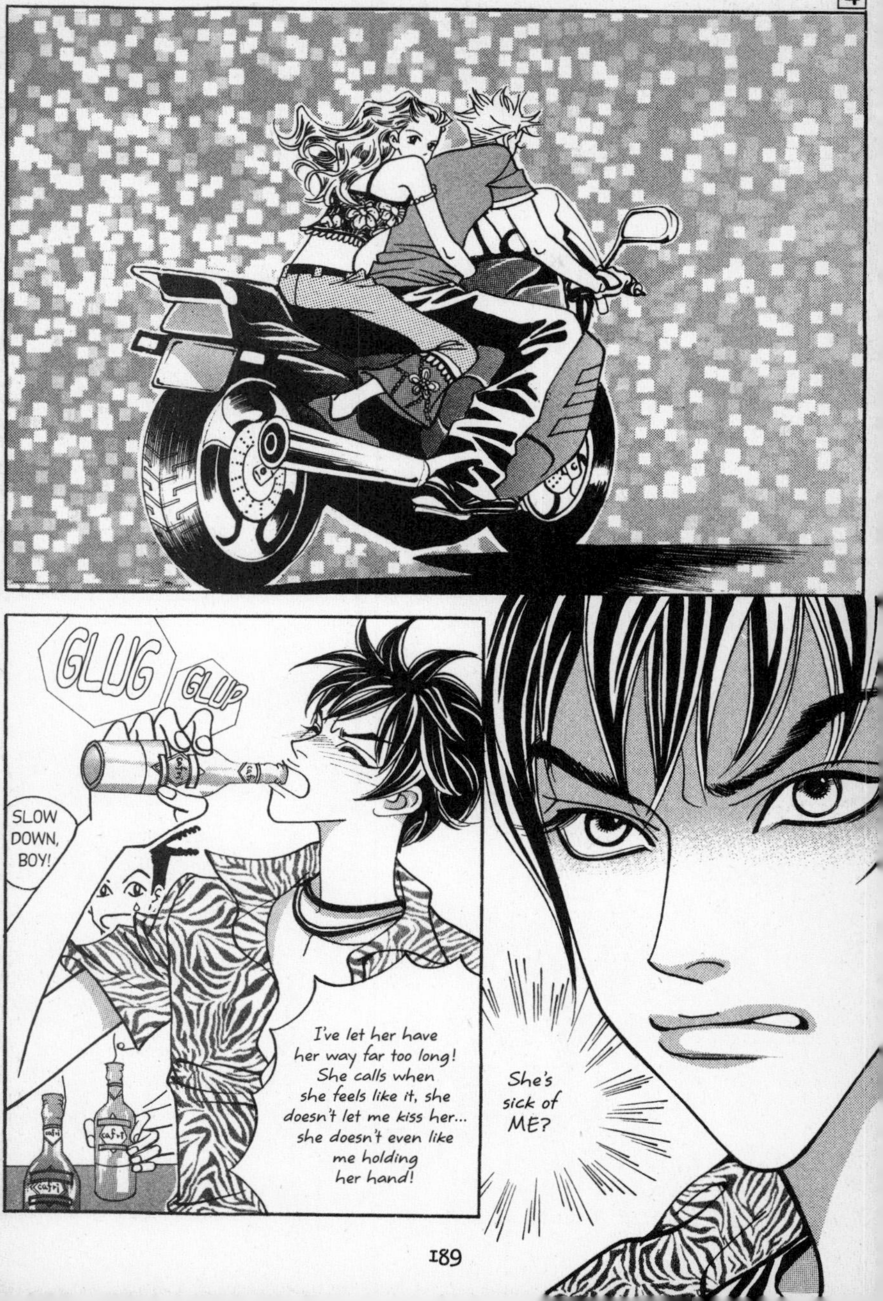
GLUG
GLUP
SLOW DOWN, BOY!
I've let her have her way far too long! She calls when she feels like it, she doesn't let me kiss her... she doesn't even like me holding her hand!
She's sick of ME?

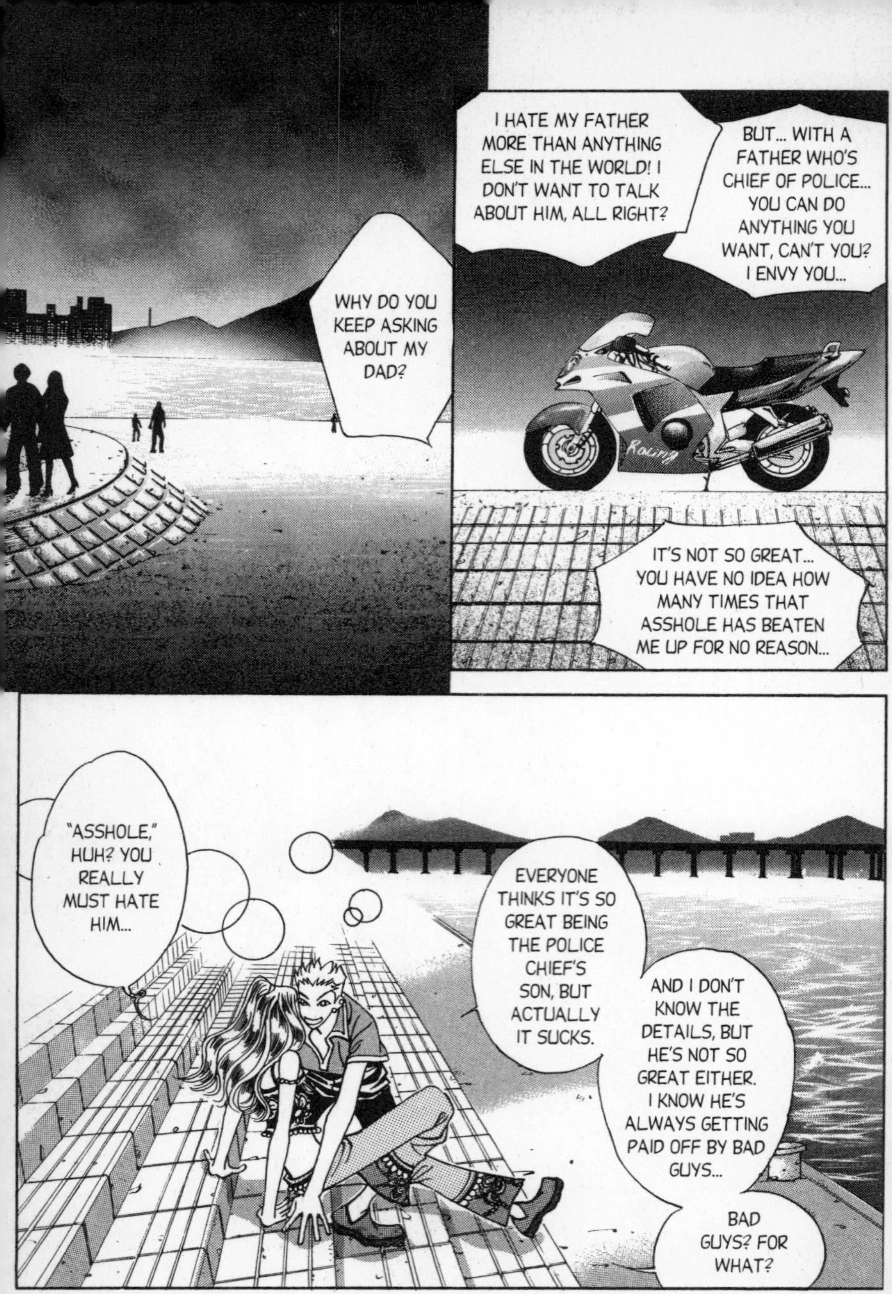
WHY DO YOU KEEP ASKING ABOUT MY DAD?
I HATE MY FATHER MORE THAN ANYTHING ELSE IN THE WORLD! I DON'T WANT TO TALK ABOUT HIM, ALL RIGHT?
BUT... WITH A FATHER WHO'S CHIEF OF POLICE... YOU CAN DO ANYTHING YOU WANT, CAN'T YOU? I ENVY YOU...
IT'S NOT SO GREAT... YOU HAVE NO IDEA HOW MANY TIMES THAT ASSHOLE HAS BEATEN ME UP FOR NO REASON...
"ASSHOLE," HUH? YOU REALLY MUST HATE HIM...
EVERYONE THINKS IT'S SO GREAT BEING THE POLICE CHIEF'S SON, BUT ACTUALLY IT SUCKS.
AND I DON'T KNOW THE DETAILS, BUT HE'S NOT SO GREAT EITHER. I KNOW HE'S ALWAYS GETTING PAID OFF BY BAD GUYS...
BAD GUYS? FOR WHAT?

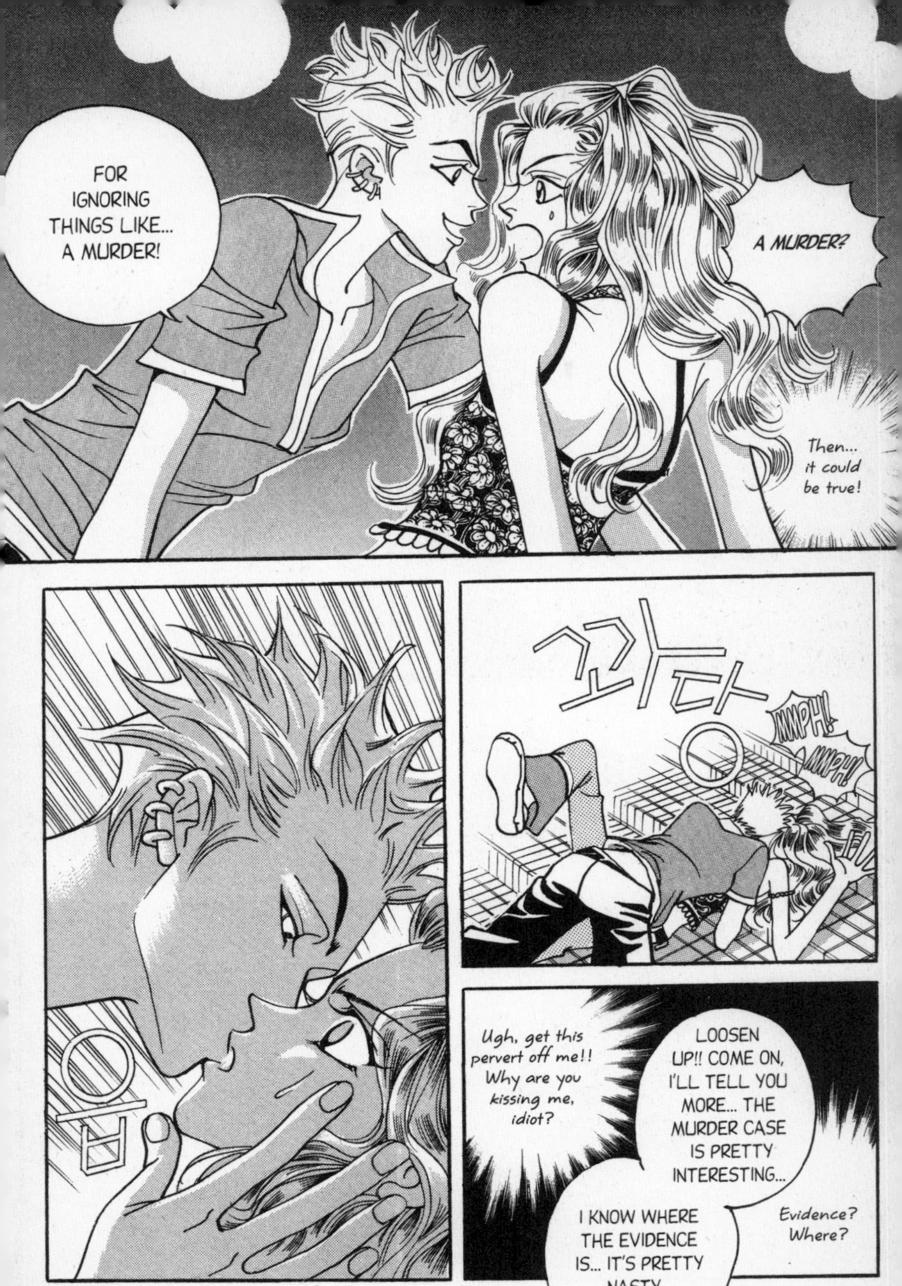
FOR IGNORING THINGS LIKE... A MURDER!
A MURDER?
Then... it could be true!
MMPH!
MMPH!
Ugh, get this pervert off me!! Why are you kissing me, idiot?
LOOSEN UP!! COME ON, I'LL TELL YOU MORE... THE MURDER CASE IS PRETTY INTERESTING...
I KNOW WHERE THE EVIDENCE IS... IT'S PRETTY NASTY...
Evidence? Where?

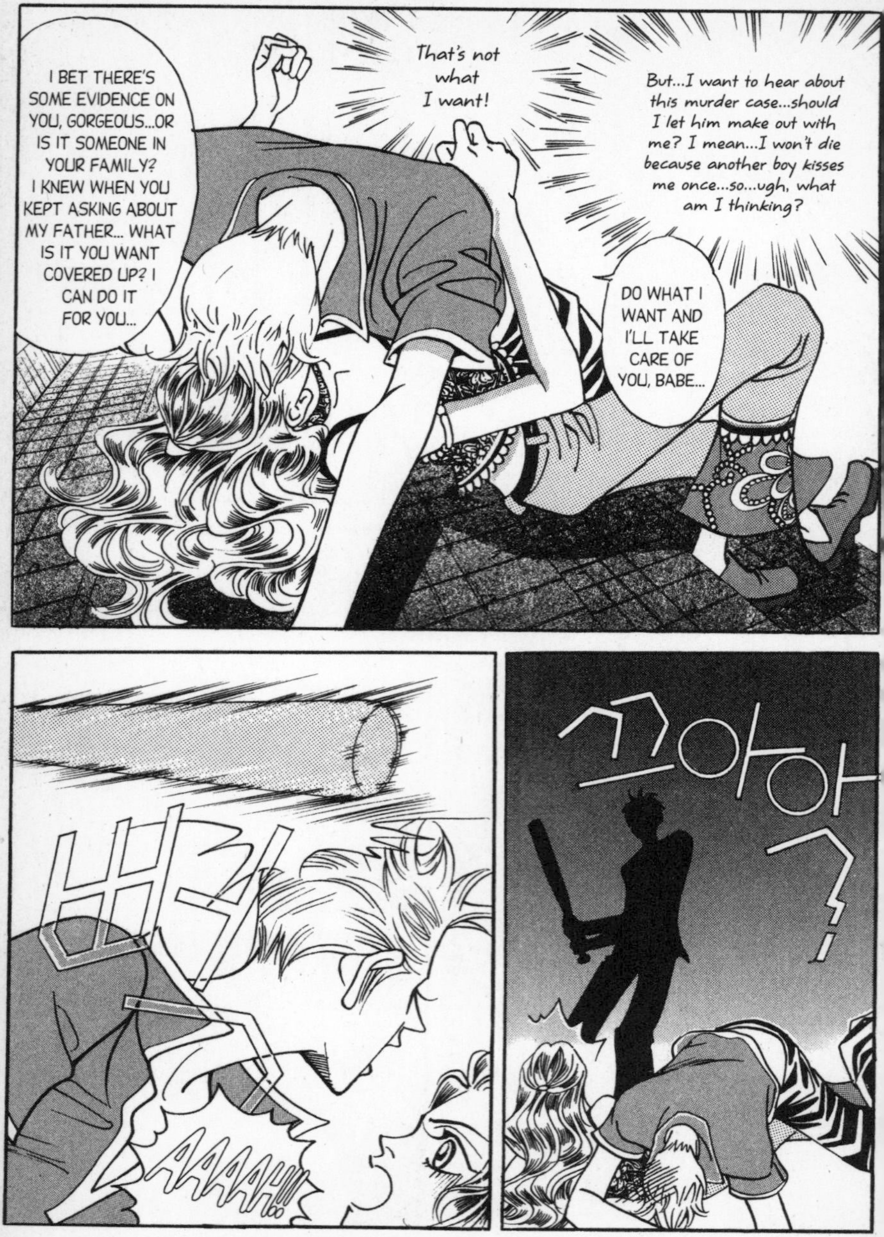
I BET THERE'S SOME EVIDENCE ON YOU, GORGEOUS...OR IS IT SOMEONE IN YOUR FAMILY? I KNEW WHEN YOU KEPT ASKING ABOUT MY FATHER... WHAT IS IT YOU WANT COVERED UP? I CAN DO IT FOR YOU...
That's not what I want!
But...I want to hear about this murder case...should I let him make out with me? I mean...I won't die because another boy kisses me once...so...ugh, what am I thinking?
DO WHAT I WANT AND I'LL TAKE CARE OF YOU, BABE...
AAAAH!!

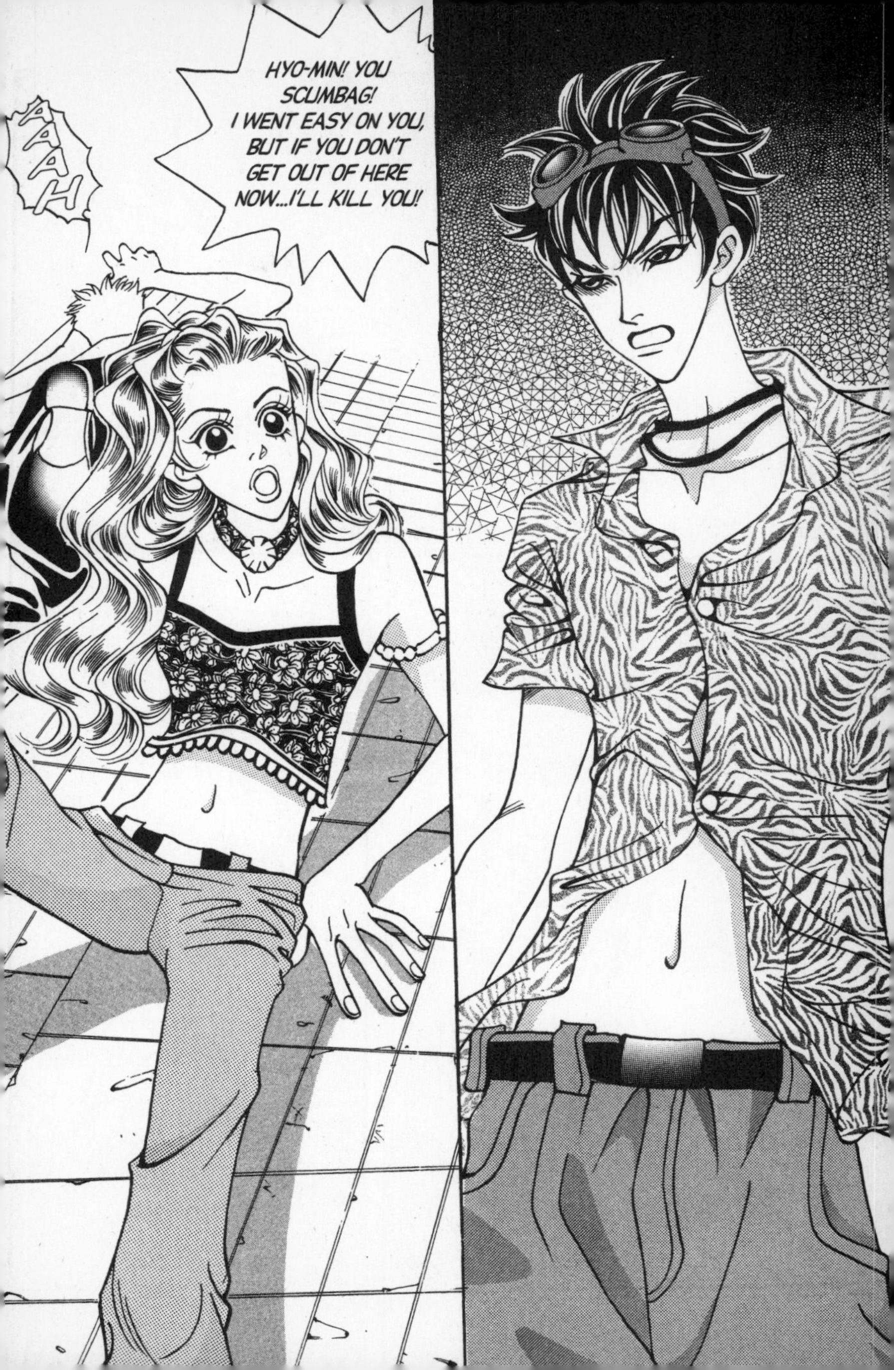
AAAH
HYO-MIN! YOU SCUMBAG! I WENT EASY ON YOU, BUT IF YOU DON'T GET OUT OF HERE NOW...I'LL KILL YOU!

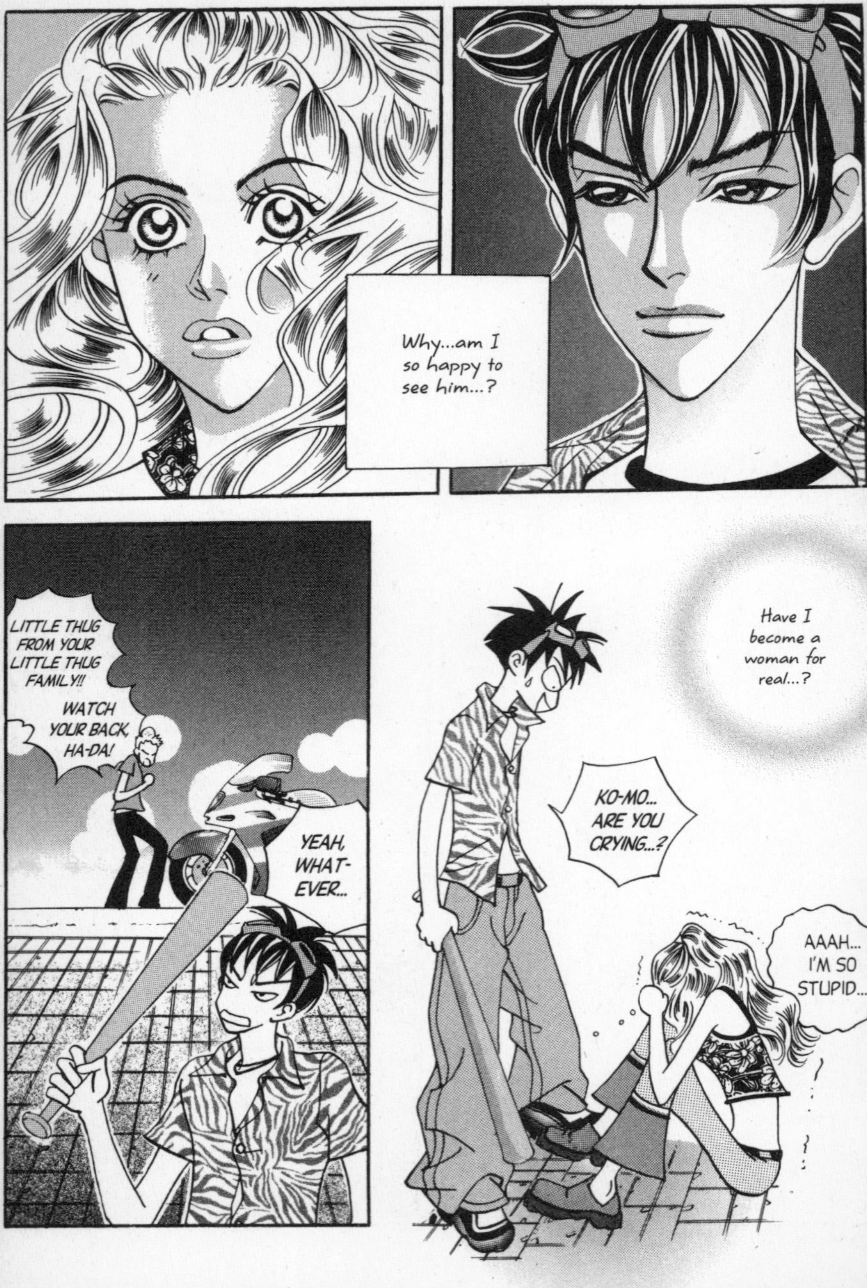
Why...am I so happy to see him...?
LITTLE THUG FROM YOUR LITTLE THUG FAMILY!!
WATCH YOUR BACK, HA-DA!
YEAH, WHAT-EVER...
Have I become a woman for real...?
KO-MO... ARE YOU CRYING...?
AAAH... I'M SO STUPID...

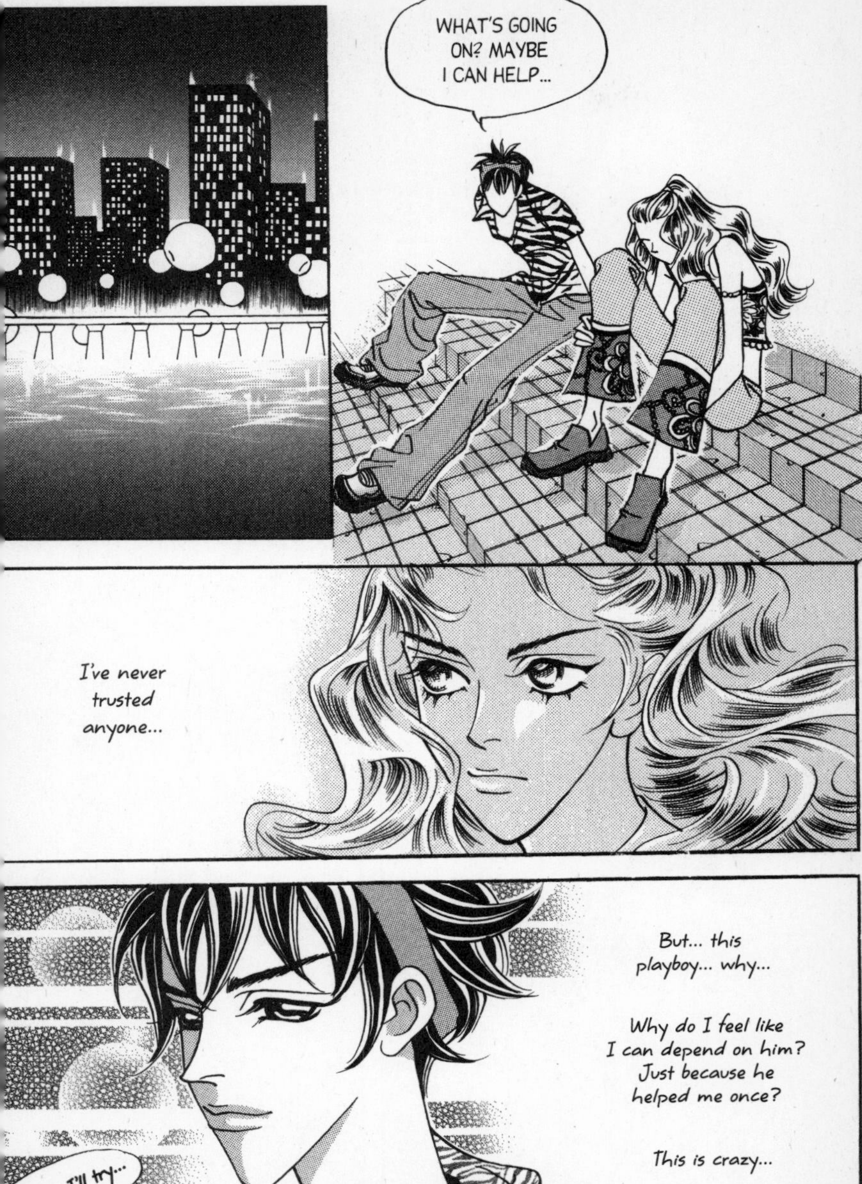
WHAT'S GOING ON? MAYBE I CAN HELP...
I've never trusted anyone...
At least I'll try...
But... this playboy... why...
Why do I feel like I can depend on him? Just because he helped me once?
This is crazy...

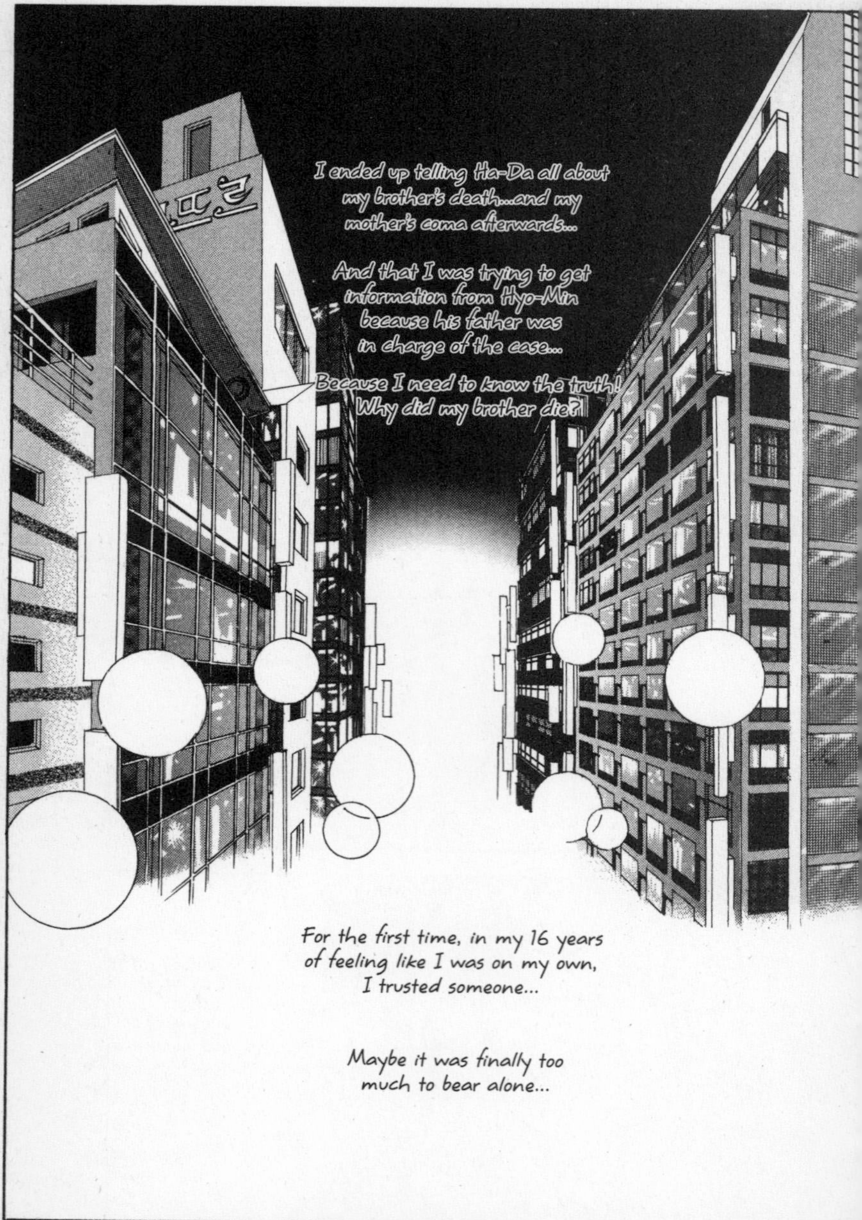
I ended up telling Ha-Da all about my brother's death...and my mother's coma afterwards...
And that I was trying to get information from Hyo-Min because his father was in charge of the case...
Because I need to know the truth! Why did my brother die?
For the first time, in my 16 years of feeling like I was on my own, I trusted someone...
Maybe it was finally too much to bear alone...

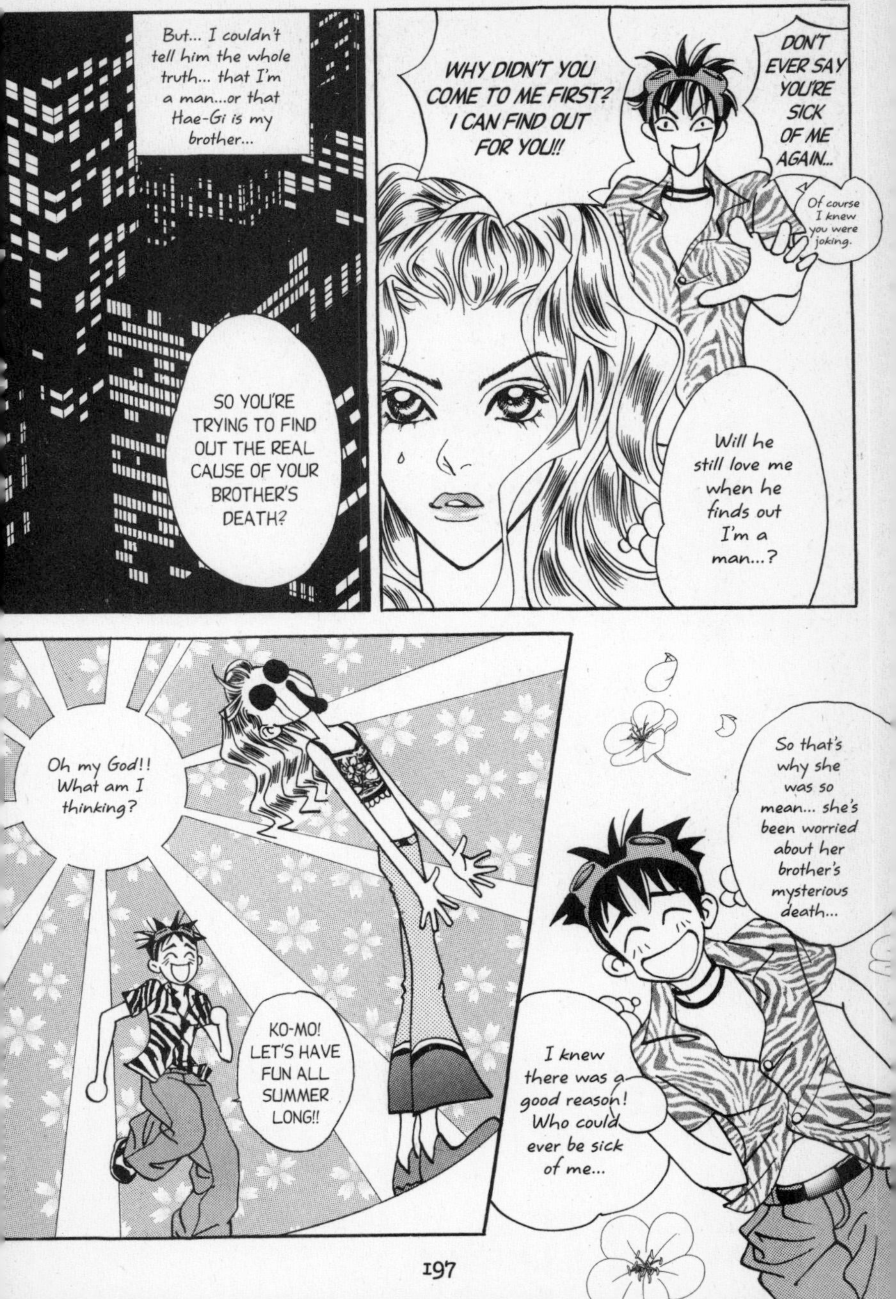
But... I couldn't tell him the whole truth... that I'm a man...or that Hae-Gi is my brother...
SO YOU'RE TRYING TO FIND OUT THE REAL CAUSE OF YOUR BROTHER'S DEATH?
WHY DIDN'T YOU COME TO ME FIRST? I CAN FIND OUT FOR YOU!!
DON'T EVER SAY YOU'RE SICK OF ME AGAIN...
Of course I knew you were joking.
Will he still love me when he finds out I'm a man...?
Oh my God!! What am I thinking?
KO-MO! LET'S HAVE FUN ALL SUMMER LONG!!
So that's why she was so mean... she's been worried about her brother's mysterious death...
I knew there was a good reason! Who could ever be sick of me...

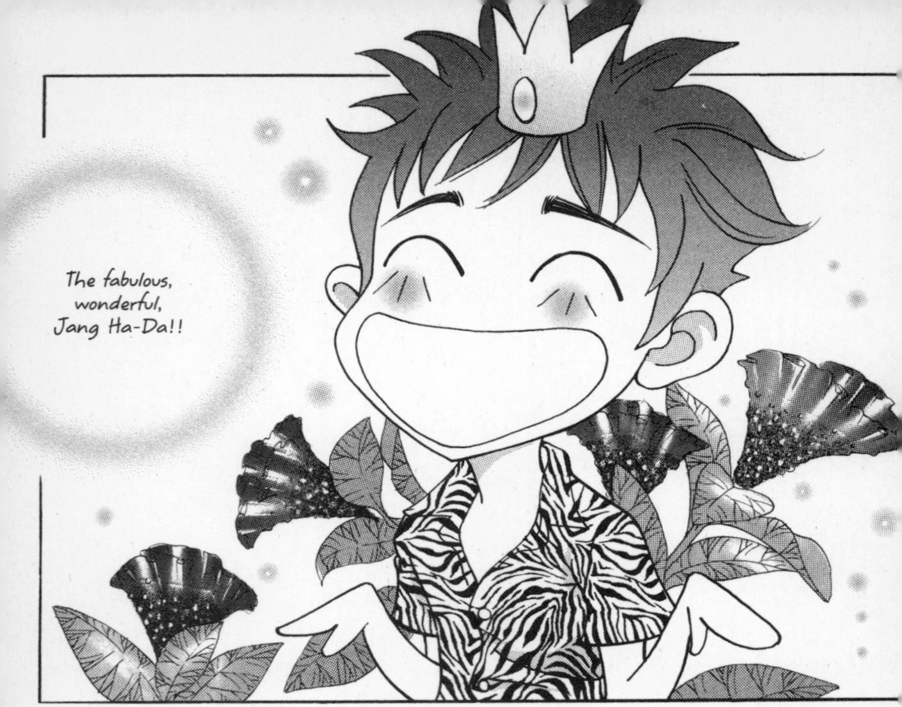
The fabulous, wonderful, Jang Ha-Da!!

And the winner of the bragging Competition... is Ha-Da!!

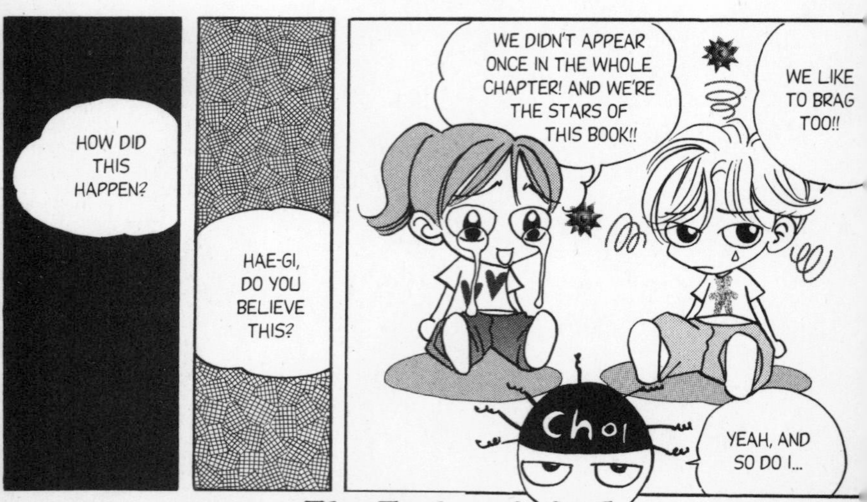
HOW DID THIS HAPPEN?
HAE-GI, DO YOU BELIEVE THIS?
WE DIDN'T APPEAR ONCE IN THE WHOLE CHAPTER! AND WE'RE THE STARS OF THIS BOOK!!
WE LIKE TO BRAG TOO!!
Choi
YEAH, AND SO DO I...

Snow Drop Volume 4 The End

Coming in September...

Snow Drop

Volume Five

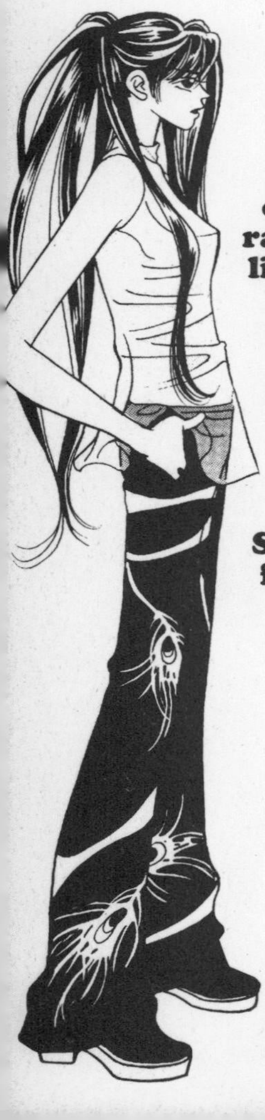

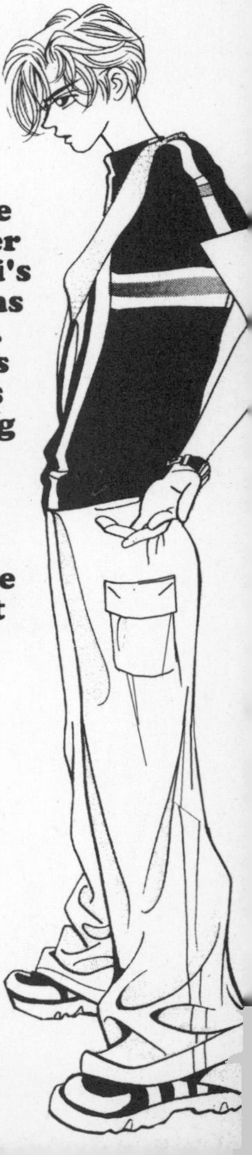

As Hae-Gi and So-Na's love continues to bloom, another ray of hope shines on Hae-Gi's life when his mother returns from her recent operation. However, not everything is coming up roses: Hae-Gi is blacklisted in the modeling industry and So-Na tries to fight off an arranged engagement! Meanwhile, Charles and ever-jealous Sun-Mi team up to crush the flowers of romance and get what they're both after-- Hae-Gi!

Drop in for SNOW DROP Volume 5!

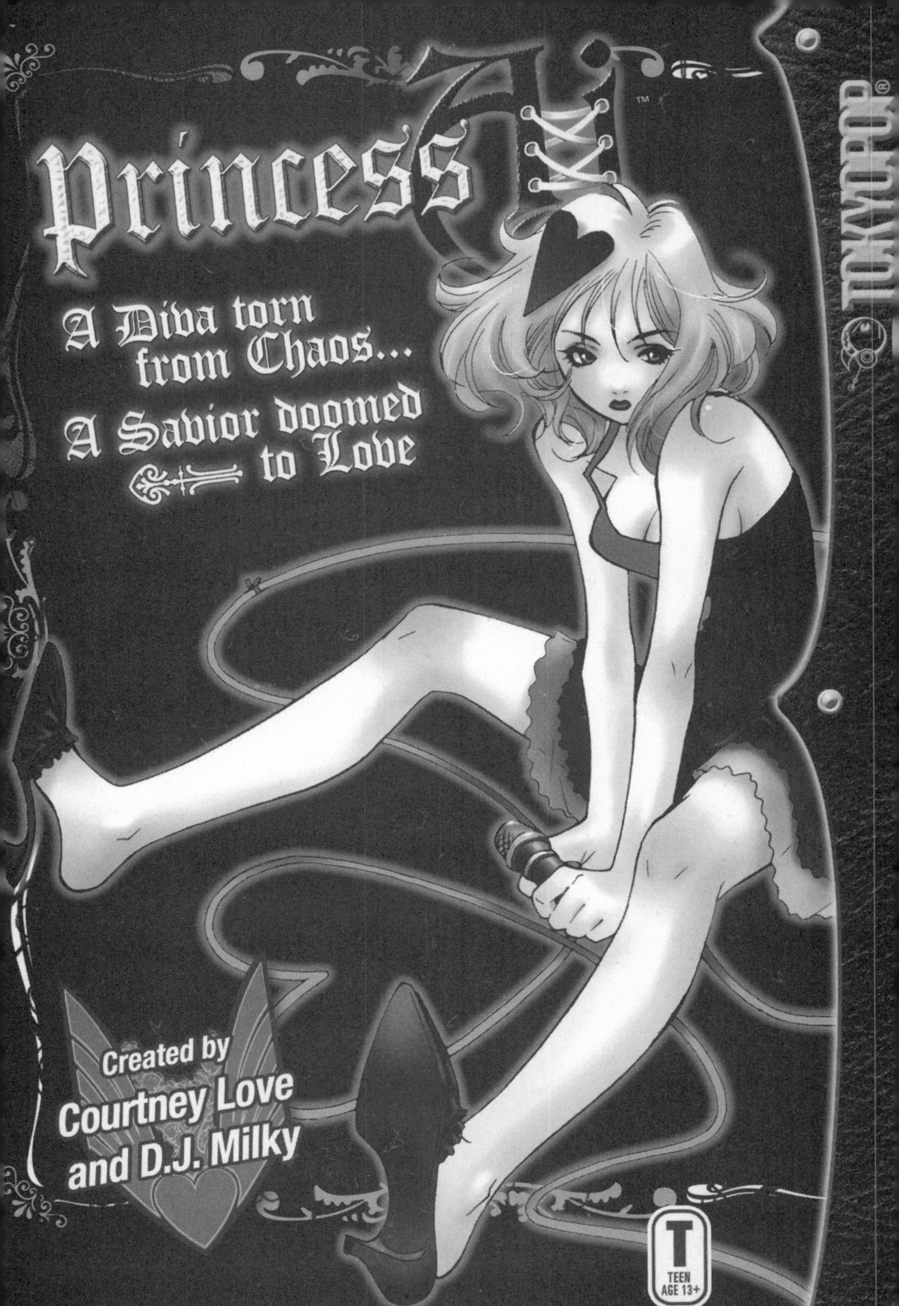

Princess Ai™
A Diva torn from Chaos...
A Savior doomed to Love
Created by
Courtney Love
and D.J. Milky
TOKYOPOP®
T
TEEN
AGE 13+

SUKI™

A like story...

by CLAMP

TOKYOPOP®

T
TEEN
AGE 13+

www.TOKYOPOP.com

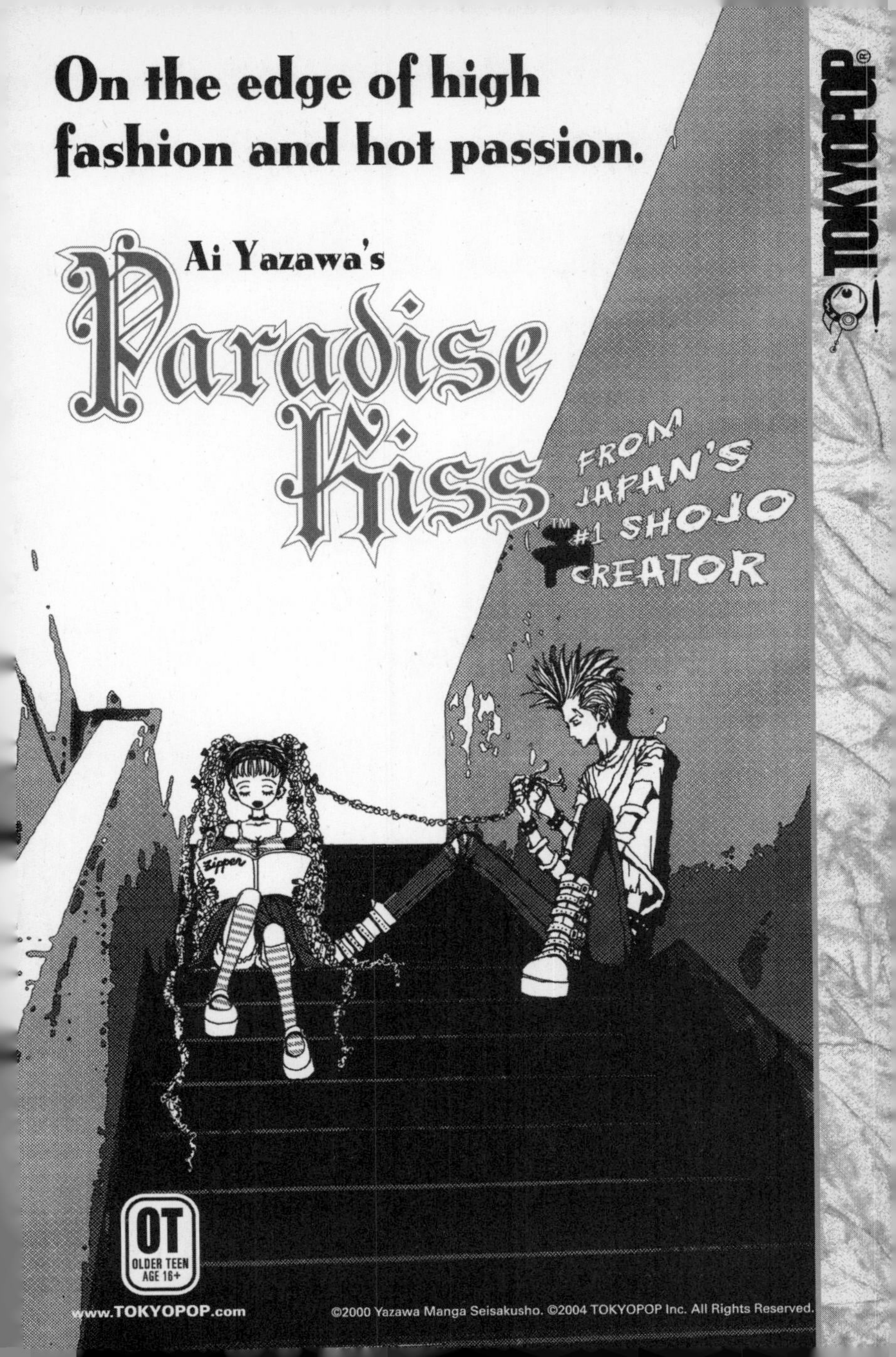
On the edge of high fashion and hot passion.
Ai Yazawa's
Paradise Kiss™
FROM JAPAN'S #1 SHOJO CREATOR
Zipper
OT
OLDER TEEN AGE 16+
www.TOKYOPOP.com
©2000 Yazawa Manga Seisakusho. ©2004 TOKYOPOP Inc. All Rights Reserved.
TOKYOPOP®

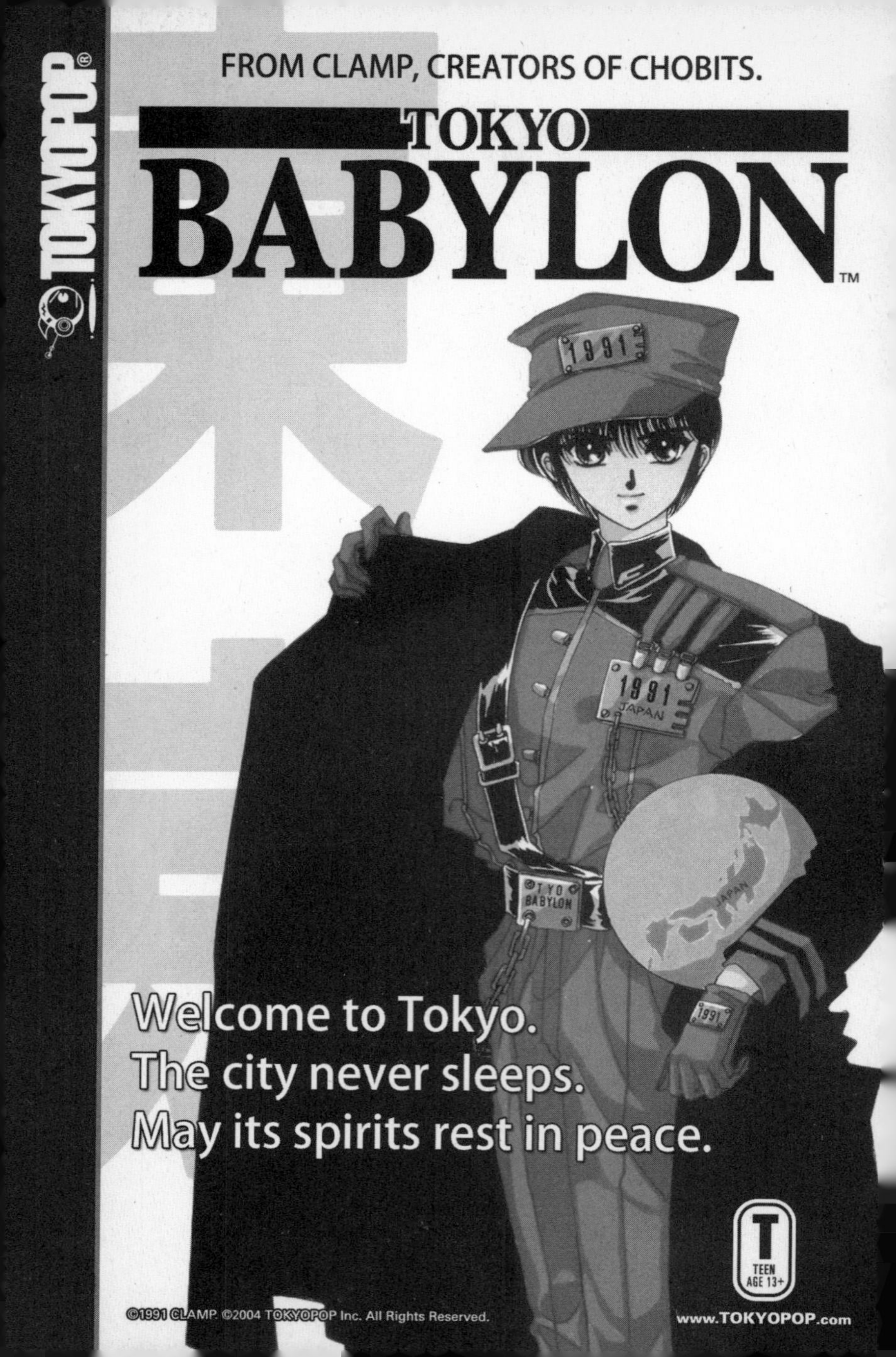

FROM CLAMP, CREATORS OF CHOBITS.

TOKYO
BABYLON™

Welcome to Tokyo.
The city never sleeps.
May its spirits rest in peace.

TEEN
AGE 13+

www.TOKYOPOP.com

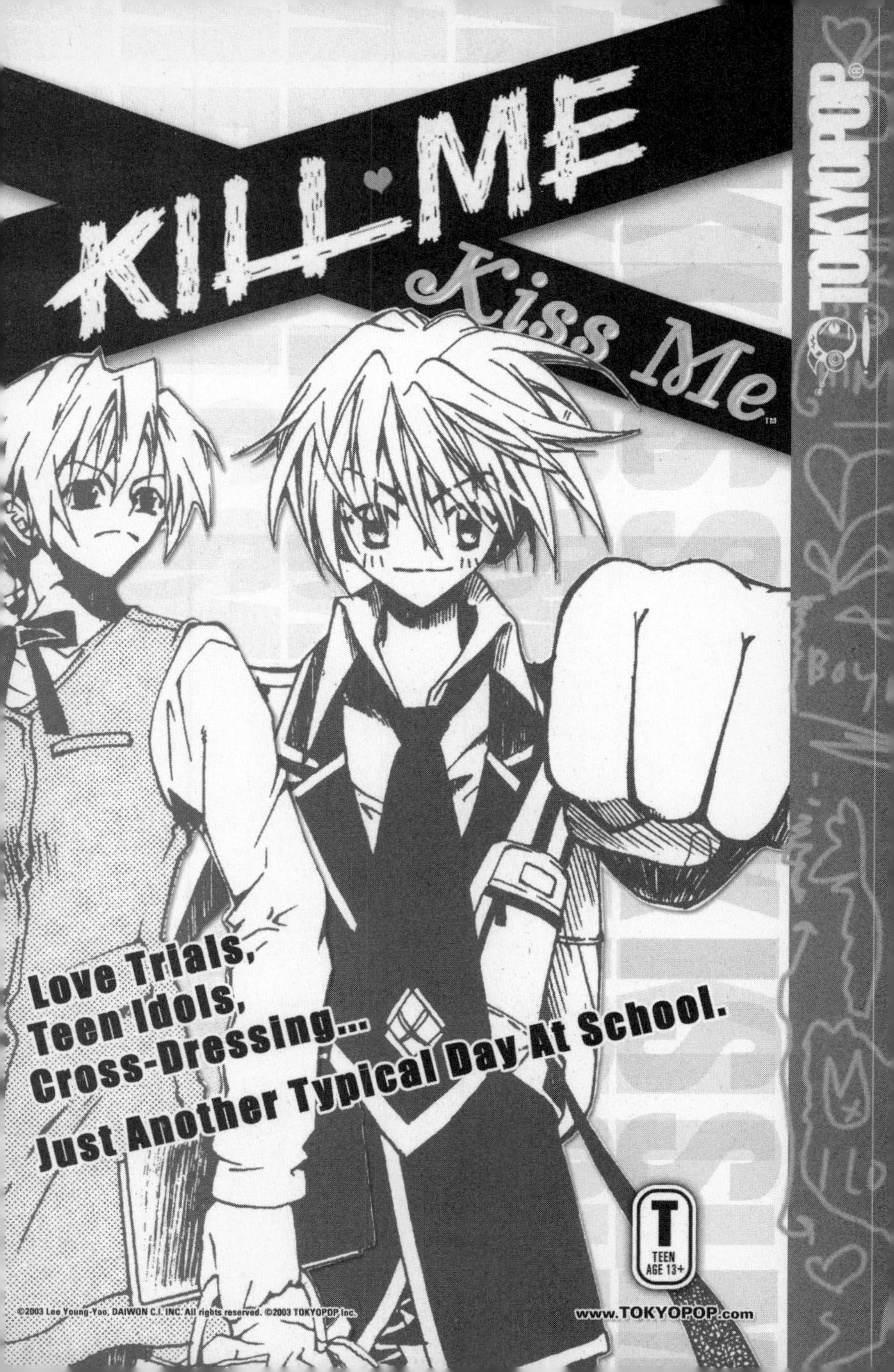
KILL ME
Kiss Me™
TOKYOPOP
Love Trials,
Teen Idols,
Cross-Dressing...
Just Another Typical Day At School.
T
TEEN
AGE 13+
©2003 Lee Young-Yoo, DAIWON C.I. INC. All rights reserved. ©2003 TOKYOPOP Inc.
www.TOKYOPOP.com

kare kano

his and her circumstances

Story by Masami Tsuda

Life Was A Popularity Contest For Yukino.
Somebody Is About To Steal Her Crown.

Available Now At Your Favorite Book And Comic Stores!

Rank	Name	Class	Points
1	???		
2	???		
3	Tomohiko T...	B	
4	Takumi ...	A	
5	Mieko T...	E	
6	Nijo Watana...	C	
7	Akemi Imafuku		
8	Mizue Ta...aka		
9	Yuki Honj...		
10	Reiko Yoko...		
11	Hiroki Sato		
12	Akira Oshima		
13	Eri Yugawa		
14	Aiko Yama...		
15	Shogo Ka...		
16	Masami H...		
17	Mizuho On...		

100% AUTHENTIC MANGA

T TEEN AGE 13+

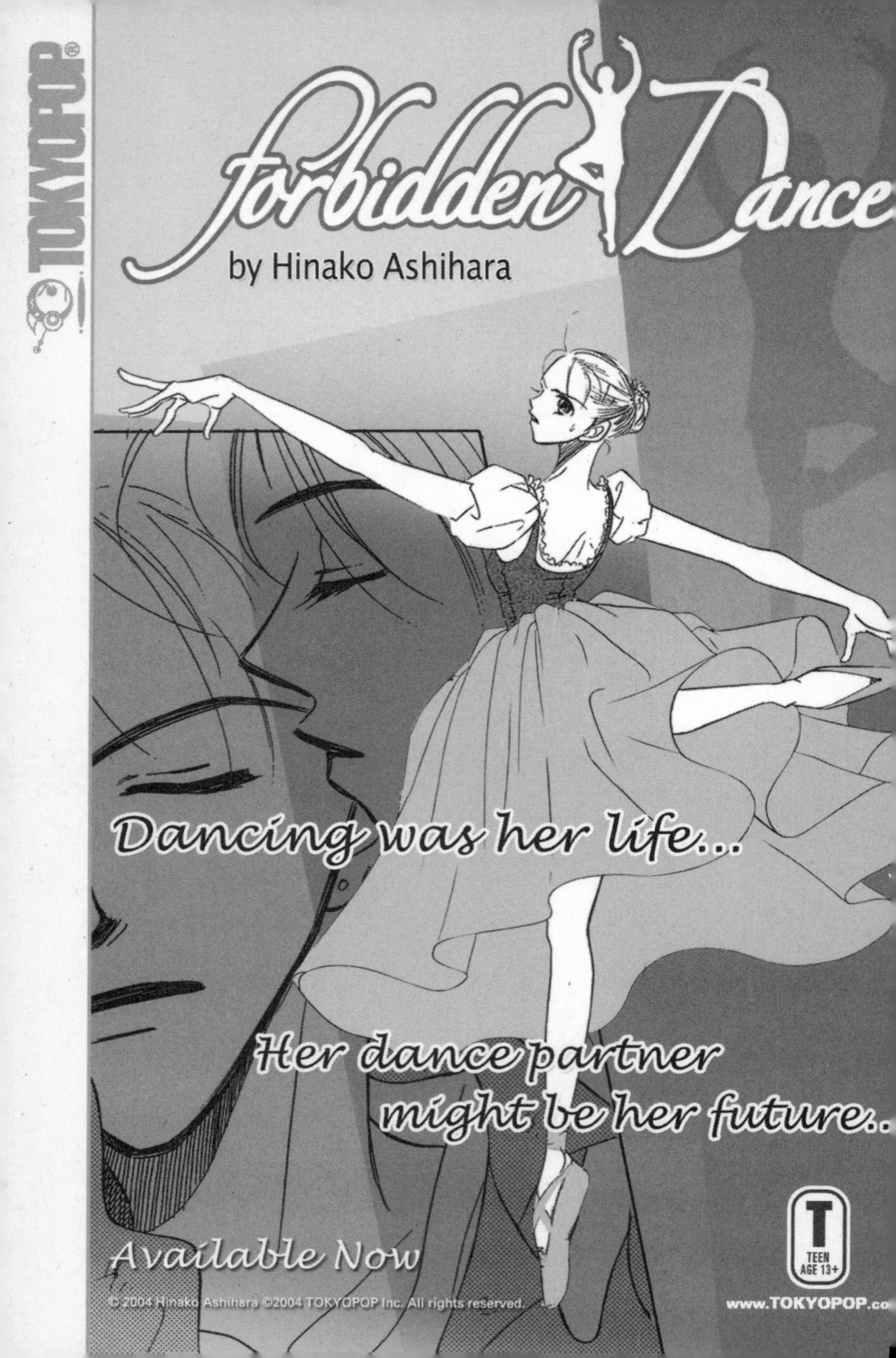
TOKYOPOP®
Forbidden Dance
by Hinako Ashihara
Dancing was her life...
Her dance partner
might be her future...
Available Now
T
TEEN
AGE 13+
© 2004 Hinako Ashihara ©2004 TOKYOPOP Inc. All rights reserved.
www.TOKYOPOP.com